# Ordinary People in God's Hands

## A Tribute to God by TEAM Zimbabwe Missionaries

## Diane Powell Hawkins

D1213312

PRESS

*"One generation will commend your works to another;*
*they will tell of your mighty acts.*
*They will speak of the glorious splendor of your majesty,*
*and I will meditate on your wonderful works.*
*They will tell of the power of your awesome works,*
*and I will proclaim your great deeds.*
*They will celebrate your abundant goodness*
*and joyfully sing of your righteousness."*
(Psalm 145:4-7)

*To the faithful prayer supporters,*
*financial supporters,*
*sending churches,*
*sacrificing families,*
*mentors and encouragers*
*who made possible*
*the work of God*
*through the TEAM Zimbabwe missionaries*

# Table of Contents

# Preface

*"Let this be written for a future generation,*
*that a people not yet created*
*may praise the LORD."*
(Psalm 102:18)

Six decades after Zimbabwe (formerly called Rhodesia) became
the eighth field of the Scandinavian Alliance Mission, forerun-
ner of The Evangelical Alliance Mission (TEAM), the number of
pioneer missionaries still living is shrinking. Recognizing the
wealth of memories these men and women carried of God's initial
work in bringing the Gospel into the Zambezi Valley, Tom
Jackson, Doug Everswick, and Donna Hendrickson Abuhl sensed
an urgency to begin collecting and preserving whatever memoirs
could still be retrieved before the opportunity for firsthand
accounts was totally lost.

This burden was quickly shared and picked up by fellow
missionaries who were willing to help accomplish this goal. The
TEAM Zimbabwe Field Council officially approved the project in
December 1999. Diane Powell Hawkins agreed to be the coordina-
tor and editor, and a committee was formed to guide the process.
Initially consisting of Wilma Gardziella Anderson, Diane Hawkins,
Don and Lynn Hoyt, and Donna Hendrickson Robinson, this group

held their first meeting in San Diego in May 2000. Bud Jackson also gave early assistance to the committee.

In establishing an overall goal for the project, the committee quickly reached a consensus to design the work as a *tribute to God* for His magnificent hand working through the missionaries whom He specifically prepared, called, and enabled for the harvesting of souls in Zimbabwe. How He intricately wove together a team of ordinary people to accomplish His extraordinary work is a story that must be preserved and passed on to future generations. The aim is not to glorify man in any way but to rejoice in the faithfulness of God in accomplishing His purposes through the most earthen of vessels, all having their individual strengths and weaknesses and traveling through their own spiritual deserts and mountaintops. Within this imperfect frame of humanity, the "greatness of the power" must be seen as God's alone (2 Corinthians 4:7).

In accomplishing this goal, the committee recognized the necessity of accepting numerous limitations. To write a complete history of the work of God through the TEAM missionaries in Zimbabwe was beyond the scope of our available time and resources; nor could we chronicle the entire life experience of each missionary on the field. Instead, our vision was to focus on incidents in the missionaries' lives that particularly revealed the hand of God at work.

While attempting to solicit contributions equally from every living missionary who served with TEAM in Zimbabwe at any time, we also realized that we could not assure that each one would be represented in a manner consistent with the scope of his or her involvement on the field. We would, of necessity, be limited by the amount and suitability of the material submitted by each one. Since our aim is to magnify *what God did* rather than the vessels He used, we decided to disregard altogether any formula for parity in representation within the book. (A comprehensive list of missionaries, which includes even those who did not contribute to the project, is found in the appendix.)

In addition to the contributions received directly from missionaries, we also drew upon a limited sampling of letters and articles obtained from the TEAM archives in Wheaton, Illinois, as well as the book *God Made it Grow* by former TEAM Director Dr. Vernon Mortenson. In spite of these additional resources, we recognize that each chapter of this present work represents only a limited sampling of the potential incidents that could be recounted to illustrate the evident hand of God in the specific area being addressed.

With over 600 pages of material collected, we regret that we could not possibly do justice to it all. As several years went by in the writing process, we recognized the need to reduce the number of chapters and subjects we had originally envisioned covering so we could bring the book to publication. We sincerely apologize to those whose material may not have been included.

Because the bulk of the book's content is drawn from the missionaries' own memories, we also cannot guarantee the accuracy of the accounts given. Although we have tried to seek verification from other sources when possible, flaws due to the fallibility of human memory cannot be fully eliminated. This is true even in the best of circumstances, let alone with the passage of many decades. We trust that the heart of the message of God's hand in the work of the TEAM missionaries in Zimbabwe will nevertheless be preserved and serve as a glorious tribute to Him.

The project was originally envisioned to benefit primarily the TEAM Zimbabwe missionaries themselves, along with their families and supporters. However, as the goal became focused on showcasing the magnificent work of God in and through this particular group of missionaries, we sensed that the book might provide valuable insight and encouragement to others interested in missions as well. Expanding the potential audience would allow praise, honor, and glory to flow upward to God from the hearts of even more readers. Therefore, instead of fashioning the book for a narrowly selected group of "insiders," we have endeavored to shape it to be of interest to a more general Christian audience.

Other more technical decisions also had to be made. For instance, surnames changed along with marital status for many female missionaries over the decades covered in this book. In general, we chose to use whatever name applied at the time of the event being described. However, at times we included the name by which the person was predominantly known on the field in order to enhance recognition. The comprehensive list of missionaries in Appendix A includes maiden, married, and remarried names for all females.

We also desired to be extremely sensitive to political issues within the country of Zimbabwe. Therefore, in consultation with both mission leaders and national brethren we decided to use consistently throughout the book the official names of places which were established at the time of the country's independence, regardless of the historical context of the event described.

Obviously the war of independence, as well as subsequent political activities, had a major impact on the lives and ministries of the missionaries serving in the country at the time. However, because of the political sensitivities involved, we have chosen to minimize focusing on these events. We sincerely regret any insensitivities that might remain in the book because of our lack of awareness of them.

We also do not want to minimize the major role that our national co-workers played in the various ministries God raised up in Zimbabwe, especially in the establishment and growth of the Evangelical Church. Included among these devoted brothers and sisters in Christ, who were equally called and strategically placed by God, are many true "heroes of the faith." Some will be mentioned in the context of stories recounted in this book, but many others will not. Their importance to the work of God or to the hearts of the missionaries must not be measured by whether their name appears in this book. Again, our primary goal in this work is to give glory to God rather than to man. Perhaps one day the Evangelical Church will write a companion volume from its own perspective, chronicling God's faithfulness through the many years of its formation and growth.

We thank God and continue to pray for the ongoing ministry of the Evangelical Church in Zimbabwe. Through this organization and many other avenues of Christian ministry, formal and informal, the firstfruits of the early Gospel witness in the Zambezi Valley continue to be multiplied from generation to generation. To God be all the glory!

> The Tribute Committee
> Diane Powell Hawkins
> Don and Lynn Hoyt
> Wilma Gardziella Riddell
> Donna Hendrickson Robinson

# Acknowledgments

*"I thank my God every time I remember you."*
(Philippians 1:3)

While it is customary in this section to express appreciation for those who contributed to the writing, editing, design, and other features of the book, the committee desires to include those who made possible the events recorded in the book as well. First and foremost, of course, our intent through the entire work is to express gratitude to God, whose unlimited love, grace, and power envisioned, directed, and enabled all that is recorded within its pages.

We also acknowledge the crucial role played by each TEAM missionary who became a vessel willing to be shaped and used to fulfill God's purposes in Zimbabwe. We honor their obedience, sacrifice, courage, and utter dependence upon the Lord for every aspect of their personal sustenance and ministry. May the example of their lives shared in this book serve as a tremendous inspiration for future generations!

In addition, we want to recognize the many individuals who together made it possible for these missionaries to become laborers in the harvest field of Zimbabwe. This includes a host of godly servants who played a vital role in building into these men and women's lives. The missionaries whose stories are told in this book reached the field because other devoted Christians brought them to a saving knowledge of Jesus Christ, discipled, mentored, and inspired them to fulfill the call of God upon their lives. The unsung heroes whose lives strategically intersected with these future missionaries include family members, relatives, pastors, teachers, youth leaders, professors, and individuals in many other positions.

We also acknowledge and honor the sacrifices made by the families of the missionaries as they released their sons and daughters, brothers and sisters, and sometimes mothers and fathers to the Lord's service in a distant land fraught with many uncertainties. Two of the early pioneers would lay down their lives on the field. Others were not available to help carry the load on the farm or to care for elderly relatives. Parents sacrificed the joys of closer involvement in the lives of their children and grandchildren, a void felt even more acutely on holidays, birthdays, and other family gatherings.

In the modified words penned to the familiar hymn "So Send I You," Mrs. Winona Carroll, a missionary in India, captured some of the aspects of sacrifice borne particularly by parents who released their children to missionary service:

> *So send I you—to give your own with gladness,*
> *To let them go unhindered to the lost;*
> *To hide the tears and every trace of sadness;*
> *So send I you—to taste with Me the cost.*
>
> *So send I you—to anxious days of waiting*
> *For word that often leaves so much untold;*
> *To nights of burdened vigil unabating;*
> *So send I you—to watch the gap you hold.*
>
> *So send I you—to walk alone when aged,*
> *To need the strength of one you cannot call;*
> *To lean on Me and on the ones I bring you,*
> *So send I you—to find in Me your all.*
>
> *So send I you—to know the joy of serving,*
> *To share the triumphs of the one you send;*
> *To reap the fruit of sacrifice unswerving,*
> *So send I you—to joy without end.*

May all the parents of TEAM Zimbabwe missionaries feel our heartfelt appreciation for the very real sacrifices you made as well as the earnest prayer support by which you faithfully undergirded those you loved so deeply.

Other indispensable individuals were those who gave of their financial resources to support these missionaries, their families, and their ministries. Some gave generously out of their abundance; others gave sacrificially from their own meager incomes. All contributed from their hearts and were used by God to enable the Gospel message to penetrate deeply into the northeast sector of Zimbabwe.

Alongside these crucial financial givers, and often included among them, were the prayer supporters who stood faithfully behind each missionary. While the financial supporters made possible the missionaries' physical presence in Zimbabwe and the tools they needed for ministry, these mighty prayer warriors enabled the will of God to be powerfully enacted *through* the missionaries, resulting in eternal fruit for the Kingdom of God.

Dr. David Johnson was profoundly gripped by the vital role of these prayer supporters when he spent a week with the early missionaries living in the primitive Zambezi Valley in 1950. While acknowledging the enormously significant task to which God had called these dedicated pioneers, his voice cracked with emotion as he added, "I would never bring my wife and young children into this Valley unless I was sure I had one thousand prayer supporters in the homeland deeply committed to pray for me."[1]

What an impact these words from TEAM's general director had on the small group of young parents who had gathered at Rukomechi for their annual conference! Russ and Marg Jackson were one of the couples who took his challenge to heart and devoted themselves to raising up 1000 prayer supporters on their first furlough. After 34 years of service on the field, Russ reported:

> *. . . I am thoroughly convinced that the Holy Spirit Himself . . . guided us to special, godly men and women along the way. . . . The Lord gave us the genuine desire of our hearts for one thousand prayer supporters and even far beyond. My heart is deeply humbled as I reflect on the faithful, loving concern of a multitude of men and women, many*

*now with the Lord, who have been committed for a lifetime to faithful prayer concern for our missionary work in Africa, as well as for our precious family. Perhaps only from eternity's perspective will Margaret and I realize fully the tremendous value of the prayers of wonderful, committed, co-laborers in ministry.*

May each prayer supporter of every TEAM Zimbabwe missionary receive the heartfelt gratitude expressed in these words! Even after many of the missionaries retired, their faithful prayer warriors have continued to pray for the Church in Zimbabwe and the many ongoing ministries raised up as a result of their powerful prayer support through the years.

In 2004, Rick Froese, Pharm.D., brought back from Zimbabwe an exciting, firsthand report of the Church, which was thriving and expanding beyond his expectations. He eagerly shared this news with his supporters, along with his recognition of the critical role they had played in making it all possible:

*The thought that kept coming back to me over and over was that all I was seeing and experiencing was made possible by those many supporters (YOU) who, over the years, faithfully contributed their prayers and support so that the Zimbabwe missionaries could labor in that great land. . . . With tears of joy and thanksgiving I can truthfully say that both your labors and ours have not been in vain. God has done and continues to do far more than we could ever ask, think, or imagine.*

In addition to the host of individuals who made possible the events described within this tribute, we also desire to recognize those who devoted their time, energy, and talents to making the book itself a reality. In this regard, we begin by extending our gratitude to the many missionaries, and some of their children, who contributed their memories for this project. We especially appreciate the candidness with which many of them opened a window into their own hearts as well as the Zimbabwe mission field.

The Tribute Committee, consisting of Diane Powell Hawkins,

Don and Lynn Hoyt, Wilma Gardziella Riddell, and Donna Hendrickson Robinson played the vital role of guiding this entire project from an idea to a reality. Their first major task was contacting all the missionaries and inspiring their participation. This involved numerous mailings and personal phone calls. In addition, Diane traveled to Florida, Michigan, Wisconsin, and Canada to interview many retired missionaries. Wilma, on a short-term assignment back at Karanda Hospital in 2001, interviewed all the missionaries serving in Zimbabwe at the time. Both of these efforts greatly increased the scope of the gathered material.

Others helped in getting all of the submissions onto computer. Tom Hawkins assisted with scanning while Wilma, Mildred Carnall, and Shirley Bradford Bennett typed whatever hard copy did not lend itself to scanning. Diane Hawkins and Betty Wolfe transcribed the taped interviews.

As the book began to take shape, the Tribute Committee continued to supply crucial input on a myriad of issues as well as extensive editorial advice. Donna Robinson's role as the official "historian" was invaluable as she researched all the historical data and did the major work for compiling the appendix.

Don Hoyt served as treasurer and conducted all matters of professional liaison in addition to arranging accommodations for each committee meeting. Carroll and Donna Robinson, Paul and Ruth Cochrane, Judy Gudeman, Phil and Barb Christiansen, and Cynthia Sander opened their homes to host committee meetings while Lynn Hoyt, Wilma Riddell, and Barb Christiansen did a superb job in providing meals.

As we came into the final stages of making the book a reality, we were extremely grateful to TEAM Zimbabwe MK (missionary kid) Tim Eichner for creating the excellent cover design. Jesse Schutt assisted in producing the map, and Dr. Scott Moose and Wilma Riddell did the major job of proof-reading the entire manuscript. We are sincerely thankful for the contribution of their respective talents and trust that each one has been blessed in the role they played to make possible this grand "Tribute" to our awesome God.

# Note from the Author

I humbly express my gratitude to God for the privilege of compiling this awesome chronicle of God's faithfulness in the lives of a small group of missionaries He called to serve Him in northeastern Zimbabwe. Adding this mammoth project to my already busy life became a truly joyous, though sacrificial, endeavor which I do not regret.

I have been deeply blessed by the opportunity to reconnect with the TEAM Zimbabwe family, who became so precious to me during a short, but meaningful, five-year segment of my life spent as a co-laborer with them in Zimbabwe. I have laughed and cried and worshipped as I've read through the many experiences these people so generously and candidly shared for this project.

I will never forget the day I sat down to ponder the structural format for the envisioned book and felt as though God virtually dictated the Table of Contents to me. As the names of the chapters poured out one after another without hesitation on my computer screen, I became more impacted than ever with what an awesome act of worship this work would truly be. Never had I seen quite so clearly how God's hand was behind every aspect of the missionary endeavor from the mundane to the spectacular, from the time He prepared and called the missionaries until the time He indicated that their work was done. Just as Christ promised in His Great Commission, He was truly *"with [them] always"* (Matthew 28:20). I feel so unworthy, and yet so honored, to be the one to hold the pen, so to speak, for the pages of this tribute to come into being.

Through this project God has also opened my eyes to the heart and soul of missions in a deeper way than I had ever grasped before. My own brief episode of filling a needed niche for a short period of time is dwarfed by those who gave a lifetime to the call of God upon their lives to bring the Gospel message to people who had never heard, no matter what the cost.

I pray that the Spirit of God will also anoint and open *your* eyes and hearts to see God—and missions—in a new way. As you read this book, it's my desire that you will join in the grand chorus of praise for His awesome power and total sufficiency in the lives of those ordinary people He calls into service in His Kingdom.

I trust that each TEAM Zimbabwe missionary will be greatly encouraged in recognizing how God used his or her own particular role in a much bigger picture, no matter how large or small, how easy or difficult, or how skilled or unskilled it seemed. Yes, there were human frailties, mistakes, disappointments, and failures, but none of these could stop the power of God from building His Church in northeast Zimbabwe through their lives!

# Map of Zimbabwe

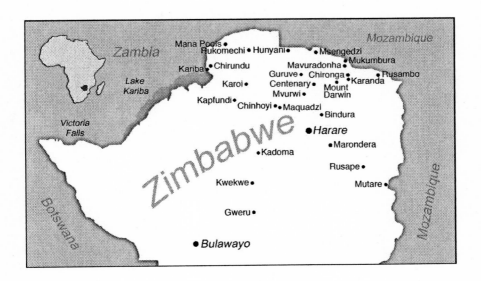

# CHAPTER 1

# God Detoured

*"Therefore go and make disciples of all nations."*
(Matthew 28:19-20)

"One thousand missionaries for China!" This was the call issued by Hudson Taylor in 1890. As it fell upon the ears of a young Swedish immigrant named Fredrick Franson, he boldly responded, "I will raise up one hundred of them myself!"[1]

Franson, already a gifted evangelist and Bible teacher,[2] immediately worked out a strategy for accomplishing this goal. On October 14 of the same year he launched his first missionary training course in Brooklyn, New York. Similar courses followed in Chicago, Omaha, and Minneapolis.[3]

As the number of recruits grew, Franson formed a committee to direct what was becoming a budding missionary organization. Because the focus was entirely on China at that point, they called themselves the China Alliance Mission.[4]

In 1891, this newly formed body sent out three teams of trained recruits to China and Japan, a total of sixty-five men and women. More followed the next year.[5]

Challenged by the growing population of the world and the soon return of the Lord,[6] Franson's vision extended far beyond these two needy countries. In 1892, missionaries were also sent to

India and South Africa.[7]

To reflect this broader vision, the China Alliance Mission became the Alliance Mission. This was soon changed to the Scandinavian Alliance Mission of North America, or S.A.M., as most of the sending churches consisted of Scandinavian immigrants.[8]

As the first group of eight missionary recruits, led by Andrew Haugerud, arrived in South Africa, their goal was to minister to the Zulu people.[9] While a series of tragedies quickly decimated this group to four women, God's hand was with them. He gave them a new leader named William Dawson,[10] and soon additional recruits arrived as well. By 1933, seventy-nine churches had been established.[11]

Being greatly encouraged by God's work among both the Swazis and the Zulus, the hearts of the South African missionaries were stirred as they became aware of "a large, inadequately reached territory just across the eastern border of Swaziland, now known as Mozambique. Several missions were active in the southern part of the country, but the extreme northern district of Tete beyond the Zambezi River was largely unreached. Here was an area eleven times the size of Swaziland with only two missionary couples."[12]

The fact that the Portuguese government was reluctant to allow additional missionaries into Mozambique did not seem to dampen their zeal to help reach the people of this country with the Gospel. When Dr. T.J. Bach, General Director of S.A.M. at that time, visited the South Africa field in 1933, the missionaries shared their burden for this neighboring country with him. Then, with Dr. Bach present at their annual conference, they unanimously agreed to recommend to S.A.M.'s board of directors that missionaries be sought for Mozambique.[13]

Eventually four individuals offered themselves for service in this new field: Mary Maluske, Magnus and Clara Foreid, and Rudy Danielson. Because Portugal at that time required that anyone applying to enter one of its colonies must first study the language in Portugal, these four proceeded to Portugal in 1938 for this purpose.[14]

During this time Rudy Danielson and Mary Maluske were married, and upon completing their language study, they sailed to South Africa in 1939 to probe for an entry point into Mozambique. The Foreids decided to stay in Portugal until the door to Mozambique was definitely open. In the end they became instrumental in opening Portugal as S.A.M.'s seventh mission field.[15]

In the meantime God led another couple to offer themselves as candidates for Mozambique. Orval Dunkeld and Helen Hughes had attended Mary Maluske's commissioning service at S.A.M.'s headquarters in Chicago and felt strongly moved to join in the same pioneer effort to which Mary had committed herself.

By the time they finished their education, joined the mission, married, and were ready to depart, S.A.M. gave them the choice of going first to Portugal or directly to South Africa. They chose to go to South Africa and arrived in March 1939, just ahead of the Danielsons.

In July the South Africa field met for their annual conference and decided to send Rudy and Mary Danielson to Mozambique's capital city, Maputo, to try to get permission for S.A.M. to bring missionaries into the country. They spent two months there pursuing every avenue possible, but to no avail. The strong Catholic element in the government was determined not to let any more Protestant missions into the colony.

Rudy and Mary returned to South Africa extremely disappointed. With permission to enter Mozambique denied for the time being, both the Danielsons and the Dunkelds became involved in the missionary work of South Africa—but not for long.

In 1940, Peter Lind, a South African working with the Zambezi Mission in Zimbabwe, heard about the Danielsons' failed effort to enter Mozambique. He contacted the S.A.M. leadership in South Africa about a vast, unreached territory in the Zambezi Valley just across the border from Mozambique. Peter explained that his mission had neither the finances nor the personnel to enter this area and asked if S.A.M. was interested in establishing this area as a new field.

The South Africa field responded positively and made an official decision at their annual conference in July 1940 to accept this invitation, assigning the Danielsons and Dunkelds to open this new work.[16] The Danielsons were freed to leave first and arrived in Zimbabwe later that year. They joined the Linds on their station at Mavuradonha, located part way down the escarpment to the Zambezi Valley, and began studying the Shona language.

When the rainy season ended in April 1941, Orv Dunkeld

joined Rudy Danielson in Zimbabwe for a six-week exploratory trip into the Zambezi Valley to choose a site for their first mission station. To reach this area from Mavuradonha, they had to descend another thousand feet down into the broad valley, some sixty miles across, through which the Zambezi River flowed toward Mozambique and the sea.[17]

Unlike the Danielson's experience in Mozambique, these men found a favorable reception from the magistrates in every place they visited. Wanting to be close to the Mozambique border, in case it should open, but also in a vicinity with a signficant group of unreached people, Rudy and Orv eventually chose a place called Msengedzi as the site for their first station.

As they made their initial contacts with the Shona people in that area, they were deeply impacted by their primitive and unhealthy living conditions as well as their animistic beliefs. This made them "more assured than ever that it was from among these people they should seek to call out followers for the Lord Jesus Christ."[18] Msengedzi was also near enough to Mavuradonha that they could maintain a "lifeline" with Peter Lind and his people should they need any kind of assistance in this unfamiliar land. After hiring some local people to start putting up poles for an African-style house for them, the men returned to Mavuradonha and Orv went back to South Africa.

In July the South Africa field officially released the Dunkelds to join the Danielsons in Zimbabwe. Due to a delay in their permit to enter the country, however, and the birth of their second child, they did not arrive at Mavuradonha until December 1941. By this time another rainy season had arrived, making travel in and out of the Valley almost impossible, so both families stayed at Mavuradonha studying the Shona language.

As soon as the rains ended in April 1942, Peter Lind and a national evangelist from Malawi accompanied Rudy and Orv into the Valley to finish the house the local people had begun building at Msengedzi. After considerable difficulty in mixing mud to the right consistency for the walls, they finally succeeded in completing the house, along with an outside shelter for a kitchen. This allowed Mary, with daughter Muriel (1 year), to move down from Mavuradonha. Helen, with sons Fred (2 years) and Dick (7 months), followed in June. They lived in a tent shelter while a more substantial house was built with sun-dried bricks for them.

The first year at Msengedzi was not easy. The rains washed out their garden and a leopard killed their goats. Malaria also struck them, with Rudy being hit the hardest. To restore his health, the two couples left the Valley for a couple months to take a break from the brutally hot summer sun.

When the hot, humid weather returned the following year, however, Rudy again became seriously ill. This time they took him to the nearest hospital, which was 160 miles away in Bindura. Here he was diagnosed as having typhoid fever. Five weeks later, on November 25, 1943, he entered the presence of the Lord.

This was a devastating loss that the others struggled to understand. Mary and Muriel returned to the United States, and the Dunkelds spent the rest of the rainy season at Mavuradonha with the Linds to avoid the ongoing threat of typhoid in the Valley.

The following April the Dunkelds joyfully welcomed Eunice Ott as a new recruit to the field. With World War II not yet over, she had bravely crossed the ocean on a troop ship. Once the war ended in 1945, other recruits followed. Norman and Thelma Everswick and Orla and Marguerite Blair arrived in 1946. Mary Danielson and Muriel also returned that year, enabling the Dunkeld family to leave on a long-overdue furlough.

In May 1947, the missionaries held their first field conference at Msengedzi with Dr. T. J. Bach, Director Emeritus of S.A.M., present. A major discussion took place over the difficulties arising from administrating the Zimbabwe field from South Africa. Therefore, upon the recommendation of both countries and Dr. Bach, S.A.M.'s board of directors designated Zimbabwe as a separate field later that year.[19] Mary Danielson became the first field chairperson.

The Dunkelds returned from their furlough in 1948, along with three more recruits, Russell and Margaret Jackson and Lillian Nelson. With their numbers increasing, the missionaries began branching out to reach other areas in the Zambezi Valley. Stations were established at Rukomechi and Hunyani. Like Msengedzi, they were both close to the Mozambique border, indicating the field's ongoing concern for that country. From each of these stations the missionaries were able to make short trips into that closed land as well as interact with those who crossed the border into Zimbabwe.[20]

In 1949, because sentiment had been growing that the name of the mission should not carry national connotations, the Scandinavian Alliance Mission became The Evangelical Alliance Mission, or TEAM, the name it carries to this day.[21] Eventually its missionaries began calling themselves "TEAMmates."

By this time the Zimbabwe field had become increasingly convinced of the need to establish a presence in the capital city of Harare. Many of the national believers from the Valley were moving to Harare to seek employment, and the missionaries were concerned about their spiritual welfare there. Most of them were living in crowded suburbs where sin abounded. Bringing a Gospel witness into these communities was seen as a great opportunity.

The missionaries also needed a better place to stay when they went to Harare to get supplies, to seek medical and dental care, and to interact with the government offices located there. Until this time they had been camping in a park on the outskirts of the city.

The school-aged children of the missionaries also needed a better place to stay while attending government schools in Harare. Muriel Danielson and Fred and Dick Dunkeld were staying in a private hostel that provided poor care, little supervision, and no Christian nurture or influence in their lives. With other children quickly approaching school age, the missionaries felt an urgent need to establish a Christian home for these children while they attended school.

In 1950, a five-acre plot was acquired in Hatfield, a suburb of Harare. This site gradually grew into TEAM Zimbabwe's head-quarters and for decades was known simply as "the Plot."

The Dunkelds repaired an old cottage on the property to serve as a hostel for the schoolchildren. They also served as the first "dorm parents," a responsibility that was frequently shifted amongst the missionaries, depending on the personnel needs on the field as a whole. In 1956-57, a much needed, larger hostel was built on the Plot with the "Old Cottage" becoming a guesthouse for missionaries coming to town from the rural areas.

As the TEAM Zimbabwe field was growing, the Zambezi Mission was having difficulty gaining new recruits from their base in England. This left them unable to continue the work they had established at Mavuradonha and Rusambo. In 1951, when presented with the option, TEAM Zimbabwe agreed to take over the work at these locations.[22]

As additional missionaries arrived, further expansion took place. In 1953, a new ministry site was opened at Kapfundi. This station was the first to be located away from the Mozambique border. The following year the mission developed ministries at Chirundu, Guruve, and Chironga. In 1955, missionaries began ministering in the small town of Maquadzi, which was located in an area with a high concentration of national farm laborers. Later, work was started in other farming areas, such as Chinhoyi in 1960 and Karoi in 1973.

Frequently, permission to establish a mission station in an area was contingent upon the missionaries being willing to open a school and/or clinic for the local people. Education and medicine thus became very prevalent means for reaching the Shona people.

Small clinics or dispensaries were quickly opened at each new station. Most were operated by trained nurses or missionaries who had taken an abbreviated medical course designed particularly for missions. Their supplies were limited, and the medical needs of the people often stretched them far beyond their level of training. Nevertheless, they were deeply appreciated by the local people.

In order to open and maintain schools, trained teachers were needed. This led to the establishment of a Teacher Training Institute at Chironga in 1955.

Soon after, a small hospital was built on the same station, moving in 1961 to Karanda, a site several miles away with a better water supply. Two years later a nursing school was established to train nationals to provide medical care for their own people. This eventually included a midwifery course as well.

Bible education was always a high priority on the field. A formal Bible school ministry began at Mavuradonha in 1953. As it continued to expand, it was moved to increasingly better facilities at Kapfundi, then Chinhoyi, and to a Harare suburb, where it became a fully accredited college. In 2004, it moved again to downtown Harare.

In 1954, Dr. Mortenson, TEAM's assistant director, came and assisted in the further organization of the field. A field council was established at this time. This elected body began having regular meetings at which the many issues incumbent upon this rapidly growing field were discussed and decisions made.

In 1955, Orv Dunkeld secured permission from the government to set up a radio network to link all of the stations, using kits obtained from the radio department of Moody Bible Institute. Having this means to communicate with each other on a daily basis was a real blessing! Before this, the missionaries often went for months without any contact between them. Now specific times were set, usually once in the morning and once in the evening, when all the stations would check in and share any necessary information. This radio system also enabled the missionaries in rural areas to talk to their children at the hostel on a regular basis and as special needs arose.

As the missionary force continued to grow and new ways to meet the spiritual needs of the people were envisioned, new ministries were developed. In 1951, Light of Life correspondence courses were established as a way to extend Bible teaching and discipleship into the rural areas and to those unable to attend a more formal Bible school. A literature ministry called "Word of Life" began in 1958. In 1959, Word of Life opened a bookstore in Harare. Two years later Word of Life Publishing was established to produce additional Christian literature, primarily for the Shona people.

With the mission actively involved in training Shona men to become biblically educated pastors and Christian leaders, Mary Danielson became burdened to train their wives. Her vision was realized in 1961, when the Evangelical Homecraft School opened its doors on the Rusambo station. Here women would be trained to be not only effective pastor's wives and women's leaders in the church but also good wives and mothers able to read the Bible and teach their children about God.

When Paul Smith returned from his first furlough in 1963, a radio recording studio was added to the Plot. Christian programs were produced in the Shona language and aired over Trans World Radio (TWR), Swaziland. These programs could be heard throughout Zimbabwe and nearby countries.

In 1964, Missionary Aviation Fellowship (MAF) began providing air service for the field. This opened the door to many new opportunities, including quicker travel for the missionaries, greater evangelistic outreach for the Evangelical Church, and expanded medical care for the outlying stations.

With its home base at Karanda, the new service enabled the doctors from the hospital to make regular visits to the outlying clinics to assist in the medical care of patients at these sites. In emergencies the plane often became an "air ambulance," flying critically ill patients in the vicinity of these other stations to Karanda Hospital, resulting in many lives being saved both medically and spiritually.

Even as God was developing this multi-faceted ministry in Zimbabwe, the missionaries' evangelistic desire to reach the people of neighboring Mozambique never abated. Any opportunity to bring the Gospel to them was eagerly embraced.

Some time after Word of Life radio was launched, programs in the language of the Mozambican people were broadcast into that country. Many responded to the offer of Light of Life correspondence courses. Released inmates from Mozambique who were reached through the prison ministry in Harare also carried these courses back into their homeland.

Eventually the growing number of people who were saved through the Word of Life broadcasts wrote to the radio station requesting help in starting a church. Stephen Bapiro, who became the head of the radio ministry, made several trips into Mozambique to help them get organized. Because the radio programs had so impacted their lives, the people wanted to name their group of churches the "Word of Life Church."

The burden for Mozambique also remained alive on the South Africa field. In 1971, Andrew and Barbara Friend were able to enter Mozambique on student visas to study Portuguese. While doing two years of extensive language study in the capital city of Maputo, they helped an indigenous pastor begin a Theological Education by Extension (TEE) school in the area. When the political instability in the country intensified, however, they were forced to leave. Their attempt to re-enter the country in 1975 failed.

In January 1983, Lee Comly succeeded in driving to Maputo with several South African pastors to assess the situation. As a result of this trip they became actively involved in bringing and sending relief into the country for the next three years. In 1986, Lee and his wife, Sandi, went to Lisbon for a year to study Portuguese, hoping to become even more involved in bringing the Gospel to the people of this African nation.

Mozambique won its independence from Portugal in 1974, but as a communist nation, it remained closed to missionaries. This abruptly changed, however, in July 1989, when the government officially declared its intent to abandon Marxist-Leninism and embrace capitalism. This major philosophical change finally brought a softer attitude towards religious ministries.[23]

Later that same year the Comlys were ready to move to Maputo and officially registered TEAM with the government. Nearly a half-century after the Danielsons and Dunkelds had been turned away, TEAM was officially welcomed into the country. The Comlys served in Mozambique until 1996 and developed an extensive TEE program in the Maputo area.

With the door to Mozambique now open, other missionaries prepared to enter the country. Phil and Karen Dubert arrived in 1991, serving under the South African field. After relieving the Comlys in Maputo during their furlough, the Duberts moved further north to Quelimane in 1993, with the objective of ministering to the Muslim population of this area.

In 1995, Don and Kyla Lester also moved from the South Africa field into Mozambique. Don had come to the Lord through TEAM's ministry in Bindura, Zimbabwe. His wife, Kyla (Kraft), had worked two years at Karanda Hospital. The Lesters ministered for five years in Chimoio, Mozambique, near to the Zimbabwe border.

With the Lesters and Duberts feeling quite isolated from South Africa, jurisdiction over the Mozambique work was transferred to Zimbabwe in 1996. This seemed to be a realistic change as the Zimbabwe field not only had a historic interest in the country but also was in closer proximity to these missionaries and had a better infrastructure in place to manage the ministry there.

Several years later the effort to bring new missionaries into Mozambique took an exciting new turn as an idea proposed by the South Africa field a decade earlier came to fruition. Their idea was to seek Brazilian Christians to minister in Mozambique since the Portuguese language was used in both countries. Thinking that TEAM's Brazil field could perhaps facilitate this, they wrote and presented their idea to them. The timing was evidently not right for this idea to germinate, however, as their letter essentially lay dormant in Brazil for 10 years.

In the meantime God was working within the heart of an independent Mozambican pastor from the town of Dondo, about 30 kilometers outside the coastal city of Beira. Pastor Massasse had been working in a cement factory there and receiving an above-average paycheck. In the early 1990's, however, he felt that God was leading him to quit his job and devote himself to the group of struggling churches he had started.

Some friends enabled him to receive short-term Bible training just across the border in Mutare, Zimbabwe. Strengthened in the Word, he returned to his country and continued establishing numerous churches.

He had been greatly encouraged in his work by a Sunday school publication from the Evangelical Christian Church of Brazil. Because he agreed with everything taught in their magazine, he decided to name his growing group of churches the "Evangelical Christian Church of Mozambique!"

While he had been using laymen to lead these churches, he quickly realized the need for trained leaders if they were to remain doctrinally sound. Not knowing how to address this need, he wrote to the Brazilian church organization several times in the 90s, sharing his burden and seeking their advice, but he never received a reply.

As the new millennium rolled in, TEAM South Africa's letter to TEAM Brazil was re-discovered. This time the idea it presented landed on fertile ground. Three TEAM couples, the Kanagys, Bachellers, and Evans, picked up the vision and began to encourage the 100-year-old Evangelical Christian Church of Brazil to consider a possible missionary outreach to Mozambique.

The idea gained such momentum that in 2001, Tim Evans and two members of the Brazilian church went to visit Phil and Karen Dubert in Mozambique to gain a firsthand look at the spiritual needs of the country. The word of their impending visit spread among the Christian community of Beira and reached Pastor Massasse. When he heard that members of the Brazilian church to which he had repeatedly written were coming to his area, he was so excited that he went to the Beira airport the day before and slept there overnight. He did not want to miss his opportunity to connect with these people!

As the visitors listened to Pastor Massasse's story, they were sure that God had orchestrated their meeting. They decided to forego exploring other possibilities in the country and to devote themselves to working with Pastor Massasse.

In May 2002, a Brazilian delegation returned to Mozambique, and extensive consultation took place between TEAM Zimbabwe/ Mozambique, TEAM South Africa, TEAM Brazil, and Pastor Massasse. Together, they proposed that the Brazilians work with Pastor Massasse in Mozambique under the supervision of the TEAM Zimbabwe/Mozambique field. After the formation of the Evangelical Alliance Mission of Brazil in 2003, a formal document was signed between this newly formed organization and the TEAM Zimbabwe/Mozambique field in October 2003.

Brazilian missionaries began arriving in Zimbabwe the following year. After spending several months being oriented to the African culture and learning conversational English, they proceeded to Dondo, Mozambique, to study the Senna language.

Just as a highway detour eventually brings the traveler back to the original road, so God had brought the detoured missionary endeavor to its original destination, Mozambique! In His wisdom and perfect plan, however, He marvelously used the "detour" to build His Church in northeastern Zimbabwe.

As the door was opening to Mozambique, the Church in northeast Zimbabwe was coming to maturity and the need for missionary involvement there diminished. Even the Karanda Hospital and Evangelical Bible College are becoming more and more indigenized. God's work continues to go forward in the hands of those He raised up through the humble work of the missionaries He called and equipped for service in this sector of the African continent. This is their story of His faithfulness to them in every aspect of their lives. To God be all the praise and honor and glory!

---

[1] Vernon Mortenson, *God Made it Grow* (Pasadena: William Carey Library, 1994), p. 25.

[2] Ibid., 28.

[3] Ibid., 25-26.

[4] Ibid. 26.

[5] Ibid., 26-27.

[6] Ibid., 25.

[7] Ibid., 27, 39-40.

[8] Ibid., 26, 38.

[9] Ibid., 40.

[10] Ibid., 51-52.

[11] Ibid., 156.

[12] Ibid., 158.

[13] Ibid.

[14] Ibid., 190.

[15] Ibid., 190-92.

[16] Ibid., 192-93.

[17] Ibid., 193.

[18] Ibid.

[19] Ibid, 650.

[20] Ibid., 649-50.

[21] Ibid., 222.

[22] Ibid., 651.

[23] Ibid., 647.

# CHAPTER 2

# God Called

*"The LORD had said to Abram, 'Leave your country,*
*your people and your father's household*
*and go to the land I will show you.'"*
(Genesis 12:1)

G od's plan always precedes God's call; but God's call initiates the fulfillment of God's plan. God's call to Abram set in motion His redemptive plan for all of mankind through the nation of Israel. In like manner God's plan for the evangelization of the people of the Zambezi River Valley in northeast Zimbabwe was set in motion by the call He began sending into the hearts of specifically chosen individuals.

## The First Pioneers

Mary Maluske was one of the first pioneers to whom God issued His call. After being led to the Lord by a teen-aged suitor, who became a student at Moody Bible Institute, Mary worked for a year cleaning houses in the Detroit area so that she too could go to Moody.

Even before she arrived, however, God opened her eyes to the spiritual need of the whole world. Her heart was deeply moved and she committed herself to become a foreign missionary. The strength of the call she felt on her life for missionary service never weakened.

After graduating from Moody, she finished her high school education at Wheaton Academy and went on to Wheaton College to train as a teacher. Through these years she was extremely active in prayer bands for missions and surrounded herself with friends who were headed in the same direction.

During this time she heard many missionary speakers and became acquainted with the Scandinavian Alliance Mission (S.A.M.). She also learned of their desire to begin a new work in Mozambique, where only two Protestant mission stations existed among five million people. This captured her attention, and God soon created within her a burning desire to join in this effort. She applied to S.A.M. and was delighted to be accepted as a missionary for this new outreach in southeast Africa.

God also began working in the heart of Rudy Danielson, son of poor Swedish immigrants in Minnesota. He too felt a strong desire to attend Moody Bible Institute after accepting Christ as his Savior as a teenager. He worked hard to earn the necessary money and was finally able to enroll in 1927, just a year behind Mary Maluske. He wrote:

*I hadn't been there long before I began to hear God's command, "Go ye into all the world and preach the Gospel to every creature . . . ." It scared me at first, for I hadn't thought of being a missionary, and to leave home and country and go to [an unreached] land with the Gospel was more than I had counted on. It was a long time before I finally came to the place of yieldedness and said, "Here am I, Lord, send me."* [1]

Upon finishing his studies at Moody, Rudy followed the same course Mary Maluske had, continuing his education at Wheaton Academy and Wheaton College. When he graduated in 1936, he had a great desire to go on to Dallas Theological Seminary. The call of God upon his heart for missionary service became so strong, however, that after being accepted, he decided to proceed towards the mission field instead.

He immediately applied to S.A.M., whose general director, Dr. T. J. Bach, had spoken at Rudy's home church. Rudy, too, was particularly interested in the fact that S.A.M. was endeavoring to start a work in Mozambique. The needs of this country had been deeply laid upon his heart years ago by a fellow student at Moody, and Rudy had been praying ever since about going there to help.

As he was ready to depart for Portugal for language study, he expressed his total dedication to this mission:

> *"I rejoice in the great privilege that is mine of bearing the blessed Gospel message to [Mozambique]."[2] "I am ready to spend and be spent that Christ's Saving Grace may be made known through my testimony."[3] "And now, farewell America! If we should not meet again on earth, we'll all join in the 'Redemption Song' up there."[4]*

Little did he know that this was indeed his final farewell to his homeland.

Helen Hughes, another of the first pioneer missionaries to Zimbabwe, felt God's call when she was only eight years old, her tender heart responding to the message of missionaries speaking at her church in Collingswood, New Jersey. In spite of graduating from high school in the middle of the depression, God made it possible for her to attend Moody Bible Institute as well.

There she met Orval Dunkeld, another student, who did not share her interest in missions at all. She described their initial relationship:

> *We were sitting next to each other at a meeting listening to a missionary speaker. As he showed his slides, Orv turned to me and said, "You can have your bugs."*
>
> *Later, however, as the missionary showed some of the Christian believers whose lives had been changed, I turned to him and said, "Is it worth it?"*
>
> *Although I didn't know about it for some time, God was seemingly hedging Orv in, moving him towards obedience to His call to missionary service as well. His roommate, Norman Weiss, "happened" to be headed for the mission field himself. That evening Orv talked and prayed with this roommate for quite awhile—and came away a missionary candidate.*

*Orv's roommate told us about the Scandinavian Alliance Mission and the prayer meetings that they had on Monday nights for their missionaries. We started attending these meetings and were very impressed by the way they prayed for their missionaries. We thought how wonderful it would be to have this kind of prayer support as missionaries.*

*One week when we went to the prayer meeting, the mission was having a commissioning service for Mary Maluske. Mr. Jensen, chairman of the South Africa field, told about the trip he and one of the other missionaries had made into Mozambique and the great need of the people in the Tete area, who were without any kind of a Gospel witness at all. Upon hearing this, Orv and I both felt that that was where God wanted us, so we applied to S.A.M. for the Mozambique field.*

God was not only giving these young people a similar vision for missionary service in Mozambique, He was also orchestrating His plans for matrimony among them. Perhaps He felt this was a better way for them to approach working so closely together on the new field to which He was leading them.

After being friends for years, Rudy Danielson and Mary Maluske began courting shortly before Mary departed for language studies in Portugal. Rudy proposed, and Mary accepted, via mail. They were married in 1938, after Rudy joined her in Portugal. Later that same year back in the United States, Orval Dunkeld and Helen Hughes were also married before heading overseas.

These were the two missionary couples who initially joined the South Africa field, hoping to begin a new work in Mozambique. After failing to gain permission to enter that country, they made their way up to the Zambezi River Valley in northeast Zimbabwe, setting up the Msengedzi mission station in 1942.

*Their plan* was to locate just across the border from Mozambique so that they would be ready to move in if that country should ever open itself to Protestant missionaries. *God's plan* was to build an extensive missionary work in Zimbabwe first, starting with their humble beginning at Msengedzi.

# Nature of the Call

What constitutes a call to foreign missions and the manner in which it is recognized can be as diverse as the people to whom God sends it. Nevertheless, at some point in time the Holy Spirit usually lays a burden for the unsaved in other lands so strongly upon one's heart that the person feels compelled by God to become personally involved in bringing the Gospel message to them.

## A Shared Burden

Often God uses an exposure to the hearts of other missionaries as a way of issuing His call. This was reflected in the testimony of almost every TEAM Zimbabwe missionary. Some were exposed as children or teenagers through their churches, youth activities, or summer camps or by having missionaries stay in their homes. Others had their first encounter with missionaries when they went to Bible school or college. As they listened to these missionaries share their firsthand experiences in the needy harvest fields of the world, God stirred their own hearts with the desire to become personally involved as laborers in His global workforce too.

Russ Jackson grew up on a farm in Western Canada and was the last in his family to accept the Lord. When God finally won his heart, however, there was no turning back for Russ. He fell in love with the Word of God and began memorizing Scripture. Then one day two years later, while plowing in the field, he stopped the horses and got down on his knees, surrendering himself completely to God and asking God to lead him according to His will.

By the time he was nineteen, he felt strongly called by God to preach the Gospel. His father's health was failing, however, so he didn't see how he could possibly leave the farm to get training. Much to his surprise, when he told his mother of his call, she told him, "God is better able to care for Dad and me than you are. You must go."

The only place Russ knew to get training was at the Salvation Army School in Toronto, so he enrolled there. Just as he was graduating, he met a young woman who really attracted his attention. She was Margaret LeGrow and was just beginning her training there. They remained in contact, carrying out a long-distance courtship regulated by many Salvation Army guidelines. They were eventually married in 1944. Both were committed to serving the Lord with their lives, but after being out on their various assignments with the Salvation Army, they mutually felt that the Lord had something else for them.

In 1946, Russ accepted a call to pastor a church in Briercrest, Saskatchewan. Here he and Marg attended the annual missionary conference at Briercrest Bible Institute, where they were introduced to worldwide missions. One day Russ described to Marg how as a lad back on the farm his greatest joy was to clear the bush away, break up the soil, and plow where the soil had never been plowed before. Then he added, "I would love to preach the Gospel in a land where the Gospel has never been heard before."

Every day they continued to listen with great interest as missionaries described their work and the challenge of reaching the lost on their particular field. Several spoke of the enormous unreached areas in Africa and the pressing need for missionaries there. Russ described their response and God's leading in their lives:

> *Back in our room at night Margaret and I would discuss all that we had heard, and then we would kneel by our bed to pray together. During these times of prayer the Lord clearly laid upon our hearts a burden for the unreached of Africa.*
>
> *A mission known at that time as the Scandinavian Alliance Mission . . . was well represented at the conference. On one occasion after the morning conference session, I approached the Canadian representative, brother Arthur Dalke, and shared with him that my wife and I were definitely interested in foreign missions and that we felt the Lord was speaking to us about service in Africa. [He] instantly replied, "Russell, you must meet Brother Bach. He is the Director of S.A.M. and he is here at this conference."*
>
> *That same morning, between conference sessions, Art Dalke led me to a group of men chatting together and introduced me to them. . . . Much to my surprise, the three men, including Dr. Bach, put their arms around me and began to pray. How well do I remember Dr. Bach's prayer! While still*

*holding me in a firm grip with his arms, he said, "Dear Lord, this young lad wants to preach the Gospel in Africa. Now, dear Lord, take him and his young wife and their baby girl to Africa and use them for your glory in reaching unreached men and women in that desperately needy field." When the men finally released me, I found myself deeply moved with a consciousness of the Lord's presence and also of His approval for our going to Africa.*

*As soon as possible I went directly to our room to share the exciting situation with Margaret. When I burst into our room, I shouted, "Margaret, we are on our way to Africa! A man just finished praying that the Lord would take us to Africa, and I've never heard anyone pray as this man prayed, and, Margaret, he is the general director of the mission!"*

*I learned later that the Canadian board met the following day . . . and our names came up. . . . A message was sent to me to plan to attend S.A.M.'s annual conference, soon to be held in Pontiac, Michigan. One of the board members, I learned, was Mr. Carl Gundersen, and he had said, "Tell this young lad 'Jackson' to be at the conference, and if he doesn't have the money for the train fare, I will personally be responsible for this."*

*. . . On the day the annual conference began in Michigan, I was there. When I arrived at the church, however, it was empty, as everyone was out for lunch. I wandered around the empty church until I found the literature table. I read several mission communications and then my eyes fell upon a brochure entitled "For Rudy So Loved."*

*The tract told of S.A.M.'s pioneer field in Zimbabwe and the story of Rudy Danielson, who went to the Zambezi Valley with his wife, Mary, to preach the Gospel to the masses of men and women living and dying in total spiritual darkness. Then it told the shocking news of Rudy's untimely death from typhoid fever just two years later. It ended with a powerful challenge: Who will go to continue the work that Rudy started? As soon as I finished reading the tract, I felt the Lord had forever settled in my mind where He wanted me to spend the rest of my life.*

The Jacksons immediately submitted their application to S.A.M. and were accepted. God wonderfully provided for their support, and in May 1948, they sailed for Zimbabwe. They were part of the second wave of missionaries that came after World War II when travel was considered safe again.

Wilfred Strom grew up in Canada as the eleventh child in a Christian family. He and his siblings were richly exposed to missionaries, who often stayed in their home. What an impact this had on their lives! Four of them became missionaries themselves.

Wilf was one of these children who definitely felt the call of God upon his life for missionary service. Upon graduation from high school, he proceeded to Prairie Bible Institute. While there, he heard speakers from many different mission fields and felt God specifically call him to go to a pioneer field.

At Bible school he also met Dorothy Pearce, who was becoming increasingly interested in missions as well. Their relationship grew and they were engaged shortly after graduating in 1949.

Dorothy had come to know the Lord through a radio ministry she listened to just before graduation exercises from high school. She had planned to go on to university, but now she feared that she might falter in her newfound faith there because of her lack of Bible teaching. She decided to go to Bible school instead, but she had no idea where to find one.

About that time one of her neighbors died. A friend of Dorothy's family had been nursing this woman and told her mother that a relative who had come to the burial spoke of a Bible school in his town. She couldn't remember, however, if the town was Two Hills or Three Hills, Alberta. Dorothy was very interested, so she wrote a letter to "The Bible School" at each of these possible towns. One letter was returned and the other bore fruit, bringing information about the Prairie Bible Institute at Three Hills.

She immediately applied and was accepted. At Prairie she heard many truths for the first time, but the two that really gripped her were the return of Christ and the spiritual need of those who had never heard the Gospel message. She began asking the Lord to allow her to go as a missionary to such a place. God not only continued to lead her in this direction, but He also brought Wilf Strom to her as a life-partner driven by the same passion.

After Bible school she and Wilf continued their preparation by attending a missionary medicine course at Pacific Bible College in Fresno, California. When they completed that, they returned to Canada and were married. Then they attended a Summer Institute of Linguistics (SIL) course at Briercrest Bible Institute.

During this time they also investigated several mission societies. TEAM told them of their vision to open a work in Irian Jaya, which greatly interested them. Because visas for other Irian Jaya candidates were being delayed, TEAM suggested that they take a pastorate while waiting for the situation to change. When their formal applications to TEAM were finalized and accepted, they were designated for the New Guinea field where Wilf would become part of a three-man team to enter and develop this new area. The other two men were Ed Tritt and Walter Erickson.

After two years had transpired with no progress at all regarding their visas, TEAM asked if they would feel at liberty to change their plans to another field. They were open to this but stated that they would really like to be involved in a pioneer work.

TEAM then sent them information about their relatively new work in Zimbabwe. As Wilf and Dorothy prayed and inquired about other fields, they felt God directing them to Zimbabwe. They resigned their pastorate, had prayer cards printed, and set up a deputation schedule, only to have TEAM inform them that it appeared that their visas were going to be granted for Irian Jaya.

Given the opportunity to go to either field, they retained their confidence that the Lord had redirected them to Zimbabwe. They felt that if God still wanted them to go to Irian Jaya, the granting of the visas could have come six weeks earlier. Little did they know that Tritt and Erickson, who did proceed to Irian Jaya, would both be murdered by their porters while making an exploratory trek inland. God had different plans for the Stroms.

## A Penetrating Message

Many missionaries can precisely reiterate a single penetrating message that God used to compel them to missionary service. It may have been a challenge given by a missionary or other respected Christian leader, or it may have been a burning message impressed upon their hearts from God's Word.

Norman and Thelma Everswick were both exposed to missionaries in their homes and Sunday schools as they grew up, but they first felt the call to missionary service themselves after they were married and attending Trinity Bible College in Minneapolis.

Norman led the mission prayer band there each week, and one day they became deeply challenged by the words of John 4:35: *"Do you not say, 'Four months more and then the harvest'? I tell you, open your eyes and look at the fields! They are ripe for harvest."* Together, they were deeply convicted that they needed to do more than pray for other missionaries. "Why wait for others to go?" they asked. "We will answer the call ourselves."

The Everswicks were also part of the second wave of missionaries arriving after the war. Because they had a child, their departure was delayed nine months while the ocean mines were cleared out and the government would permit a child to travel on a troop ship. They eventually sailed on the same ship with Mary Danielson and her daughter, Muriel, as they returned to the field after Rudy's death.

Carl and Donna Hendrickson grew up attending the Evangelical Covenant Church of Los Angeles, in which missions was heavily emphasized. In 1947, as teenage sweethearts, they attended a summer camp in Forest Home, California. While there, they were both deeply impacted by the missionary speaker and particularly the verse he used, which was John 20:21 (KJV): *"As my Father hath sent me, even so send I you."* As a result, they both dedicated their lives to serve God in missions and, more specifically, in Africa.

Lynn Hoyt clearly remembers her pastor, Dr. Charles W. Anderson, teaching that *everybody is called to go into missions unless God keeps you home.* This had a major effect on her life. Later, as she attended Gordon College, she was also impressed with the zeal of soldiers who were returning from Korea and wanting to return there as missionaries.

Wilma Gardziella and Diane Powell were both impacted by the statistics that 90% of all Christian workers were ministering to the 10% of the world that spoke English while only 10% were ministering to the 90% of the world that did not. These figures were dramatically likened to a heavy log being carried by nine men on one end and only one on the other end, followed by the penetrating question, "Which end do you want to help carry?"

Judy Everswick heard a similar message from a missionary speaker at a high school youth conference. As she heard her speak of how those in the United States have so much opportunity to hear the Gospel while much of the rest of the world had never even heard the name of Jesus, Judy was so moved that she committed herself right then to serving God in Africa.

Joe Reimer was greatly influenced by the godly example of his parents, who spent five years as tentmakers in Mexico while he was a child. As he grew into his teen years, he continued to be impacted by his father's belief that Christians were to be ministering to the spiritually and physically underprivileged. This was one of the major factors leading Joe to a commitment to missionary service himself.

## A Growing Conviction

While some missionaries can point to a precise moment of time at which they received their call to missions, others experience it as a slowly growing inner conviction of the heart. In some instances God seems to weave together a web of circumstances that eventually leads the person to make a firm commitment to personal involvement in missions. For others, an initial commitment is made but waxes and wanes awhile before becoming solidified.

Barb Christiansen experienced a call to missions that developed through a number of incremental steps. She wrote:

> *From my earliest years my family attended the First Baptist Church of Pontiac, Michigan, which always had a strong emphasis on missions. . . . I remember anticipating Uncle Ralph's weekly missionary story told with great passion and expression in children's church. We also had frequent missionary speakers as well as an annual missionary conference. The Scandinavian Alliance Mission occasionally held its annual conference in our church, and my parents often hosted missionaries in our home.*
>
> *As a very young girl, I witnessed Orval and Helen Dunkeld's farewell service as they headed for Africa. I also listened with great interest to their reports when they returned on furlough. I was too young, however, to take note of their mission board or their specific field of service.*

*When I was fourteen, I was very impressed with a young missionary candidate named Lillian Nelson, whom we had as a guest in our home. She seemed so young and had such an engaging personality. I felt drawn to her and always remembered her. Again, however, I was not really aware of her mission board or field of service.*

*Our church encouraged us to use our musical and other abilities for the Lord in our youth programs. I loved playing the piano and was very seriously devoted to it, being enrolled in the Sherwood Music School and eventually achieving a teacher's certificate. I even had a youthful dream of becoming a concert pianist.*

*My plans to make a career of music were challenged, however, when our high school Bible club had a guest speaker named J. Stratton Shufelt, an accomplished vocalist who traveled with evangelistic teams. His testimony really touched my heart. I was greatly impressed that he had given up a secular career in music to serve the Lord. In my spirit I was sensitive to the Lord's leading and wanted to serve Him too.*

*This man's challenge continued to ring in my ears as I returned home to study for a geometry exam. I could not concentrate or shake off the conviction I was feeling until I knelt by my bed and gave my whole life to Christ, telling Him that any musical ability I might have was His to be used for His glory. At that point I committed myself to go wherever He might lead. Soon after this I found and claimed Psalm 32:8 [KJV] for myself: "I will instruct thee and teach thee in the way which thou shalt go. I will guide thee with mine eye."*

*Putting my musical ambitions aside, I began to feel drawn to nursing as a profession, knowing I could use that to serve the Lord in many ways, including perhaps on the mission field. I therefore enrolled in West Suburban Hospital, which had recently begun a 5-year program for nursing in conjunction with Wheaton College.*

*My interest in Africa developed over time, beginning with those weekly missionary stories by "Uncle Ralph." With all the exposure I had to missions in our church, Africa seemed to stand out in my mind more than any other field. Because of my interest in missions and Africa, I joined an outreach program at Wheaton College to the African-American children of south Chicago. . . . In this ministry I met Phil Christiansen, who had a similar background and interest in missions.*

*After our marriage and completion of schooling we applied to TEAM, which we learned was the former Scandinavian Alliance Mission. We were very excited when Dr. Vernon Mortenson told us about a new hospital being planned in Zimbabwe. We thought this would be a perfect place for both of us, as Phil had trained as a medical technologist.*

*That summer we attended a TEAM picnic and met some of the TEAM Zimbabwe missionaries. One young-looking, blonde missionary on furlough looked very familiar to me. Yes, it was Lillian Nelson—now Lillian Austin! I was completely amazed, having had no idea she was serving with TEAM in Zimbabwe too.*

Don Hoyt's obedience to the Lord's call on his life for missions also went through several stages. The American Baptist Church he grew up in was not significantly involved in missions, leaving Don quite unfamiliar with the whole concept. The church's youth ministry often interacted with other churches in the county, however. Through this means Don met Pastor Emil Gaverluk from another church. Sometime during his senior year in high school, this man confronted Don with a poignant question. "Don," he asked, "have you ever considered the ministry for your life?"

Don was totally taken aback by this, as such a thought had never crossed his mind. His plans at that time were to go to Bucknell University to study business. The pastor's question struck a responsive chord in his heart, however, and this became the beginning of God's calling him to foreign missions.

As Don redirected his path towards preparing for the ministry, it was a total step into the dark for him. He was clueless as to what that would involve.

Since Pastor Gaverluk had attended Gordon College of

Theology and Missions in Boston, Don decided to go there too. This is where his exposure to missions began. Early in his freshman year he responded with the conviction that he could not see a reason why he should not be involved in missions, and that conviction stuck with him for the rest of his life.

At Gordon College he met Lynn Grigg, who was also preparing for missions. They were married after Don's second year, and both continued their education, Don in business and Lynn in education.

During that time Dick and Marge Winchell, TEAM missionaries who had just returned from South Africa on their first furlough, spoke at their church. Don and Lynn were drawn to them, and they ended up spending a significant amount of time together. Through them, they became interested in TEAM as a mission board. The Winchells also shared their burden to establish a literature ministry throughout South Africa and spoke of the need for bookstore managers. With Don's training in business, this seemed like a potential "fit" for the Hoyts.

After completing his business degree, Don had a discouraging year seeking further theological training. This resulted in his turning away from the goal of missions and seeking employment in business.

God did not let go of His plans for this couple, however. As they attended the annual missionary conference in their home church, the pastor poignantly addressed the audience one night, saying, *"There are couples sitting in this audience today who have committed themselves to overseas missions, and you need to give the Lord a good reason for why you are still here."* Don was so affected by these words that he felt like his heart was going to explode.

He and Lynn went home, got down on their knees, and recommitted themselves to missions. They then drove to TEAM headquarters and talked to the director, Dr. Vernon Mortenson. After listening to their story, he specifically challenged them to consider the need for a bookstore manager in Zimbabwe to take Martin Uppendahl's place.

They prayed about this on the way home and were soon overwhelmed with the assurance that God had been preparing them for just this. They raised all their support and arrived in Zimbabwe less than eighteen months later.

Pat Mortenson was another missionary whose call evolved over time as she overcame a number of hurdles and misconceptions about missionary life. She wrote:

*As a child of missionary parents in China, missions to me meant war with bombs, fleeing from an enemy, famine, and winter spent in the mountains far away from home. When I left China at five years of age, I never wanted to see it again.*

*En route back to the USA we spent six months traveling across India to reach Bombay, where we would board our ship. We stopped at many S.A.M. stations, and I began to get a broader exposure to missions. As I experienced the warmth, the flowers, the fruit, and the abundance of food, I thought I was in heaven.*

*One station was operating an orphanage for little Indian girls who had been saved from the refuse pile of society. I was deeply impacted by Gladys Hendriksen and wanted to grow up and be a missionary "mother" to orphans just like her. She became my early role model, and I started praying for several of the little girls in her orphanage and following their life stories.*

*After we returned to the States, we lived at S.A.M. Headquarters in Chicago. Here I had the opportunity to meet most of the missionaries who were returning from their fields as well as the new missionaries going out. Conversation around our dinner table was always interesting and challenging, and I could not think of anything I would rather do than become a missionary too. Gradually my ambitions shifted from being an orphanage "mom" to being a missionary nurse.*

*When I was nine, I had a Sunday school teacher who had been a missionary in Africa for a short time. She challenged me to choose a life verse for myself, and I chose Proverbs 3:5-6 [NKJV]: "Trust in the Lord with all your heart and lean not on your own understanding. In all your ways acknowledge Him and he shall direct your paths." This was my first real commitment to serve the Lord as a missionary, if He should so direct.*

*Learning how to trust the Lord to direct my paths was not without its hurdles. As I thought of actually being on a mission field, I had to confront some of the negative aspects of what this would mean and what I might miss out on.*

*When I was thirteen, my father made a mission visit to Zimbabwe. In a letter he told us about camping in the bush and shooting at what he thought was a small antelope. It turned out to be a lion that started to charge at him. Fortunately, the other missionaries were able to take it down before my father was hurt. I also knew Eunice Ott, who was bitten by a rabid dog and died there. This all made Africa seem like a fearful place to me. At that point I told God that I would go anywhere but China or Africa.*

*A close friend of mine in nursing school, however, was Muriel Danielson, the daughter of Rudy and Mary Danielson. She loved Africa even though her father had died there and she had to leave home at age five or six to attend a non-Christian boarding school. Many Zimbabwe missionaries coming through Chicago would visit Muriel, and I was able to meet them. I believe these were people that God put in my path to change my mind about Africa and eventually draw me to Zimbabwe.*

*As I approached the end of my nurses' training, I had a period of time in which I began to question whether missions was just a childhood dream of mine or the true leading of God in my life. I believe this is an important question to resolve for a "missionary kid" (MK). I attended the Urbana '61 missionary conference that year, and through several speakers there, including an African Bishop from Uganda, I felt God confirm His call to me.*

*When I applied to TEAM, I was encouraged to go on to graduate studies in Bible and missions. It was at Columbia Bible College that my call to missions really matured. As I learned much more of the greatness of God's love to me, the richness of His grace, and the marvelous plan that He had for reaching all of mankind, I became truly "constrained" by the love of God to be a part of that plan (2 Corinthians 5:14).*

*I attended TEAM Candidate School in 1964, still undes-
ignated as to what field I would go. The following year as I
was ready to embark upon deputation, Orla Blair,
Zimbabwe field chairman at the time, wrote and asked me to
consider coming to the Karanda hospital nursing program
in Zimbabwe. Shortly after receiving his letter, I attended
TEAM's annual conference, and while there, I became
comfortable with this request being God's leading for me.*

*As a Zimbabwe "appointee," I put together a selection
of slides from that country, including one of the great
Victoria Falls. As I reflected on its majestic power, God led
me to use it as an illustration of 2 Corinthians 5:14-20 and
the final stage of my call. As the rather lazy Zambezi River
is suddenly "constrained" by the rock formation around it
and transformed into an incredibly rushing force plummet-
ing with a mighty roar into the narrow gorge below, so
God's love constrains and empowers us as believers,
compelling us to enter into His plan of reconciliation and
become ambassadors for the King of Kings. How well this
represented the change in my own life as my eyes became
fixed, not on the temporal sacrifices, adjustments, stresses,
and strains of cross-cultural ministry, but on Christ and His
plan for all people of the world!*

## Time of the Call

God calls individuals to missionary service at all stages of life.
Some, like the prophet Samuel, hear His call at a very tender age. A
few hear it immediately upon salvation. Many sense it as they move
into their teen years and begin to consider what direction to take
with their lives after high school. In some cases God uses an
increased exposure to missionaries while in college or Bible school
to direct a person's path into missions. Some do not hear God's call
until they reach early adulthood and are searching for the right
place to "put down roots."

Others are well established in various occupations when they
feel God asking them to change direction and use their particular
skills on the mission field. God even calls some when they have

retired from successful careers and are entering a time of greater freedom in their lives.

## At Salvation

Ruth Anderson Regier grew up in South Dakota as the youngest of seven children, who loved to sing together. They did quite well and were often invited to sing at various gatherings. When she was twelve, they sang at a young people's camp. That night the Gospel message penetrated her heart, and she accepted the Lord as her Savior. Immediately, she knew in her heart that the Lord was calling her to be a missionary in Africa.

While she didn't really live for the Lord in high school, God again corralled her heart at a summer camp. This time it was a Free Church camp in Medicine Lake, Minnesota. Here she got her focus back onto God and rededicated her life to serving Him.

After graduating from St. Paul Bible College in 1951, she applied to TEAM, as she was most familiar with this mission through her church and family. She was accepted and went to Candidate School in 1952 and then went on to earn a teachers' training degree. In February 1955, she arrived in Zimbabwe.

Dottie Larsen's family hosted many missionaries in their home. She also had an uncle serving with TEAM in India. With all this exposure to missionaries Dottie could not help but be impacted. From the time she was saved at age 10, she felt strongly that she wanted to be a missionary nurse.

As she matured, Dottie also drifted away from the Lord for awhile. When she returned, however, she felt God renew this call. The verses that really challenged her at that point were Isaiah 6:8-9 (KJV): *"I heard the voice of the Lord, saying, 'Whom shall I send and who will go for us?' Then said I, 'Here am I; send me.'"*

Pat Dunkeld felt called to missions even *before* she "officially" accepted the Lord as her Savior when she was 12. She wrote:

> *For almost as long as I can remember, I felt the tug of missions on my heart. Growing up in a Southern Baptist church, we had "Lottie Moon" offerings and occasional missionary speakers, including our own pastor's daughter and her husband. I was greatly impressed, even as a young*

*child, to hear of the very real persecution they faced when preaching the Gospel in Brazil and yet their apparent joy in continuing on and seeing God at work.*

*Two years after I was saved, I dedicated my life to serving the Lord wherever He wanted me to go. By the time I got to Moody Bible Institute, having heard a lot more missionary stories and being more aware of some of the harsh realities of cross-cultural living, I decided that I would keep things simple and go as a single person. At that time Europe seemed to keep coming to my attention as a destination.*

*My best-laid plans were turned upside down, however, by a certain MK who not only seemed quite well adjusted but who also had a great desire not to run from, but to return to, what he considered his home country of Zimbabwe. Good-by singleness! Hello marriage! Good-by Europe! Hello Africa!*

*I'm certainly grateful that God knows best—and accomplishes His will when we allow Him to lead. Thirty-five years later I am still blessed with the memories of those years of being Mrs. Dick Dunkeld and doubly blessed to remain part of the Dunkeld family even after Dick went home to be with the Lord in 1972.*

Chris Goppert was nineteen when he was saved and reported that he, too, immediately felt called by God to be a missionary. He shared this testimony:

*On the night of my conversion it occurred to me that many, many thousands of people were in a similar position as I in never having heard the Word of Grace. It was then and there in an attitude of prayer that I said, "Lord, I want to present my life in service to you, as a tribute and as a sacrifice of thanksgiving for what you have done for me."*

Later, Chris found 1 Samuel 12:24 (KJV), which he felt expressed the motivation of his heart on that night so well: *"Only fear the LORD, and serve him in truth with all your heart: for consider how great things he hath done for you."* This is what launched Chris towards his missionary career and continues to keep him going day by day.

## In Childhood

Marlene Georgia wanted to be a missionary from the time she was a very young girl, primarily because of the many missionaries she heard speak at her church. When she got to Taylor University, however, and had to decide whether to go forward in this direction or to move into a teaching career in the States, she struggled with the Lord a little over taking this final step.

As she prayed about it, however, she felt God wanted her to relinquish herself totally to His will and to say from her heart, "Anywhere, Lord." Responding positively to this confirming word from the Lord, she set her course on missions.

Lynne Hawkins had talked about being a missionary to the orphans in Korea since childhood. This never changed for her as she grew up.

After graduating from BIOLA and applying to TEAM, she went to Candidate School in 1965 designated for Korea. While there, however, she learned that orphanages were being phased out in Korea, as the need was decreasing. Not knowing what to do, she told Candidate Secretary Delbert Kuehl to select a field for her. He, however, urged her to wait on the Lord and see how He would lead her.

As Candidate School progressed and she heard reports from various countries, she began to feel the Lord leading her towards Zimbabwe. She prayed about this over the summer and gradually became convinced that this was indeed where God wanted her.

Arriving on the field in 1967, her varied ministries have included working with orphans and other needy children. House of Hope, where Lynne now ministers, has rescued many girls off the streets and given them a place to live and an opportunity to reshape their lives in a Christian environment.

Nancy Everswick was only nine years old when she felt God call her to be a missionary. She was deeply moved at a missions conference at her church as one of the speakers challenged the audience to be willing to go wherever, and be whatever, the Lord wanted. As she made this commitment within herself, she immediately thought of Africa as the place that was most needy.

## In Teen Years

Carol Olsen Austin remembers her father praying that God would use one of his children on the mission field. As a young child, she would think to herself, "I will probably be that one." The idea of leaving home and family to go so far away was something she struggled with for quite some time, however. She wrote:

> *Over the years God kept working in my heart. . . . When I was sixteen, my parents took my brothers and me to a missionary meeting at Moody Church near downtown Chicago. The Reverend Oswald Smith from Toronto, Canada, gave a very challenging message for missions and then invited young people to come forward who would "be willing" to go to a mission field if the Lord called them. Before I knew it, I was up and out of my seat and walking down the aisle. . . . Reverend Smith prayed for us, and as I turned around to rejoin my family, I remember seeing a big smile on my dad's face. Mother, too, was glad for me and was the one who became my encourager in the years to come.*

Knowing that she would need Bible training, Carol applied to Moody Bible Institute. World War II had just ended, however, and Moody was filled with returning servicemen. She then applied to Northwestern Schools in Minneapolis. She and her cousin Norma were both accepted and became roommates. Norma always wanted to be a nurse, but that was the farthest thing from Carol's mind. Nevertheless, they both got jobs as nurse's aides at a nearby hospital. Here, much to her surprise, Carol "fell in love with nursing."

After graduating from Northwestern, she was eager to apply for nurses' training. Her father's congestive heart failure had worsened, however, and he was now bed-ridden under her mother's care. Carol offered to put off going to nursing school in order to help her mother care for her dad.

"Absolutely not!" her mother responded. "You need the nursing degree to use on the mission field, and I will not have you delayed in your plans."

With this word from her mother, Carol proceeded to enroll at Swedish Covenant Hospital in Chicago. Here she was delighted to learn that ten of her classmates were also preparing for missionary service.

During her senior year she began attending TEAM's weekly prayer meetings and became acquainted with the staff and other missionary candidates. One week Dr. Mortenson asked her why they hadn't received her application yet, and she knew it was time to take this final step. When she heard the news that she was officially accepted as a candidate for Zimbabwe, she did not even know where the country was located.

God also gave Helen Smith an interest in missionaries from the time she was a little girl. She remembers hearing about the sinking of the ZamZam in the Atlantic Ocean during World War II and being concerned about the missionaries on board.

This early interest in missionaries did not become a personal call, however, until after she graduated from high school. One evening she accompanied some people from her church to a missionary banquet for the South Africa General Mission. At the end of his presentation, the speaker asked, "If there is anyone here who is willing to go to the mission field if the Lord should so lead, will you stand to your feet?" Helen felt as if something was literally pushing her out of her seat. She stood up and determined from that time that she would go to the mission field.

While attending Northwestern Bible School, Helen met Paul Smith. God had stirred his heart with an interest in missionary radio when he heard Clarence Jones from HCJB speak at a missions conference near his home in Iowa. This was solidified when he listened to Austin Paul from Africa Inland Mission speak at Northwestern. Paul's inner response was, "I can do that!" and from that moment he committed himself to move in this direction.

Paul and Helen were married in June 1950. As they began thinking about possible mission boards, a friend suggested that they apply to TEAM. The few people from TEAM that Helen had met seemed like such "spiritual giants" in her mind, that she was sure TEAM would never accept them. Nevertheless, they applied and were accepted. In 1957, they arrived in Zimbabwe.

Dr. Roland Stephens began to hear God's call when he was in junior high school. He reported:

> *Our pastor at that time had been a missionary in Angola for forty years. The great regret of his life was that he had not gotten medical training so that he could have ministered to the physical needs of the people as well as their spiritual needs. That was the beginning of my interest in medical missions.*
>
> *As I continued to prepare for this, I was very interested in going to Irian Jaya. However, because there was no hospital set up there yet and there was a great need of a surgeon to join the other two doctors at Karanda Hospital in Zimbabwe, TEAM asked me to consider going there instead.*

Roland accepted this recommendation. Little did he, or TEAM, realize that both of Karanda's other doctors would soon need to return permanently to the States. He and his wife, Kathy, arrived on the field in 1962.

## In Early Adult Years

Betty Mason Wolfe didn't hear the true Gospel message preached until after she had graduated from high school. When she was saved, however, she was so thrilled to know she was going to heaven that she wanted to spend the rest of her life doing whatever God wanted her to do.

Feeling so far behind the others in her church in Bible knowledge, Betty began to contemplate going to Bible school. As she did, she put out a fleece, praying that if God wanted her to go, she would be fired from her job because someone more efficient was found to take her place. This is exactly what happened.

Since her Sunday school teacher at that time had attended the Bible Institute of Los Angeles (BIOLA), she applied there and was accepted. At BIOLA she heard a different missionary speaker every week. When she heard someone from South America, she wanted to go there. When she heard someone from Africa, she wanted to go there. When she heard Dick Hillis from China, she said to herself,

"I would never go there!"

When she came home for summer vacation after her first year at BIOLA, a fine Christian young man wanted to court her. She felt much too immature emotionally for romance at that point, but her mother almost forced her to write to him after he shipped out with the army.

This upset her so much that she became desperate to know the Lord's will for her life. As a result, she reported, "It was almost like a voice spoke to me only one word—'China.'" She argued with the Lord about that for the rest of the summer, but by the beginning of the next semester she went back to BIOLA with the intent of preparing to go to China, even enrolling in an evening class in Chinese.

After graduating from BIOLA, she went to nurses' training. As she neared the end of this, she learned that her good friend, Dorothy, from BIOLA had gone to the Tibetan Frontier under TEAM. Betty thought, "If TEAM accepted Dorothy, maybe they would accept me too." So she applied and was accepted.

By this time, however, China was closed to missionaries. Not feeling called to any other specific country, she told TEAM that she was willing to go wherever they needed a nurse. Knowing the need in Zimbabwe, TEAM assigned her to go there. Betty did not even know where this country was located in Africa, so she quickly bought an atlas to find out.

Emil Rilling was born with a heart defect. His health was not normal and his father prayed that God would either heal his little boy and take him to the mission field or to take him to be with Himself.

One day when Emil was barely two years old, his father was treating the infected eyes of a horse and didn't see Emil standing behind the horse. As the horse reacted to the medication, it jerked backwards with its hoof landing right on Emil's chest.

His father quickly picked up the unconscious little boy and headed by horse and buggy to the doctor some miles from their farm in rural Canada. While in the waiting room of the doctor's office, Emil regained consciousness and started to play with his father's fingers.

When their turn finally came, the doctor examined Emil and told his father, "I don't see anything wrong with this boy. Take him home." From that time on Emil had no more heart problems and developed normally.

God answered the prayer of Emil's father in both healing him and sending him to the mission field. The route to the latter was not straight and direct, however.

Emil was exposed to missions quite extensively as he lived near Prairie Bible Institute and attended functions there as a teenager. He eventually joined the Canadian Air Force and drifted away from a clear focus on the Lord for a few years.

When he returned to the farm, however, God challenged him concerning what he was going to do with his life. Rather than just wasting it away, Emil decided that he wanted his life to count for something, so he got serious about his relationship with the Lord and enrolled in Prairie Bible Institute with the intention of becoming a missionary.

At that time the student body included many other veterans, and the very first year he was there the Lord visited the school with a powerful revival. A deep spirit of conviction spread quickly among the students. Once again God met Emil in a special way, pointing out a number of areas of his life that needed cleansing. Each of these, Emil believes, were things that would have kept him from the mission field had he not dealt with them.

After graduating from Prairie, he enrolled in the School of Missionary Medicine at BIOLA in California. Here he met Phyllis Casebolt, who had graduated from Multnomah School of the Bible in Portland, Oregon.

Phyllis had been richly exposed to missionaries during her childhood. "By the time I was fourteen," Phyllis shared, "there was nothing in life that I wanted more than to go out and reach some people who heretofore had not heard the Gospel. This never changed."

Emil, too, wanted to go to an unreached area. Their lives were drawn together, and as soon as they completed their course at BIOLA, they were married.

In the process of selecting a mission with which to serve, Emil was impressed with TEAM's prompt way of doing business, their worldwide focus, and their desire to open new areas to the Gospel. Both he and Phyllis had also been blessed by the ministry of Dr. T. J. Bach at their Bible schools. This led them to apply to TEAM, and they were pleased to be accepted.

Emil was initially interested in going to Irian Jaya, but he also had a vision for work in Africa. Soon they began preparing to go to Zimbabwe. They arrived in 1953.

Clarence Cedarholm's call to missions came while serving in World War II as a medical corpsman onboard the USS New Mexico. When a kamikaze (Japanese suicide plane) hit the ship, many of his fellow crewmen, including his medic partner, were killed. Clarence himself carried shrapnel in his body for the rest of his life. While he never talked much about the event, he decided he had been spared for some reason.

He was also appalled at how immorally his shipmates acted toward the native women when on shore leave. It bothered him so much that he committed his life to serving the underprivileged of the third world who knew nothing of Jesus and had been taken advantage of and treated so poorly by American soldiers. He wanted to show them that mankind is not all evil, that some men were truly capable of doing good.

Chuck Pruitt also felt called to be a missionary while he was serving in the Armed Forces during World War II. As a Marine on the USS Idaho operating in the Pacific theater, he had come to the Lord through the Navigators. Every night he met for Bible study with some of the other men on the ship.

One of these men learned that the people on a nearby island had had some Christian teaching and asked Chuck to accompany him there to hold a Gospel meeting. The ship was not going to this island, but his friend had arranged for a PT boat to drop them off and pick them up.

Now Chuck was an athlete who was planning to become a professional ball player like his father, who was a pitcher for the White Sox. The day that his friend wanted him to go to this island to preach to these natives was the day of the biggest ball game of the Pacific. His coach was a very ungodly man and expected him to play. What a quandary Chuck was in! Should he play in this important game, or should he go to the island?

As he prayed about it, he decided that God wanted him to go. Of course, he then had to tell his coach that he wouldn't be playing in the big game. He prayed about that too.

When he broke the news to his coach, he fully expected him to respond harshly. What a surprise it was when the coach simply said, "Well, Chuck, I guess you better do that then"!

As the PT boat dropped the two men off at the island, they were told to be back at the dock in an hour for pick up. However, they had to walk inland to get to this village. Then when they announced that they were going to hold a meeting, the islanders exclaimed that they would all have to go and wash in the bay first before hearing the Word.

After the whole village went down to the bay, bathed, and came back, the men's hour was almost used up, and they still had to get back to the shore to catch the boat. They decided to trust God and hold their meeting anyway, praying earnestly that the boat would somehow be delayed.

After the meeting all the people had to shake hands with them and walk them out of the village and part way back to the shore. When they said their final good-bys, the two men ran the rest of the way back to the dock where the PT boat was to pick them up. They were now two hours late and extremely worried, as being AWOL during wartime meant time in the brig.

Just as they got to the dock, they saw the PT boat arrive. The skipper explained to them that he had been delayed by the rough water. Chuck and his friend knew that it was God who had detained the boat for those two hours!

As they returned to the ship and had their usual Bible study that night, they were in for a big surprise! The coach came and joined them. God had been working in his heart that day as well, and by the time they finished their study, he accepted Christ as His Savior.

This whole day had such an impact on Chuck that he decided to become a missionary rather than a ball player. What greater joy could there be than to see folks come to know the Lord?

When he got out of the service at the end of the war, he went to Moody Bible Institute and became the prayer leader for the island world, thinking he would return there as a missionary. Soon, however, he began to feel God leading him to go to India with World Evangelism Crusade (W.E.C.) instead. He proceeded in this direction, but after being on deputation for a year, he learned that visas for India were not available at that time.

Chuck then went to visit TEAM. While there, Dr. Mortenson

asked him to pray about going to Zimbabwe. He went home to pray about this and did not get back in touch with TEAM for a whole year. When he did, Dr. Mortenson recognized him and immediately asked, "Have you prayed about going to Zimbabwe?"

Chuck replied, "Yes, I believe that's where God wants me." After applying and being accepted, he attended Candidate School and again went out on deputation to raise support.

When he returned to his small home church in Illinois, he met a Scottish gal, Elizabeth Elliott ("Scotty"). She had just started attending there after feeling called to the mission field herself that summer. Coming from a rich generational heritage of missionaries, pastors, and pastor's wives going as far back as the Revolutionary War, this might easily have been expected of her as well. Yet receiving her own personal call from God was absolutely necessary. This came as she attended a Youth for Christ Conference at Winona Lake, Indiana.

God put them on a fast track towards marriage as Chuck needed to be in Zimbabwe within six months of receiving his visa. Immediately after getting married, Chuck and Scotty attended TEAM's annual conference, followed by Candidate School. Chuck then needed to introduce Scotty to his supporters, as he had already been on deputation for three months before they were married. God's hand was very evident as they quickly received double support without ever asking for it.

Dr. Sam Wall also heard the call of God to missions while in military service. His life is a tremendous testimony of the work of God's grace in the most unlikely of candidates. In the words of his wife, Emily, Sam was a "goof-off" who frittered away his high school years with no goal in mind and barely-passing grades.

Working for Firestone Tire and Rubber Company after graduation and about to be drafted, he enlisted as a medical corpsman in the Navy. While serving at a naval hospital in Hawaii, God placed the desire in his heart to become a missionary doctor. With his background he knew such a goal was reaching for the stars, but he was willing to trust God to make it possible.

Unbeknown to Sam at that time, God had chosen him to establish a hospital for TEAM in Zimbabwe and to serve as its first doctor. Therefore, God took this unprepared, but willing servant, who was lacking college entrance requirements, and overcame one obstacle after another for him, leading him successfully forward to fulfill this call on his life. Eleven years later, in December 1957, Dr. Sam and Emily Wall and their three children departed for Africa. Four years later Karanda Hospital became a reality.

Mildred Rogers Carnall was 23 when her mother died suddenly at the age of 48. Although they had not been particularly close, Mildred felt a tremendous loss of security when this happened. She had been working at the Pentagon and was having a great time living in Washington, DC. Now she had to leave her job and return home to Marianna, Florida, to help her father care for her younger siblings. She wasn't very happy about this but did what was expected of her as the oldest child.

Her bad attitude spilled over in her new job, and eventually she was fired. She recalled:

*I came to the end of myself and contemplated turning to drink or committing suicide, although neither option really appealed to me. My aunt had been sending me Christian literature for years. In my depression I told her that I would like the book* Peace of Mind *by Liebman. My aunt sent the book* The Way *by E. Stanley Jones instead. It was written to the non-Christian and spoke to my need.*

*I learned that I could pray for deliverance from smoking and it would happen, so I tried it. I went for a whole day without wanting to smoke, and that was enough to convince me that Jesus was indeed alive, real, and concerned about me.*

*I had learned John 3:16 as a child and quickly went to this verse to see what I needed to do to be saved. The verse said just to believe, so I prayed, "Lord, I believe."*

*His life came into me, making a radical change in my attitudes, outlook, and practices. I could have exploded with joy in knowing that my sins were forgiven. I wanted to tell everyone what had happened to me, but since I didn't really understand it well myself, I had difficulty putting it into words.*

*I have often thought that God corralled me, bringing me to a place where there was only one way to turn and that was to Him. When I did, He really took hold of me, and I was strongly moved to give my whole self to Him.*

*Less than a year after I was saved, my aunt paid for me to attend a Ben Lippen Conference in Asheville, NC. She wanted me to be strengthened in my faith. The week I went "happened" to be missionary week. I sat for a whole week listening to outstanding missionaries tell of how God had worked miracles in their lives and their ministries. I found myself longing to know God the way they did.*

*The last night an invitation was given. Dr. McQuilkin, founder and President of Columbia Bible College, made it clear that the Great Commission was in the Bible, and it meant every Christian should be willing to go to the mission field. He said that if we had nothing standing in our way of going, we should commit our lives to do so. I had already committed my life to do God's will, and I willingly made this commitment as well.*

Donna Kahlstorf came to know the Lord when she was seventeen. Her call to missions came several years later. She had graduated from college and taught for a year when a friend encouraged her to go with her to Northwestern Bible College in Minneapolis. Recognizing her need for Bible study, she went.

After her first year there she volunteered to spend her summer teaching DVBS and doing camp work, neither of which she had ever experienced herself. At camp each counselor was supposed to give a missionary challenge. She was given some material to read and instructed to challenge the kids about being willing to go to Africa.

As she was doing this, the Lord spoke very clearly to her, *"You're telling them to be willing to go, and you know that you're not willing yourself."* She was so deeply impacted by this that she took it as God's call upon her life. From that moment on she began to prepare for mission service in Africa.

In October 1958, Dr. Rick and JoAnn Froese were struck by the definition of a call they read in a book entitled *The Bible Basis of Missions* by Dr. Robert Hall Glover. Rick wrote:

*Dr. Glover quoted the "logic of facts that had appealed to Keith Falconer, that heroic Scottish nobleman who blazed the Gospel trail into Arabia, who stated that 'the need, knowledge of that need, and ability to meet that need constitute a call.' Falconer also wrote, 'While vast continents still lie shrouded in almost utter darkness, and hundreds of millions suffer the horrors of heathenism. . . the burden of proof rests upon you to show that the circumstances in which God has presently placed you were meant by Him to keep you out of the foreign mission field.'"[5]*

*Glover also quoted James Gilmour, the brave pioneer among the nomads of Mongolia, who spoke in words no less forceful and convicting: "To me the question was not 'Why go?' but 'Why not go?'"[6]*

Shortly after this, while serving as an Air Force lieutenant in Great Britain, Rick attempted to contact his college roommate's brother, who was serving with TEAM as a medical doctor in India. In the process someone sent him a page from TEAM's *Horizons* magazine giving the address of TEAM's field headquarters in India. Also on the page, however, was a list of all of TEAM's fields and the various personnel needed on each one.

Rick's eye was caught by the stated need for a pharmacist and a nurse on the Zimbabwe field. He responded by writing a short note to Dr. Sam Wall, who was listed as the contact person, asking for more information. Several weeks later he received a reply from Dr. Wall, explaining his need for a pharmacist to help in drug procurement and in setting up a pharmacy for the new Karanda Hospital as well as for another nurse and someone trained in hospital administration.

Rick wrote:

*I sat there at my desk, reading and rereading that air form. I was a pharmacist serving as the Medical Supply Officer at this airbase in England and had also been trained by the Air Force in hospital administration. JoAnn was a registered nurse. I couldn't help but think of Dr. Glover's words: "The need, the knowledge of the need, and the ability to fill the need constitute a call."*

*JoAnn had been interested in missionary nursing from the time I met her. I myself had written to several mission organizations inquiring about the need for a pharmacist on the mission field. After receiving nebulous or negative answers, I had assumed that the Lord had no need for me overseas.*

*With the letter still in my hand, I got up from my desk and walked out of the Quonset hut into the foggy, dark, cold weather of the East Anglican countryside. My mind was captivated with one thought: "Was this where God would have us serve in the days ahead?" As I walked down the path, I was aware of a lovely sound piercing the fog. A skylark was singing its heart out in the sun above the clouds and mist. I took this as a confirmation.*

*That evening I shared this all with JoAnn. Together, we decided to step out in faith and write to TEAM about ourselves and our interest in filling this need in Zimbabwe.*

*After several weeks a reply came. We'd have to attend seminary after getting out of the Air Force. . . . Our stint in the Air Force was shortened . . . and soon we were in seminary. . . . God guided our every step. . . . We were in Zimbabwe for the opening and dedication of the new Karanda Hospital in 1961.*

Judy Gudeman was also a young adult when she felt God's call to be a missionary. After finishing nurses' training, she went to visit her brother Stan, who was a missionary in Venezuela at that time. There she became acquainted with Irene Garrett, one of his co-workers. When Irene came on furlough, she invited Judy to go with her to Founders' Week at Moody. Judy wrote:

*I was in prayer that during that week the Lord would give me direction for what He wanted me to do with my life. I was quite disappointed when I went through the whole week but felt no specific leading from the Lord.*

*The following Sunday evening, however, my pastor spoke on the subject of sacrifice. All through the service I sensed he was going to give an altar call, though I had never known him to do it before. Sure enough, he did. First, he asked for parents who were willing to give their children to the Lord if*

*He should call them into service. Then he asked for those who were willing to do what God asked and go to the mission field. My heart was pounding. This time I knew that God was speaking to me, and I had to respond. I knew instantly in my heart that God wanted me to go to Moody Bible Institute and then to the mission field somewhere.*

*I wanted to go to Moody for just a year, as I was already older than most of the students by this time and wanted to get involved in missions soon. Since my brother was a TEAM missionary, I knew Dr. Mortenson and decided to ask him for advice. As I went to see him, I told the Lord that I would do whatever he recommended.*

*Because single gals on the mission field usually have to do more speaking and carry greater spiritual responsibilities than those who were married, he strongly advised me to take the full, three-year missions course at Moody. This is what I did.*

*While there, I attended area prayer meetings and decided I was most interested in Irian Jaya. I did not want to go to Africa, as so many seemed to be heading that direction. As I tried to get more involved with the Irian Jaya Prayer Band, however, the Lord closed the door.*

*When I had been living at home, I would read the prayer letters that my brother received from other missionaries and then send them on to him. One of them had come from Bill and Joyce Warner in Zimbabwe, telling of their marriage and Joyce's need for support. As I read the letter, I felt led to take on a bit of her support.*

*Now at Moody I received a letter from her asking me to tell her about myself. I wrote back, saying that I was a nurse attending Moody in the missions program and seeking the Lord's direction. I thought I had written all this to her before, but evidently it hadn't been God's timing for it to register with her.*

*She immediately gave my letter to Dr. Wall, the doctor at Chironga at that time. Very quickly I received a letter from him, asking me to consider coming to the hospital in Zimbabwe. This was all so unexpected that I knew the Lord had to be in it. Too many circumstances came into play to cast the thought out. Suddenly both the mission board and the field I was to go to came into clear focus.*

*I applied to TEAM, went to candidate school, raised my support, and left for Africa by the end of the year. As I look back, I can see the Lord's hand in all the details. I was not used to having them all fall into place so quickly as they did. This served as a real confirmation to me that this was indeed God's will.*

For some individuals a call to missions is received early in life, but various factors come into play to postpone the response they are able to make to that call. Noël Liddle was 21 when he surrendered to God's call to missions while living in Northern Ireland. Ann Liddle was a senior at Asbury College when God called her through the preaching of Bill Gillam of O.M.S. International. After Noël came to the United States for further studies, he and Ann were married in 1953.

When Noël completed his Th.D. degree, they applied for overseas missionary service. Noël was unable to pass the medical examination, however, because of his severe ulcers. Thirty-two years later Noël had coronary bypass surgery, and as a result his ulcers were also suddenly and unexpectedly healed.

He was working as a school administrator in suburban Chicago at that time. God spoke to Noël and Ann during a Sunday morning service at Moraine Valley Baptist Church. One of the young people, Janet Anderson, gave a five-minute report on how she had served the Lord as a "summer missionary" in Zimbabwe. For eight weeks she had taught English at TEAM's Mavuradonha High School.

As the Liddles listened, Noël turned to Ann and said, "I have my summer months free. If that youngster can teach on the mission field for eight weeks, we can do it too."

Ann's immediate response was, "Let's go."

With their extensive training and experience in both Bible and teaching, they set their sights on the possibility of teaching for a summer at TEAM's Bible college in Zimbabwe. As the summer of 1985 approached, however, they received a letter from Dale Everswick, the Zimbabwe field chairman, asking them if they would consider staying longer than a summer, as they were looking for someone to replace one of the Bible college teachers who was returning to Canada.

As they thought about this and took the request to the Lord in prayer, they were impacted by the words of Ephesians 3:8 (KJV): *"Unto me, who am less than the least of all saints, is this grace given, that I should preach among the Gentiles the unsearchable riches of Christ."* They took this as direction from God and adjusted their plans from being missionaries for one summer to serving for a full year. "Actually," Noël wrote, "unknown to TEAM, we were now committing ourselves to being missionaries 'until the Lord returns.'"

John Ulrich had served as Youth Pastor at Messiah Baptist Church in Wichita, Kansas, for five years when God intervened and started moving him and his wife, Kelley, towards the idea of serving on the mission field. While at Dallas Theological Seminary, Mike Pocock had been John's missions professor. The Ulrichs had no interest in missions at the time, but John developed a good relationship with Mike, a former TEAM missionary.

Their friendship continued even after John graduated. They both shared a passion for fishing and set an annual date for fishing every May. During these times Mike would tell John exciting and exotic stories about fishing on the Zambezi River.

On one of those visits Mike asked John, "If you could do anything for God, what would it be?" John answered immediately, "I would teach at a Bible college or seminary." Mike simply commented that there were places all over the world that needed teachers.

At their church the Ulrichs were responsible for leading the annual missions week. Their prayer goal this particular year was for God to call one couple from the church to become missionaries. When the end of the week came and no one had responded, they told their best friends, "We thought *you* would be the ones."

They immediately responded by telling John and Kelley, "And we thought *you* would be."

When they shared this with Mike, he suggested that they and the other couple form a Prospective Missionary Fellowship. Following his advice, they met for a meal every Thursday evening and read *Operation World* and *Perspectives on the World Christian Movement* together. Pretty soon they found themselves getting excited about what God was doing in Africa, and their friends were developing an interest in South America.

Kelley wrote:

*We decided that we wanted to take a missions trip some-where and see God's work firsthand. We contacted dozens of mission agencies to try to organize a short-term trip, but nothing was working out. We were positive at the time that TEAM wasn't working in Africa, so we didn't even try to contact them!*

*Finally, our friends asked us to contact TEAM on their* behalf, *and we got Bev Tindall on the phone. She was incredibly friendly and helpful and informed us that TEAM had a workshop called "EXPLORE," which was designed to help people determine if they are suited to cross-cultural ministry. This seemed to be exactly what we needed, so all four of us signed up. We also learned that TEAM was indeed working in Africa.*

*At the end of the workshop we met with some of TEAM's administrative staff and received several green lights to move forward. We then met with Lynn Everswick, who was TEAM's representative for the Africa fields. He suggested that we take a short-term trip to Zimbabwe.*

*I was pretty apprehensive about this at first. I had seen travel brochures about South Africa and thought I could probably handle that, but I had never even heard of Zimbabwe. Nevertheless, we set up a trip in which we would spend four weeks in Zimbabwe and two weeks in South Africa.*

*That was in October 1996. The following January we and our two children (ages 3 and 1) were on a plane to Zimbabwe.*

*When we arrived, John only needed two days of teach-ing at Harare Theological College before he was totally sold on the idea of applying for full-time missionary status. Since I was having to wash clothes in the bathtub and walk a couple of miles to the grocery store, it took me a little longer to be convinced! By the end of our four weeks, however, we had both come to love Zimbabwe so much!*

*As we went to South Africa to finish our trip, for the first time in years the colleges we visited had enough teachers and didn't need us! We took that as our final confirmation that God wanted us in Zimbabwe.*

## In Retirement Years

Richard ("Dad") and Inez ("Mom") Grigg, Lynn Hoyt's parents, visited the Zimbabwe field in 1962. As they toured the various mission stations, they were very attracted to the ministry being carried out by the Zimbabwe TEAMmates. They returned to the United States and began making plans to go back to Zimbabwe as associate missionaries when "Dad" retired from his job as an insurance company administrator in 1964.

By 1967, they had sold their house, moved to Zimbabwe, and built a new home on the Plot. Dad Grigg took over the mission bookkeeping, releasing Marian Wilterdink to follow her calling to teach Bible classes in the government schools on a full-time basis. While "Mom" Grigg was not well much of the time, she was always eager to offer hospitality to the missionaries.

After nine years they returned to the States. "Mom" passed away in 1981. In 1983, "Dad" returned to Zimbabwe and served for another two years, working once again with the bookkeeping in the office.

As Sam and Dorothy Cook approached retirement, two missionary couples who were home on furlough from Zimbabwe visited them. They both asked what the Cooks planned to do in their retirement. When they said, "Fish and travel," the missionaries immediately invited them to come to Zimbabwe and help them there.

Dorothy had worked as a nurse at Contra Costa County Hospital in the Los Angeles area for 20 years, the last 15 as an operating room supervisor. Back in the '50s she had learned about Karanda Hospital in Zimbabwe from Dr. Sam Wall, a resident who had shared with her his plans to go as a TEAM missionary to build a hospital at Karanda.

In time, Dorothy herself became interested in doing what she could to help this new bush hospital. She started accumulating, packing, and sending out whatever hospital supplies she could salvage from her workplace. Her "goodies" included lots of sutures, pans, pots, trays, and many things that were no longer valuable in California but would be very useful in the African bush. She also repaired broken instruments to be "recycled" at Karanda. As salesmen learned of her project, they sometimes contributed wonderful samples for her to send as well.

In spite of all this, when Sam and Dorothy were invited years later to go to Karanda themselves, they didn't see what they could possibly do to be of help there. God knew differently, however, and He began to show them how Dorothy's hospital experience and her training of surgical technicians as well as Sam's two decades of work in a hardware store would be very valuable at Karanda.

As this picture came into clearer focus for them, they reached a decision rather quickly. "We've been blessed with good health," they said, "and the Lord has opened a door of service for us in Africa. We had anticipated being involved in some form of Christian ministry in our retirement, and this is it."

They applied to TEAM, were accepted, attended candidate school, and ten days after Dorothy officially retired, they left for Africa. While they had been accepted for an eighteen month short-term, they hoped to stay longer. They ended up spending three years as associate missionaries at Karanda.

Welton and Betty White had owned and operated an Army/Navy surplus store for 20 years when God started redirecting their path. They had decided that when their lease expired in 1974, they would not renew it.

The thought of "what next?" was rolling around in their heads when Lynne Hawkins, a TEAM Zimbabwe missionary, spoke at their church in Garden Grove, California. After church they invited Lynne over for dinner to talk with her some more about her ministry in Zimbabwe. As they visited that afternoon, a seed was planted in Welton and Betty's minds. Slowly it took root and germinated, and they knew that God had answered their "what next?" question.

George Smazik was also planning to serve the Lord in some way when he retired. In anticipation of this he began taking evening classes at Moody Bible Institute when he was 45. His plan was to take an early retirement in 1983, when he was 55, trusting God to direct him into the ministry of His choice.

What was not in his plans was his wife's death in July 1980, about a year after he graduated from Moody. While grieving this deep personal loss, George continued to set his sights on early retirement and Christian service.

Through his home church George had known Dr. Dave Drake, another doctor serving at Karanda, for years. In December 1980, Dave made an unexpected phone call to George and invited him to come to Karanda—not in three years, but NOW! "If ever you were needed here," Dave said, "the time is now!"

George was just learning how to iron shirts and live as a single person again. He really felt the Lord's leading in Dave's invitation, however, so he decided to take an even earlier retirement from his job at Illinois Bell Telephone and put his house up for sale.

Because he had a pension, George did not really have to go on deputation to raise support. TEAM's African representative advised him, however, that having other folks support him financially would also give him an important prayer support base. Almost without asking, George was fully supported, and by March 1981, he left for Zimbabwe.

## Second Generation Missionaries

The TEAM Zimbabwe field is unusual in the number of MKs ("missionary kids") who fell in love with the country to which their parents had been called and caught a missionary vision themselves. Many returned to Zimbabwe as short-term or career missionaries. Others became missionaries to other countries.

Those returning to Zimbabwe had the distinct advantage of already being familiar with the culture and language of the Shona people and the nature of missionary life in that country. On the other hand, they had to face the major adjustment of becoming co-workers with those they had grown up calling "Auntie" and "Uncle."

Personally hearing God's call for missionary service in Zimbabwe was just as important for them as for any other missionary. In some respects it was perhaps even more so.

God led each of Norman and Thelma Everswick's children to

return to Zimbabwe as career missionaries. They all testified of how profoundly they were impacted by what they observed in their parents.

Their oldest son, Lynn Everswick, said:

> *Becoming a missionary was always on my heart because of the love I observed my parents to have for the ministry. They would often say that there was nothing better to do in the world than to serve the Lord. I greatly admired them.*
>
> *During my Bible college years as I began praying about my future, missions became a personal call for me. When I married Judy Sherman, who specifically felt called to serve in Africa, Zimbabwe naturally attracted me.*
>
> *Wanting to be very sure that this was the Lord's direction for us, we asked Him to set up roadblocks if this was not His will. When nothing happened, we were sure that Zimbabwe was the place that God wanted us.*

Dale Everswick also recalls the tremendous influence of his parents. He wrote:

> *One of my earliest memories was of lying in bed at Mavuradona waiting for my dad to come home from his weekly meeting at Kamtsenzera. When he returned, he would come into my room, sit on my bed, and tell me all about the worship service. It was held in a schoolroom lighted by a pressure lamp and usually the benches were full. The singing was unaccompanied but hearty and beautiful. Then Dad would preach, and invariably one or two or three came forward to give their lives to Jesus. This, of course, was the highlight of the evening, and Dad and I would pray and thank God for the new brothers and sisters who had joined God's family.*
>
> *My mom and dad were so content and fulfilled with their station and mission in life, and I can remember thinking that there could be nothing better than to be a messenger of the Gospel in a needy world. That feeling was born early in my*

*life and carried me on to Bible school and then back to Zimbabwe with TEAM.*

Sharing this same heritage, Joyce Everswick Goppert wrote:

*All my life growing up in Zimbabwe, I had wanted to be a missionary nurse. With Mom and Dad being so committed to missions, it was the most natural thing in the world for me to feel led in the same direction. Mom and Dad never pushed their will on us kids but constantly assured us that the Lord would lead us where He wanted us to be. Dad was fond of saying, "The safest place you can ever be is in the center of God's will." As I grew up, I found it easy to rest in that truth and let the Lord show me the way.*

*While I was at Northeastern Bible College, Dr. Charles W. Anderson (the President) made a trip to Africa. When he returned and shared his great burden for that continent with the student body, my heart was moved. I felt God was confirming to me that this was where He wanted me to go.*

*That same year I met Chris Goppert, another student who was committed to full-time Christian service and seeking the Lord's direction. As I felt the Lord leading us together, I wanted him to be free to sense God's leading totally apart from any influence from me. When God put Zimbabwe on his heart as well, that gave me complete assurance that this was God's place for us to serve.*

Doug Everswick reported that he always had a clear sense of wanting to return to Zimbabwe as a missionary. He never felt any change in that call. As he attended Northeastern Bible College, he met Nancy Osmun, who also had felt specifically called to Africa. They were married in 1977 and arrived in Zimbabwe 1984.

Russ and Marg Jackson also had two of their children return to Zimbabwe as missionaries. Their eldest son, Bud, initially returned to work for the Ministry of Internal Affairs. He described how the Lord used this experience to call him into missionary service:

*During my seven years as a civil servant, I was stationed in semi-rural towns situated in the outlying mining and farming districts of Zimbabwe. Much of my work took me into the traditional tribal areas, but I also had the privilege of building friendships with people of various races living in the administrative centers of these districts. Over time, I became burdened and challenged by the lack of evangelical witness among the multi-racial mix of people living in these towns and communities.*

*When TEAM missionary Bonnie Lanegan invited me to speak at a young adults' retreat on two separate occasions, I found my appetite for teaching and preaching being whetted. This opened brand new possibilities for me. I recognized that perhaps I myself had the means to connect in a meaningful spiritual way with the Zimbabweans in these rural communities.*

*When I told my wife, Mandy, that I sensed the Lord was leading us to a significant shift in vocational direction, she shared that the Lord had been putting similar thoughts in her own mind. To find that the Holy Spirit had been leading both of us in the same direction at the same time served as a significant point of confirmation for me that this was the Lord's leading.*

*After much prayer and some significant heart-to-heart talks with my dad, we continued to feel God's leading in this direction. Then one day we were attending the evening service of a missions emphasis Sunday at Elgin Road Baptist Church. As the visiting missionary spoke, I sensed a strong moving of the Spirit upon my heart, again without any perception that Mandy was feeling the same.*

*We were ending the service with a time of communion, and just before partaking of the elements, Mandy turned to me and asked, "Have we any choice?"*

*I knew exactly what she meant, and my answer to her was, "No."*

*From that moment we knew we were going to travel to North America to pursue further Bible training. Then we would return to Zimbabwe as missionaries.*

As Tom Jackson, Bud's younger brother, grew up in Zimbabwe, he so identified with the people his parents were ministering to that when he was in the twelfth grade, he was baptized by Pastor Kadzingatsai, joined the national Evangelical Church, and proudly wore his member's pin. He entered Northeastern Bible College with the intention of preparing to go back to Zimbabwe as a missionary, asking God to stop him if this was not His will.

Dr. Dan Stephens, son of Dr. Roland and Kathy Stephens, always wanted to be a missionary doctor like his father, but he envisioned going to some country other than Zimbabwe. He shared:

> *Being the son of missionaries, I was always impacted by how busy their lives were and how few workers were in God's harvest field. I also felt eternal values were more important than temporal ones, and I wanted to make my life count for the Kingdom of God. I covenanted with God that if He would enable me to become a doctor, I would return to the mission field. Through various miraculous acts of God, I became a general surgeon with good training in general medicine as well and had no debt to pay off when I finished my training.*
>
> *I felt quite strongly, however, that I did not want to return to Karanda Hospital. I wanted to make my own way and not follow too closely in my father's footsteps. At candidate school everyone thought Julie [daughter of Carl and Donna Hendrickson] and I would naturally be going to Zimbabwe, where we had been raised, but we told them we weren't being drawn in that direction.*

Dan's wife, Julie, reported that she had considered being a missionary like her parents ever since childhood. While at college, however, she began to sense in a much stronger way that this was what God wanted for her too. She said, "I looked at life in the United States. and saw people so caught up in the 'American Dream' and doing what everyone else was doing. I wanted to do more than that with my life." Like Dan, she didn't necessarily expect to go back to Zimbabwe.

Dan continued to recount how God led them:

*While we were still at candidate school, we learned that due to significant problems in the area, the Zimbabwe field had voted to turn the hospital over to the government. The directive was then given that all prospective medical missionaries for Karanda were to be redirected elsewhere. We felt this was a real confirmation from the Lord regarding our own decision to pursue another field.*

*Initially, we felt a strong leading to go to Nepal, having heard some speakers tell of a specific need for a surgeon there. However, no visas were available at the time. We were then drawn to a new opportunity that became available in Sri Lanka. Shortly after candidate school several missionaries from Chad also crossed our paths and encouraged us to go there. We learned, however, that they desired a whole medical team from the U.S., not just one physician.*

*The next few months were filled with uncertainty as I prepared for my surgical board exams. We were not happy with the decision to go to Sri Lanka and we didn't feel Chad was the place either.*

*Then we learned that the Zimbabwe government had made an emphatic statement that they strongly desired TEAM to continue operating the hospital at Karanda and would do everything possible to eliminate any potential interference in this. President Mugabe even made a trip to the station to register his support.*

*While this was a very welcomed outcome, it posed an immediate problem, as the current doctors were already planning to leave the country, and no replacements were available. Recruitment efforts had stopped at the time the Zimbabwe field had decided to turn the hospital over to the government. Needing to resolve this situation as quickly as possible, Field Chairman Lynn Everswick called us and asked if we would consider coming to Zimbabwe.*

*Here was an immediate and urgent need and a specific request from the field. Both Julie and I had immediate peace that this was God's direction for us. Over the next eight months our support poured in, and we were able to reach the field by August of 1991.*

Ann-Britt Byrmo Smazik grew up as an MK in both South Africa and Zimbabwe. Her parents, Martin and Margaretha, had served with the Swedish Alliance Mission in South Africa for 16 years. Then, in 1961, they felt led to move to Zimbabwe to minister to the Zulu and Ndebele people living in the southern part of the country.

Not wanting to feel completely isolated from other missionaries in Zimbabwe, her father explored and succeeded in working out an affiliated relationship with the TEAM Zimbabwe field that was acceptable with their mission as well. This enabled them to have a measure of fellowship and accountability with the TEAM missionaries and yet retain their status with the Swedish Alliance Mission.

During their 17 fruitful years as church planters in the Bulawayo area, the Byrmos made yearly trips to Harare for the annual TEAM conferences. Even the children loved these occasions of interacting with the large TEAM family. Ann-Britt, who testifies that she "always felt called" to be a missionary, was so impacted by these experiences that she decided TEAM would be a nice mission with which to serve one day.

Years later, when she returned to her home country of Sweden for nurses' training, she turned her back on this idea, however, telling the Lord that He had had enough missionaries from her family. Having seen all that her parents and grandparents had been through on the field, she decided that working as a nurse in Sweden would be a much nicer option for her. "All I wanted was to stay in Sweden, get a cute little apartment, work my shifts, and go to Spain for my vacations," she wrote.

God's call on her life did not change, however. After finishing her nurses' training, she decided to go to Moody Bible Institute. Here, as a young adult, she heard God's voice clearly calling her to missions once again. That was all she needed to turn her path back towards the whispers she had heard from Him as a child.

Though many years had passed, she knew exactly where she wanted to serve. She contacted TEAM, applied, was accepted, and left for Zimbabwe to serve as a nurse-midwife at Karanda Hospital in 1973.

# Missionary Recruits from Zimbabwe

Another significant group of missionary recruits came from among the people that the missionaries interacted with in Zimbabwe as they carried out their ministries. Another frequent point of contact were the churches that the missionaries attended when they came into Harare for supplies and other business.

Les Austin grew up in a rather impoverished home in London, England. His mother was a Christian but not his father. He was exposed to the Gospel at a Baptist church where he joined the Boys' Brigade. He and his brother, Reg, also became very close to another Christian family who became like "second parents" to them. Les became a bricklaying apprentice when he was fourteen, following in the footsteps of his father.

During World War II, Les was impacted with the precariousness of life as he and his family had several close calls during the "Blitz" (bombing of London). They escaped death, thanks to the small bomb shelter they had in their front yard, but their home was destroyed.

Shortly after the war his family took advantage of free passage being offered to anyone willing to resettle in South Africa. Eventually Les became more interested in moving up into Zimbabwe, so the family relocated to Harare instead. He was nineteen at the time and got a bricklaying job there. His family also began attending Central Baptist Church.

Here he had his first contact with American missionaries and was quite intrigued with what they were doing. The Blairs, Jacksons, Everswicks, and Lillian Nelson all attended there when they came into Harare for supplies.

As Les pursued a growing relationship with them, he eventually went out and helped to build the church at Msengedzi, where Lillian Nelson was stationed. When Lillian was transferred to the Hunyani station with the Blairs, Les began carrying fresh fruit and the mailbag out to them about once a month by motorcycle.

Les and Lillian developed a special relationship, and eventually Les spoke with the TEAM leadership about marrying Lillian. They were agreeable if he would become a missionary and would attend Moody Bible Institute on their first furlough. Les agreed to this and he and Lillian were married in 1951.

Reg Austin, Les's younger brother, remained in South Africa when his family moved to Zimbabwe, as he had begun an apprenticeship there as an electrician. When he later went to Zimbabwe to rejoin his family, he too became active in Central Baptist Church.

There he met an elderly couple from India who asked him to help them in starting a church among the colored (mixed race) people in Harare. Reg accepted this invitation and began going out on Sundays with them to teach Sunday school to the children. He was surprised at how well he could relate to them and enjoyed teaching and befriending them. He also thoroughly enjoyed the encouragement and fellowship of this elderly couple, who were a very positive influence in his life.

At Central Baptist Church he, too, began meeting many of the TEAM missionaries. His family learned that they had to live in tents in a camp grove way out on the city limits when they came to town to get their supplies. For families with little children this was particularly difficult, especially during the rainy season. Reg explained his family's compassion:

> *My mother was a very generous and hospitable person. She told us boys, "If you see missionaries, and they're hard pressed for somewhere to stay, what we have is not much, but they're welcome to it." So our house became a kind of resting place for the missionaries or a temporary storage place for their supplies.*

Through Les, Reg became more acquainted with the TEAM missionaries. The two of them would often be invited out to their stations as they both had skills that could be put to use. Reg described the impact of these experiences on him:

> *We were taken in kind of as "sons" of the missionary families, and we would frequently spend week-ends out on their stations helping them. The Mungers, Knapps, Blairs, Everswicks, Uppendahls, and Jacksons became dear friends who shared their beds, tables, and food with us. We were so accepted by them. Some of their love and interest rubbed off*

*on me, and I decided that I would go to Moody Bible Institute and prepare to become a missionary.*

John Wolfe was born in South Africa but had gone to London to try to get into the theater. While there, he was approached by an elderly man in a subway station who very politely asked if he would take a little booklet to read, entitled *The Way of Peace.* John accepted the booklet and put it in his overcoat pocket without reading it.

Dissatisfied with his experience in London, he returned shortly after this to South Africa and then traveled up to Zimbabwe to take a job in Bulawayo. He worked there only a few months and then accepted a job to work on a friend's farm near Guruve.

On day he was returning from a supply trip to Harare in a severe thunderstorm and feeling a real restlessness of heart. He was delayed a day in getting back to the farm because a rear wheel of his vehicle came off en route. When he finally made it back to the farm, he told his employer that he had a great desire to go down to one of the mission stations in the Zambezi Valley where he had heard there were missionaries.

He wrote:

*My knowledge of missionaries, and certainly of the Word of God, was minimal. The farmer for whom I was working seemed sensitive to my desire to go to the valley, however, telling me of having made a commitment to Christ himself while visiting missionaries there. Due to social pressures he had not continued in the faith, but as I look back, I can see God using my friend to encourage me to make that trip.*

*At that time the [Guruve] area and the Zambezi Valley were very primitive areas. Roads were mere tracks and could be traversed only during the dry season. Even then, trucks going into this area were few and far between, primarily belonging to farmers seeking to employ labor from across the Mozambique border or adventurous hunters. The few TEAM missionaries at Msengedzi and one couple at Hunyani were the only permanent residents other than government rangers and the Shona people who lived there.*

*You can imagine the District Commissioner's horror when I walked into his office in [Guruve] requesting a local man who could accompany me to the Hunyani Mission Station on foot—since I had no transport. "Wolfe," he said, "You are mad."*

*I had my gun and my dog, Jock. It was the dry season, and I had made rough sketches where the water points were. I was prepared to make the trip on foot, but God intervened. In the commissioner's office was a born-again Christian man who invited me to spend the night with him and his wife before I set off on my trek. He, too, was an encouragement to me, being sensitive to my seeking, which was evidently clear to him.*

*The following morning, just as I was preparing to leave, God intervened again. A truck arrived and offered to give me a lift right to Hunyani.*

*Upon arriving at Hunyani, the driver dropped me off right at the station, where Les and Lillian Austin were living. One of my first observations of this dear couple was their material poverty. I learned later that they were under-supported and short of food and supplies—except for an abundant supply of Ovaltine.*

*Their gracious hospitality was outstanding, however. I was welcomed and made to feel quite at home. They could see the hand of God in leading me to their doorstep. Les, having only a few years previously immigrated from London to Zimbabwe, was able to relate to me quite well. The relaxed atmosphere between us enabled me to receive his encouragement and help in my time of spiritual need.*

*During the short time that I was at Hunyani, Les began explaining to me God's way of salvation. Strangely enough, even as an unbeliever, I always traveled with my Bible that was given to me as a child. For the first time I began to look up Scripture verses that were given to me. I also found the little booklet that had been given to me in London, which I had never read. In so many ways God was preparing me, and my heart was beginning to respond. Soon my life would be completely given to following and serving Christ.*

*Not long afterwards I accompanied Les and Lillian on their supply trip to Harare, about 200 miles away, and was invited to stay with them at the mission hostel. During this time Les and I prayed together in the kitchen of the old cottage, and I gave my heart to the Lord. Old things passed away. Everything became new.*

*For the next year I served on a volunteer basis with TEAM, first with Russ and Marg Jackson at Rusambo and then with Warren and Lois Bruton at Mavuradonha. Russ and Warren became my spiritual fathers. I grew much during that year spent with them and am very grateful to God for them and especially for Les.*

During this time John was also building a relationship with Betty Mason, who was stationed at Msengedzi. After his year of volunteering he moved to Kalk Bay, South Africa to attend Bible school. In December 1954, he and Betty were married, just a day or two after receiving his official acceptance as a missionary with TEAM.

Roy Carnall was another Englishman who ended up in Zimbabwe. Having grown up in the Anglican church in Devonshire, he found the Lord only after leaving home.

From the time he was a child, Roy was greatly interested in travel books and big game hunting. He worked for awhile with a man who loved to talk to him about his travel to different parts of the world, and Roy loved listening.

When he was presented with an opportunity for free passage to South Africa in exchange for three years of work, he eagerly accepted it. After eighteen months in South Africa he was transferred to Zimbabwe to work in the Turk mines outside of Bulawayo. Here he met a man, Chovi Svanda, who asked him to buy some Bibles for him.

Roy reported:

*I got him some Zulu Bibles, but my conscience kind of pricked me. Here was a man who had had about a third grade education, but he wanted to have a Bible study, and here was I not doing anything. I wasn't even going to church because the nearest English-speaking church was forty miles away.*

When his three years of service were over, Roy never returned to England. Instead, he went to Harare. Here he met Sydney Hudson Reed, the pastor of Central Baptist Church. Roy continued

*My first Sunday at his church he asked me home for lunch. I said, "Oh, this is a wonderful church!" I went back another Sunday, and a lady named Bessie Till asked me home for lunch. So I said, "Oh, this is a wonderful church! I'm going back here again!"*

Through the Tills, he met some of the TEAM missionaries. The warm hospitality of Orla and Marguerite Blair greatly impacted him. Having tea with them one day, he also met Mildred Rogers, who was in from her Hunyani station for a few weeks.

When Roy told them he was a builder, they mentioned the building project going on at the children's hostel. Since Roy had access to building materials, he graciously donated some doors to the hostel.

His relationship with Orla continued to grow, and Orla took him around to visit several of the mission stations on the week-ends. This gave him the opportunity to gain a firsthand look at missions and also to see the needs that existed on these stations.

Roy explained:

*I never had a definite, dramatic call to be a missionary. It was kind of a growing conviction that a certain course of action was right for me. I fought it, but that was biblical too because Paul fought against the "pricks" as well.*

Roy talked about this "growing conviction" with Pastor Reed and began progressing toward becoming a missionary himself. First, he enrolled in a lay preachers' course in Harare. Then he went to Kalk Bay Bible School in Cape Town, South Africa.

While he was there, he applied to TEAM and was accepted. When he returned to Zimbabwe, he was delighted to marry Mildred Rogers. It must have been something that Marguerite sprinkled in that tea!

Cherith Till's family had moved back to Zimbabwe from South

Africa when she was nine years old. Her first exposure to missions came as a teen-ager when Orv and Helen Dunkeld spoke at her church camp in Kadoma.

When her family later moved to Harare, they became acquainted with more of the TEAM missionaries. Her parents, Cecyl and Bessie Till, began assisting at TEAM's annual missionary conferences, working with the children while their parents were in meetings. Cherith, who was working at the time, occasionally went with them. This was the beginning of what became a very close relationship between the Tills and the TEAM missionaries.

Cherith began developing friendships with the single women missionaries. One day when she went to the Plot to see Lorraine Waite, she and Dr. Wall were looking over plans for the new Karanda Hospital. Quite unexpectedly, Dr. Wall turned to her and said, "You should take your nurses' training and come and help us!" Within a short time two other people suggested the same thing to her.

Once planted, this idea took root in her mind and would not die. It interrupted her thoughts again and again throughout the day. Finally, one day as she was having devotions, she told God that she would at least begin moving in this direction and see what He did in leading her forward.

The first step was to apply for nurses' training. She was sure that she would not be accepted as she had been brought up to think that she was sickly. She had also completed only three years of high school and then had enrolled in a one-year business course. She was totally surprised when the nursing school she applied to did not consider her to be sickly and also accepted the business course as her fourth year of high school.

During her nurses' training, she continued her friendships with the TEAM missionaries, taking vacations with some of the single gals and visiting them on their stations. One day on such a visit she accompanied one of them in visiting some of the nearby villages to invite them to some special meetings. As she was doing this, she felt God saying to her, "I want you to be a missionary here." At that moment the idea suggested by others became a personal call from God upon her life.

After finishing nursing school, she went to Canada to attend

Briercrest Bible Institute, where God confirmed this call. She then applied to TEAM and was accepted but was advised by the Zimbabwe field to take a midwifery course in South Africa before beginning her missionary service.

# Struggles with the Call

The call of God to leave home and family and all that was familiar to go to a strange land for the cause of the Gospel was not always eagerly embraced initially. A serious consideration of the cost involved is by no means out of place, however, as Jesus emphatically urged this somber deliberation of anyone who would become His disciple (Luke 14:26-33).

Within the hearts of those who struggled with His call, God worked gently and gradually in His own unique way to move them into a clearer awareness of His voice and a willing and obedient heart (Philippians 2:13). Marian Wilterdink described the process that God used with her:

*I took a business course in high school with the intention of working in an office and getting married. As I approached graduation, the senior class prophesied that I would be a missionary to Africa. I really laughed at that, as being a missionary was the last thing I ever wanted to do.*

*Then one week in church all of the Sunday school classes gathered in the auditorium to listen to a missionary from Africa. While he was speaking, God softly asked me if I would be willing to go to Africa to present the Gospel to the national children there. Knowing it was God who was asking me to go, how could I refuse?*

*Nevertheless, I went through a period when I thought I could serve God just as well in the States. During that time He never gave me any inner peace, however.*

*Each time I saw the word "Africa," the letters seemed enlarged and a soft voice said, "That is where I want you to go." When I began a job in an office, I found only one thing in the desk to which I was assigned, and that was a map of Africa. One night I attended a meeting in a church, and the speaker was from Africa. Through these and many other ways the Lord continued to remind me of His call for me to go to Africa. I had no inner peace until I surrendered my life to His will. Then He gave me inner peace!*

God continued to give Marian a consistent inner peace about her call that remained throughout her 51 years in Zimbabwe. She had no doubt that she was where the Lord wanted her to be. She said, "I loved the work and I loved the kids."

Bob Medaris was a partner in a construction company that built custom homes in Phoenix, Arizona, when the Lord spoke to him about using his abilities on the mission field. When he shared this with his wife, Fran, however, she was shocked! They had just gotten their home in "tip-top" shape for their retirement, and now Bob was suggesting that they leave it and go to a foreign country! "What kind of a house would we possibly live in there?" she wondered. "What if it had a thatched roof that harbored insects and other crawling creatures?"

Fran had anything but peace about this prospect. She did go and talk to her pastor's wife about her feelings, however. This lady gave Fran a copy of Isobel Kuhn's book *By Searching*. Fran had hardly read half of the book when the Lord spoke to her, and she realized that she was placing her priorities in the wrong order by focusing on material things.

She told Bob that she was ready to go anywhere but to Africa! Her next lesson was to learn that when God calls you, you don't tell Him where or when. As God continued to work in her heart, Fran reported, "I soon was brought to the place where I could say as the song does 'Where He leads me I will follow.'"

God then graciously helped her make the next step. Dr. Al and Donna Clemenger had returned from serving at Karanda Hospital in Zimbabwe and were in their church. They were able to give the Medarises a wealth of information about Zimbabwe. Fran's ears really perked up when they told her, "If you like growing flowers and vegetables, Zimbabwe is the place for you."

As she heard this, Fran was touched in recalling God's promise in Romans 8:28 that He works all things together for good for those who love Him and are obedient to His call. She said, "When I realized that I could not only serve the Lord in Zimbabwe but could also enjoy growing things, I said, 'All right, Lord, I'm willing to go to Zimbabwe.'" Peace then flooded her heart.

Fran was able to rest in the assurance that God had a plan for her life that would be "good," and He did! In looking back over her life, she now values the years she and Bob spent in Zimbabwe as the very best ones. God is so faithful to His Word!

When she was a teenager, Betty Endicott responded to an invitation given by a missionary speaker at her church to be willing to go into full-time Christian service. Most of her entire youth group went forward. Betty, being one of the youngest, was more hesitant and unsure about ever leaving her family to go overseas if that was what God wanted. She finally did follow the others, however, agreeing to go anywhere the Lord led—except Africa!

Because of her poor health Betty left high school in her junior year and took a course at a business school instead. She then got a job at the Philadelphia Gas Works, met Bob Endicott, a printer, at a Sunday school picnic, and married him seven months later. With her education cut short and her marriage to a printer, she abandoned her thoughts about going to the mission field and didn't even tell Bob about them. She was just going to settle down and be an ordinary wife and mother at home.

After a few years, however, Bob dropped what Betty considered a "bombshell" on her, telling her that he felt the Lord calling him to full-time Christian service. Tearfully Betty told him of her earlier decision as well. Together, they went and talked to their pastor. Betty was very relieved when he told Bob that since he already had a wife and two small children, getting the necessary education to become a pastor would be extremely difficult. So Bob and Betty went home and continued life as usual.

Roy Eichner was one of the other youth who had gone forward with Betty's youth group as a teen-ager. He had proceeded to get married and go to Zimbabwe as a TEAM missionary. When Roy and Lydia returned to the States on furlough, they visited the Endicotts.

While they were there, Roy was asked to speak to the church's youth group. Roy agreed and Bob went with him. As Roy spoke, he turned toward Bob and said, "God can even use a printer."

This remark stirred Bob's thinking. Eventually, he wrote to the Eichners, asking them if printers really were needed on the mission field or if Roy was just speaking generically, using a printer as a rare example just because Bob was standing there. With Eichners in the midst of preparing to return to the field, the letter seemingly never reached them. Once again Betty was relieved and life continued as usual.

Then another missionary serving with SIM in Liberia spoke at their church and invited those who were interested to stay for a slide show afterwards. In the midst of the show was a slide of an idle printing press, which was accompanied by a plea for a printer to run it.

This nearly knocked Betty off her chair! She was certain she would never get out of this one. Sure enough, after the slide show Bob had a lengthy discussion with the missionary. Betty finally got near enough to hear that some information would be coming to Bob in the mail from the mission.

Day after day Betty watched the mail for that information to arrive. Finally, a thick brown envelope addressed to Bob from SIM came. Bob read the material and laid it on the dresser before going off to work. After he left, Betty was so curious that she read the material too. Her heart sank as she learned that printers were indeed needed on the mission field.

As she thought about all the drastic changes that becoming a missionary would mean for her and her family, she became overwhelmed. She looked at her daughters, her home, her church, a special couples' Sunday school class, her extended family, her friends, and even the dog (couldn't desert him). Everything was so comfortably in place for her, and she did not want to disrupt it. So she told the Lord that she was no longer willing to be a missionary.

During the following year each of the things that Betty had viewed as more important to her than heeding the Lord's call to the mission field suffered a major blow. The dog died of cancer, the girls both got mononucleosis, their church split with even their friends being divided, her mother started showing signs of dementia at an unusually early age, and problems erupted with their house as well. It was the worst year of Betty's life.

After the church split, the Endicotts felt led to help in forming a new church. On New Year's Eve the pastor gave a message on

"Redeeming the Time," which really challenged Betty. Suddenly she got a new perspective on her life and priorities and realized that everything that she had lost in the last year was not as important as she had thought.

In fact, she came to view that awful year as God's chastening of her, which according to Hebrews 12:11 (KJV), at the time seems grievous but afterwards *"yields the peaceable fruit of righteousness unto them which are exercised thereby."* God was working in her life and she was recognizing it.

One Sunday shortly after this her pastor was leading the congregation in singing, "I'll Go Where You Want Me to Go." Before beginning the second verse, he told them that to continue to sing this hymn if one did not mean these words would be a lie. The words had already been speaking to Betty's heart. With tears in her eyes she continued singing, telling the Lord that she finally was willing to follow wherever He led.

She felt quite strongly that that was to the mission field, but to be absolutely sure, she decided not to tell Bob of her renewed commitment. Instead, she asked God to give Bob "no peace" until he also made a definite decision in this direction.

Two weeks went by with nothing happening; yet Betty continued to pray. One day after working the night shift, Bob woke up earlier than usual and began talking to Betty about the many things they had recognized as the Lord's leading in their lives. Then he told her how during a rare slow period at work the previous night he had had "no peace" as his mind was continually drawn to thinking about the mission field.

When Betty heard those words, she knew God had answered her prayer. With tears pouring down her cheeks, she went to the kitchen to prepare dinner. Bob followed her and asked the meaning of her tears. She was only too happy to tell him how the Lord had dealt with her heart too.

When they shared this with their pastor, he encouraged them to push forward through the doors leading in this direction and to keep going as long as they were open. Since they would need some Bible training, he also helped them map out courses to take at Philadelphia College of the Bible, where he had previously been on staff.

He also went to the missions department and secured a list of 17 missions they could explore. When they wrote to each of these missions, 10 responded that they needed a printer on one of their fields. Bob and Betty didn't know how they were going to determine which one God wanted them to fill. They took the list and arranged it in order of their preference with all of the openings in the United States first and with TEAM Africa last. Very quickly all of the possibilities were eliminated for various reasons—except for TEAM.

Accepting that TEAM was the open door they were to walk through, they were still unsure of what country God had in mind for them. Somehow their own expectations leaned more towards the Colombia-Venezuela field. Therefore, they were quite surprised when they arrived at Candidate School and found "Zimbabwe" written on their folders rather than "Undesignated," which they saw on some of the other candidates' folders.

Going to their assigned room, they found that they would be sharing a unit of rooms with three other couples. After meeting each other, the group decided to have a prayer time together before attending classes each morning.

The first day of classes went well, but that evening an experienced missionary told Bob and Betty that having two teenaged daughters might affect their ability to raise support. Their daughters might also have difficulty in adjusting to the field at their ages.

The next morning Bob and Betty shared their concerns over what they had been told the night before with their prayer group. Together, they all prayed that God's will would be made clear to them.

In their first class that morning they were deeply moved by the devotional. They felt it gave them the clear message that they were to continue on through the doors that the Lord had opened for them.

After the devotional the leader asked if anyone had any questions. Only one question was asked. An unidentified person in the back of the room, who knew nothing about them, asked, "Are printers needed on the mission field?"

The answer was, "Most definitely," and the class proceeded.

Bob and Betty could hardly believe their ears. They felt that this, too, had been orchestrated by God specifically for them.

At Candidate School they were required to read the brochures on each of TEAM's fields. When Betty opened the one for Zimbabwe, the first words were "Redeeming the Time in [Zimbabwe]." This was the message Betty had heard on New Year's Eve that caused such a major change in her heart.

These and many other confirmations came during those three weeks to assure them that they were definitely on the right path, and Zimbabwe was where God wanted them. By the end of Candidate School they were given final acceptance as TEAM appointees to Zimbabwe.

Betty wrote:

*In every area we can now look back and see how anything we gave up, God gave back many times over and blessed our lives as a result.*

Both of their daughters also testify that their experience in Zimbabwe was life-transforming.

## Singleness

A major struggle in responding to the missionary call for some was the issue of singleness. Mission fields and single women seem to go hand-in-hand with an occasional single man found as well. Some of these individuals have the "gift of being single" and are grateful to have a life unfettered with the cares of a family so they can devote full attention to ministry. Others do not feel they have this "gift." While they too can devote much more time to ministry, they struggle emotionally with unfulfilled longings for a mate and family.

Why God expects even those without the "gift of singleness" to live in that state on the mission field is a difficult question to answer. We do know, however, that God clearly states that many sacrifices concerning family are necessary for those who would truly be His disciples (Luke 14:26). He expects devotion to Himself to be an absolute priority above everything else, including the desire for a mate.

Several of the Zimbabwe missionaries opened their hearts to share how they struggled with the idea of being single missionaries. Each one can be commended for following God's call in spite of the unfulfilled longings she carried deep within her heart.

Wilma Gardziella Anderson wrote:

*As a child I heard lots of missionaries giving their reports and decided from a very young age that I was going to be a missionary. This never changed.*

*When I went to college, I declared a Christian Ed. major. I changed this to pre-nursing in my second year, however, as I had a boyfriend who was also going to be a missionary. As I contemplated marriage, I wondered how we would manage in the middle of the African bush far away from any kind of medical care. So I went into nursing primarily to prepare me to be a better wife and mother on the mission field.*

*By the time I finished college and started nursing school, we were engaged, knowing it would be another three years before we could get married. My fiancé eventually decided, however, that that was too long for him to wait. Therefore, we broke our engagement, and I finished my nurses' training, as dropping out at that point would have left me with nothing to show for the five years of education I had already completed.*

*I really struggled that year as I asked the Lord why He had led me into nursing if I were not going to be married. Certainly He knew how strongly I did not want to be single! Obviously, He had other plans for me.*

*I continued on my path to the mission field, as I truly believed that that was God's call upon my life. I hoped with all my heart, however, that God would bring another man into my life who shared that call.*

*Gradually God showed me that if I were to teach nursing, I could multiply the effect my one life could have on the field. This insight led me to turn my course towards nursing education. God confirmed this new direction for me by opening a wonderful opportunity for me to teach for two years at the University of Kansas School of Nursing. This provided invaluable experience to take to the field with me.*

*I had applied to TEAM in my senior year of nurses' training and was accepted as an "undesignated candidate." The day I went to see Dr. Delbert Kuehl, the Candidate Secretary, to be assigned to a particular field, I had mixed emotions. I knew that four of TEAM's fields wanted a nursing instructor. New Guinea, Pakistan, and Zimbabwe all wanted to begin nursing schools. South Africa already had a school but wanted more teachers.*

*I had asked the Lord to show me which field was His choice, but my own desire was to go to South Africa where I already knew June Salstrom, who was teaching nursing at TEAM's hospital there. I had what I thought were good excuses for not going to New Guinea and Pakistan. I also could not see Zimbabwe as being a viable option as I did not feel experienced enough to start a school on my own.*

*I decided, however, not to tell Dr. Kuehl of my desire to go to South Africa but to ask him where TEAM could best use me, having my excuses for the other possibilities. To my surprise, the moment he said without any hesitation, "Zimbabwe," the Lord seemed to speak clearly to me as well, "That's where I want you," and I had perfect peace with that decision.*

When Karanda Hospital closed in 1978 due to the war, Wilma remained in the country until the end of 1980, having served 20 years in Zimbabwe. God then gave her the desire of her heart. In May 1981, she married Homer Anderson and enjoyed nearly 20 years of marriage to him until he passed away in 2000.

God surprised her again as He brought Bill Riddell into her life. They were married January 1, 2003. This time Wilma gained not only a husband but an extended family, including children and grandchildren.

Kiersten Hutchinson also described how she wrestled with her call to missions and the possibility of going to the field single:

*After spending a summer in Zaire during my college years, I knew that God was leading me to missions, but I confess that going single was not part of that agreement!! I had it all planned out. I would get a medical profession, some experience in that profession, pay off debts, get married, and then go to wherever God called us.*

*I even made certain choices that were specifically*

*designed to accommodate marriage. I chose to be a Physician's Assistant instead of an MD, in part because I felt that I would not be able to sustain both marriage and the demands of being an MD at the same time. I preferred to have less money in order to have time for a marriage.*

*I also kept my mind open as to where in the world God might send me. I felt that as long as I was following God's will, He would provide a complementary man who shared my passion for missions and perhaps had his sights set on a particular people group. I was willing to go wherever my husband felt led to go.*

*I was also prepared to put my work on hold while rais-ing children. Therefore, as I was looking at mission agencies, I checked out how they viewed MK education, since I did not want to be "forced" to send my kids away at age six to a boarding school.*

*Being a fairly stubborn person with an independent spirit, I knew that an act of God would be required to find a mate for me—but nothing is impossible for God, right? I continually kept my eyes open for men who might share my interest in missions. I dated several wonderful Christian men, but none of them shared that passion.*

*As time progressed, all the other areas of my "plan" were in place—except the husband part. I had been patiently and obediently following what I understood to be God's will for my life, but He was not coming through with His part!*

*Finally, I had to face the reality that God was, in fact, calling me to the mission field single—which was deeply troubling to me! He really wanted me to give up all of my dreams of marriage! Hadn't I given Him most of my life already? Wasn't marriage the reward for obedience? These issues weighed heavily on my mind and spirit.*

*God knew how He made me, however, and He did not give me a burden that was too heavy to carry. Instead, He used a wonderful women's retreat to encourage me to place ALL on the altar for Him—including my desire for marriage. I actually went through a time of mourning for the husband and children that I might never have. While that may sound somewhat melodramatic, that was how much I was looking forward to marriage.*

*Even though I consider myself an independent person, it was because I have always had loving relationships with family and friends to support me. If you take those away, I am really quite a coward! I had always pictured myself on the mission field with a husband. Now that God wanted me to go single, it was a whole new decision for me.*

*Satan used this time to plague me with fear. Was God really strong enough to sustain me without the benefit of a husband? Was I strong enough to act in faith, trusting that He was? I really had a crisis of faith! One that I did not expect! Did I really believe all the things that I had been spouting all these years about the all-sufficiency of God?*

*Then, just when I had come to terms with singleness, let go of my desire to be married, AND decided that I could trust God to take care of and provide for me on the mission field, a man came along!!! Isn't this just the way others have experienced it??? When you finally release your desires to God and are willing to give them up for Him, He fills them? Wow!*

*This guy had all the qualifications too. He was a missionary pilot with a good agency (and attractive). We also had some similar interests. Things were rolling!*

*In fact, things were rolling too fast! I said, "Okay, God, when you answer a prayer, you really answer a prayer! Please God, I am only going to do this marriage thing once, so make it real clear if this is the one or not." I knew what all the wrong ones looked like, but I wasn't sure if I knew what the right one should look like.*

*Plans progressed. I would apply to his mission agency. Then we would have a spring wedding, followed by language school, and then off to Africa! Wow!*

*God answered my prayers for direction, however, and said, "No, this is not the one."*

*"What? Did I hear you correctly, Lord?"*

*"Yes."*

*Crash! Another blow to my faith. "Okay, God, are you*

*just jerking me around here or what? I said I was willing to give up marriage for You. Now You have brought up all my desires again only to leave them painfully unfulfilled?" Although I still do not understand the reasoning for His timing, I chose to trust God's goodness. I worked my way back to that sense of contentment that I had found prior to this unexpected curve ball.*

*Once again I readied myself to launch out into missions as a single person. Am I really able to do it? Of course not! Is God able to do it through me? Absolutely! Am I willing to act on this truth? Slowly. God knew that if He led me in baby steps, I would make it.*

*First, He opened the door for me to go to Zimbabwe for two months. God was so gracious! Not only did I like Karanda very much, but the other missionaries actually liked me too (no small feat for the stubborn person that I am)! The doctors knew how to utilize a Physician's Assistant and the hospital had a good balance. I felt that I could be used there. The impossible was slowly seeming possible.*

*The next step was to return for two years—which again was a step of faith for me. The first year was so full of new and exciting things that I hardly had time to miss a relationship with a man. The second year was much more of a challenge. I would get lonely. I would struggle with my sense of femininity since there were no available men to take notice of me. Every once in a while I would mourn once again for the marriage and family which I felt would never be.*

*I also came to enjoy the other single women who shared my feelings. We would have "ro-tic" nights together (that's "romantic" without the "man")! Once they planned a hilarious birthday "date" for me with the male CPR mannequin!*

*We grow to trust God in new and deeper ways. I remind myself of the Israelites, who were not satisfied with their Divine King but rather wanted a human one. They got what they wanted—and a lot of misery too. I pray that daily I will have the faith to allow God to continue to be my "husband." I never quite stop looking, though, just in case God decides to change His mind! I still have a long way to go, but at least I know that I can trust the One leading me.*

Going to the mission field single does not always mean lifelong celibacy. Quite a number who, in obedience to the Lord, went to Zimbabwe single, met their "special someone" on the field.

In many other cases God provided husbands when they retired from the field. God blessed many with not only a spouse but also with a ready-made family of children and even grandchildren. God is good and He loves to give good gifts to His children. The road of obedient sacrifice often leads to great blessing from His hand.

---

[1] *The Missionary Broadcaster*, 1935.

[2] Ibid.

[3] *The Missionary Broadcaster*, Oct.-Dec., 1937.

[4] *The Missionary Broadcaster*, 1935.

[5] Robert Hall Glover, *The Bible Basis of Missions* (Los Angeles: Bible House of Los Angeles, 1946), 138-39.

[6] Ibid.

# CHAPTER 3

# God Prepared

*"For we are God's workmanship,
created in Christ Jesus to do good works,
which God prepared in advance for us to do."*
(Ephesians 2:10)

God's hand working in the lives of His chosen missionaries often began long before they sensed His call to carry the Gospel to another land. Knowing the nature of the challenges that lay ahead for them, God used various means to teach them important skills and to sculpt their lives into prepared vessels, able to accomplish the "good works" for which He had ordained them.

## Preparation for Primitive Living

Many of God's early missionaries to Zimbabwe grew up in homes lacking electricity, central heating, indoor plumbing, hot running water, or refrigeration. Only in retrospect could they appreciate how well this prepared them for the primitive living conditions they would face on the mission field.

Betty Mason Wolfe described her early childhood home in Indiana:

*The house was quite old, but adequate for the five of us. It even had indoor plumbing, which many of the farmhouses didn't. There was a crack in the cistern, however, so we couldn't flush the toilet in the usual way. We had to take a bucket out the back door, pump it full of water, carry it in, and pour it down the toilet. We did that for many years.*

*There was also no hot running water, so on bath night (Saturday) we put the copper boiler on the gasoline stove and filled it bucket-by-bucket until it was full. Then we all took turns bathing in it. . . . On washday we heated the water in the same way and then filled both the washing machine and the two rinsing tubs bucket-by-bucket.*

*We had no central heating. The coal cook stove in the kitchen and a heating stove in the large dining room were used to keep us warm in the winter. Cold food storage was a big problem as there were no freezers. I was eleven or twelve when we got our first refrigerator. Until then we used the cellar to keep things cool in the summer.*

Joe Riemer stated, "Olga and I both feel that what helped us the most in adapting to the mission field was our primitive lifestyle during our formative years." They both grew up on Canadian farms with no modern conveniences at all.

God prepared Thelma Everswick for life on the mission field in a slightly different manner. Her mother had been told that if she didn't live outdoors for months at a time, her pleurisy would turn into tuberculosis. With five children to raise, she could not let this happen. Therefore, every summer from the day after school was out until school reopened, she took her family camping at High Point Park in New Jersey. Thelma recalls doing this from the time she was six-years-old until she was fifteen. Her father would join them on week-ends.

They really roughed it during these times, hauling their own water and firewood, cooking on an open fire, and scrubbing their own clothes. They had to walk to a public toilet, battle mosquitoes and other insects, and deal with thorns and stubbed toes since they were barefoot most of the time. Thelma, who later became a nurse, learned how to clean a wound and bandage it from her mother during those days. She now recognizes how well this whole experience prepared her for missionary service in the Zambezi Valley.

Bob and Betty Endicott described how God used their first home in New Jersey to introduce them to conditions they would experience in Zimbabwe:

*We lived with the barest of necessities with most stores being miles away and with electricity that would go out for days at a time after storms. We also had to deal with a problem septic system and flying ant invasions coming from heating ducts that ran under our cement slab floor. Wet or winter weather drew the ants through the dirt under the slab toward the heat and then out through our floor registers, getting into everything, including our food on the table and Nancy's diapers on a shelf under the changing table. Little did we know then that God was using this to prepare us for all the creatures we would later encounter in our Chironga home during our eight months of language school.*

Growing up during the depression was another significant factor that prepared many of the early missionaries for the less-than-affluent lifestyle that missionaries tend to live. Mildred Carnall reported:

*The "pioneer" living we experienced on the mission field was not too far removed from what I had known as a child growing up in a poor family during the depression.*

God used working in the inner city Chicago to prepare George Smazik for the poverty he would encounter on the mission field.

## Development of Work Skills

Establishing, developing, and carrying out the overall ministry God desired His servants to have in Zimbabwe would require knowledge and experience in a broad array of skills, including construction, mechanics, education, medicine, accounting, business, administration, printing, and radio. A retrospective look again reveals the marvelous way that God worked "beforehand" to develop these necessary skills within His chosen servants.

## Farm Related Skills

A particularly fertile training ground, especially for the early missionaries, was the farm. Within this environment many young people acquired a vast range of physical skills and mental disciplines that proved to be invaluable on the mission field.

As the son of pioneer farmers in Canada, who labored hard to break up new land and make it productive, Russ Jackson learned many skills that would serve him well on the mission field. What a tremendous help and encouragement he was to the other missionaries when he and Marg arrived at Msengedzi in 1948!

Up to that point no one had been very successful in growing vegetables in the extreme heat of the Zambezi Valley. Drawing upon his experience as a pioneer farmer, Russ took a sample of the soil to Harare for testing. When he returned, he knew exactly what it needed in order to be productive. With the help of an elderly local man he was able to establish a wonderful garden by the Msengedzi River, giving the missionaries a much appreciated source of fresh produce.

The women of the station had also been complaining that the men did not know how to care properly for the wild game they shot to prevent the meat from becoming tainted. They were so delighted that Russ knew how to do this too.

Martin Uppendahl also found his farm background to be of "immeasurable help" on the mission field, especially during his first term in the early fifties when he was surveying new areas for outreach and helping to open additional stations. He valued the experience he had gained not only from the typical farm operations of fieldwork, gardening, and care of livestock but also from the subsidiary activities of construction, roadwork, and mechanics.

Joe Reimer, who arrived at Karanda in 1976, echoed this same appreciation of his farm experience:

*My farming background gave me insight and experience that helped me on the field in building, repairing, improvising, and coping with many different situations that arose.*

A particularly valuable skill gleaned from the farm was the knowledge of mechanics. Knowing how crucial this would be on the mission field, especially on the early rural stations where repair facilities for vehicles, generators, pumps, and kerosene appliances were simply not available, God prepared numerous men with this particular expertise.

Wilf Strom's farm experience was enriched by working alongside two of his older brothers who had taken a course in mechanics at a technical college. They were able to explain things to him exceptionally well, he reported, passing on many "tricks of the trade." He recounted two examples of how he was able to use this knowledge to resolve specific problems he encountered on the field:

> *In the Zambezi Valley the missionaries' vehicles were not used during the rainy season, so their batteries were not well charged. I recall the first trip we made to Harare after the rainy season the year that we were in language study at the Hunyani station. We were traveling with the Cedarholms, and the riverbeds we had to cross were deep with sand. At the bottom of a steeply banked river the Cedarholm's truck stalled. The battery didn't have enough of a charge in it to start up, and the bank was too steep and soft for us to try to pull it out.*
>
> *Then I remembered a "trick" from my farm experience. We jacked up a rear wheel and wrapped a rope around the tire several times. Then we put the car in gear and turned on the ignition. We had two or three local men run with the rope, making the wheel turn fast enough to cause the engine to turn over and start. What a relief it was to see the truck's motor take hold and drive up the other side of the riverbank!*

Another time George Dee's truck had somehow gotten "out of timing" and wouldn't start, so he had requested that Wilf come down to Hunyani to see if he could fix it. Wilf reported:

> *I rode my motorbike about a hundred miles down into the valley, ruminating all the while on how I could possibly*

*remedy the problem with the limited resources that I would have. By the time I arrived, I had an idea. I removed the spark plug from the first cylinder and turned the motor over. With my thumb on the spark plug hole, I determined when the piston was coming up on compression. Then I inserted a wire that I held in my hand so I could feel the exact moment when the piston started going down. I could then set the distributor so that the timing was right. When I put the spark plug back in and started the truck, it ran fine—greatly delighting both George and myself!*

Ray and Myrtle Finsaas were also grateful for the mechanical skills Ray learned growing up on the farm so that he could keep their well-used truck, as well as other engines on the station, in good repair. They and other missionaries used their trucks in many aspects of their lives and ministries, so keeping them in good repair was vital, especially with all the travel done on isolated and rugged rural roads. The Finsaases used their truck to get supplies from town, to transport their children to and from the hostel where they stayed during their school terms, to bring seriously ill patients to the station clinic, and to carry nationals to minister in the outlying villages with them.

Emil Rilling expanded the skills he had learned on the farm by taking a course on diesel mechanics during one of his furloughs. While God also used Emil in teaching short-term Bible schools and planting churches, he became an extremely valuable asset on the field because of his expertise in both mechanics and construction.

These skills were put to good use while the Rusambo station was being expanded. He also served as Karanda's maintenance engineer for a number of years in the 1970's, keeping their diesel generators going and doing other mechanical repairs. While there, he also maintained and improved the water system and kept the sewer system running in a manner that produced a thriving vegetable garden for the nursing students.

No matter what type of ministry a "farm-grown" man intended to have on the mission field, his wide range of farming skills were sure to be used as well. Dave Voetmann's primary role on the Zimbabwe field from 1964-1974 was serving as the Missionary

Aviation Fellowship (MAF) pilot. However, he drew upon his farm experience to fill many other important roles at Karanda, where he was stationed. This included overhauling the water pumps, maintaining the generators, supervising the hospital's work crew, and spearheading several building projects.

Even some of the medical personnel, such as Dr. Al Clemenger, Dr. Dave Drake, Dr. Rick Froese, and Phil Christiansen rolled up their sleeves to address mechanical needs when needed. Dr. Clemenger wrote:

*I recall the early days at Karanda Hospital when the patient load was not too heavy and both Sam Wall and I were there as physicians. There was a need for someone who could drive a tractor and work with machinery. Since I had the farm experience and mechanical knowledge, I was elected to do that while Sam cared for the patients.*

Rick Froese, who came to Karanda Hospital to serve as a pharmacist, also did a lot of mechanical work, which he had learned from assisting his father, who was a school bus mechanic. This included maintaining, repairing, and overhauling the station's diesel generators as well as the gas engines on the Maytag washers used for the hospital laundry. Rick wrote:

*Many times Phil Christiansen and I would work all day installing an elaborate filtration system down at the river or overhauling machinery, go home for supper, and then be down at the hospital doing our medical duties until late into the night.*

Construction skills learned on the farm were also invaluable as the various mission stations and ministries were established. Dick Regier recalled that while building the Bible school at Kapfundi, he and Ken Munger, who had both grown up on farms, were able to tackle many jobs and resolve problems that seemed quite challenging to those without this experience.

Emil Rilling worked with Clarence Cedarholm in building the Teacher Training Institute at Chironga. He then supervised a crew of local men in building the Homecraft School at Rusambo as well as in expanding the Mavuradonha Primary School. When the Bible school moved to Chinhoyi, he worked with local men to transform an old Bible school building at Kapfundi into a functional clinic.

Wilbur Beach also gained experience in construction from growing up on a farm. In fact, his father was recognized as a gifted creator of almost anything out of wood. Wilbur learned from him and went on to gain further experience as well. He wrote:

*Following my army days I purposely took jobs in construction in order to improve my knowledge and skill. While a student at Prairie Bible Institute, I was fortunate to be able to work during my summers building dorms under a journeyman who was a perfectionist in construction. This on-the-job training was just what I needed on the field.*

Bob Medaris was another man whom God prepared to be used in construction on the mission field. After growing up on a farm and being a farmer himself for the first few years of his marriage, Bob became a partner in a construction company and worked in that capacity for ten years.

When he and Fran arrived in Zimbabwe in 1967, his first assignment was to supervise the building of an out-patient wing for Karanda Hospital. This was followed by building a missionary duplex and a men's dormitory and classroom block for the nursing school. When the need arose for a new dining hall at Mavuradonha High School, he commuted there by MAF plane to direct the building of this as well, flying over on Monday and back to Karanda on Saturday. He then went to Harare to remodel TEAM's offices, build another duplex for missionaries, and make bunk beds and desks for the hostel.

Clarence Cedarholm didn't grow up on a farm, but his father was a carpenter by trade, and Clarence received excellent training from him. One dry season he led a crew in putting up twenty-seven buildings at the new Chironga station. This included the Teacher Training Institute, staff and missionary houses, and the dispensary.

God developed specific construction skills in several other men through apprenticeship programs. Roy Carnall, who grew up in

England, spent four years as an apprentice carpenter and went to evening school for three years to study the theory aspect. His carpentry skills were, in fact, what introduced him to the TEAM missionaries in Harare. The hostel was being built at the time, and he helped lay the parquet floor in the lounge. Later, as a missionary, he used his particular skills to make built-in dressing tables/vanities, shelving and drawers, pelmets, and kitchen cabinets at various places where they were needed.

Roy also taught a building construction class at the Mavuradonha High School, teaching the theory of brickmaking and bricklaying and supervising the students' practical work in constructing latrines. Some students also gained experience in electrical wiring and water supply.

Les and Reg Austin, two brothers also from England, not only learned much from their father, who made his living in construction, but Les also took an apprenticeship as a bricklayer and Reg as an electrician. As a result, God was able to use Les in doing considerable construction work on the Hunyani station as well as with the children's hostel in Harare.

Upon joining the TEAM Zimbabwe missionary force, Reg Austin set his course on becoming an educator, but his electrical training was put to good use at times too. He did all the wiring for the hostel complex as well as some of the electrical work for the new Evangelical Bible School campus in Chinhoyi.

During his training to become an electrician, Reg also developed an interest in architecture and gained experience in drawing house plans. Tapping into these skills, he did some of the architectural drawings for the Bible school in Chinhoyi and worked with Dr. Sam Wall in drawing the architectural design for the Karanda Hospital.

Men were not the only ones to learn valuable skills for missionary living from growing up on the farm. Judy Gudeman described learning to garden, can, and butcher chickens on the farm as well as to sew and bake. Not being able to run to the store when something was needed also helped prepare her for the isolation of bush living, she reported.

## Medical Skills

Individuals trained in various medical skills were greatly needed on the field, as medicine became a prominent vehicle for drawing the people of the Zambezi Valley to hear the Gospel message that the missionaries desired to share. Starting with nurses working out of small dispensaries and rural clinics, this ministry eventually expanded to include the 150-bed Karanda Hospital, requiring an even broader range of medical personnel. Training to fill these needs was certainly not difficult to acquire in North America, but many of those whom God called to this line of work in Zimbabwe can look back and see special circumstances that God seemed to design to prepare them for their particular roles on the field.

Carol Olsen Austin greatly appreciated the year that she worked with the Chicago Visiting Nurses Association while waiting for TEAM to decide on her field assignment. Nursing people from many different ethnic groups and of all economic levels was a real eye-opener for her and invaluable in preparing her for the mission field.

God opened a very unlikely, but opportune, job for Wilma Gardziella that proved extremely helpful in broadening her skills as a nurse educator. She now recognizes how God orchestrated that in order to prepare her for the teaching role that He planned for her to have with the student nurses at Karanda Hospital. She wrote:

> *Having decided that the Lord was possibly leading me into teaching nurses somewhere on the mission field, I went for a quick week-end visit to a friend who was teaching at the University of Kansas Medical Center at the time. Marie did not tell me that her faculty was having a progressive dinner that evening, thinking this would keep me from coming. So after our first burst of conversation, she informed me that I was accompanying her to this event. Being a senior student at West Suburban Hospital at the time, I did not feel comfortable in going but was more or less forced to go anyway.*
>
> *I am sure Marie had told the Director of Nursing about me, as we had several conversations in the course of the evening. Before the event was over, she offered me a teaching job there for the next school year. I was stunned; yet I*

*have looked back with much gratefulness at the way that God led in opening that door for me. I had been trained in a three-year diploma program, had my Bachelor of Science Degree from Wheaton College, and was able to teach in a four-year academic program, which had very different approaches to nursing and gave me a whole new dimension in my nursing experience.*

Judy Gudeman also saw God's hand at work in several steps of her journey to the mission field. Working in an office for three years before going to nurses' training prepared her for doing the necessary office work at Karanda Hospital before they had a full-time secretary. Then, after completing her nurses' training, she worked for four years in a hospital where she was in charge of a small, eleven-bed unit. Not only did she gain significant experience in caring for medical and surgical patients, but running the ward also helped to prepare her for the supervisory roles she had at Karanda Hospital. She also worked in the Health Service Department while attending Moody Bible Institute. There she became familiar with treating malaria, as one of the students had grown up in Kenya and had severe bouts of malaria, a disease very common in Zimbabwe as well.

In a similar way Dr. Roland Stephens recognized how God specifically arranged circumstances to give him the types of experience that would be most valuable in preparing him for his role at Karanda Hospital. He wrote:

*I feel that my surgical training was God-directed. I had not specifically planned on going into surgery, but as I neared the end of my internship year, I received my commission from the army to go to Korea. I learned, however, that at that time the draft board would not be calling up anyone for about a year. Therefore, I decided to turn in my commission and take my chance with the draft.*

*Knowing that I had a year before I might potentially be drafted, I decided to use it in getting some surgical training. I began a surgical residency in Chattanooga, and by the end of my first year the Korean War had ended. I stayed on and completed my residency, doing eye surgery on my day off.*

*By the time I finished the three-year residency, I had performed 35 cataract surgeries. All of this turned out to be ideal preparation for the vast array of surgical cases I would face at Karanda, including many cataracts.*

When Roland committed himself to join the staff at Karanda Hospital, he anticipated being the third doctor there, working primarily as a surgeon. However, after only four months Dr. Sam Wall left for furlough and Dr. Al Clemenger had to leave the field unexpectedly for medical reasons. Suddenly, Roland became the *only* doctor.

He went on to explain another way in which He could see God's hand had been preparing him specifically for this:

*After I finished my residency, I "just happened" to read an advertisement in the Christian Medical Society Journal concerning an opening for a physician at a small county hospital in Michigan. Out of four doctors who applied, I was the only one accepted.*

*This hospital had only three doctors. Because we had no specialists to fall back on, as we had had in residency, we helped each other learn things, which would have been impossible in a larger hospital. I also began getting used to having less equipment to work with there, which was very good preparation for going to Karanda Hospital.*

*Academically, my residency had been more broadly based than most General Surgery residencies. Between the residency and that year of practice before going to the field, I obtained invaluable experience in Obstetrics, Gynecology, Orthopedics, Vascular Surgery, and Ophthalmology, all of which proved extremely helpful at Karanda.*

Sam and Dorothy Cook, who went to the field in their retirement years, could also look back and see how God was preparing them for missionary service at Karanda. Sam's twenty years working in a hardware store enabled him to move quite readily into the role of directing the maintenance crew while Dorothy's experience as Surgical Supervisor and overseer of Central Supply Services at

Contra Costa County Hospital in Martinez, California, prepared her for training nursing students in this area at Karanda Hospital. She was particularly grateful for the teaching skills she had learned and the visual aids she had developed in training surgical technicians.

Diane Powell became extremely grateful for the timing of her training in medical technology, coming as it did just as laboratory medicine was transitioning from manual methods to automation. She was in one of the last classes to be taught the manual, as well as the automated, methods for conducting most tests. This was absolutely crucial to her being able to function in the laboratory at Karanda Hospital.

She also recalled that in her year of practical experience before going to the field, she delighted in working in the blood bank and having three emergencies going on in the hospital at the same time, all requiring blood to be cross-matched as quickly as possible. Little did she know that God was preparing her to handle the multiple, serious casualty patients that would be flown into Karanda Hospital during the war, all requiring x-rays, blood transfusions, and surgery "as quickly as possible."

## Other Skills

God used specific types of job experience to prepare individuals for other roles on the mission field as well. Bob Endicott worked 18 years as a printer before heeding God's call to the mission field. While he was never without work for a day, he had many changes in employment. This resulted in his gaining experience in all areas of printing. In addition, he was frequently chosen to replace his supervisor when he was absent. Only in retrospect could Bob see how well God had orchestrated this to prepare him for his role in Zimbabwe as Director of Word of Life Publications from 1970 to 1974.

George Smazik also came to the field later in life after a 33-year career with Bell Telephone where he progressed from being a phone installer to training managers and becoming a supervisor. He arrived in Zimbabwe in 1981, just in time to play a major role in the reconstruction of Karanda Hospital after it had been shut down and damaged during the last two years of the war. Through the management skills he had learned at Bell Telephone, he was able to lead the work crew to a higher level of performance as well as make good use of his administrative skills in the hospital itself.

Lynn Hoyt came to recognize God's hand at work in even some of the seemingly minor learning opportunities she had had, such as her volunteer work in teaching English to Chinese immigrants and her study of special education methods at graduate school. She found herself drawing on these skills as she taught English to students at Mavuradonha Secondary School. She explained:

*Much of the Shona students' learning experience had been through rote memory. They parroted back what they had memorized without really understanding it. I was able to incorporate new learning methods involving more than memory, which helped the students learn more quickly and with greater understanding.*

## Development of Ministry Skills

God's hand in orchestrating the development of various ministry skills in His future missionaries was also evident. This occurred through many academic and practical ways that are too myriad to cover. A small sampling will suffice.

Betty Mason Wolfe was not saved until after high school, but her life was immediately and dramatically affected. She wanted nothing more than to serve God. Every Friday evening she went with a group from her church to hold a street meeting on the court-house square. Here she gained experience in giving her testimony publicly. After graduating from BIOLA, she worked for awhile among the Navajo Indians in Arizona under the Brethren Home Missions Board, feeling this too would give her practical experience in preparation for a foreign field.

Carl and Donna Hendrickson, who had both committed themselves to missionary service at a summer camp, also began ministering together as members of a Gospel team of First Covenant Church in Los Angeles. Through this group they shared their testimonies of salvation and life in Christ in places such as a juvenile home, an honor farm for minor offenders, county hospitals, and city missions. Carl gave his first sermon at age sixteen in one of these city missions.

About two years before leaving for Zimbabwe, the church asked

Carl to plan and coordinate a Saturday Morning Club in the multi-racial neighborhood of their church. In this valuable, cross-cultural ministry experience they saw much growth take place as they taught the Word of God and introduced these kids to Jesus Christ.

God started preparing Phil Christiansen for cross-cultural ministry while he was attending Moody Bible Institute. There he became active in release time and street ministries in the South and West-side Chicago areas. When he went on to Wheaton College, he again found himself working on the south side of Chicago, this time with a Sunday school at Maxwell Street YMCA. Here he participated in leading a Sunday school of three hundred kids who were gathered every week from the surrounding neighborhoods. This is where Phil met his future wife, Barb. They both really enjoyed working with the African-American kids and came to appreciate them and their culture.

God used several experiences in Mildred Rogers Carnall's life to prepare her for the vigorous nature of rural ministry in Zimbabwe. She spent two summers working at Rehoboth Mountain Mission in Kentucky where she had to learn to drive a Jeep through a dry riverbed in order to get to an up-creek location for Sunday school. This, she said, was very similar to the driving challenges she faced in rural Africa.

Later, she taught at the Christian Grade School of the West End Presbyterian Church in Hopewell, Virginia. There, all of the teachers had to do visitation during the summer holidays and were specifically required to do it *on foot*. This was hard, she said, but it was good preparation for rural evangelism on the field.

God was preparing Lorraine Waite for ministry in Zimbabwe long before she even knew what a missionary was. Growing up on a farm in Michigan, she and her sister were the only children to survive out of her mother's eight pregnancies. As a result, her parents were somewhat over-protective of them. For instance, they were not allowed to have anything with wheels on it, such as tricycles, bicycles, or roller skates, so that they would not be tempted to play on the road.

Instead, Lorraine and her sister gathered a collection of about fifty dolls and spent hours playing by themselves. While they had a few store-bought dolls, most of their dolls were made out of corncobs, stick clothespins, and tobacco sacks. Lorraine describes how these dolls were integrally involved in her learning to study and to teach the Bible from the time she was saved at age eleven and how God put an intense hunger for the Word into her heart and that of her sister:

> *When my sister and I became Christians, all our dolls became Christians with us. My doll Betty was the Sunday school teacher. We went to our real Sunday school at the Gospel Hall at 1:00 in the afternoon, but in the morning after we finished our chores, we had doll Sunday school. By the time we had taught the Sunday school lesson to fifty dolls, we knew it very well ourselves.*
>
> *My sister's big corncob doll, Barry, was the preacher, and on Sunday evenings our dolls would have a church service. A preacher was coming to the Gospel Hall at that time and preaching on Revelation on Sunday evenings, but because our parents didn't allow us to go out at night, "Barry" preached on Revelation at home. Somebody had given us a Scofield Reference Bible, and we looked up all the cross-references in each chapter as we went through it. Many of these were to the book of Daniel, so when we finished going through Revelation, we went through Daniel.*
>
> *My sister and I also memorized a lot of Scripture together. We even tackled Psalm 119 as well as many other chapters of the Bible. You see, when we became Christians and told our folks about it, their first reaction was, "Well, they'll get over this soon." Then, when this didn't happen, they started giving us all the objections to Christianity that the world gives, which drove us to find answers in the Bible. As we did, this ignited within us an even greater hunger to know the Scriptures.*
>
> *We started reading a chapter or so when we got up in the morning, and in the evening before we went to bed, we took turns reading out loud six to ten chapters. We would start in Genesis and go through to Revelation. I have no idea how many times we did that.*
>
> *One time when I was reading the Bible, I was struck by Jesus saying that if His followers were ashamed to confess*

*Him in this sinful and adulterous generation, then He would also be ashamed to confess that they were His followers before the angels in heaven. I certainly didn't want that, so I started witnessing to our neighbors and schoolmates. At first it was with trembling knees and much trepidation, but as they listened to me, it helped me get braver.*

God continued to lead and prepare Lorraine's heart for a very special ministry in Zimbabwe through nursing, youth ministry, and community health work.

# Development of Character

Building character into future missionaries was as important to God as developing their technical and ministry skills. Once again, the farm proved to be a particularly fertile ground for building these traits.

Dr. Al Clemenger testified that growing up on a farm instilled into him a sense of responsibility that carried over to other areas of his life and ministry. The cows had to be fed and milked on time; the chickens had to be fed and eggs gathered on time; the pigs had to be fed and their pens cleaned to prevent the spread of illness; clean water needed to be available at all times for the animals; and crops had to be planted and harvested on time to reap the maximum yield.

The farm also played a significant role in teaching many future missionaries a strong work ethic. George Dee and Dave Voetmann reported that from their early adolescent years they learned to work hard all day long on the farm, even in the hot summer heat. Stew Georgia stated, "An eight hour day was an unknown. We learned to work until the job was done." He also recalled Dr. Rick Froese saying, "No one ever told us the job was impossible, but rather, 'Here is the job,' and we got on with it." This was a very important mindset on the mission field.

Bev Asa described how she learned the importance of teamwork from a very early age through her farm experience:

*Growing up on the farm helped to give me a good work ethic. Each child in the family had certain responsibilities.*

*There were small jobs for small children. As a young child, I watched my dad dry dishes as my mom washed. My father helped my mother and my mother helped my father. As we grew older, those dishes became the responsibility of my sister and me. I had wonderful parents who worked hard and we all worked together.*

Dr. Dave Drake spent many summers working on a farm where he too developed this strong work ethic as well as a sense of self-sufficiency, which was another vital preparation for the mission field. Of necessity, he learned how to fix things and to improvise when what was needed was not available.

Dave Voetmann also learned self-sufficiency on the farm, including how to make the best use of resources and eliminate waste. Therefore, when he saw all the food that was being thrown away from the nursing school at Karanda, he bought some pigs, thinking that the discarded food could be fed to the pigs and then recycled back to the students in the way of pork. He also started planting beans in a further effort to help the nursing school become more self-sufficient.

Karen Longnecker described other valuable lessons she learned growing up on a farm:

*It helped me learn to face a variety of circumstances and develop a sense of independence. Having to depend on the Lord to bring the right weather for the crops to grow and thus provide our necessary income helped to prepare me for depending on the Lord for His provision as a missionary.*

God also used various types of youth clubs to build character and leadership skills into future missionaries. Martin Uppendahl reported, "I believe that the Lord used the Boy Scouts in a major way to help me develop leadership experience as well as outdoor camping and living skills."

Thelma Everswick described how being in the Girl Scouts taught her not only many practical skills but also gave her the opportunity to develop important people skills; such as getting along with others, respecting leaders, and following orders. She also learned how to set specific goals and work toward accomplishing them.

Sometimes God used difficult experiences to prepare individuals for specific issues they would face on the mission field. Twice Cherith Till went through the disappointment of failing to pass her final exams in nursing. Later, on the mission field she recognized God's hand even in this as she was uniquely prepared to identify with and encourage the nursing students at Karanda who failed their exams and had to re-take them.

As children of God, we have the joy of knowing that our lives are always in the hands of the Master Planner. If our eyes were opened to all that God does in our lives to prepare us for future events, we would stand in awe of His love and His sovereignty. The incidents recorded above would be seen as but the tip of the iceberg of His wondrous and mysterious workings in our lives.

# CHAPTER 4

# God Gave Grace to Adjust

*"In all these things we are more than conquerors
through Him who loved us!"*
(Romans 8:37)

As God's obedient servants arrived on the mission field, they came with a wide range of expectations that often didn't match reality. Betty Mason Wolfe believed that the whole of Africa was one vast jungle with lions and tigers roaming the streets. Dorothy Cook, on the other hand, was surprised to see that out in the "bush" people really did live in mud huts.

Rusty Sherwood naïvely offered to write a series of articles for his hometown newspaper in Beloit, Wisconsin, in exchange for a six-month subscription—to be shipped to him in Zimbabwe! He wrote:

*After a long trip down into the Zambezi Valley we spent our first months with Orv and Helen Dunkeld at the Msengedzi station in language study. In these early days the mail only came when you sent a bicycle rider up the escarpment to get it. This was only done every month or so. You can imagine my chagrin when the first load of post came back and 90% of the huge postbag was packed with DAILY newspapers from Beloit!!! Needless to say, I was not the rider's favorite missionary!*

Whatever the missionaries knew, or did not know, about the country to which they were called, they all faced a period of adjustment as they embarked upon their new lives in it. In addition to the many cultural differences they would face, Zimbabwe posed a much more difficult manner of life which was fraught with significant new challenges, especially in the undeveloped rural areas.

Almost without exception, however, these brave and committed fledglings viewed these as hurdles to be conquered in their goal of winning the hearts and souls of the Shona people for the Kingdom of God. Their faith in Him carried them forward. His grace was sufficient, and through Him these "ordinary people" became "more than conquerors."

# Nature of the Country

Located in southern Africa, the country of Zimbabwe itself confronted the missionaries with physical realities that were new and different. They would have to adjust to the many living creatures prevalent in the country and learn how to protect themselves from the dangers involved. Living in a sub-tropical climate with new kinds of seasonal changes was potentially challenging as well.

## Living Creatures

The very word "Africa" evokes images of exotic, but dangerous, wild animals. Lions, elephants, hippopotami, buffalo, rhinoceroses, zebras, wart hogs, hyenas, and baboons abound in many parts of Zimbabwe. For some, this promised the ultimate in game spotting and hunting adventures, while others found it extremely frightening.

Living in close proximity to Africa's wild life was an adjustment, especially for the early pioneer missionaries. Russ Jackson said he would never forget his first night on the Msengedzi mission station. He and Marg were shocked to hear the chilling laugh of the hyenas around the house in which they were sleeping. Sometimes it seemed as though they were right under their windows.

Lions and leopards and occasionally even elephants and hippos were known to visit the early mission stations as well. Cliff and Jeanette Ratzlaff recalled having leopards grunting outside their bedroom window at Chironga. They could also hear lions roaring at the nearby Ruia River. Other "visitors" included baboons, monkeys, mongeese, wart hogs, civet cats, and various kinds of antelope.

Probably evoking more fear, however, were the smaller creatures that could enter one's living space unnoticed, such as the many varieties of insects, spiders, scorpions, lizards, and snakes. Merle and Kay Bloom reported, "We sometimes would find snakes in our bedroom, centipedes in our beds, and scorpions in our shoes."

Some of these smaller creatures were feared for the pain, disease, or death they were capable of inflicting. Others were disdained for their unwelcome intrusions into the house or food supplies, while some were just a nuisance.

Gladys Cedarholm expressed her feelings as she was introduced to perhaps the most common and innocent of these intruders that are virtually inescapable in Zimbabwe:

*One thing that I detested was the geckos that would crawl up and down the walls in the cottage. They were harmless, but I still didn't appreciate them. I was glad for the mosquito nets we could sleep under at night. I made sure they were well tucked in because I really wasn't keen on having a gecko crawling in bed with me.*

Unfortunately, those mosquito nets did not always work in keeping such creatures on the outside. Phil and Barb Christiansen described one of their first experiences sleeping under one in language school at Msengedzi:

*We got the kids to bed and then went to bed ourselves, carefully tucking the mosquito net under the perimeter of the mattress. We were just settling down when we heard a scratching sound. The ever-present torch (flashlight) revealed a three-to-four-inch centipede crawling up the inside of the net! There was quite a commotion as we quickly attempted to get the netting untucked and ourselves out of there. (Have you ever tried to pull the net out from under the very spot on which you are kneeling?) We are happy to report that the centipede was eventually terminated without any harm done to the human occupants of the bed.*

Mosquito nets were a necessity in Zimbabwe, especially in the era of more primitive housing. Their purpose was primarily to protect against the malaria-carrying anopheles mosquitoes. This particular species makes no sound and is not even felt when it bites. It can only be identified by the way it stands on the skin.

Malaria was a real and constant threat for the missionaries in the Zambezi Valley. Precautionary measures were imperative, including taking anti-malarial prophylaxis on a regular basis. Even then, many missionaries contracted the disease.

The tsetse fly also posed a problem in some areas of Zimbabwe. This insect often carries the parasite which causes sleeping sickness, a potentially fatal disease. It was especially prevalent at TEAM's Rukomechi station. Bud Jackson wrote of his experience there:

> *I have vivid recollections of traveling to Rukomechi, which was situated right in the "fly belt." Tsetse flies were particularly bad on the last stretch of road going in to the house. The moment our truck would slow down to cross a stream or a particularly bad part of the road or stopped altogether, the tsetse flies would swarm into the cab. I can remember one occasion when Mom was trying to help us fight the flies off while Dad was outside working to get the truck unstuck.*
>
> *We quickly learned how difficult it was to kill these hardy relatives of the horse fly. You could try to crush them against your bare skin, but invariably they would fall to the floor and proceed to crawl up your leg again and bite you.*

Fortunately, no TEAM Zimbabwe missionary ever contracted sleeping sickness.

Parasites in the water were another problem to which the missionaries had to adjust. Schistosomiasis, or what is called "bilharzia" in Zimbabwe, was the most common threat and was virtually endemic in the area. These parasites burrow through the skin and can cause numerous intestinal and bladder problems as well as anemia, malnutrition, and lethargy. Prevention entails avoiding having any skin contact with standing water (some believed flowing water was safe) and boiling all water before drinking it. Missionaries taught their children not to play near any river or pond.

Bot flies are also a nuisance in Zimbabwe. The female bot fly catches a blood sucking insect, such as a mosquito, and lays its eggs on the insect's abdomen. The larvae then hatch from these eggs, and when the mosquito finds a human to feed on, the larvae burrow into the human's skin and form a small, boil-like lesion.

Apparently, the larvae can also be transferred from the mosquito's abdomen to other wet surfaces it should happen to light upon, such as laundry hung out to dry. If a person should wear an infested piece of clothing or lie on infested sheets, the larvae can then penetrate into the skin through this means as well.

The pustule formed by the larva grows as the larva grows. At some point the larva will begin to bite its way out of its confinement. This is the worst part according to Diane Powell, who had personal experience with five of these unwelcome creatures during language school. "Each unexpected bite of the larva," she said, "felt like a sudden stab of a needle!"

In order to avoid bot fly infestation, meticulous ironing of all laundry that hung outside was strongly recommended. Even this was not fool-proof, however, as a number of missionaries can attest.

Scorpions were also feared, mostly for the pain they afflicted. Lynn Hoyt, who accidentally stepped on one at Mavuradonha, said that the pain felt like "a knife going through my toe."

One's reaction to a scorpion bite seemingly depended on the type of scorpion involved as well as the person's degree of toleration to the venom. Russ Jackson was stung on the forehead when a scorpion fell from an overhanging tree limb, and his whole face swelled up with one eye going completely shut. Debbie McCloy's entire foot and leg swelled up after she stepped on one at Karanda.

When Merv Driedger was stung by a large scorpion that darted out from under a board he was moving, he recounted, "It hurt intensely, sending shooting pains through my arm that seemed to stab my very heart." In his case, he was rushed to Karanda Hospital where Dr. Roland Stephens gave him a shot of calcium gluconate to counteract the effects of the poisonous bite. This, Merv reported, caused the pain to subside, and he suffered no further consequences.

The duration of the pain also varied. Marlene Georgia was stung by a scorpion at Mavuradonha, and although the sting was very painful, her discomfort only lasted for an hour or so. Roy Carnall's arm was swollen and painful for three weeks after he unknowingly put his elbow down on top of one at Mavuradonha.

Bud Jackson described the adjustments many of the missionaries made to protect themselves against getting stung by these venomous insects:

*Scorpions were something else we grew to respect. We developed a habit of looking in our shoes before putting them on every day. We always had a flashlight handy, too, for when we had to walk to the outhouse at night, as much for the scorpions as for the snakes. We never put our fingers beneath a log or rock in order to lift it without first checking to see if there was a scorpion under it.*

Large, ugly tarantulas were also found in Zimbabwe and could be intimidating when unexpectedly encountered. Lynn Hoyt wrote of Don's mother's visit to the field in 1963:

*We heard her scream and, upon investigating, found that she had discovered a large, hairy, orange tarantula crawling up the side of a kitchen cabinet. Don was able to make short work of it with his pellet gun.*

A breed of hairy caterpillars in Zimbabwe can also cause misery for those who come in contact with them, as their tiny hairs detach and become embedded in the skin like tiny fishhooks. Mary Ann McCloy spent hours removing all the hairs from her daughter Debbie's hand when she touched one at Chironga.

Numerous types of ants are also problematic in Zimbabwe. Fire ants are known for their intense sting. Debbie McCloy had her encounter with these too. They got her as she was going up to the Dunkeld's house one day. As they started stinging her legs, she innocently sat down on the ground to brush them off and was attacked by even more of them!

White ants, or termites, are also very prevalent and destructive, feasting on more than just wood, as Donna Hendrickson soon discovered. She described her early experience with them after arriving in Zimbabwe:

> *While in language school we lived at the Plot in Hatfield in a condemned, two-room building, which had been used for storage. Our bedroom walls were lined with boxes containing our earthly goods, which had to be moved every week to clear away the accumulated white ants [termites].*
>
> *One week I came down with a dreadful case of malaria, which hit me like a triple flu, and the boxes did not get moved. When I finally got my strength back and could move the boxes, I found that many of the clothes and pieces of material inside had huge holes in them, especially at the folds. This was our introduction to living with white ants.*

Dick and Mary Ann McCloy reported that their biggest adjustment was learning to tolerate the inch-long flying ants which came at the onset of every rainy season. These were totally harmless, seasonal insects that were eagerly caught and devoured as delicacies by the local people. To the missionaries they were more often a major nuisance, as Mary Ann described:

> *During language school at Chironga we left a kerosene lantern on in the bathroom for getting up with the kids in the night. This probably attracted the flying ants. No matter how hard we tried to block every space under the windows and doors, in the morning there would be* wings *all over the floor. "Where were the* bodies?*" we wondered. "Where did they go?"*
>
> *By the time flying ant season came the next year, we were living at Rusambo, and God had helped us adjust to these intruders to the extent that we actually watched them with interest. By the time we moved to Chinhoyi ten years later, we even looked forward to them.*
>
> *Only once after that first year did the nuisance level of these creatures surpass our tolerance level. That was the year we were in Mabelreign and singing in a Christmas Cantata at Calvary Baptist Church. As we sang, the ants*

*starting flying into the church. Someone brilliantly decided to turn off the lights over the audience. You guessed it; they all came up to the platform with us!!! We had ants in our hair, ants in our ears, and even ants in our mouths!!! This obviously affected our ability to sing, but we were able to complete the concert—to the glory of God!*

Weevils also abounded in the hot climate of Zimbabwe and often infested food supplies. This too was an adjustment for many of the female missionaries. Helen Dunkeld laughingly recalled the first time she found a weevil in the flour and almost threw the whole supply out. While Tupperware eventually became highly valued for its ability to keep out the weevils, most missionaries adjusted to the rather ubiquitous presence of these harmless invaders of many of their food staples.

The greatest fears in regard to Zimbabwe's living creatures were probably reserved for its snakes, many of which were extremely poisonous. Gladys Cedarholm described this well as she and her family adjusted to life at Msengedzi in 1954, after six months of language school:

*Settling into our grass roofed, mud brick house with lizards scooting up and down the walls playing hide-and-seek gave me the shivers. Then a big clump of white ants fell all at once from the grass roof and landed right in the middle of our bed. There were just hordes of them. That was unpleasant, to say the least, but when a snake crawled out of its nesting place in the grass roof and dangled above the crib where our nine-month-old daughter, Lois, was tucked in for her afternoon nap, I was horrified! Thankfully, it was startled when I entered the room and withdrew into the roof again. How we thank God for His care in the midst of that rather trying adjustment period when we were so new on the Msengedzi station!*

Merle and Kay Bloom also lived at Msengedzi about that time. They reported:

*We shall never forget the time a huge cobra crawled into the house of the Dees who lived next door to us. We heard some screaming and shots. Merle hurriedly ran to see what was happening. As he approached, they cried, "Cobra!" He opened their door and looked around the corner. Sure enough, there it was with its head reared up and ready to spit its venom. Needless to say, Merle made a hasty retreat. After much confusion George Dee was finally successful in shooting it.*

Stew and Marlene Georgia found a green mamba curled up on their washing machine engine outside. Shirley Bradford opened a dresser drawer, and a cobra raised its head and spat at her. Fortunately, she was wearing glasses, which protected her eyes from damage.

Goldye Gustafson, who came to the field on a short-term assignment in 1971, was greatly in need of God's grace to help her conquer her horrible fear of snakes. She wrote:

*I was very excited when I received the letter from Dr. Mortenson offering me the opportunity to go to Zimbabwe for a year as the secretary in the field office, taking Shirley Bradford's place while she was on furlough. She would then replace me as Dr. Mortenson's secretary. My only concern was my ability to cope with the snakes I knew were in that country. I quickly rationalized, however, that to my knowledge no TEAM missionary had ever died due to snakebite in the history of the mission.*

*Nevertheless, when I arrived in Zimbabwe, I found that I still had to battle my fear of snakes, and it seemed that I was hearing snake stories all the time. My fear grew until one night I prepared for bed by first moving my hands all over the top of the covers to see if I could feel anything beneath them. Then I threw the bed linens back as far as possible to look under them, and when I got into bed, I stayed curled in a ball the whole night. I knew at that point that I could not continue in Zimbabwe if my intense fear of snakes persisted.*

*The following morning I picked up* Our Daily Bread *and*

*opened to the Scripture for the day. It was Psalm 91. As I began to read, the tears rolled down my face: "He that dwelleth in the secret place of the Most High shall abide under the shadow of the Almighty. I will say of the Lord, 'He is my refuge and my fortress: my God; in Him will I trust'" (vss. 1-2; KJV).*

*As I continued reading through the psalm, I could only say, "Thank you, Lord." "For He shall give his angels charge over thee, to keep thee in all thy ways. . . . . Thou shalt tread upon the lion and adder: the young lion and the dragon (snake) shalt thou trample under feet" (vss. 11, 13; KJV).*

*A few days later I returned to my duplex and saw a snake in the corner of the verandah. I was able to open the door and go in without panic. I then called Wilf Strom, who came and killed it.*

*God met me in a powerful way through his Word that morning, or I would not have had almost twenty happy years as Mrs. Cecyl Till!*

While in Zimbabwe, Goldye met and married Cecyl Till, a widower who had generously volunteered his numerous skills in service to the TEAM missionaries for many years.

## Climate

The climate of Zimbabwe was another factor in the adjustment process of the missionaries. Wilf Strom said his greatest adjustment was the lack of seasonal changes that he had known in Canada. There was no winter snow nor spring thaw nor autumn colors. Christmas coming in the middle of summer was also an adjustment to many.

While Zimbabwe did have a summer and winter of sorts, its climate was more often differentiated as the rainy season and the dry season. The hottest time of the year was right before the rainy season began. In fact, October is referred to as "suicide month" because of the extreme heat and humidity that builds up before the rains begin. Because of its lower elevation, the Zambezi Valley was at least ten degrees hotter than the capital city, Harare.

Betty Wolfe wrote:

*During our second term we spent four years at Hunyani in the Zambezi Valley. As we drove down into it, we would get about two-thirds of the way down the escarpment and then a wave of heat would hit us like an oven door being opened in our faces. The only trouble was that we couldn't shut the oven door.*

*Our house had an asbestos roof with no ceiling over the kitchen and dining/living room, which made it rather like an oven. One year we hung a thermometer outside in the shade, and it registered 110 degrees (Fahrenheit) every day for a month. In the middle of the night it cooled down to 96. We left water in the bathtub, and often in the middle of the night we would go and sit in the water for awhile to cool down enough to sleep for a couple hours.*

*I often had to write letters with a towel under my arm to soak up the perspiration. We had a very large dispensary at the time, which meant working hard all morning. After lunch we usually took a short rest in the heat of the day. By the time I got around to studying or writing letters, it was so warm that I really did "sweat it out." Sometimes I had to do these things in the evening, which was even worse with a hot kerosene lamp on the desk.*

Ray and Myrtle Finsaas also found studying very difficult in the heat. They learned to get up at 4:00 in the morning to study while it was cooler before the sun came up.

The heat posed an even more uncomfortable situation for Dorothy Strom. She and Wilf arrived at Hunyani for language study in September 1953, just as the sun was becoming its hottest. She attributes the almost constant headaches she had in the valley to not being able to perspire in the extreme heat. She said, "I often felt like my head was going to explode. It was a real challenge to clear my head for language study!"

Even in elevated areas, however, the heat could be oppressive, and the Zimbabwean custom of an afternoon siesta was readily embraced by many. Dr. Rick Froese described his first encounter with the debilitating effects of the mid-day sun:

*While in language studies I also helped with the finishing touches of the construction of the Karanda Hospital. The first few days I wondered why things moved so slowly and why everyone took a rest after lunch. Soon, as the heat and direct sun overhead took its effect, I too was looking for shade at noonday. I even brought a folding camp bed and put it on the hospital veranda so I could take a few "zzzs" at noon!*

Other missionaries told of hanging wet Turkish towels over the windows during the hottest hours of the day in an attempt to cool any breeze coming in as they took their afternoon "siestas." At night many would lay wet towels over their bodies in order to sleep. Judy Everswick reported that her family would sometimes lie on their cement floors in the hot weather. Russ and Marg Jackson sometimes lay on a reed mat on their floor.

# Way of Life

Besides adjusting to the many features inherent to the country itself, the missionaries were also confronted with a drastically different way of life. The changes were not so pronounced in the cities, but conditions were rather primitive in the rural areas, especially for the early pioneers.

## Living Conditions

Almost all of the early missionaries were assigned to a rural station for language study and cultural orientation, even if they were later placed in a more urban ministry. This is where culture shock usually hit them the hardest.

Phyllis Rilling described the magnitude of the adjustment she felt when she and Emil arrived at Mavuradonha in 1953:

*I think my first big hurdle was going out to Mavuradonha with a baby (William) under six months old and finding that our kitchen was a round, pole and mud hut separate from the main house. Our kerosene refrigerator and all but a few cooking utensils were in the house. We also ate in the* house, so it seemed like I was doing a lot of running between the house and this outside kitchen. I also had to learn to control a wood stove, which was new for me. All the dirt and dust in that outdoor kitchen was trying at times as well.

I remember the first time I baked bread in that kitchen. I had never baked bread before, and learning to do so in a wood stove was quite challenging. I was so proud of my very first loaves as I took them out of the oven and then left them in the "kitchen" to cool. You can imagine how I felt when I returned and found that a village dog had made a lunch of one of the loaves! Where he had come from, I don't know, as we had not seen any dogs around before.

Another problem was that we were told to iron everything to kill the eggs of the bot fly! I had never heard of such a preposterous thing—to iron sheets and all! Not only that, but the ironing had to be done with a flat iron kept hot on the wood stove in the outside kitchen. Otherwise we ran a huge chance of getting the bot fly larvae under our skin.

Oh, yes, and we had to boil all of our drinking water on the outside wood stove for ten minutes. We did this tea kettle by tea kettle, and I thought I would surely spend all my time doing nothing but keep us in boiled water. I was very grateful when Emil came up with a solution to that problem and enabled us to boil it by the drum.

Emil made all of our furniture the first week, using our shipping crates as well as poles from the woods. He also cared for the two or more types of wick lanterns that we used for light as well as the kerosene refrigerator.

We did have a village girl, not so very big, to help us with some of the work. She would sweep the floors and do our laundry, using a washboard and galvanized tubs for wash and rinse water. However, communicating with her to tell her what to do and how to do it was very difficult at first when we knew so little of the language.

A week after we arrived, we began language school along with Chuck and Scottie Pruitt. To top it all off, quite *unexpectedly I found I was pregnant again, and the nausea and vomiting from that set in too. We also had mostly tinned or dried foods to eat, and I had such an extraordinary longing for fresh food. The rains had set in, however, and no one could travel to town for another three months.*

*I quickly realized that I had to cut back on all that was required of me at that time, or I would not be able to cope. Therefore, I stopped ironing the sheets, pillowcases, and nappies (diapers). It wasn't that I wanted those larvae biting us under our skin, but there was just no other way I could survive!*

*At the end of that season little William had gotten one larva, which was enough, but the rest of us had none. At the same time the father of another family which faithfully ironed everything with the help of a well-trained, adult male helper had eight larvae. With those results, I went merrily through the rest of our missionary years giving no heed to the supposed need to iron "everything." At some point Emil also had a single larva. Otherwise, we had none.*

*In all these totally new things, the Lord helped us. He gave us good common sense, a trust in Him, and Emil's background. None of these things were new to him, as he had grown up on the farm in Canada during the depression when they had very little and before any of the farms had electricity. I was extremely grateful that I had him to support and teach me as I adjusted.*

Ray and Myrtle Finsaas also wrote of their adjustments upon arrival at Msengedzi for language study in 1957:

*We found it hard to adjust to the station at first. The heat, new language, and primitive conditions were challenging. Our houses had grass roofs and cement floors. We had to haul river water, put it in a drum, and boil it for twenty minutes for drinking. We bathed in small, galvanized tubs. The adults wore sun helmets, and the children wore felt hats. We used kerosene lamps, irons, and refrigerators, which were difficult to use and keep clean.*

Marian Wilterdink had her first experience of living in primitive housing when she moved to Kapfundi with the Uppendahls in 1953 to open the station there. She wrote:

> *I did have to live in a mud hut there, but it was nicer than I had expected. It had a mud floor that was hard to sweep, so I sprayed it with water before I swept it. There were big holes in the walls for windows but no glass in them, so I got pieces of screen to tack over them.*
>
> *The hut had log crossbeams to support the roof. Every night the rats would run back and forth on those logs. Bats would also take over the kitchen at night, leaving their droppings on the stove.*
>
> *Wood bores were also a problem. These black, hard-shelled bugs would drill holes into the poles, which was especially bothersome over my bed. I didn't dare open my eyes lest dust fall in them. The roof leaked right over my bed too, so I took old cardboard cartons and made a ceiling across the whole top of the house, which helped a lot.*

When Don and Lynn Hoyt moved to Mavuradonha after their first three-year assignment with the literature ministry in Harare, they were faced with a major adjustment. Living in Harare had not been much different than living in the States. Moving to Mavuradonha, however, meant replacing all of their electric appliances with those using kerosene, propane, and wood. They were not nearly as easy to maintain as their electric counterparts. The fridge and freezer needed constant attention as soot would build up on the wick and exhaust pipe. Learning to maintain this "temperamental" equipment was just one of the new experiences that lay ahead for the Hoyts at Mavuradonha.

Don wrote:

> *The transition was challenging—nights under mosquito netting; limited electric power; kerosene lamps; hot water*

*supplied from drums heated by wood; a running battle with termites and spiders, occasional snakes, lizards, and scorpions in the house; constant attention to the water pump; the night symphony of hyenas, leopards chasing baboons, and village dogs; and the morning overture of the guinea fowl.*

*But it was the greatest place in the world to live. We loved it, and so did our children. They are richer for the rural experiences.*

Even as conditions improved from the early pioneer years, the adjustments to rural living, usually encountered during language school, proved to be a major culture shock to new missionaries. Lynne Hawkins, who arrived in 1967, reported:

*I really wasn't prepared for how different the living situation was going to be. In language school I lived in a house with a grass roof, and I never knew what was going to fall from it next. It took me awhile to adjust.*

## Cooking

Learning to cook in the Zambezi Valley was another big adjustment for many of the women. Not only were supplies limited, but many had never cooked on a wood stove before. Helen Dunkeld had her first experience in this while she was still in South Africa. She expressed her frustrations as follows:

*Because the pots became rounded on the bottom from continued use, you had to take the cast iron plates off the stovetop to cook. Then the flames would come up around your hands. I found it very difficult.*

She also learned how to make yeast and bake bread.

When she and Orv moved to Mavuradonha in Zimbabwe, she again had to learn new cooking skills. She explained:

*I wasn't able to work the wood stove, although I had been used to a wood stove in Zululand. This one was different, and food after food failed in the oven until I finally learned how to work it. I also had to learn to cook with new ingredients in Zimbabwe. I realized afterwards, however, that through all of this God was preparing me to be better able to help the other new missionaries when they arrived.*

## Water

Water was not a commodity to take for granted on the early mission stations. Usually considerable effort went into obtaining it and making it suitable for household use. This, too, was a significant adjustment for many missionaries.

In the beginning water had to be hauled from the river and boiled to make it safe for drinking. This was a tremendous inconvenience. Even as various means of pumping water from the rivers to the missionary homes were developed, the water arrived muddy at times.

Once metal roofs replaced thatched ones, rainwater was often collected off the roofs into large cisterns for drinking and washing. Of course, this supply depended upon the adequacy of the rainfall in a given season.

On some stations, such as Rusambo and Karanda, the adequacy of the water supply was often insufficient for the need, requiring water to be rationed, especially during the dry season. The missionaries had to adjust to using water for two or three purposes before discarding it. Sometimes even bath water was shared!

## Domestic Help

The Zimbabwe missionaries typically hired local nationals to assist them with house, yard, and garden work as well as childcare. This was another area of adjustment for many of the women.

Donna Kahlstorf recalled her struggle with this at Chironga. After being raised to be so self-sufficient, she had a difficult time getting used to having someone else in her kitchen cooking her food, etc. Eventually she came to appreciate it, however. With her full schedule at the Teacher Training Institute, she found it quite nice to come home and find the floors polished, the dishes washed, and her food on the table. She also came to recognize that taking care of one's house was much harder in the bush with all the dust that accumulated from the grass roof and dusty surroundings.

Keeping the wood-burning stove going also took significant time and energy, which she was glad to be able to direct towards ministry instead.

## Isolation

The isolation felt on the various mission stations was another adjustment for many. Wilf Strom said, "I loved living in the bush, but at times I felt isolated from the outside world with no radio, no newspapers, and mail only a couple of times a month." His wife, Dorothy, also struggled with this initially, feeling that the isolation from the outside world, compounded by the language barrier, made for loneliness.

When the early missionaries began branching out to open more stations, they usually sent a couple by themselves to begin the ministry in these areas, compounding the sense of isolation. Russ Jackson reported that when they went to Chirundu, the Everswicks to Rukomechi, and the Blairs to Hunyani, they rarely saw each other for months at a time, perhaps only once or twice a year. In those early days the annual missionary conference held at one of the stations was an especially wonderful time for the scattered missionaries to join together for fellowship and planning.

Every year the rainy season would essentially lock the early missionaries into the Zambezi Valley, increasing their sense of isolation. Travel out of the valley by road was generally impossible during these months.

Roy Eichner described how greatly this increased the magnitude of his family's adjustment to rural living:

> *We arrived in Zimbabwe before the first rains in December of 1957, looking forward to language study and our first assignments. How well I remember driving through the Zambezi Valley on the way to the Msengedzi station. It seemed as if we were driving to the end of the world. Miles and miles of unpaved dirt roads spread out before us as we passed scattered villages.*
>
> *Little did we realize when we went into the Zambezi Valley that we would not be coming back to a town until language school was over five months later. Here we were,*

*straight from the suburbs of Philadelphia. We were used to speaking with dozens upon dozens of people in the course of a week at school, work, and church. Now, suddenly, we could converse with only a handful of missionaries and national teachers. No one else could speak English. We would not be able to speak with other people until we had learned their language. The situation seemed impossible, but God's grace was sufficient!*

Later, during the war years of the seventies, travel by road became very dangerous with the possibility of land mines planted at any point. Even walking off the stations in the rural areas had to be curtailed, once again heightening the sense of isolation.

This was the situation when Joe and Olga Reimer arrived at Karanda in 1976. Olga wrote:

*My adjustments were difficult mainly because of the state of war in which we were living. We couldn't drive in and out of the station. We could only travel via the MAF the plane, and we weren't used to flying, especially in such a small plane. Living confined in the security fence that was built around Karanda was also an adjustment.*

Phil Christiansen found the repetitive nature of his lab work day after day and the limited access to other professionals an adjustment. He explained:

*I immensely enjoyed those rare days when we would have a visitor come who was even remotely interested in lab work. I remember when a urologist came out. It was just fantastic to have this guy bring a breath of fresh air into the hospital because he was an outsider.*

## Travel

Traveling within Zimbabwe was another tremendously different experience from what the missionaries were used to in North America. Their first challenge was learning to drive on the left side of the road, which also meant training themselves to look for traffic coming in the opposite direction from which they were accustomed.

While streets were generally paved in the towns and cities, this was not always true in the rural areas. In some places roads consisted of two tarmac (asphalt) strips, which were just wide enough to accommodate the tires of a car. When passing, each car moved over to the left strip so that the front and back right wheels were on the strip and the left wheels were over to the side on the dirt. It was an improvement over dirt roads in that during the rainy season you weren't as likely to get stuck in the mud.

Until more recently the most of the rural roads were dirt. These could be a real challenge. Potential problems included rocks, ruts, corrugations, sand gullies, and unexpected livestock. The greatest difficulty, however, was the lack of bridges over the many rivers and streams they would cross. These crossings were known as "spruits." In the 35 miles between the small town of Mt. Darwin and the Karanda station the missionaries had to navigate 17 spruits.

During the rainy season one would not know how deep the water would be in these spruits until arriving at them. If it was relatively low, people could drive through with little problem. If the water level was too high, however, they would have to wait until it receded. Usually this occurred in a matter of hours, but for some spruits it could stretch into days!

When it was finally low enough to cross, vehicles could still get stuck in the mud and require quite an ordeal of digging, pushing, and pulling to get unstuck. Sometimes help could be recruited from local villagers. Once in awhile a truck or large tractor would happen along and pull disabled vehicles out. What a blessing that was!

Often the missionaries were totally on their own to get out of their predicament. Orv Dunkeld described laying down tree branches in front of the wheels to provide traction or putting chains on the vehicle's tires. Dave Drake recalled going backwards through spruits at times to take advantage of the vehicle's rear-wheel drive.

For the early pioneers, the roads were even less developed. Often they had to wind their way through what could hardly be described as more than a bush trail or blaze a new road altogether. Rudy and Mary Danielson described their trip down into the Zambezi Valley from Mavuradonha in a letter dated May 26, 1942:

*About three miles from the Mavuradonha Mission Station
we turned off the main road onto a [bush] trail that has been
cleared wide enough for the car to pass. The [District]
Commissioner uses this road on his patrols, so [he] sent
word out for the [local people] to hoe the road and fix the
dry stream beds for him to cross . . . In some parts we drove
for miles through the forest with the road winding in and out
among the trees like in a park.*

In another letter dated April 1, 1943, they described the considerable work that had to be done after the rainy season was over in
order to get out of the valley:

*Now the rainy season has come to an unceremonious end,
but there will be several weeks yet before we will be able to
get the car across the Msengedzi River. [We also have to] fix
the endless number of smaller river beds as well as two
other larger rivers, one a dry sand bed and the other a wide
expanse of standing water—we hope not too deep to drive
through. There are swamps, too, that have been standing
under water for months that must dry out enough to drive
over. These are grown over thick with grass twelve to fifteen
feet high. . . .*

Helen Dunkeld described the experience she and Orv had when
they returned to the Valley after spending the rainy season at
Mavuradonha in 1944:

*Finally, around April 5th we felt the road was dry
enough that we could head home. That was a happy day for
us. We found the road very badly grown over during this
rainy time. The people were starting to clear it, but we just
drove through where we could. We had to sleep about fifty
miles from Mavuradonha when we got stuck in the river and
couldn't get through.*
*Then we got stuck again about fifteen miles further on
and had to unload. That was one of the difficult things. When
we got stuck, we had to take everything off the truck and get*

*some men from the village nearby to help push and pull and get the car across. Then we had to carry the things across and load up again. It was quite time and energy consuming.*

*Finally, we got down to the Msengedzi River and, of course, it was running. We couldn't drive across, but the local men were there to help carry the load across. I started to wade the river. It was only about knee deep and seemed very nice, but suddenly it dropped off into the current. It was still only about waist deep, but I was surprised at how swift it was. It just about swept me off my feet. One of the men grabbed my hand and pulled me through that swift part.*

Glenn and Dorothy Hotchkiss learned that trucks could some-times be unloaded with great ease in the midst of these spruits. As new missionaries on the field, they had just purchased the furniture, groceries, and other supplies they were going to need for their next few months at Msengedzi. They loaded these onto their small pick-up truck, along with the school, medical, and personal supplies requested by other missionaries on the station.

Off they went in caravan with the Dunkelds, the Smiths, and the Finsaases. All went well until they got to the last, most difficult stretch of road, which was rough and narrow with many curves and hills. As the truck went down into a particularly deep spruit, Glenn put the truck into low gear so he would be able to make it up the steep incline on the other side. Then, just as he was ready to begin the ascent, he accelerated quickly. Suddenly, there was a loud crash! Looking behind him, he discovered that the whole load had slid off the truck into the spruit. Fortunately, it was dry and he had lots of help already with him to reload the truck. Glenn learned very quickly the necessity of tying the load to the truck and not just to itself in the truck.

Sometimes the missionaries gambled with the rains and the state of the roads when special occasions demanded it. Gladys Cedarholm described an extremely challenging journey she and Clarence had in getting back to Msengedzi from Harare just as the rains were beginning:

*Following our language study at Hunyani we were asked to take over the ministry at Msengedzi while Orval and Helen Dunkeld went on furlough in 1954. In preparation for the rainy season we were instructed to get our supplies in by October or November. However, John Wolfe and Betty Mason were to be married in Harare in December, and they had asked our son David to serve as their ring-bearer, and we had agreed. Therefore, we decided to hold off until then to get our supplies rather than making two separate trips into town.*

*When we left the station in December, the rains had not started, and our hope was that not too much rain would come before our return. During our time in town, we encountered much rain, however. We even had to use umbrellas at the wedding, which was otherwise very beautiful.*

*After shopping for our long list of personal, station, and ministry needs, we were ready to return to Msengedzi with our heavily loaded truck. The Beaches and Pruitts, who had also come to town for the Wolfes' wedding, were going to travel with us.*

*When we checked with the Guruve police, they informed us that it had rained a few days in the Valley, but they felt we could make it through. We thought we were doing well until the last 35 miles into the station. It took us a whole week to go that distance!*

*The road was saturated with mud and enormous puddles everywhere. The spruits were all full. Getting the three trucks through was most difficult. Each day we would master a couple of miles, and then down they would go again in the mud. The men, along with local villagers, would work hard to get them out each time.*

*At night we pitched a tent and some slept in it with others in the cabs of the trucks. One night the children (David and Lois) and I were offered a hen hut to sleep in at a village while the others slept in the cabs of their trucks or under the stars. I cringed at having to share a hut with hens of all sizes and didn't get a wink of sleep. The children thought it was great fun and slept well.*

*One day a local man on a bicycle offered to alert the*

*Guruve police of our dilemma. We welcomed his suggestion and gave him some of the bacon that we had purchased to last us through the rainy season. Unfortunately, the police never came, but the bacon* chipo *("gift") must certainly have pleased the [would-be] messenger.*

*We finally arrived at Msengedzi on Christmas Day exhausted and dirty. . . John and Betty Wolfe returned the following day. You can imagine how we felt when they told us that they had encountered no road problems at all! The sun had come out in full force and dried up the roads, and the streams and rivers had receded. Nevertheless, we all felt that God's grace had cared for each of us involved in that difficult journey back to Msengedzi.*

Chuck and Verna Knapp experienced quite a range of travel adjustments as they arrived in 1953:

*Our first experience in Zimbabwe was our encounter with customs coming into the country from South Africa. We were traveling in convoy with the Everswicks, Blairs, and Mungers as well as Jean Schmidt and Marie Schober. Everyone had to unload their vehicles and wait for what seemed like hours. Then, to our amazement, the last truck got by without even having to take off the tarp.*

*After getting through customs, we had our first experience driving on those tarmac (asphalt) strips. A little farther north we crossed a river and then decided to stay in a "hotel" for the night. Verna and the other ladies were terrified when something fell from the grass roof that evening.*

*The next morning we learned that we were between rivers, and the water was too high over the crossing ahead of us, so we couldn't go anywhere. Norman Everswick (God bless him!) decided to use the time to start us in language study. When we finally started out again, we found that the bridge we had to cross was still covered with about a foot of water, but we were able to drive through this.*

*We were in for another adventure when we embarked upon our trip out to the Rusambo station. We thought we had a perfect day for travel. Little did we know that we would not even reach our destination that day! We encountered a washed-out gully and had to fill it in before we could cross it. After spending the night in a village hut, we finally reached our new home the next morning.*

*We soon learned that traveling in the rural areas was full of all sorts of surprises and challenges. Not only were there the many spruits to navigate, but you never knew when you might come around a bend and encounter a herd of animals in the road. At times we had to travel on unseen roads with the grass taller than the truck. Of course, the greatest misfortune was to have a mechanical breakdown, such as a broken spring or a bent tie rod, with the nearest repair garage 150 miles away!*

In 1956, Carl Hendrickson was asked to move Eunice Ott from Mavuradonha, where she had been teaching, to her new assignment at the Teacher Training Institute at Chironga. The rainy season had not yet ended, but they made it safely to Chironga and unloaded Eunice's household furniture and belongings.

After having tea with the missionaries there, Carl began his return trip to Mavuradonha. As he drove towards Mt. Darwin, a major storm struck. He had two river-bottom "bridges" to cross in order to get home, but they were already overflowing.

Being blocked in that direction, he thought maybe he could detour to Harare instead. Again, he was blocked by an overflowing river. Next, he tried making his way to the Rusambo station but was deterred by another high river. He ended up being stranded for an entire week in Mt. Darwin, a small town with only a few homes, a post office, a gas station, and a couple of small stores. By God's grace the postmaster, who was a friend of the missionaries, warmly welcomed Carl into his home.

With no radio communication yet available on the mission stations, Carl's wife, Donna, and their children waited at Mavuradonha, hoping each day to hear his truck driving onto the station or some word of his whereabouts. Finally, on Donna's birthday Carl was able to get through. What a great birthday celebration they had, thanking God for taking care of Carl and using their postmaster friend to meet his needs!

The Sherwoods also had difficulty moving to Chironga from Rusambo during the rainy season. Rusty wrote:

> *I was driving my one-ton truck over to Rusambo to bring back another load of furniture, etc. On the way I encountered a couple of long puddle areas that looked very negotiable, so I plowed into the first one and promptly sank down to the axles.*
>
> *Suddenly I was confronted with the very unpopular chore of getting "unstuck" in the rainy season. I dug into the mud and threw rocks and branches under the wheels. Finally, I extricated myself and went merrily on my way to Rusambo where I picked up my next load of furnishings.*
>
> *As I headed back toward Chironga, I approached that nasty wet area saying to myself, "Self, be careful now, and don't go through that nasty wet area." Then I proudly drove around it and continued on my way, not realizing that I had miscounted, and the nasty wet area I had navigated around was not the one I had bogged down in before. What did I do but plunge right back into the same one!*
>
> *I was so mad at myself that I stepped out of the truck,* slammed *the door, untied a bike from off the load, got on it, and headed to Chironga without even looking back. When I arrived and told my story, Reg Austin took pity on me and came back out to help me get unstuck again.*

This was not the last time that Rusty Sherwood would find himself exasperated traveling this same stretch of road. He told the following story as well:

> *We had just arrived back from furlough with our new Ford truck which had five of those new-type gadgets called "TUBELESS TIRES." I didn't trust them, so I installed tubes in them, which were woefully under-inflated. The under-inflation made the tubes pinch and wear out—like fast!!*
>
> *Anyway, the young males of the species "Everswick" and yours truly were traveling from Rusambo to Chironga*

*for some reason. We had no more left Rusambo when one of the Everswick boys banged on the roof of our cab shouting, "Uncle, you've got a flat tire!"*

*No problem. Just hop out and put on the spare. Job done. Off we go.*

*A few miles on—BANG, BANG, BANG! "Uncle, you've got another flat!"*

*Jump down. This time repair flat (I'm out of spares), and we are on our way again.*

*A little more down the road—BANG, BANG, BANG!*

*"Yeah, I know. Another flat!!" Out. Fix. On our way.*

*BANG! Out. Fix. On our way.*

*BANG, BANG, BANG!*

*"O.K. So stop with the banging already! I know! I know!"*

*"But, Uncle, this time two are flat!!"*

*That's it! Sanctification is now gone. I slam the truck door, take off all the tires, and stack them in a pile in front of the truck and send word on to Chironga for help.*

*So we wait, and finally one of the missionary cars pulls up and stops—but no one gets out! We go over to the car, and the guys are doubled up with laughter at my plight.*

## Lack of Resources

Another shock for some of the missionaries was the greatly reduced resources available for the jobs they had come to do. Rather than being deterred by this, however, they usually just put on their "thinking caps" to figure out how they could improvise and meet the various challenges upon them. God again was faithful to give them the grace and resourcefulness they needed in making these adjustments.

Thelma Everswick described her initial reaction to the clinic at Msengedzi where she was to begin her experience of nursing in this rural setting after just ten weeks of language study in 1946:

*Going from nursing in New Jersey where doctors were available to write orders for medications and treatments, and supplies were plentiful, clean, and sterile to a clinic in the Zambezi Valley was a major adjustment for me. The clinic building was a pole and thatched hut with a mud floor and a space for a small window. It had no electricity, no running water, no phone, very limited medicines and supplies, and a box for the patient to sit on while being treated, to say nothing about the heat and flies that had to be coped with as well.*

*Somehow God gave grace to make the necessary adjustments. With no doctor or phone available, I was frequently on a "hot line" to the Lord when I needed help in knowing how best to treat and cope with unusual cases. The Lord helped, and many recovered physically. The Gospel was shared daily with all who sought medical help, and some found spiritual healing as well.*

Phil Christiansen was accustomed to state-of-the art laboratory equipment in the States. Arriving in 1959 as the medical technologist for the Karanda Hospital, was like moving back into the Dark Ages of laboratory medicine, he reported. He basically had to build the lab from scratch.

Joseph Horness, one of TEAM's board members, generously donated all of the laboratory furnishings, which was a tremendous blessing, but the lab still had very little in actual equipment for doing the work. Little by little Phil built it up. It wasn't much, but it turned out to be the third best lab in the entire country.

Even so, Diane Powell, his successor, went through a very similar type of culture shock when she arrived in 1971. She wrote:

*I remember walking into the laboratory for the first time and exclaiming to myself, "I'm supposed to do WHAT in here?" In spite of the impressive looking professional countertops my quick survey of the room revealed only the most rudimentary of laboratory equipment: a microscope, a centrifuge, a primitive looking spectrophotometer able to read one test tube at a time, and a huge, outdated Van Slyke $CO_2$ apparatus. A fairly decent flame photometer was one encouragement.*

*The incubator used for bacteriologic cultures as well as*

*cross-matching blood had been ingeniously constructed by Phil Christiansen. It was a homemade, double box made of plywood sitting over a small Bunsen burner. "How could it possibly maintain a consistent temperature?" I thought. But it did! A home-style pressure cooker usually used for canning served as the only sterilizer.*

*There was basically nothing available for doing any kind of quality control, an absolute "must" in the States. Even the simple things like notepads or tissues to remove excess blood or reagents from pipettes were not to be found. Needles and syringes were recycled over and over again. Forget about sanitary paper towels! One large green terry cloth towel hung by the sink to be used by all. I couldn't help wondering how long it went between washings.*

*A whole new ward had been added to the hospital to house tuberculosis patients. This meant I would have to handle sputum specimens from these patients, but there was no protective exhaust fan under which to work with this virulent matter. I would just have to trust God for protection from disease.*

*He was faithful not only in protecting my health but also in helping me adjust to the reality of my resources. I soon learned that I had a laboratory to be envied in the whole northeastern corner of the country. I never contracted TB or any other serious illness. I only ended up with an Ascaris worm in my gall bladder after I had returned to the States. "Where did that come from?" I wondered. Then I remembered the old green towel!*

Bob Medaris was equally challenged when he arrived at Karanda to build a new wing for the hospital in 1967. He wrote:

*When we got out to the hospital station, I looked over the plans for the new addition and asked Dr. Stephens, "Where do I buy the bricks?" He said, "You make your own!" After letting that soak in a bit, with a glint in his eyes, he informed me that all I had to do was to let it be known to the local builders that I needed some bricks, and the "grapevine" would go to work.*

*For a little while I wondered, "What am I doing out here?" I had been a partner in Shields Construction in Phoenix, Arizona, that made custom-built homes. There I would just call different companies and place an order, and the needed supplies would be delivered to me. I was somewhat skeptical of Dr. Stephen's instructions at first, but I put the word out, and before I knew it, several men came wanting to make bricks for me. We needed a lot of bricks, as they were to be used for partition walls instead of two-by-fours. The outside walls were cement blocks, which we also had to make.*

# Cultural Adjustments

In addition to coping with the physical realities of life in Zimbabwe, the missionaries also had to adjust to two very different cultures. While expecting this in regard to the Shona people, many were caught by surprise at the adjustments needing to be made to the European population in Zimbabwe as well.

### European Culture

Carol Olsen and Carl and Donna Hendrickson were introduced to some of the British customs on the ship en route to Zimbabwe. At mealtimes the officers attempted to teach them how to eat European style with a knife in the right hand and a fork with tines down in the left hand. Food that needed cutting was cut with both instruments and then immediately eaten with the fork in the left hand—in its tines down position. Softer food was often pushed with the knife onto the back of the fork and eaten in the same manner. Once missionaries got the knack of this eating style, many decided it was much more practical and readily adapted to it.

Becoming familiar with the various British tea customs was another area of adjustment for most missionaries. Betty Mason described the unexpected introduction to these that she, along with Marian Wilterdink and Effie Byrd, experienced at the hotel in which they stayed when they arrived in Cape Town, South Africa:

*The hotel staff must have had a few good laughs at our igno-*

*rance. . . . They asked if we wanted tea or coffee in the
morning, and we told them coffee, not realizing that their
custom was to serve tea or coffee in the room before breakfast. When they came knocking on the door at six in the
morning, we got quite a scare and told them to go away.*

Noël Liddle was rather astonished by what he called the
"almost sacred institution of 'Tea Time'" that he experienced in
Zimbabwe. He wrote:

*All of Africa stops daily at 10:00 a.m. for "Tea." . . . In the
bush, on the farms, and in government offices in the city no
one interferes with "Tea." Even the Civil Service clerks in
many instances have their "Tea" served to them at their
desks![1]*

Missionaries also had to adjust to the British vocabulary, and in
the early days, the British monetary system as well. Rusty
Sherwood described his first cultural challenge upon arriving in
Cape Town:

*I was asked by the travel agent there to give him a "tingle"
about "tenish" on the phone. I was to use a "ticky" in a
phone booth that looked more like a large fireplug with
windows.*

Chuck and Verna Knapp encountered this new British vocabulary when they first went shopping in Harare in 1953. They wrote:

*We had to learn new words for familiar things, such as
"cotton wool" for "cotton balls" and new pronunciations
for words like "tomato." We also had to get used to using
pounds, shillings, and pence instead of dollars and cents.*

Sometimes English words were used for something totally
different in the British culture. Lynn Hoyt shocked a saleslady at OK
Bazaar when she asked for draperies to hang in the windows of her
house only to learn that "draperies" refer to women's underwear.

Even adjusting to the British and Afrikaans accents was difficult at first for some. Diane Powell panicked when she arrived in the Johannesburg airport and could not understand the Afrikaans announcer, who was speaking English. She immediately requested that someone else inform her when her flight was called.

## The Shona Language

The Shona people living in the northeastern part of the country were the original focus of ministry for the early missionaries. Therefore, learning to understand their language and culture was most important. This was an adjustment of varying difficulty to the new missionaries as they arrived on the field.

The Danielsons and Dunkelds, as the initial pioneers, began to study Shona at Mavuradonha. At that time the station was operated by the Zambezi Mission, and Peter and Nancy Lind, who were stationed there, tried to help them. Helen Dunkeld reported:

> *Peter was very good at the language, but he had just picked it up from the nationals. He did not understand the grammar nor have a knack for teaching. The best he could do was to tell us how to say specific things. We were very keen to learn the language and were studying each day. Apart from Peter's help we had only a very poor grammar book and translation of the New Testament.*
>
> *When we got down to Msengedzi, we became quite confused, as what we were hearing from the people there was different from what we were reading in our grammar book. We learned later that this was because we had moved amongst a group of four villages that spoke quite a different dialect from the rest of the country. As a result, the Shona we learned was a mixture of what we read in the grammar book and what we heard from the people.*
>
> *I was trying hard to get as much of the language written down as possible. Our messages at that time were carefully prepared and written down word-for-word. We would then read them. If we tried to branch off and say something we didn't have written down, we were in trouble.*

Russ and Marg Jackson, who arrived in 1948, were extremely grateful that they had attended Wycliffe's Summer Institute of Linguistics. "This course was invaluable in our ability to pronounce the strange sounds in the vernacular," Russ reported.

Soon after arriving in Zimbabwe, Russ also felt moved by God to begin memorizing many of the great Gospel texts from the Shona New Testament. "This proved to be an immense blessing for my ministry in the years ahead," he testified.

Merle and Kay Bloom described their experience in learning the Shona language in 1953:

> *At first the language seemed impossible. The structure of the words and sentences were so different from English that they didn't seem to make sense. Learning the long lists of vocabulary words was easy, but being able to use them in an intelligible manner took a long time.*
>
> *After awhile we began to make progress. We were able to make or translate simple sentences and to do some reading in the Shona Bible. Then, just as we thought we were getting somewhere, our confidence had a setback. We found that even through we could carefully think through what we wanted to say and speak simple sentences, our ears refused to comprehend what the nationals said.*
>
> *We struggled on for a few months, and then one day we realized that we were beginning to understand, and even think in, the Shona language. That was a very thrilling experience, and from then on we began to make greater progress.*

In 1953, after three months of language study at Msengedzi, George and Pat Dee were sent to the Hunyani station on their own. As brand new missionaries with no English speakers around, they wrote out their messages in English and used a Shona-English dictionary to translate them. Then they read them verbatim at the clinic or church.

The people told them later that they couldn't understand a word they said when they first started, but they were happy that they were trying to learn the language. George expressed his feelings about this difficult learning process:

*It was hard when you're a college grad and everyone's laughing at you for all the mistakes you make, but you have to struggle through that in order to master the language.*

George and Pat eventually became extremely fluent in Shona, which greatly impacted their reception in many places after that. Many of the people they ministered to on the farms in the Bindura area in the '80s and early '90s were from the Zambezi Valley. When they heard a white man preaching in their dialect, they came to listen. The Dees were able to plant 49 churches there in 11 years. None of this would have been possible without their 26 years of previous experience learning to understand and communicate with the Shona people.

Lorraine Waite told of the embarrassing time she had while learning Shona:

*While I was still in language study, I went to visit Baba John's wife, Rufina. I wanted to start practicing my Shona, but I couldn't do very well. Rufina finally got across to me that I should not come again without bringing someone who knew more Shona. I was hurt, but I waited until I could communicate better.*

Spending a designated number of months solely in language study and orientation before entering into ministry was the normal requirement for new missionaries. Sometimes, however, the demand for their services in other areas cut this short or greatly compromised their study time, leaving them struggling with communication throughout their service on the field.

Joe Reimer, for instance, arrived at Karanda in 1976 to take Emil Rilling's place in managing the station's work crew. Emil had left a month earlier, so work had already piled up waiting to be done immediately upon the Riemers' arrival. Joe reported:

*My hardest adjustment to the field was learning to speak Shona. I had no time for formal language training, so I always struggled in trying to communicate with the work crew I was supposed to supervise. While we were able to spend mornings with Helen Dunkeld for a few months to get the basics, it was never sufficient for me to feel comfortable in communicating. I was quite frustrated in not being able to do either the maintenance job or the language study adequately. Both needed my full-time attention, which I was not able to give.*

Even those who had grown up on the field faced unexpected language challenges when they returned in the capacity of missionaries. Lynn Everswick explained:

*I thought that language would not be a concern to me since I grew up speaking Shona. However, I quickly discovered that what I learned was more of a colloquial version of the language, so I really had to start over in learning the proper way to speak it.*

Learning any new language demands that you step out at some point and start using it, no matter how confident or inadequate you feel. Even those missionaries who became most proficient in speaking Shona had to go through this stage. Obviously, many mistakes were made, some hilarious, some embarrassing, and some just leaving the listener confused. Wilma Gardziella told of some of her experiences along this line:

*After an abbreviated language course, due to the sudden departure of my language teacher, June Munger, I was sent to the hospital to begin my work as a nurse. My first assignment was to take histories from patients coming to the outpatient department. My language informant had helped me make a little notebook of questions to ask for various symptoms the patients might mention. I had a page of questions for "cough," "fever," "diarrhea," etc.*

*On one of my first days doing this, I had a patient who I thought said "cough," so I turned to my questions for "cough." Then, from my list I asked, "Do you cough more at night or during the day?" knowing that night coughs were a symptom of TB, which was prevalent in the area. The man replied, "Ndinokosoraba." I knew that "Ndinokosora" meant "I cough," so I continued asking more questions, and to all of them he answered the same, "Ndinokosoraba."*

*Eventually I asked someone why he was not answering my questions, and I was told, "But he is. He is saying he doesn't cough!" That was the first time I remembered hearing that the little suffix "ba" tacked on the end of a verb form creates a negative. I had only remembered that the "ha" put onto the beginning of the sentence made it negative! From that day on I never forgot that little suffix of "ba"!*

*Then there was the little old ambuya ["grandmother"] accompanied by her granddaughter, who was about eight years old. In response to every Shona question I asked the grandmother, she would turn to her granddaughter and ask, "What did she say?" I then heard the granddaughter tell her exactly what I thought I had said. The ambuya would then turn to me and answer my question.*

*After I had determined her history and was about to send her on to await the doctor's exam, I asked her one last Shona question, "Why don't you answer my questions directly?" She replied, "Handinzwi chirungu" ("I don't understand English"). I thought my Shona was improving, but she obviously heard only my poor accent and thought I was speaking English!!*

## Shona Customs

Learning the customs of the Shona people was just as important as learning their language. The Danielsons and Dunkelds recognized this from the beginning, so even as they were struggling to learn Shona, they were also trying to observe the manners and customs of the people. Helen Dunkeld reported:

*Some of their customs we were very slow to pick up. Later they told us, "We knew that you didn't know, so we excused you," but after we had been there for awhile, we were expected to know them.*

*We learned that in their culture you always hand things out with your right hand. This is because, not having water in*

162

*abundance, they did all the dirty work with the left hand and the clean work with the right hand. Therefore, to hand something to someone with your left hand would be quite offensive.*

*At first we thought that they were rude because they never said, "Thank you," when we gave them things. Then we learned that they said, "Thank you," in actions rather than words. They would clap their hands together and then receive the gift with two hands. If you accepted a gift with only one hand, you would not be showing full appreciation for it. If one of your hands was dirty or full, then you were to touch that hand to the elbow of the arm with which you received the gift to show that you were receiving it whole-heartedly.*

Greetings are also extremely important to the Shona people. To start a conversation before going through a greeting ritual is considered rude. The correct greeting to give varied according to the time of day and how long it had been since you last saw the person. Specific actions were often expected to accompany the greetings as well. These differed according to whether you were male or female and whether the person you were greeting was younger or older than yourself.

Another major adjustment that missionaries had to make in working with the Shona people involved the perception of time. Those in the rural areas grew up with the concept of time relating only to the changing position of the sun through the day. Therefore, they are much more event and people-oriented than time-oriented. They take whatever time is necessary to fulfill what is expected in personal interactions. Church and other meetings are viewed as events that start when the people arrive and end when all that is intended to be accomplished is over. Obviously, this contrasted greatly with the highly time-oriented western culture of the missionaries.

Nevertheless, the pioneer missionaries gradually learned and adjusted to these and many more Shona customs. As new missionaries arrived on the field, they reaped the benefit of what the pioneers had learned. Being taught these customs as part of their orientation to the field, they were able to put them into practice much more quickly.

# Missionary Life

Other adjustments came out of the dynamics of missionary life and the necessity of working together as a team for the common goal of evangelism and church planting. For this to occur in an effective manner, a structure of leadership was put in place for the field as a whole as well as for each mission station and institution formed.

Basically, this took the form of a Field Council and a Field Chairman being elected to serve a two-year term as overseers of the entire Zimbabwe field. Each station then had an appointed station head. As various ministries were developed, directors were appointed for each of them as well.

Learning to subjugate one's personal desires within the team structure was a significant adjustment for some missionaries, especially those who had been accustomed to making their own ministry decisions prior to coming to the field. Submitting to authority sometimes meant accepting assignments that did not fit with their original expectations or even with their particular gifts and experience. The second-generation missionaries had a rather unique adjustment issue as they became peers in ministry with the very people they had grown up calling "aunties" and "uncles."

Missionaries also had to learn to live within a close community on the various mission stations. They did not always get to choose their housemates or close co-workers and had to learn to live and work amicably with different personality types.

Marg Jackson wrote:

*For our first few months on the field we boarded with the Dunkelds, as we didn't have funds to set up housekeeping for ourselves. This was an adjustment for us as we waited until funds arrived so we could live on our own.*

Chris Goppert, who had grown up as an only child and had been married for only 18 months, expressed similar feelings: "Not having our own home where Joyce and I could enjoy some privacy during language school at Chironga was a big adjustment for me."

Missionaries also had to grapple with how to balance ministry with personal and family needs. This adjustment was particularly difficult for mothers whose young children needed a significant amount of their time. How could they be both a good missionary and a good mother? Which role was to be given higher priority? "It wasn't easy balancing these roles," said Phyllis Rilling. Many felt guilty when meeting home and family needs kept them from being more involved in ministry.

Those living in rural areas faced another struggle when their children reached school age. The expected norm was to send them to school in Harare. Before TEAM built its own hostel, the only option available there was a non-Christian boarding school that left much to be desired. Even after the TEAM hostel was built and operating, the separation involved was a big adjustment for both the children and their parents.

Julie Stephens expressed her struggles along this line:

> *My biggest adjustment was coming to the field with a three-year-old, a seven-year-old, and twins who were eleven. The twins immediately went into the hostel, which continued to be an adjustment every time they had to leave.*
>
> *When Davey was five, an unexpected place opened in Gateway School, where we had had the children's names on a waiting list. If you didn't take a place when it was offered, there was no guarantee you would get one down the line, so we had to send Davey, our youngest, in at age five. One blessing God had in place for us just at that time was that my mother, Donna, and her husband, Bert Abuhl, were hostel parents that year, which made it easier for all of us.*

## Role Definition

Missionary spouses often had an adjustment in finding their role in ministry when the couple was assigned to a particular area because of the gifts and training of one of them. Julie Stephens, as a doctor's wife, struggled to find her place as a non-medical spouse on a hospital station. Non-medical husbands often became involved in maintenance areas, but where could she fit in and have a significant role? She eventually resolved her dilemma by filling the need for a first and second grade correspondence school teacher for the staff children on the station.

Judy Everswick described the struggles she had in finding her role as a missionary wife:

*My parents had invested considerable time in helping me to develop a strong sense of self-confidence. The attitude they instilled in me was, "You can do whatever task is set before you."*

*That was the spirit in which I arrived in Zimbabwe. I immediately tackled language school and learning how to bake bread. I saw those things as challenges and goals that I could take on and master.*

*However, when we moved to Kapfundi four months after language study, I found myself facing a very different kind of challenge. Even though I had received a higher grade on my final language exam than Lynn, I could hardly make a prolonged conversation. Having grown up in Zimbabwe, he could talk to anyone and even preach. I was not used to being unable to communicate.*

*On top of that the pastor of the Evangelical Church there was quite insistent that a missionary wife not "take over" Ruwadzano, the women's ministry. He did not want the group to depend upon the leadership of a missionary because he feared that it would falter when the missionary moved away.*

*Therefore, role definition became a huge challenge for me in my early years as a missionary. I was not a nurse or a teacher. I was the wife of a school manager, a station head, and a church planter. It was not a clearly defined role at all.*

*I found that the wives of the national teachers made friends slowly. After we had one couple over for dinner and I tried to set a "date" for another dinner, the wife told me, "No, we cannot come a second time until you have had all of the teachers and their wives a first time."*

*Relationships were very important to me, and I found it difficult to adjust to missionary life with the language barrier, the cultural barrier, and the expectations of the national church. Eventually, the Lord gave me other areas in which to develop a ministry, but moving into "missionary" status was not the easy move that I had anticipated.*

## Flexibility

Another major adjustment for many of the missionaries was the seeming necessity to move frequently from one station to another or even from one ministry to another. Gladys Cedarholm described the situation in her era:

*During our first term on the field we had to learn to be flexible in our ministry assignments and go wherever we were needed. Conferences at that time were referred to as "fruit basket upset" time. We all held our breath, waiting for Field Council to announce who would be transferred and to what location.*

*At one particular conference we were asked to go to Harare as the new hostel was ready to be roofed. Clarence was assigned to this job as well as to build the kitchen cabinets. We had to prepare for a three to six-month stay, which meant we would be required to take along all necessary furnishings, appliances, tools, and machinery. Yes, it was an adjustment, but God enabled us to carry out what we had been called upon to do, and we praised Him for His continued faithfulness.*

Ray and Myrtle Finsaas, with their two children, had to move four times in just their first year on the field. Arriving in April 1957, they first spent a month living on the Plot in Hatfield. The field was waiting for some other new recruits to arrive so that they could all begin language school together.

While waiting, the Finsaases were sent to Chironga where Ray helped Emil Rilling in the building taking place there and Myrtle helped Jeanette Ratzlaff with the dispensary. By July, all of the expected new recruits had arrived, and the Finsaases picked up and moved to Msengedzi for language school.

Because food supplies were only able to be purchased in Harare every three or four months, Russ Jackson encouraged Ray to buy 100 baby chicks so that when they went to their next assignment, they would have a source of meat and eggs.

When their four months of language school were finished, they were sent to help with the work at Mavuradonha. The partially grown chicks were able to be transported in the side boxes of their truck. Soon after arriving at Mavuradonha, the chickens started laying eggs, so the effort of raising them and transporting them was finally paying off.

Then, at Field Conference the next April the Finsaases were sent to Kapfundi to take care of maintenance and the dispensary there as well as to work with a village church. By this time, moving was even more of a challenge as the chickens were full grown. Ray had also built a playhouse for their girls. They described this final move of their first term:

> *We gathered all our belongings, supplies, groceries, kerosene, petrol, and medicines in the truck. Then the chickens were placed in the playhouse on top of the load. What an interesting sight it was!*
>
> *We made it fine to Kapfundi. The chickens survived, got a new home, and furnished us with many eggs and meat for a long time. And the girls, Ruth and Joy, got their play house back.*

Factors other than changes in ministry assignment required Karen Longnecker to move numerous times during her first term on the field as well. She reported:

> *I had several moves during my language study. Then, because my house at Mavuradonha was not finished, I had to move into the "Y" in Harare for several weeks. When I finally moved out to take up my teaching assignment at Mavuradonha, the war of independence escalated in the area, and everyone eventually had to evacuate that station. I then had to move into a flat [apartment] in town until Field Council decided where to re-assign me. That turned out to be Karanda, which was my final move of the term. This repeated "pulling up of my roots" was a major adjustment for me.*

Missionary life required flexibility not only in changing the location in which one served but also in the roles one was required to fill. At times when no qualified person was at hand to meet a specific need, others had to "pinch hit," regardless of their prior experience. Many times this took missionaries out of their comfort zones, but it also gave them the opportunity to see God minister His enabling grace to them in a special way.

Marian Wilterdink, who had had two years of nurses' training but whose heart was set on teaching Bible to children, was sent to Harare to learn anesthesia when the hospital was being built. Phil Christiansen and Diane Powell, both trained medical technologists, had to branch out of the familiar territory of the laboratory and learn to operate the x-ray department of Karanda Hospital. Diane even had to fill in as a nursing instructor for a few weeks as personnel transitioned on and off the field.

Missionary nurses often had to perform duties that went far beyond their training or what would be permitted in North America. Carol Olsen Austin described her first such experiences as a nurse:

*After finishing a year of language school and knowing enough vocabulary to get by in the clinic, I was sent to Chironga to start a clinic for the people of that area. They had never had a clinic or a nurse before, so this was new to them too.*

*The first morning the clinic was open for patients I remember apprehensively wondering if anyone would come for treatment. One of the very first patients was a lady who needed a tooth pulled. I felt incapable of doing this, but I had to try anyway. Unfortunately, her jaw dislocated in the process. Then I was even more at a loss to know what to do.*

*The Lord helped me to remember that Clarence Cedarholm, one of the other missionaries on the station, had been a medic in the navy during the war, so I hurried out to find him. After I explained the situation, he said he thought he could help. As soon as the lady's jaw was unlocked by a very simple procedure, she gave me a strange look, ran to the door, and never came back. I didn't blame her!*

*A day or two later a father rushed into the clinic carrying his small daughter, who was not breathing normally. I looked into her mouth and thought I saw what could have been diphtheria. (I had seen it once at the Contagious Disease Hospital in Chicago.) The child died shortly thereafter as I could do nothing to save her. I became quite upset emotionally about that.*

*Later, when sharing this experience with Phyllis Rilling, she gave me some good advice. She told me that I would have many such experiences in which people would die because I could do nothing or very little to help them, and I mustn't let myself fall to pieces at these times. The Lord knew my limitations, and I thanked Him for the peace He gave me to carry on and to grow in my own level of confidence as I relied on His strength and wisdom for each day.*

Dr. Dan Stephens has had an ongoing struggle to adjust to the reality of having to fill "too many shoes" at Karanda Hospital. He reported:

*I have to do the work of the doctor, the surgeon, the hospital administrator, and station head. This leads to overwhelming busyness and the feeling that I'm unable to do all of them well.*

*I also have the frustration of feeling that I'm not having any spiritual ministry. Someone pointed out, however, that at least I was making evangelism and ministry possible for a number of others by what I was doing. That helped a bit.*

Sometimes it paid to have a sense of humor when approaching a task you had no idea how to perform. Possibly the humor came only in retrospect, but Rusty Sherwood had a particular knack for turning a challenging experience into a hilarious story. He wrote:

*Orv and Helen Dunkeld had left my wife, Jo, and myself all alone at Msengedzi when they went on furlough. Now what was I, as a city boy, supposed to do with all those cows? Especially when the time came to butcher one for the pot?*

*Well, first I shot the cow with a .22 rifle. Then, beneath the shade of a tree with an encyclopedia propped up before me and open to a picture accompanying a section entitled*

*"Cow; Sections Thereof," I proceeded to carve the cadaver into "steaks," "roasts," "T-bones," "ribs," etc. The only problem being that when I was done, it all looked pretty much like mince [hamburger]!*

## Effectiveness in Ministry

Almost every missionary was eager to see the ultimate goal of bringing souls into the Kingdom of God actually happen. Just as the medical personnel had to adjust to the reality that they could not save every physical life, those involved more directly in evangelism and church planting had to adjust to the reality of not always seeing the spiritual results for which they hoped. Phyllis Rilling shared some of her feelings along this line:

*When we were stationed at Rusambo, I began to feel even more keenly the disappointment in seeing the Gospel given daily at the clinic with so little response! I went home crying a few times as it seemed like the Word of God wafted over the people's hearts like water rolling off a duck's back.*

While much patience was needed in sowing and watering the seed, in God's time the fruit came. How rewarding it was! All praise and honor and glory goes to God, who gave each missionary the grace to conquer an abundance of adjustments to become effective workers in His Zimbabwe harvest field!

---

[1] Slightly modified from Noël Liddle, *"A Million Miles of Miracles"* (Bulawayo, Zimbabwe: Baptist Publication House, 1995), p. 62.

# CHAPTER 5

# God Gave Grace to Adapt

*"I can do everything*
*through Him who strengthens me."*
(Philippians 4:13)

What a challenge the early missionaries faced in figuring out how to live, work, and minister far away from all the conveniences they were so accustomed to in their homelands! Though isolated from modern civilization, they were never really on their own, however. God had promised that He would surely be with them as they took the Gospel to the uttermost parts of the world.

Over and over again He gave them the resourcefulness to use the limited materials they had on hand and adapt them to fit the need of the moment. As God continually showed His faithfulness in this way, the missionaries learned to respond to problems or needs that arose by praying and then "putting on their thinking caps," fully expecting God to guide them.

## Living Adaptations

Wherever the missionaries arrived to establish a new station, their most immediate needs were for the basic essentials of life: food, water, and shelter. None of these came easily, but the dedicated pioneers were undaunted by the challenge. Through hard work they applied themselves to doing whatever was necessary to secure these things, and they succeeded—with God's help.

## Housing

Regardless of previous experience, the early missionaries had to build their own homes. In most cases, especially in the beginning, they were limited to using only the materials that were on hand in the natural habitat that surrounded them.

The first house that Rudy Danielson and Orv Dunkeld built at Msengedzi was made of poles, mud, and grass, just like those of the villagers. The only differences, according to Orv, were that "it was a bit bigger so that you could stand up in it without bumping your head on the roof, and it had a wide verandah around it." No home-land experience could have prepared these men for constructing a house of these materials, but the local people helped and taught them in the process.

Rudy had actually hired village men to start building the house for the missionaries when he and Orv made their exploratory trip into the Valley in 1941, choosing Msengedzi as the location for their first mission station. When the men returned to Msengedzi after the rainy season the following year to make the necessary preparations to move their families and establish residency there, they were pleased to find that the local men had followed through in putting up the pole structure for a house, topped with a grass roof.

The men then had to fill the spaces between the poles with mud, both inside and out. Being their first experience in making "plaster" out of mud, they had a bit of difficulty getting the mud the right consistency. In the end, however, when they put a coat of whitewash over it, they were quite pleased with how it looked.

After moving in, Rudy and Mary Danielson described this first "home" of theirs in a letter dated May 26, 1942:

*The hut is roughly finished, as the mud plaster on the walls and the mud floor did not turn out so well with many cracks, but nevertheless we have a shelter until we are able to build something better. With the floor covered with [reed] mats, which the [villagers] make and use for sleeping mats, and with pictures on the walls, we have made it as homelike as possible. . . . When one gets in beds, chairs, table, and box cupboards, as well as the many other smaller items, it is a case of utilizing every square inch. The stove was set up in the middle of the yard for awhile, but now [the men] have built a shelter around it of sticks and grass. We hope to build something better when we get time.*

As the Danielson's hut was being finished, Rudy and Orv were contemplating what kind of temporary structure they could put up for the Dunkelds that would enable them to move down to Msengedzi with the Danielsons as soon as possible. In the end they decided to construct a crude annex to the Danielson's hut,

Orv described this initial shelter:

*We put some poles up for the walls. Bundles of grass were then tied together and bound to the poles to make the two walls extending out from the Danielson's house. We also had poles going out from their house over the top of this structure. Then we extended a large canvas from their roof over the top of the poles and down the opposite side. It wasn't quite long enough to reach to the ground. We had to accept that or make a smaller room. We needed the space, so when the truck was available, we parked it by that wall to help close the gap.*

*We had no door, so we had to leave an opening in one of the grass walls. That made for some interesting nights, as we never knew what was going to go by that opening. I remember hearing strange sounds and sometimes watching a hyena or a leopard walk by.*

*When we put in our double bed and beds and dressers for the children and grass mats on the floor, it was not too uncomfortable. We shared the Danielson's kitchen and ate our meals with them while we lived in the shelter.*

Orv began sleeping in this shelter as soon as Rudy brought Mary and one-year-old Muriel down from Mavuradonha to move into their temporary hut. On the next trip, about six weeks later, Orv brought Helen and two-year-old Fred and seven-month-old Dick down to join them. The Dunkelds lived in the shelter for nearly two months while their house was being built.

In order to build more durable, permanent houses, the men had to learn how to make bricks. Kimberley bricks could be made more quickly than burned bricks, so the men decided to make the Dunkeld's house out of these. Orv described how they were made:

*The first bricks we used were just mud bricks called Kimberley bricks. They were about 6 inches by 9 inches by 12 inches. The mud for the bricks was made in a large pit. The men got in the pit and mixed up the clay and the sand and water with their feet, then tossed the resulting mixture up on the bank where other men put it into molds.*

*The molds were then carried to an open area where the bricks were carefully dumped out on the smooth ground. They were left there to dry but had to be turned every day so they would dry evenly.*

*When they were dry and ready to use, they were laid in a mud mortar, which was a mixture of mud and sand. Laying these mud bricks in a straight line was rather challenging.*

The site on which these pioneers chose to build their houses was solid shale with just a shallow layer of top soil over it, so they didn't have to worry about digging a deep foundation. They just dug a trench into the shale and started laying the bricks in it.

They had to compromise with the workmen on the shape of the house. The local people didn't know how to thatch a square house, and the Dunkelds weren't too anxious to have round walls because furniture doesn't fit well against round walls. In the end they decided to make a six-sided house, which worked out very nicely.

When they were ready to put the roof on, the Dunkelds decided they wanted a thatched roof of a style they had seen during their time in Zululand, South Africa. It was a much thicker roof and therefore kept the inside of the house cooler, which was greatly appreciated in the Valley. Essentially, the 10-foot tall grass stalks were laid with the tips pointing up instead of down.

Because the local people were unfamiliar with this type of thatching, Rudy and Orv had to do most of the work themselves.

They made an 18-inch needle out of mahogany to use in sewing the bare grass stalks in place. One would be inside the house pushing the "needle" up, and the other would be on top of the developing roof, pulling it up.

Orv described a little more of how the roof was made:

*We put the grass through a rake and combed it so that all the fuzz was taken off, leaving just the grass stalk. These were then sewn onto the purlins with the big end down. As we went around with each row, we would take a wooden beater, which was like a stepped trowel, and we would beat the grass so the ends were evened off. It gave us a very even roof.*

Their next job was to put window and door frames in and cover them with screen so that air and light could come into the house. Needing lumber, the men found a large, dead mahogany tree a couple of miles upriver, which they floated down and pit-sawed into lumber.

They had learned to use a pit saw when they were initially staying at Mavuradonha with the Linds. The Danielsons described this process in the same letter of May 26, 1942:

*Just now the men are busy trying to saw up a huge, dry mahogany tree about two miles up the river to make door and window frames for the Dunkelds' hut. They are cutting it into boards with a pit saw. This is done by digging a large pit under the log after it has been supported on heavy poles that can be moved forward and backward out of the way of the saw as the cutting progresses. The actual sawing is done by two men, one down in the pit to pull the saw down and the other standing on top of the log to pull the saw back up and to guide it as it cuts. As soon as it is possible, they are planning to use an old automobile engine to run a saw as this primitive method is too slow and difficult. . .*

The following year the men went up to Zambia and were able to buy about 1900 pounds of teakwood planks, which were delivered to Harare. The men had to haul them down into the Valley, but this wood was dressed and ready to use, which was a welcome relief after all the work they had had to do in cutting those mahogany logs.

Finally, the Dunkelds' house was finished and they were able to move into it. Orv described what it was like:

> *When we finally got moved into this one-roomed, six-sided house, it seemed like a palace. We had painted the walls and had a cement floor, windows with screens on, a screen door in front, and a nice verandah with a mudded floor.*
>
> *We had an outside kitchen, which was really just four grass walls. We set the stove up inside of this, and that is where Helen did the cooking.*
>
> *. . . For furnishings I made a table and cupboards for the kitchen out of boards we had there or bits we brought out from town. When we went into town, we would go to auctions. When we would see something we wanted, we would buy it, so our house was gradually getting furnished.*
>
> *Later, we decided that we were a bit crowded in our single room, so we were able to expand our house to provide more room for us. On our six-sided house, every other wall was blank. The others had windows or the door. The encircling verandah was five feet wide, so we started closing in sections of the verandah where the blank walls were. We used burned brick for this, which would take the rains better.*
>
> *First, we made a bedroom for Fred and Dick. Then we made an attached kitchen. The third room we added served as a pantry. "This enlarged the house quite nicely and gave us a very practical building."*
>
> *. . . Later, we opened up the side of the boys' bedroom and built on an extension. This provided a bedroom for the boys, a bathing room with a cement tub and wash basin, and then a bedroom for ourselves.*

The men also built a new brick house for the Danielsons. Their house had a combined living room/dining room, a bedroom, a kitchen, and an open verandah, which was later screened in.

A problem the men faced was how to keep the prolific termites in the area from devouring their houses. Orv described what they devised to resolve this problem:

*In using the unburned Kimberley brick, we would lay a couple of rows of brick above ground level, and then we would put a layer of tar right across the plaster and bricks and everything else, and the termites couldn't chew through that.*

*Later, when we started building a guest house so guests would always have somewhere to stay, I suddenly realized that we were going to run out of tar. So we simply took the drum itself and cut the drum into strips and used them in place of the tar. It was the way we had to make do with whatever we had on hand. . . . Eventually, we realized how impossible it was to keep the termites out of the Kimberley bricks, so we went then almost exclusively to burned brick.*

*These were more or less the same size as the bricks we have in the States. They were about 3 inches by 4½ inches by 9 inches, so the finished wall was about 9 inches thick.*

*Of course, we first had to make the molds for the bricks. You could buy them, but they were rather expensive, so part of our mahogany tree went into making brick molds. We put scrap iron around the molds so they didn't come apart.*

*The bricks were stacked loosely in such a way as to form a large kiln with interspersed fire tunnels through them. These tunnels were then stacked with wood. Once we started burning the bricks, we had to keep the fire burning all the time, day and night, until fire came out through the cracks between the bricks at the top of the kiln. Then we sealed the entire kiln by mudding it over to let it cool slowly. This is how we got our burned bricks.*

*Some of the bricks were burned real well and some not so well. We used the poorer ones on the inside of the wall and the good ones on the outside of the wall where they would withstand the rain better. These burned bricks were a lot easier to lay. Once we learned how to make them, we used burned brick for all our buildings.*

When their houses were finished, Rudy and Orv decided they needed a building to shelter their vehicles from the sun and rain and provide a place for a workshop. Orv described this project:

*We decided to put up a big roof, what the local people called a musana we nzou, meaning the "back of an elephant." That is what it looked like with these big poles standing upright and then a big thatched roof on top of it. We made it approximately 30 by 40 feet—big enough to get three vehicles in and have room at the end for a workshop.*

This new shelter never actually got to be used for its original purpose, however, as a small church formed at Msengedzi and needed a place to meet. Then, the need for a school came along, and it started meeting there too.

In order to make benches for the church and school, the men put forked poles in the ground and then set straight poles across the forked ones. This made nice round benches for them. They used this *musana we nzou* for the church and school for a long time.

As new missionaries began arriving after World War II, the potential to spread out to reach other parts of the Zambezi Valley was excitedly embraced. In 1955, Russ and Marg Jackson and their three children went to establish a new mission station at Chirundu, where a large sugar estate had opened up, employing thousands of nationals. Marg told of their arrival at Chirundu:

*At the time Tom was two, Paul (Bud) was five, and Lynette was eight. We arrived at Chirundu with all of our earthly possessions, including our chickens, in our truck. All that was there was a mark on a tree to indicate the site that the men who had initially scouted out the area had chosen for our house.*

*Little Tom seemingly expected to find a house already there for us. By the time we had unloaded the truck and no house was in sight, he became quite upset and started to cry, "But where is mine house?"*

*We tried to explain to him that we would have to build our house and proceeded to pitch our tent to use in the meantime. When the tent was pitched, Tom wrapped his arms around the tent pole and said, "Here is mine house."*

They lived in the tent while Russ hired workmen to build a 12' by 24,' grass-roofed shelter made of poles, river reeds, and chicken wire. Russ then wrapped heavy, black paper (used to wrap tobacco for shipping) around this structure and over the ground as a floor covering.

He described living in this temporary shelter and building their permanent home:

> *This became our living and dining room and bedrooms all combined. There were no regular windows, only a large square opening at each end of the one small room. As soon as possible we covered the window openings with mosquito netting, and Margaret managed to provide a substitute for curtains to give some privacy. We also built a small grass shelter nearby, which was our kitchen. We lived in this temporary dwelling for several months until our permanent house was built.*
>
> *We had drawn up our own plans for this home with a seven-foot veranda all around it so the children would have a place where they could play out of the hot sun. The site was overlooking the beautiful Zambezi River.*
>
> *My first task was to locate several local men to make bricks. Trees and bush also had to be cleared away on the new building site. The men made sun-dried, mud Kimberley bricks, together with some small ones, which would later be burned in a large kiln. These burned bricks were for the outside walls and pillars of the house and veranda because they could withstand the rains better.*
>
> *All the water with which to make the bricks had to be hauled from the nearby Zambezi River in 44-gallon drums. This was a rather time-consuming task, as the water had to be carried by hand in buckets up from the river to where the truck was parked. Margaret learned to drive at Chirundu and became very proficient at driving the truck filled with drums of water.*

*Sufficient grass had to be cut for the roof, and this was done mostly by the local women. Poles also had to be cut and treated for the roof. We took great pains erecting the roof structure and making sure sufficient thatch was put on to keep out the rains during the rainy season.*

*Floors were made of cement, and we put colored powders into the cement so that we had red living and dining room floors, green bedroom floors, and a black kitchen floor. Margaret wanted a black and white kitchen, as the ladies of the Greensboro Church had purchased a small wood cooking stove from Sears for her kitchen, and it was white with black trim.*

*Our lifestyle in the Zambezi Valley was totally different but also immensely interesting. I am still amazed at how Margaret, growing up in the large city of Toronto with all the conveniences, could manage to adjust to this kind of living so readily. To God be the glory!*

Lynn Everswick, who grew up on the field with his parents in the early fifties, explained how the men learned from each other in building their homes:

*Some of the men learned a bit about building a house while in language school with more senior missionaries. Helpful information was also shared on the two-way radio, especially if someone ran into problems. Any "tricks" that were learned were shared by radio as well.*

*At times "trial and error" was the only teacher. For instance, bathtubs were built inside from bricks and coated with cement. One missionary built his bathtub so big that he then had a problem filling it with enough water since the water had to be hauled and boiled first to kill the bilharzia parasites.*

*Learning a lesson from this, another missionary made his so narrow that a good, healthy person could get stuck in it. Another decided to paint over the dull brown cement of his bathtub with white enamel. This, however, resulted in bathers picking peeled white paint off their bodies after each bath for the next few months!*

Keeping their houses cool during the hot summer months was a major concern for the missionaries. The brick walls and thatched roofs of the early houses were a big help along with the wide verandahs that were usually built around them to keep the sun off the walls. Some of the houses were built in an L-shape so that they could catch the breeze from all directions.

Don Hoyt recalled a whitewashed, burlap ceiling hung under the grass roof of his home at Msengedzi. This not only served to catch the "critters" dropping from the roof but also provided a further reflective barrier to the heat absorbed by the grass roof. Later, when houses were built of total masonry construction, they had high ceilings and screened air vents in the walls near the ceiling through which the hot air could escape.

Many hung reed mats in front of their windows or at the perimeter of their verandas. Mary Ann McCloy wrote:

*They could be rolled up if desired or let down to make shade. In the very hot season we would have our windows and doors open at night to catch any breeze. Then, early in the morning we would close everything up, pull the drapes, and let the reed mats down to keep the sun out and the house as cool as possible.*

When electricity eventually became possible during limited hours of the evening, some missionaries were able to start using fans in their houses. Dave Drake enlarged the attic access in his hallway and mounted a large exhaust fan in the opening to blow air into the attic. When he opened the windows in the evening, the fan would draw the cool evening air into the house while pushing the hot interior air into the attic and out through the roof tiling cracks. "It made the house quite comfortable," he reported.

Dave also had a humidifier of sorts that he used during the hot summer months. It was basically a fan with a reservoir that dripped water onto a bed of straw lying on a screen in front of it. As the fan blew air over the wet straw, the water would evaporate and have a cooling effect on the air.

During the cold season the missionaries had the opposite challenge of trying to make their houses warmer. Most of the later houses were built with fireplaces, which provided nice heat as long as the fire was kept burning. Hot water bottles were sometimes used to warm up beds at night.

George and Pat Dee described what they did in their house at Hunyani:

> *Our brick walls made the house very cold during the winter season. The high grass roof over our bedrooms also drew any heat upward, making them the coolest of all.*
>
> *Before going to bed, we would build a wood fire in a small metal drum and bring it into the house overnight. It sat quite safely on our cement floor, and the hard mupani wood burned very slowly, almost like coal, creating little smoke. We really appreciated this make-shift, "moveable fireplace" on those cold nights.*

Gradually the quality of the missionary homes improved as God brought more experienced builders to the field and transportation in and out of the stations improved. By the mid-sixties most of the new missionary dwellings in the rural areas differed little from those in the towns except for the lack of hot, running water and 24-hour electrical service.

## Outhouses

With no indoor plumbing available, outhouses were an essential part of the early stations. Marg Jackson recounted some of her memories from this era:

> *When we arrived at Msengedzi, the Blairs and Everswicks were there, each with two children. The Dunkelds returned from furlough with us with two children, and we had one at that time. With all these children, we had only one outhouse. Russ and I made our home in a storehouse near the outhouse, and every morning we would watch the parade of dads come and empty their nighttime "potties."*
>
> *. . . We were always conscious of snakes and vermin and would take a good look down the hole before we sat.*

Apparently bats sometimes took refuge in the outhouses too. They could be quite startling if they emerged from one hole while someone was using the other.

Dorothy Strom described the rather sophisticated outhouse that her family had at Kapfundi:

*We had one of the nicest outhouses at that time. It was called an "aqua-privy." The pit was dug and lined with a cement wall and top, which was also the floor of the outhouse. Off of the pit, a drainage field was prepared with rocks and sand. A shaft went down from the toilet bowl into the pit, and a pail of water was poured down it about every other day. The theory of this outhouse was that the contents in the pit would become liquefied and seep out through the drainage field.*

*The important thing was that no paper was to be put down into the pit, so beside the toilet hole was a good sized, covered, square tin that was set into the woodwork. That was where the used toilet paper was deposited. (It was frequently taken out and burned.)*

*The great thing about this toilet was that it was odorless and without flies. It looked like every other outhouse when entering it, but it had a very prominent sign not to put paper down the hole and had an obvious marking indicating where the paper was to be put.*

Roy Eichner described some interesting experiences with outhouses as well:

*When Lydia and I were in language school at Msengedzi in 1958, we lived in a brand new dispensary because all of the missionary houses were already occupied. Since it had no "proper" outhouse, a temporary one was built for us with pole-and-grass walls and roof. The only problem was that the grass walls were quite close and short. Because of my height, my head would often hit the grass roof.*

*One day I heard a swishing sound not too far from my head. I turned to see what it was, and much to my surprise, I found myself staring eye-to-eye with a snake on the pole along the top of the grass wall. Needless to say, I made the fastest exit you could imagine!*

Once when Mildred Befus made a nighttime visit to the outhouse at Kapfundi, she had difficulty opening the door. When she lifted her lantern to see why, she discovered that the outhouse had sunk several inches into the ground.

The Rillings had an even more startling experience with their outhouse at Rukomechi, a rather spacious one that the Everswicks had built. One day, only about ten minutes after Phyllis had left the outhouse with her boys, she heard a tremendous explosion-like sound.

"What was that?" she exclaimed.

"The outhouse must have fallen down its hole!" Emil responded.

Sure enough! That was exactly what had happened! Record rains had fallen that season, and the soil was evidently more unstable they had realized. As the sand had washed away in the rains, the outhouse gradually lost its foundation until it met this untimely end.

As the missionaries developed ways to pipe water into their houses, indoor plumbing soon followed. Myrtle Finsaas recalled how delighted everyone at Kapfundi was when her husband, Ray, and Glenn Hotchkiss put plumbing into each house. "We all bought our own sinks, tubs, and toilets," she explained. "We were getting modern! No more outhouses!"

## Electricity

Bringing electricity into their homes was another major step forward in convenience for the missionaries. Prior to this they had to rely solely on candles and kerosene lamps for light at night. Joyce Everswick Goppert remembered her father filling their lanterns and trimming the wicks outside on a table each night before it got dark.

Myrtle Finsaas also described how electricity came to the Kapfundi station:

*When we came out to Africa in 1957, Ray brought an Onan light plant with us from America, which we used to provide power for our washing machine. Then, when we moved to Kapfundi, he used it to provide electricity for the entire station. He was able to get free remnants of wire on big spools from the Kariba Power project, which was putting electricity across the country, and used these to wire all the missionary homes and the Bible school.*

*We turned the generator on at about 6 p.m. for four hours. At about 10 p.m. we blinked the lights, and everyone had five minutes to get ready for the electricity to go off. The missionaries split the costs each month to pay for the petrol to run the generator.*

Roy Eichner, living on the station, recalled:

*So often we would be engrossed in an activity and completely forget about the time. When Ray gave the five-minute warning, no matter what we were doing, we stopped. We would either try to get in bed quickly before the lights went out or pump up the kerosene lamp so we could see in order to finish what we were doing.*

When Christmas came, Dottie Larsen was delighted to have electricity for those few evening hours at Kapfundi. She had brought Christmas tree lights from home and was able to find an evergreen tree of sorts, which she brought in and trimmed. What an attraction that was! Word got around, and everybody had to come and see it.

George and Pat Dee also brought a generator with them to use in their house at Chironga. This made their home a popular place for game night and other station gatherings. Pat wrote:

*Everyone would come to our house and enjoy the luxury of the bright lights. Sam and Emily Wall were great game play-ers, especially Emily. She and George and Reg Austin would play Monopoly late into the night, shouting with great enthu-siasm, "Down with the houses! Pay me my rent!"*

Later, a Lister diesel generator provided electricity for the entire station, including the Teacher Training Institute and the teachers' houses.

Soon all of the rural stations had generators to provide electricity. They were usually run for only limited hours, however, and sometimes broke down, so the need for candles and lanterns was never totally eliminated. Even after the Kariba Power Project brought electricity into vast areas of the country, the steady supply of current was often interrupted. The missionaries always had to have a back-up plan in place.

The Karanda station had two generators, a large one that provided electricity for the entire station and a small one that kept the lights on at the hospital through the night. The large one was generally run for four hours each evening, on surgery day, and for brief periods when x-rays were needed.

Dave Drake described how 24-hour electricity was eventually brought to the Karanda station.

> *I frequently pursued getting the main line from the Kariba Project into the station, but it was too expensive. Eventually, the line was brought a short distance up the Chesa Road to the Chiunye school. We tried hard to get them to bring it up to the station from there, but it was still far too expensive.*
>
> *Sometime later, during the war, the line was extended up to the Rushinga Army Camp, and out of the blue the Kariba Power people came over to Karanda and asked if we still wanted the line brought to Karanda. Needless to say, we gave them a resounding yes! It still cost us $1,000 per kilometer from the Chesa Road, so we sent out a fund-raising letter, and the cost was covered by the time the project was completed.*
>
> *Then we had 24-hour electricity! I was amazed to see how quickly our schedules changed to accommodate this new luxury!*

## Furnishings

The missionaries generally furnished their homes with what they could bring with them from their homelands or purchase in Harare. Funds were often limited, however, and in the early days, especially, they had to be creative in using whatever materials they had on hand to construct their own furniture.

Orv Dunkeld described more of his creative efforts along this line:

> *Fred, who had started doing correspondence school, needed a table, so I took some of the teakwood we had and made a couple of little chairs and a small table. This provided a nice place where both Fred and Dick could do their schoolwork.*
>
> *I also made a sofa, using some more of the teak and a cushion from the old Ford pick-up. The Ford cushion became the seat part, and Helen made some other cushions for the back. It had nice wide teak arms and made a very nice piece of furniture. You never had to worry about termites because they don't like teak at all.*

Many missionaries used the wood from their shipping crates to make furniture. By adding a little hardware and some screening, Emil Rilling made wonderful screened-in beds for young Art and Bill. He and Phyllis could put their sons into their beds, close the lids, and know that they would be safe from mosquitoes, spiders, scorpions, snakes, and other crawling creatures capable of entering the house.

Other missionaries used their plywood shipping crates to make cabinets for their kitchens, bathrooms, and bedrooms. Merv Driedger described making kitchen cabinets for his house at Chinhoyi: "I sanded them down, applied a few coats of paint, and installed them. They served us well." Donna Hendrickson covered the cabinets her husband made with colorful fabric she had brought from the States and was very pleased with the outcome.

Bob and Betty Endicott were quite adept at improvising what they could find on hand to help furnish their home. While in language study at Chironga, Betty planned to make curtains for the many large windows of house they would move into in Hatfield when they finished.

She had brought an electric, zig-zag sewing machine with her from the States, which she liked very much. However, the generator, if it was working, was only on for a few hours in the evening, limiting the time she could work on this major sewing project.

To remedy the situation, Bob adapted Betty's modern zig-zag machine to fit on the treadle base of an old Singer sewing machine that had been left in the house they were living in at Chironga. This enabled her to sew at any hour of the day.

In addition to the curtains, Betty made a circular tablecloth out of the same brocaded fabric she used to make the living room drapes. This was designed to cover one of their large shipping drums, giving them a nicely coordinated table for a living room lamp.

Bob and Betty also found an old, unused, wooden desk on the Plot which they cut apart and redesigned for the bedroom of their daughters. After joining the drawers from each side of the desk, Bob cut a piece of plywood to form the top of this new "dresser" and then extended the same piece of wood into a corner desk. They painted it white, covered the drawer fronts with dark, wood-grained adhesive vinyl, and added fancy gold handles, making it a useful and attractive piece of furniture.

Bob also remodeled the front entry of their home, using their shipping crates to build an enclosed, double-door closet with upper storage compartments. After painting it to match the hall, Bob and Betty were very pleased with this permanent addition to their home.

## Water

The availability of water was always a crucial consideration in choosing sites for mission stations. Significant quantities of water were needed on a daily basis for many purposes, including drinking, bathing, washing dishes, doing laundry, growing a garden, and making bricks.

Not only did the missionaries need a good source of water nearby, but they also had to find a way to transport it to where it was needed. Orv Dunkeld described how the first pioneers obtained their water and how they gradually developed more efficient and convenient ways of doing so:

> *At first we had local women carrying water in buckets or clay pots on their heads. We paid them each day with a cup of salt, as they had difficulty getting salt in that area. Later, we made a donkey wagon from an old car, and we*

*used it to carry 44-gallon drums down to the river, where the women would fill them. The drums could be covered and sealed and then conveniently placed outside our houses or wherever else they were needed. . . .*

*In very hot weather we would pour water into a couple of big washtubs so we could take a bath. When we finished, we saved the water and used it the next day to make mud for laying bricks.*

*Eventually we decided that we needed a better water supply, so we began looking for a spot where we thought we could get water if we dug a well. After choosing a site, we dug down as far as we could until we hit rock. Then we used dynamite to blast through the rock. We repeated this process as many times as necessary until we reached water.*

*At first we brought our 44-gallon drums to the well, filled them, and hauled them back to our houses. Later, we were able to install piping and could pipe the water onto the station itself. Ultimately, we put up a storage tank and ran the water by gravity right into our houses.*

*Our next step was to get hot water piped into our homes. For this we followed what nearly all the rural farmers did. We built a brick structure to support a 44-gallon steel drum lying on its side with a fire hole underneath and a chimney at the back. By building a fire under it, we were able to heat 44 gallons of water. We then piped this right into the bathroom, which was very nice.*

Dottie Larsen described the system by which her house in Kapfundi was supplied with hot water without a drop being wasted:

*On the outside was another fireplace supporting a 44-gallon drum filled with water. . . . The drum was placed on a slant so the water would run by gravity into a cement bathtub inside the house. The bathtub was also on a slant to drain the water out by gravity. Instead of going to waste, however, it went out and watered the poinsettia trees. This worked very well, . . . and it felt so good to be able to take a hot bath at the end of the day.*

Some missionaries devised a way to assure a more continuous supply of hot water by placing two drums, one on top of the other, over the outside fireplace. Stew Georgia explained this system:

*As water was used from the lower drum, water from the upper drum would drain into it and be heated. When the upper drum was empty, it could be refilled without inter-rupting the availability of hot water, as we still had 44 gallons of hot water in the lower drum.*

Eventually some of the houses had propane geysers installed in their kitchens. These heated water very quickly to provide hot tap water on demand.

When metal roofs began to be used on the missionaries' homes, a large covered water tank was sometimes placed where it could catch and store the rain water that ran off the roof in the rainy season. "This was a real blessing," Mildred Carnall said, "and could be used for drinking and cooking without boiling."

Having an adequate water supply was a particular challenge on the Karanda and Rusambo mission stations. The TEAM hospital was relocated from Chironga to Karanda in 1961 because it seemed to promise a better supply of water from the Ruia River. A 100-foot borehole was drilled between the hospital and the river. This was supposed to put out more than enough water for the station's needs. The water was pumped up into a 25,000 gallon storage tank on a ridge alongside the station and distributed by pipelines to the hospital, nursing school, and houses. Being well water, boiling was considered unnecessary for routine use.

This worked for awhile, but the output of the well soon decreased and could no longer keep up with the needs of the developing station and hospital, which required up to 25,000 gallons of water a day! Eventually a diesel pumping station was put in to pump water directly from the Ruia River up to the holding tanks. A second 25,000-gallon tank had been added by then.

Getting water from this source meant that it once again had to be purified before consumption. In addition, the water was often muddy in the rainy season when the river was in flood stage.

Dr. Rick Froese wrote:

*The Lord brought a solution to this through a government "hydro-expert" who passed through the area about that time. During his tea break visit at the hospital we mentioned our water problem. He suggested that we build a filter bed in the river to remove the silt, mud, and bilharzia parasites before piping the water up to our storage tanks. He then sketched a diagram of what he was proposing on an old paper bag for us. The next day Phil Christiansen and I started on the new project!*

Phil described the major effort it took to implement this plan:

*With the hope and expectation that we would be able to have clear, adequate water all year around, Rick and I, along with the hospital work crew and some hired labor, laid a 40-foot long, hand-dug, sand-and-tile filter system directly in the river bed. It was designed to allow filtered water to flow to the point from which the pump collected water for the station.*

*In spite of sandbagging, we had a constant battle with inflowing water carrying sand back into the excavation area. We worked on the project for three months, putting in half of the tile needed before the rainy season began and halted our work.*

*We came back to the project the next year when the water level had sufficiently receded again and worked another three months to complete it. When we finished, we were delighted to see beautiful, clear water being pumped up to the tanks. We filled the first tank and then switched the lines to pump into the other tank.*

*You can imagine our dismay when we looked back into the first tank and found that the water had turned rust brown! The soluble iron picked up from the river sand had combined with the air to form a rusty precipitate.*

Rick described how they remedied this:

*One of my supporters, who was a US federal water engi-*

*neer in San Francisco, sent us terrific plans for a filtering system that would solve the problem. To implement it, we had to build a large holding and filtering tank.*

*We added lots of chlorine to this tank, which quickly changed the pH of the water so the soluble iron salts became insoluble and precipitated out. The tank had baffles in it which created a path for the water to snake around as the precipitate settled in the tank. We then transferred the cleared water by gravity into the two other holding tanks.*

The water still had to be heated when hot water was required. This usually meant using fire to heat it by the barrelful at its destination. Some of the missionaries, however, devised ways to tap into solar power to heat water. Rick had a sheet metal worker in Harare construct a heating panel made up of sheets of corrugated iron which were soldered together with spacers in between and holed pipes on both the top and bottom. He then placed a 44-gallon drum on his roof, insulated it with fiberglass, and attached pipes from the top and bottom to his "solar heater."

He wrote:

*It worked great. During the cooler months and on more cloudy days, I found that placing a 1000-watt tea kettle heater in the base of the drum worked real well. With a little electricity from the generator during the evening hours, we had warm water on cloudy days as well.*

Dave Voetmann laid a 100-foot length of black plastic piping on the hospital roof and ran it into hot water faucets in the lab and the operating room. The water in the rooftop pipe was heated by the abundant Zimbabwe sun and provided hot water on demand in these two hospital departments. He also built solar heating boxes on his own roof to supply hot water and save on the diminishing supply of firewood.

Water was also a major problem at Rusambo, one of the stations which TEAM took over from the Zambezi Mission. Chuck and Verna Knapp reported having to drive several times a week to fill their water drums at a site five miles away. They were delighted when the government began surveying the area for a place to construct a dam. When they chose a site that was quite a distance from the Rusambo station, Chuck showed them another very suitable location closer to the station and was successful in convincing them to build the dam there.

A side-benefit of the dam construction was that the government also made a new road to bring in the heavy scrapers and bull-dozers needed for the project. Previously, the road was so poor that traveling the five miles to the nearest store took a half hour. With the new road it only took a few minutes.

The dam was completed in 1956, and two years later Carl Hendrickson supervised laying a pipeline from the dam to the mission station. "We were extremely grateful to have water available right on the station—even if it was coffee-colored," Donna Hendrickson wrote.

Rusty Sherwood described how during the dry season he and Carl put in a filtering system at the dam site in an effort to get cleaner water:

*We dug a large ditch out into the dry dam area and laid our pipe in the ground. Then we put a layer of rocks on top of it, then a layer of smaller rocks and finally a layer of aggregate stones. It must have worked because we eventually got relatively clean water.*

Rusty and Carl also built a tower for the water tank on the station with a small room at the base for keeping equipment. The door frame ended up being slightly askew as they each were laying bricks on opposite sides of the frame without a level. When they met in the middle, they had a good laugh as they discovered that Carl's side was leaning slightly out and Rusty's slightly in.

Rusambo's water problems were still not over, however. In 1965, Roy and Mildred Carnall came to Rusambo, and Roy got permission to make the dam wall higher as he was having to pump water several times a day to get enough for the station's needs.

Then a flood came and broke the wall, and the government had to rebuild it. Roy explained:

*The original wall was built on rock. The flood caused it to slide off the rock. When the government rebuilt the wall, they drilled holes into the rock to reinforce its mooring.*

Because local cattle often kept the water stirred up and muddy at the dam site, the station pump needed frequent cleaning and repeatedly broke down. Dick McCloy described the challenges the station faced when he arrived in 1972:

*When we arrived, a back-up plan was in place to handle the water problem. If the pump broke, we would drive the tractor down to the pump station and use the tractor's power take-off to drive the pump. This was great—until the housing holding the oil in the tractor split!*

*We then had to use my Peugeot station wagon and trailer to haul water up to the station in 44-gallon drums. I was unwilling to spend my whole day doing this, so we converted the trailer that the tractor pulled into a "scotch cart" and hired a team of oxen from the villagers to pull it.*

*On the station we placed a large galvanized tank at the foot of a small embankment so the oxen could pull the trailer alongside it. The men would then empty the drums into it.*

*Sometimes even this system failed, however, and the young women attending the Homecraft School had to carry their own water on their heads. From time to time the MAF plane came to our rescue by flying in drinking water to us.*

In 1973, Dick's father, George McCloy, came to Rusambo with his wife, Edith, for the specific purpose of working on the water problem. One of his projects was to build new, cement storage tanks for the station. He hired women to crack rocks with sledge hammers in order to have stones for making concrete, paying them by the bucketful. Mary Ann reported:

*They would work away with their babies tied to their backs. When they had a bucketful of stones, they would carry it to the top of the rock heap in their bare feet and pour it into a barrel at the top.*

George also added 18 inches to the height of the dam and ran plastic pipes from the dam up to the tanks. He ordered the materials from Harare, and when they arrived at the station, he discovered that one end of the pipes was metric and the other end was imperial. He was too far from town to return the pipes, so he devised a system whereby he heated the larger end of the pipe with a small gas torch to expand it. Then he inserted the smaller end of another pipe, and as the larger pipe end cooled, the connection became tight.

## Food

Becoming self-sufficient in their food supply was another challenge for the early missionaries. They were able to purchase their basic staples and a short supply of more perishable foods in Harare, but trips to town were generally only made several times a year.

On some stations missionaries could buy a limited amount of certain items, such as eggs, milk, peanuts, beans, a few types of fruits and vegetables, and chickens, from the local people. Eggs were usually given the "float test" for freshness before buying, and milk was generally boiled and strained before using it. The village chickens were generally very tough and not purchased very often.

In order to keep their families adequately fed, the missionaries had to supplement what they could obtain from these sources by hunting for wild game, raising their own animals, and/or growing their own vegetables. For those who grew up on farms, this came easily, but for others it was a completely new experience.

Permission to hunt in the Zambezi Valley was readily obtained as it was part of a zone the government was trying to clear of game to control the spread of the tsetse fly. Thelma Everswick reported:

*For 11 years we were given permission to "shoot for the pot" as needed. We lived for those years on wild meat, such as kudu, impala, duiker, bush buck, wild pig, and guinea fowl. I would pressure cook the meat in quart jars to preserve it, and it would keep for many months on my pantry shelf.*

Wilf Strom explained:

*The game of choice for eating was duiker because it was smaller and more tender. When a larger animal, such as a kudu, was shot, we would share the meat among several families.*

Mildred Rogers Carnall told how George Dee kept his family and her supplied with various types of antelope meat at Hunyani, adding:

*Once he brought home a bush pig, which was a welcome change. Another time he returned with elephant meat. This was dried by fire underneath platforms made with branches of trees. The platform was erected in my back yard and the smell was not appetizing! We didn't eat the elephant meat but gave it to the local village people.*

Merv Driedger recalled occasionally hunting for food in the Zambezi Valley from 1970-76. He wrote:

*I have shot impala, water buck, kudu, duiker, sable, wart hog, cape buffalo, and zebra. Apart from gifts to friends, we as a family ate all of these except for the zebra.*

An alternate source of meat was available by raising animals, such as cows, chickens, ducks, geese, goats, or even rabbits. Chickens matured quickly and also provided eggs while cows and goats provided milk as well.

Gardening was essential but not always easy. Russ Jackson, being raised on a farm, was a great help in this regard when he and Marg arrived at Msengedzi in 1948. He took soil samples from potential garden sites around the station and had them analyzed in Harare. The results revealed that the rich soil along the riverbank was ideal for raising vegetables. With the site chosen, Russ went to work preparing the garden. He described the process:

*Baba John and I, along with several other village men, went into the bush to cut a number of 8-foot posts and a load of long, thin, mupani poles. We carried these back to construct a framework for shading the garden from the hot Valley sun.*

*When this was finished, we went down to the river and cut huge bundles of 15 to 20-foot river reeds. The men made large mats by tying the reeds together about one inch apart with bark. We then rolled these mats out on top of the poles, completing our sun screen.*

*Next we dug several holes in the ground where we could put empty gasoline drums for water. Then we built a bed of poles in the river bottom and secured a hand pump to this, allowing us to pump the river water and fill the drums for the garden.*

*Finally, we were ready to measure out rows of vegetable beds and plant the seed. The station was soon able to enjoy a wide selection of fresh vegetables but not before several sad experiences convinced us that we needed to erect a strong fence around the garden to keep out a variety of hungry animals.*

Russ also felt that the missionaries at Msengedzi needed a steady supply of fresh eggs, so he set out on another project. He wrote:

*Every village had a large tree house made of woven river reeds where chickens could be safe from leopards and a variety of other predators. The chickens in the Zambezi Valley were all exactly the same size and color. They were very small but very sturdy and able to survive by finding their own food in the village. They were also used to the Valley heat. The problem was that these hens only produced enough eggs for hatching.*

*Being a farm boy, I had an idea to improve the situation. The village people were anxious to get clothes of any kind, so I asked Margaret to gather up all she could find, and I began to trade old clothes for some of their chickens.*

*I built a strong brick hen house for them with a fenced-in chicken run. Then, on our next trip into [Harare] I bought a beautiful, pure-bred, leghorn rooster. I used it to produce a large flock of "half-breeds." Then, much to my dismay, my lovely rooster suddenly toppled over in the heat and died.*

*By the time the "half-breeds" were ready to lay eggs, I managed to purchase another purebred, leghorn rooster. The hens from the second generation were terrific layers and were also able to survive the hot Valley climate. My endeavor was at last successful in producing a sufficient daily supply of fresh eggs.*

*Soon the village people were anxious to purchase one of my "half-breed" roosters. In time this unusual breed of white chickens was found in many villages, some at quite a distance from Msengedzi.*

Keeping perishable food was another challenge for the early missionaries. While still in South Africa, Orv and Helen Dunkeld learned how to make a "food-safe" that would keep food somewhat cooler in hot weather. It consisted of a large wooden frame on legs, which were set in water with kerosene floating on the top to keep ants out. The wooden frame was covered with screening overlaid with burlap sacking. On top of it was a coffee can filled with water. The can had a hole in the bottom so that the water would drip down over the sacking. The air blowing over the wet sacking would evaporate the water, and this would provide a cooling effect on the contents inside. The coffee can would be refilled with water several times during the day.

When they described the "food-safe" to their supporters back home, someone apparently felt sorry for them and sent them $80 to buy a "real" refrigerator. Orv described their continued experimentation with non-electric refrigeration in South Africa:

*We went to Durban and bought a refrigerator that was recommended to us called an "Icy Ball." The basis of the whole thing was a big glass dumbbell that had the refrigerant in it. Each evening we would put one end of this glass unit into the fire. As the liquid refrigerant in this end turned to gas, it would drive the remaining liquid to the other end—the other glass ball. Then we would put the dumbbell back in the refrigerator, and as the gas turned back to liquid during the night, it would cool the inside of the refrigerator.*

*We could regulate the degree of cooling this device would provide by how much we heated the one end at night. The only problem was that we had to guess what the weather was going to be like the next day. On a rainy day we might heat it less, producing only a little gas. Then the next day would be scorching hot and the fridge would warm up. Or we might heat it a lot only to have the next day be cooler, and everything in the fridge would freeze. We weren't satisfied with this, so we sent that refrigerator back and got another one.*

*The second refrigerator had the compressor on top of it with a kerosene flame burning constantly under it. This arrangement somehow seemed to raise the temperature in the house at least 10 degrees, so we took that one back too.*

*We ended up with a four cubic feet Electrolux. It was a small square box with a little wick burner underneath that burned constantly. We could regulate the temperature inside by adjusting the flame under it. That one worked real well. In fact, that is the one we took with us to Zimbabwe. We used it there for many years until we could get a larger one.*

## Personal Needs

The missionaries could not possibly foresee or prepare themselves ahead of time for all the personal needs that would arise while they lived on the isolated mission stations. Therefore, they often found themselves without a needed item and once again had to rely on God-given resourcefulness to provide an acceptable alternative.

Orv Dunkeld described what he did when Helen's shoes wore out long before a trip to town was possible:

*I took some rubber from an old tire we had and stripped it down to make it a bit thinner. Then I trimmed two pieces to match the soles of her shoes and took them to a local shoemaker, who sewed them on with his hand awl. When he finished, Helen had a pair of shoes that I don't think would ever have worn out.*

Giving haircuts and home perms was another skill often acquired out of necessity on the mission stations. Helen Dunkeld described the first haircut she gave Orv:

*It didn't turn out too wonderful. I got it too short in some places, leaving some whitish spots on the back of his head. He had an important event to go to, so I took a pencil and filled in those spots. It didn't look too bad then.*

Joyce Everswick Goppert reported that the teenage girls learned to cut each other's hair and would regularly do so at the hostel. They even offered their services to the adult missionaries. She wrote:

*At one conference we set up a "Beauty Parlor" in the hostel where the missionary ladies could come and receive a full line of hair services. We shared the tips we earned and were very pleased with the success of our endeavor.*

Because of his interest in photography Orv Dunkeld brought solutions for developing photos with him to Msengedzi. This enabled him to develop family photos as well as to make enlargements and reprints without having to wait for a trip to town. He just had to make a few adaptations in the process. Lacking a dark room, he worked at night, and when he needed to dry the prints, he used the oven.

One night as he was developing a batch of 50 prints of a family photo to send to supporters, a large spider started running around his workspace. He instinctively grabbed his flashlight and started chasing the spider, only to have the realization dawn on him that he had just spoiled the whole batch of prints by turning on the light.

Children's needs had to be cared for on the mission field too, including the provision of enjoyable activities with which to occupy themselves. Adaptability was often required in this area as well.

Helen Dunkeld described how she and Orv made toys for their children at Msengedzi:

*We took pieces of wood left over from the building, sanded them, painted them, and made up sets of blocks for the kids.*

*Orv also got patterns from a company in the States and made cars and games for them. A lot of our presents to the kids on Christmas and their birthdays were hand-made, and they were always very, very happy with them.*

Chris Goppert told of some of the toys he and Joyce made for their children:

*One of Kim's first toys was a plastic, camera lens container in which we put colored "lucky beans." She enjoyed the bright colors inside and used it as a rattle.*

*We also obtained off-cut wooden blocks from a local furniture factory which we used as a substitute for Lego blocks. We had several hundred of them, so we built houses, bridges, walls, and many other structures with Kim and Sonja. It was great fun and stimulated our imaginations. We even kept one of the blocks as a memento.*

Commonplace items often took the place of sophisticated toys for the children. Old tires hung from trees became swings, and simple cardboard boxes provided hours of fun for imaginative children, who used them to make forts, tunnels, doll houses, etc. Karen Drake wrote:

*Heather had hours and hours of fun from the playhouse we cut out of a large appliance box. She used it for a long time with her little playmates until one day it got soaked in the rain.*

*Brad and his friends would line up lawn chairs to form their very own "747." They would spend hours "flying" to who knows where.*

*When their uncle came for a visit, he built the kids a swing set with an elevated platform. While they enjoyed the swing, the elevated platform really spurred their imaginations and was transformed into a multitude of uses.*

Animals were another source of fun for many children. Marg Jackson wrote:

*The animals were our children's toys. At various times they had guinea pigs, rabbits, kittens, dogs, a small monkey, a baboon, and even baby duikers and baby leopards.*

When the Eichner's house burned down at Kapfundi, they didn't have the funds to replace their children's toys. Roy wrote:

*Steve and Debbie really liked playing with frogs. Lydia and I decided to allow them to bring little frogs into our living room in the evening to play with, as long as they were sure that all of them were put outside before they went to bed. These were great toys, and the frogs did all kinds of things without even winding them up or feeding them.*

Some of the women made dolls and doll clothes for their daughters. Karen Drake wrote:

*I made Heather a Raggedy Ann Doll—complete with the "I love you" sewn over the heart. When we gave it to her for Christmas the year she was two, it was bigger than she was.*

*I used material left over from her bright bedroom curtains to make a basinet for her dolls. I also sewed and knit lots of clothing for her Cabbage Patch dolls, which often matched the clothes or sweaters I made for her.*

Some of the men used their building skills to make toys for their children. A number built doll houses or doll beds for their daughters. Clarence Cedarholm made little carts and wagons for his sons.

Dr. Roland Stephens made a harness to put on a goat so it could pull a wagon. His children enjoyed riding in this around the station. He also built a "foofy slide" (zip line) for them on the hill behind their house.

Ray Finsaas built a playhouse for his girls out of the wood from his family's shipping crates. Then he made a wooden airplane for his son that was large enough for two or three children to ride in while another pushed. His wife, Myrtle, remarked, "They always prayed before 'take off,' just like they saw Uncle Dave Voetmann do before MAF flights."

Ray also made his kids a metal tractor and trailer powered by a Briggs and Stratton washing machine motor. Myrtle explained, "The trailer was just right for Jewel to ride in as her brother, Raymond, drove the tractor around the station and often to the airstrip to watch the MAF plane land." (Raymond is currently a missionary pilot in Papua New Guinea with New Tribes Mission.)

"Aunties" and "Uncles," the endearing designation used by the children for other adult missionaries, often contributed to the children's enjoyment too. Nancy Hendrickson developed a special relationship with "Auntie" Lolly Fritz because of her love for birds and arts. Nancy wrote:

> *I would go bird watching with her and learn the names of the different birds and how to identify them by their calls. Then we would go to her house, and she would draw pictures of the ones we had seen for me to color. I was fascinated with how God had made each type of bird unique.*
>
> *I also remember collecting flowers and leaves of different shapes and sizes and Aunt Lolly showing me how to press them so that they kept their color. Then we would arrange them and use them to make cards.*

Even without the help of adults, the MKs (missionary kids) demonstrated considerable adaptability in finding ways to have fun on their mission stations. They really didn't need an abundance of toys. They were surrounded by a fascinating environment that beckoned their exploration and provided many unique resources to be transformed into exciting "playthings." Their active imaginations took them in many directions, sometimes being inspired by activities they enjoyed in their homelands and sometimes imitating what they observed in the Shona culture around them.

Dr. Dan Stephens was exuberant about his childhood experiences in Zimbabwe:

> *To me, Zimbabwe was a boy's paradise, a place where we could live out the Tom Sawyer and Huck Finn aspirations present in every boy's heart. We had the opportunity to do and use so many things that were impossible for many*

*American kids.*

*We could go on daily hikes through the hills and along the river beds with our slingshots, pellet guns, and, later, .22 rifles to "rid the world of" doves, lizards, and so forth. As we grew older, we advanced to guinea fowl, rabbits, and baboons. Who needed Tonka trucks?*

The boys on the Karanda station also built a substantial tree house on the hill behind the Stephens' house.

Norman and Thelma Everswick's oldest son, Lynn, expressed similar feelings:

*I loved coming home on vacation from the hostel and getting back to my Shona friends. We would spend hours out hunting in the fields for doves.*

*We also loved to go down to the river where the masau trees were loaded with little red berries. We would find the longest stick we could to knock down the ones left high up in the tree and always came home with our pockets bulging.*

Wes Hendrickson described how the boys made their own slingshots from tree branches and rubber taken from old inner tubes and how they would roast their bounty after their "hunting expeditions." Sometimes they would also have target shooting competitions with their various types of "weapons."

Steve Eichner remembered watching some of the older boys devise creative ways to catch small birds that came out towards dusk to feed on grain. He himself was fascinated by many other creatures he found in his environment around the mission stations. He wrote:

*I would catch all kinds of insects and bugs. I still remember eating flying ants and roasting my first—and last—locust to eat with a friend of mine. I loved to kick over large white ant hills (often more than 3 feet tall) and then watch the ants meticulously rebuild them. During the rainy season I would catch frogs and play with them.*

*Some of the creatures around the station were dangerous, such as the scorpions and snakes, which made it all the more exciting to catch a glimpse of them. I still remember when a snake slithered down our hallway and into the bathroom where it wound itself around the base of the toilet.*

Wes told of how the boys at the hostel would play with masasa beetles:

*We would tie a thread to a leg of the beetle and then let it fly like it was our own airplane. We also set up "gladiator battles" with rhino beetles, camel or cut worms, ant lions, or other critters.*

*During the rainy season, when the flying ants came out of their clay "homes," we would catch them, remove their wings, and roast them in an oven or fry them in a skillet with a little oil and salt for a wonderful, tasty snack.*

Dr. Dan Stephens expressed his fascination with ant lions:

*After it rained, we loved to catch ant lions. These little insects, about 3-4 mm. in diameter, would make a little pit in the sand and position themselves at the bottom of it. Ants that crawled into these pits would fall to the bottom and become food for the ant lion. After it rained, you could see all these little pits in the sand, and if you took a little stick and put it down into one of them, the ant lion would grab hold of it with its claws, and it would be yours.*

Even the girls were drawn to some of the little creatures of Zimbabwe. Nancy Hendrickson wrote:

*I was fascinated by all the bugs and their different shapes, colors, legs, eyes, and antennae. I liked to watch how they moved, how they built their homes, and how they collected their food. I would also think about how each one was created by God to have its part in keeping the balance of nature.*

*At the hostel many of us girls had silk worms, which we kept in shoeboxes. We would collect mulberry, cabbage, beet, and other kinds of leaves to feed them. The kind of leaves we fed them determined the color of the silk they would produce when they spun their cocoons. Once they did that, we would carefully unwrap the silk onto pencils and make little bookmarks and other things from it, which we often sold.*

Nancy was also intrigued by the agates and other stones she found at various places where her family went camping. She wrote:

*I was amazed at how they changed from their rough form and became so much more beautiful when we washed them and had the boys polish them with their stone polishers. The boys had learned how to make these stone polishers using bicycle wheels in one of their science fair projects at school. This gave them a way to make a little money off of us girls wanting our stones polished. We girls would then make jewelry from our polished stones to give as gifts and/or to sell.*

Nancy went on to describe other creative activities she enjoyed on the mission stations where she lived:

*We loved to roller skate on the verandah at Rusambo and would work up "shows," skating forward and backwards and doing little "tricks" and group arrangements that we thought were worthy of an audience. Then we would dress up and invite the missionaries for cookies and a "show."*

*At Kapfundi we had a "marching band" and would proudly parade through the station playing our instruments. We strapped pots and pans around our waists and beat them with wooden spoons for drums. We used pot lids for cymbals. Someone had a harmonica, and at least one of us would have a comb with plastic around it to play. We had an African flute and some kind of pipe that we blew through for a horn-like sound as well as wooden blocks that we banged together. We also had an mbira ["thumb piano"]. This had flattened nails mounted on piece of wood, which were plucked with one's thumbs. The leader always had a whistle. With the Stroms, Finsaases, and Fritzes all living on the station, we had quite a few children to make up our band.*

Joyce Everswick used to make her own paper dolls. She would first draw the figures she wanted and cut them out. Then she would make paper clothes to dress them.

Debbie Eichner told of the creative tea parties she had with her Shona nanny:

*My "playmate," as I saw her, picked me up in the mornings and patiently watched over me as I discovered my world around me. It was from her that I learned how to have the best tea parties ever! She taught me how to take leaves from these huge trees and bend them, carefully piercing the halved, soft leaf with a little stick, and somehow attaching a base to create a tea cup. We would make several "cups and saucers." Then she would make a "teapot," and together we would have a "tea party." I loved those times with her.*

Many of the girls were influenced by the Shona culture of their playmates. Heather Drake and her friends spent hours playing with a small cooking pot, making *sadza* and *muriwo* (staples of the Shona diet). They would gather whatever leaves they could in the garden and cut them up for their *muriwo*.

Kris Georgia pretended to make peanut butter African-style, using a "pounder" to smash and grind the peanuts in a pot. She also made "real" mud pies, which she heated over a fire like she observed the village women doing, and carried her dolls wrapped on her back with a towel.

The plentiful supply of sand and dirt on the stations also lent itself to the children's play. Wes Hendrickson wrote.

*It made a wonderful playground for "dinky" [Matchbox] cars. We would build roads and elaborate "towns" in the dirt and play with our "dinkies" for hours in the imaginary settings we created.*

Even some of the girls had "dinky" cars. Joyce Everswick Goppert, growing up with three brothers, recalled:

*Growing up as an MK, I don't remember having many "real" toys other than a doll or two, but I vividly remember my "dinky" car. It was blue, and I would play for hours making roads for it in the dirt with my second and third fingers. Those two fingers made the perfect sized track for my car, and I could drive it all over: through "spruits," around boulders, and over hill and dale. There was always plenty of dirt, so the scope was endless.*

Wes also described the wire cars he would make with some of his Shona friends:

*We made them from single strands of large diameter fence or chicken wire, bending the wire into various shapes resembling real cars (Datsun, Toyota, etc.). The cars were typically about 18 to 24 inches long and 9 to 12 inches wide. Some of the more fancy versions were created by pushing the large wire through bamboo sticks to create a "woody" look.*

*After bending the large diameter wire into the appropriate shapes, we attached the various pieces together with small diameter wire, using empty shoe polish tins for the wheels. The last thing was the steering wheel. This was made of coiled wire and attached to the front axel by means of a long shaft of wire so that it could actually turn the front wheels of the car.*

*When it was finished, we could walk behind the car, pushing it and turning corners by means of this extended steering wheel. The cars even had springs and would bounce along as we "drove" them around the mission station.*

Wes also told about the airplanes he and the other boys would make at the hostel:

*We designed and made our own airplanes out of balsa wood. We flew them by attaching string to the wings and*

*turning ourselves around in circles while we guided the
planes up and down, just like radio-controlled planes.
Some of us even made airplanes with gas engines.*

Several of the MKs told about forming "clubs" and building
clubhouses using whatever materials they could find. Wes wrote,
"We made numerous 'forts,' which we usually dug out of the
ground, using scrap metal and wood for the outer walls and roof."
His sister Nancy reported that she and the other girls on the station
often used their family's truck camper as a clubhouse when it was
on the ground.

Steve Eichner described similar activities:

> *We made our own tents out of burlap sacks and hung out
> our sign "No Girls Allowed" with a skull and crossbones on
> it. Were we cool or what!?! The girls retaliated by building
> their own exclusive clubhouse.*
>
> *We also built "forts" in piles of bricks at a construction
> site or up in trees. Once we built a partially underground
> slide that descended into a big hole covered by metal roof-
> ing, which we covered in dirt to try to hide it. After we had
> worked on it for days out in the open, everyone knew where
> it was, but we imagined we were doing a "top secret"
> project.*
>
> *We even built our own church and put together our own
> "kid's services." Somehow my sister, Debbie, always ended
> up as the preacher. At Christmas we acted out the Christmas
> story with a real sheep and donkey.*

Steve also told of how the boys would make their own balls out
of clay and then try to build an underground kiln in which to fire
them. They were convinced that they could make "super-hard" balls
this way, not realizing that a fire needed oxygen to burn effectively.

He also recalled playing soccer with kids in a village using a
ball made of plastic bags wrapped in twine and another game using
small stones and holes dug in the dirt (Mancala). Lynn Everswick
had similar memories of playing soccer for hours with his Shona
friends using a tennis ball.

Sometimes the MKs' creativity was directed towards devising pranks to play on other people. Wes described one of his favorites:

*We had an amusing game we played called "Snake." We would cut an old bicycle tube in the middle, tie off one end, fill the tube with dirt, and tie off the other end. Then we would attach a long (10-30 feet) piece of fishing line to one end.*

*At dusk we would position our "snake," hiding it right next to a road or path. Then we would hide and wait until someone came along, either walking or riding a bike. A designated "runner" would then pull the "snake" across the path or road just before the person walked or rode by. We always got a good laugh as the "victim" screamed and ran from our "snake."*

The adaptability these children learned in finding ways to have fun on the mission field carried over into their adult lives. Steve Eichner wrote:

*Last week I organized a Wet and Wild game night for about 40 teenagers at the church I am pastoring in Philadelphia. I had four tribes competing with each other. All evening the kids kept asking who came up with the crazy games. I could have told them they came from someone who grew up as a kid in Africa learning how to invent fun the way that only kids can.*

Adult missionaries had to find ways to relax and have fun too. Many did this by going on walks, having picnics and cook-outs, hunting, camping, or climbing nearby hills and rock formations. Some stations also had tennis courts and/or soccer fields for those so inclined.

One year Anne Watson and Diane Powell bought horses for a recreational diversion at Karanda. They rode around the station, on the airstrip, to nearby villages, and occasionally to other mission stations. What stories they could tell about some of their horse escapades! They also allowed other missionaries, MKs, and the nursing students to ride their often temperamental horses. For some it was a brand new experience.

Social gatherings were important for the missionaries. Many of those living on isolated stations for months at a time learned to be creative in devising their own social activities. Game nights were popular on many stations as were special meals featuring home-made versions of American foods unavailable in rural Zimbabwe, such as ice cream, tacos, or fondue. These often became hilarious opportunities to let off steam and relieve stress. As Pat Dee said, "The missionaries had LOTS of fun!"

The single gals at Karanda enjoyed dressing up for some of the special dinners and birthday parties they planned. If the meal followed an ethnic theme, they might even try to dress appropriately for that particular country, such as draping long lengths of material around them to serve as saris for an Indian meal.

Anne Watson, having grown up as an MK in Japan, once fixed a Japanese meal, including home-made tempura and "fortune" cookies with Bible verses in them. An empty house happened to be available, and she was able to get the men to bring in unhung doors and cement blocks or bricks on which to lay them to provide Japanese-style tables around which the guests sat cross-legged on the floor.

Holidays were always a time for festive gatherings. At Karanda the men would be totally in charge of making Thanksgiving dinner for the entire station. With Roland Stephens generally in charge, they would "pull out all the stops" to make it as special as possible. Occasionally they roasted a whole pig on an outdoor spit and transferred it whole, with an apple in its mouth, onto the table. The women would greatly anticipate attending this gala event, being served by the men, and not having to do any of the work.

Christmas was another special holiday, but it was never quite the same on the mission field as at home, especially for the single missionaries, who felt their separation from family more keenly at this time of year. Even in the midst of their loneliness and disappointments, however, the missionaries showed remarkable adaptability, as demonstrated by this story of Eunice Ott's:

*A week before Christmas, I received two large parcels in the mail. I was so excited—until I discovered that they just contained bags of old clothes. The three of us [Eunice, Donna Kahlstorf, and Carol Olsen] decided that even "old clothes" could be festive, however, so we pretended they were our Christmas gifts. We opened them and tried on everything that we could. We laughed until we cried, as many of the items were old crepe dresses that had been washed and had shrunk up to nothing. We couldn't wear a thing, but the fun we had really lifted our spirits.*

Through God's grace these undauntable missionaries managed to transform their disappointment into fun.

## Transportation Adaptations

### On Land

When they arrived in Zimbabwe, the Danielsons had a Ford car and the Dunkelds had a Chevy pick-up. They soon realized, however, that they needed another form of transportation down in the Valley as these vehicles were limited in where they could go. Because Msengedzi was in a tsetse fly area, no oxen were allowed, so the two couples bought some donkeys and made a most unusual "cart" for them to pull.

The idea came when Rudy and Orv purchased an old, broken down Ford pick-up for about $35 in Harare. They primarily wanted to use the engine to power a large circular saw for cutting boards, but in those days their minds were keenly tuned to finding a use for any available materials. Therefore, they couldn't let the rest of the vehicle go to waste. The seat cushions, they quickly decided, could be used to make couches for their homes, so they were removed for that purpose.

Then they took off the top of the cab, and Orv attached a tongue to the front of what remained of the pick-up so they could hitch their donkeys to it and have them pull it like a cart. With the seat cushions removed, they made a modified seat so one of the workmen could sit behind the steering wheel to steer it. What an interesting sight it was! This became the station's primary means of transportation for fetching water and wood.

Rudy and Orv also learned how to make a drag to smooth out some of the roads they used around the station. Orv reported:

*We got a big log and split it in half with the pit saw. Then we used the sharp edge as our drag. We set the log so it would drag at a 45 degree angle, and that did a good job of smoothing the road.*

Orv also rigged up a bicycle charger to serve as a back-up to the station's wind charger, which they used to charge their car and radio batteries. He described this:

*We set the rear wheel up and used a pulley to connect it to the charger. Then we had workmen sit on the bicycle and pedal away. The harder they pedaled, the faster the battery would charge.*

Later, when the Dunkelds decided they wanted a canopy over the back of their Chevy pick-up, Orv built posts up on the sides and put a sheet of galvanized iron across the top. He explained how this made the truck more versatile:

*If we were carrying a big load, we could take the canopy off, and if we were carrying a small load, we could put it back on. If we were going out camping or visiting in the villages, then we could sleep in it if we wanted.*

With virtually no type of auto service available on the many miles of bush roads over which the missionaries traveled, they often had to think of adaptive ways to resolve their car problems when they broke down. Ray and Myrtle Finsaas shared some of their ingenuity on the road:

*Because the roads were bad and we had to cross over rivers to get to the villages where we held services and clinics, we made sure we had water, tea, and sandwiches along in case of an emergency. Once, as we were driving through a riverbed on a mat of river reeds, one of the reeds poked a big hole in the radiator and all the water drained out. Now what?*
*Ray went to a nearby village and asked for some daga.*

*This was a clay-like mud which the women used to mud the floors and walls in their huts. He used this to plug the hole in the radiator. He also asked for a bucket of water, which they gladly gave him. The daga worked quite well, although we occasionally had to add more water to the radiator.*

*Later, as we were going to Harare up the escarpment from Hunyani, the radiator began leaking again. This time Ray got some sadza ["thick corn meal mush"] from a local village to repair the hole. We finally made it to Harare, where he had the radiator repaired properly.*

Another time the clutch went out on his truck as he was driving to an outlying village. To remedy this problem, Ray borrowed a small ax and whittled some small mupani pieces to widen the clutch, which served very well in getting him home.

## On Water

With the Msengedzi station lying on the far side of the Msengedzi River, transportation was also needed for crossing the river, especially during the rainy season. At first the missionaries and the local people visiting them were able to use a dug-out canoe that some villagers upstream had for this purpose.

One day, however, the canoe sank, leaving no means to cross the river. This hindered not only the missionaries in their evangelistic efforts but also the local people who wanted to come to the station for medicines and other purposes.

Orv Dunkeld decided the only solution was for the missionaries to make a boat, and he proceeded to embark upon the task. He reported feeling a bit like Noah, however:

*I was laughed at very, very much as I tried to construct a boat out of the materials we had on hand, but I just kept going. I used a couple of the teak boards we had gotten from Zambia for the sides and the ends. Then I took some tongue-and-groove flooring boards we had gotten for making doors and used them to make the bottom of the boat. After putting seats in it, I painted it, caulked it, and painted it again. Then I floated it.*

*Everybody had come down to watch this crazy mission-
ary building his boat, but it worked! As it began to make
regular trips back and forth across the river, the laughing
stopped, and everyone was eager to use the missionary
boat.*

## In the Air

In 1964, Missionary Aviation Fellowship (MAF) assigned a
plane and a pilot to serve the TEAM Zimbabwe missionaries.
Stationed at Karanda, this new service offered an alternative to road
travel. Because of expense it had to be used judiciously, but the
great decrease in travel time and elimination of driving woes that it
offered were greatly appreciated.

To prepare for this new opportunity, airstrips were cleared on all
of the stations. Betty Wolfe described how her husband, John,
prepared the airstrip at Hunyani:

> *. . . He selected the longest, level area that he could find
> on the station, which happened to run between the church
> and the dispensary. Then he and the workmen went to the
> nearest mupani woods and cut and trimmed heavy logs,
> which they made into a raft-like drag.*
>
> *After clearing all the trees and bushes from his selected
> location and leveling the ground as well as possible, he then
> graded it by pulling his mupani drag behind the Land Rover
> up and down the strip repeatedly until it was quite useable.*
>
> *He named the airstrip Chikafa after the headman in
> our area and put up a windsock with this name on it. Then
> he whitewashed it so that it would be easy to identify from
> the air.*

Because of the hilly terrain, the airstrip at Mavuradonha had to
be built on a slope. MAF pilot Ted Ludlow wrote:

> *It was a "fun" airstrip. You had to land uphill and take off
> downhill. Once the plane was rolling, you were committed
> to fly as there was no way to abort a takeoff.*

One day Ted was flying a local government official into Mavuradonha. As they came in for the landing, the commissioner said, "Ted, I wouldn't fly a helicopter into this tiny strip." The TEAM missionaries were always grateful that the MAF pilots were well trained to handle such adverse conditions.

Once Dave Voetmann flew Dr. Dave Drake and one of the nurses to Hunyani for a clinic visit. Upon landing, he discovered that a thorn had pierced and flattened one of the tires on his Cessna 172.

He wrote:

*For some reason I did not have the customary spare tube along, posing a major dilemma of what to do in order to get back the 130 miles to Karanda before nightfall with only one good tire. Praise the Lord for those faithful White Cross missionary society ladies who so methodically tore old bed sheets into endless yards of roller bandages and sent them out to needy missionaries. If they only knew the many ways in which we used them!*

*The supply of roller bandages at the Hunyani clinic saved the day. I removed the flat tire, unbolted the split hub, cleaned out the shredded tube, and stuffed that "baby" as full of tightly rolled bandages as possible. Then, with Dave Drake sitting on the hubs, we bolted everything back together and mounted the tire on the plane. It really didn't look too bad. The right wing was only a bit low as we rolled down the Hunyani runway with the ailerons cranked all the way to the left to get that tire off the ground as soon as possible.*

*The flight home was smooth as silk without a single bump or complaint out of that bandage-stuffed tire. However, we left a trail of roller bandages down half the length of the Karanda runway as we touched down as gingerly as possible and brought the plane to a safe stop. A huge thanks to those White Cross ladies and their prayers as they laboriously tear up sheets!*

# Medical Adaptations

In the medical field the adaptations that God helped the missionaries make were often life-saving. Whether at the station clinics or the hospital, the medical staff continually had to call upon God for help and do the best they could in improvising for equipment or supplies they lacked. Again and again God gave them the resourcefulness they needed and blessed their work in the most inadequate of situations.

## At Clinics

Thelma Everswick told of a time when an unconventional means enabled her to resolve a woman's pain at Rukomechi:

> *One day an elderly woman came and sat at our doorstep early in the morning. She had two molars that needed extraction and was miserable. I gave her aspirin for the pain and explained that I had no dental pliers, so I was unable to help her further.*
>
> *She never left our doorstep all day. Finally, Norman asked me, "What is that lady still waiting for?"*
>
> *When I explained my lack of proper dental pliers, he quickly offered, "I'll get the pliers in the truck."*
>
> *I was horrified and quite reluctant to use such a large and unsanitary tool in her mouth. Nevertheless, with Norman's encouragement and the Lord's help, I was able to use those mechanic's pliers to pull the two molars. The woman was so happy and I was very thankful to the Lord! We then shared the Gospel with her before she returned to her village.*

At Kapfundi a baby was born with severely deformed legs that were bent back over her head. Dottie Larsen felt that the baby could not survive in the village without straight legs. With no x-rays or orthopedic surgeon available, she decided to do what she could. After explaining the situation to one of the men on the station, he made a flat, body-shaped splint to which the baby could be strapped, keeping her legs in a normal position.

By six months the baby was sitting up with straight legs! Dottie testified:

*Praying with the mother and showing her I cared and that God loved her and her baby gave me the opportunity to lead her to Christ. The results achieved with this baby also made a big impression on the local people, which was very helpful in my gaining their trust and willingness to listen to the Gospel message at the clinic.*

On another occasion Dottie improvised to help save the life of a two pound, premature baby. Lacking an incubator, she put the baby in a cardboard box with hot water bottles positioned around it on the outside. "By the grace of God the baby survived," Dottie reported.

God also helped Lorraine Waite develop a system for keeping premature babies alive at the Kapfundi clinic that yielded a better success rate than that of any hospital around. She described her procedure:

*When I arrived at Kapfundi, I found a home-made incubator that had been made by one of my predecessors. It was a blue painted box the size of an orange crate. About a third of the way up from the bottom, ropes were suspended and stapled to the sides to support a folded blanket or thin, make-shift mattress on which the baby was laid. Hot water bottles were put in the space beneath the ropes. A thin sheet was laid over the top of the incubator to let air in.*

*We had a special hut that was designated for premie babies, and only the nursing staff, the mother, and one grandmother were allowed in it. The mother and grandmother would stay with the baby constantly. The grandmother was included so that the mother didn't have to be on 24-hour duty with the baby. If visitors came, either the mother or grandmother could go out and inform them of the baby's status.*

*I taught the mother and grandmother proper handwashing and the importance of keeping germs away from the baby. I also gave them an alarm clock and taught them how to set it to go off every two or three hours so they could feed the baby.*

*For feeding, the mother would use pumped breast milk. I put an NG tube through the baby's nose into its stomach. Then I gave the mother a syringe without the plunger, which could be attached to the NG tube and serve as a measuring funnel so the mother could give the baby the proper amount of milk. At first the milk was diluted with sterile water but eventually it was given straight. They began by feeding the baby every two hours and then, as the baby progressed, every three hours. The mother, grandmother, and baby would stay in this special hut until the baby was a little over five pounds.*

*I also taught the mothers how to take care of their babies when they went home. I believe the careful teaching of the mothers was responsible for the good results that were usually achieved.*

The clinic nurses were greatly encouraged when MAF service began. Not only could they call for the plane to take critical cases to the hospital, but they could also look forward to monthly visits by a doctor. Usually a doctor, accompanied by one of the missionary nurses from Karanda and a student nurse, was flown to one of the outlying clinics every Saturday. The nurse there would have all of her difficult cases waiting for the doctor to see. At times he even did surgery at the clinic.

As the MAF pilot waited through the day, he willingly lent a hand wherever needed. Dave Voetmann described one of those days:

*I can remember being on a clinic trip to Kapfundi with Dr. Roland Stephens when he operated on a woman out in a village. We tacked a sheet to the rafter poles in a grass-roofed hut to keep the spiders and dirt from falling on the patient, who was lying on a crude table. Then by the light of a kerosene lantern and a flashlight held by myself, Dr. Stephens removed cataracts from the woman's eyes.*

Dave's successor, Ted Ludlow, also gave his impression of a surgery he watched:

> *I remember Dr. Roland Stevens doing what I considered a very complex surgery (I think it was an amputation) on a trip to the Valley. He had no real help, no blood supplies, minimal equipment, and did it all on a bare wooden table under a thatched roof. Amazingly, the next clinic trip found the patient thriving.*

## At the Hospital

Extensive medical adaptations also had to be made at the hospital. The first one, built at Chironga in 1959, was extremely primitive by all standards of comparison.

Phil and Barb Christiansen described the surgical "suite":

> *The building was grass-roofed and, as such, housed a large variety of insect and small animal life. In order to keep these little intruders from dropping into the surgical field during a procedure, a whitewashed burlap "ceiling" was suspended from the pole rafters and tacked to the walls. IV's were also hung from the pole rafters using roller bandages. A goose-necked lamp was used for lighting.*
>
> *A major job on hot days was to mop Dr. Wall's forehead to keep perspiration from dripping into the incision site. Lorraine Waite would also go around swatting flies so they wouldn't get into the "operating room."*
>
> *Through the Lord's grace and the excellent care of the nurses, post-op infections, even in this very primitive setting, were amazingly few and far between. God's hand was definitely evident.*

For Dr. Wall, this was a time of practicing "make do" medicine. With virtually no money to buy new instruments and equipment, the medical staff had to do its best with the limited "cast offs" donated by US doctors.

Phil, who arrived in Zimbabwe in 1959 to serve as the medical technologist at the hospital, became especially resourceful in constructing needed hospital equipment out of materials at hand. In order to do bacteriology studies, an incubator that could hold cultures at a constant 37 degrees Celsius was needed. If it could also provide a lowered oxygen environment, it would be even better. Phil was able to devise such an incubator. He described what he did:

*I made a small incubator consisting of a two cubic foot, double-walled box with a door in front. The bottom of the case was open to accommodate a flat porcelain pan with sand in it, which served as a heat diffuser. Below the pan was a small propane micro-burner, which was adjusted higher or lower to regulate the temperature in the box. This arrangement produced a reduced oxygen level in the box and was perfect for growing organisms. It was used with very good results for nearly two decades.*

It also provided a 37 degree environment for cross-matching blood, testing for venereal disease, and performing other chemical analyses of the blood.

In order to have electrical power to run his lab equipment during the day, Phil used the generator power that provided lights for the hospital during the overnight hours to charge a 12-volt car battery. This then provided power during the day to run his microscope lamp and a centrifuge originally made for petroleum field use. Later, through an inverter, it also powered some other small 110-volt lab equipment brought from the States. "This system was also used for years and served very well," he wrote.

Phil also told of a delightful experience in which God provided a specific need just when it was needed to enable him to perform a bacteriological procedure for which the lab was otherwise unequipped:

*We had a patient come in to the hospital with a large leg ulcer. The doctor wanted a culture of it, thinking there might be an anaerobe there. Our lab had no capabilities for providing an anaerobic environment to culture such strains of bacteria. However, I knew that back in the States I had*

223

*learned to culture anaerobes by using some Seratia bacteria on a blood plate and then sealing the edges with wax. It just so "happened" that I had noticed some red clusters of Seratia growing on another culture I had done that day. I had never seen this organism out there before. So I was able to use it and was successful in getting an anaerobic organism to grow.*

Another time a patient came to the hospital having been severely beaten by his wife after he had threatened to harm their child in a drunken rage. Both of his arms and legs were broken. He needed a fracture frame bed that would allow his limbs to be held in traction until they healed.

Phil quickly went to work to construct what was needed. He wrote:

*One of the materials that was used extensively in making desks and tables in the early days in Zimbabwe was Dexion. This was painted, perforated angle iron of a not-too-heavy gauge that could be bolted together much like an erector set. I used this to make a frame for his bed and then attached pulleys to the top of the frame. Weights on ropes suspended over the pulleys were used to provide the desired traction on his limbs.*

Wilma Gardziella Riddell added:

*A graduated set of weights was made by putting various amounts of cement into cans. While the cement was still wet, a hook was partially submerged in the top for attaching the weight to the pulley rope. Sometimes multiple weights were put on one rope for a large person!*

As this particular patient rested in the men's ward for several months, he heard the Gospel daily and eventually accepted Christ as his Savior. This is what made the medical work with all of its challenges so worthwhile.

Phil also helped make somewhat up-graded incubators for

premature babies. These usually consisted of two wooden boxes, one placed inside the other. The needed temperature was maintained in the inner box by light bulbs or hot water bottles placed under it. Oxygen and moist air were piped in through tubes, and a peep hole was made in the top of the outer box and covered with celluloid. Later, George Smazik added a chicken house thermostat to regulate the temperature.

Dr. Dave Drake also devised some needed medical equipment at the hospital, including cool mist machines, which were used to save many young lives. Measles was a prevalent disease in Zimbabwe, which often led to death in malnourished children. Often the disease had progressed into serious laryngeal-tracheal-bronchitis or pneumonia before the children were brought for treatment.

Dave described the cool mist machines he made to help these children recover:

*For the first ones I made, the mist was created by a large droplet hitting a spinning propeller. I made the unit portable with a battery and a converter so that it could be used even if the generator was not operating. Later, I was able to get a proper cool steam generator and this was much more efficient.*

When using the cool mist machine, a plastic tent was draped over the child's crib to contain the mist. It helped to make breathing easier for those with respiratory conditions.

Dr. Dave Drake also made a special "cryo unit" out of an old disposable syringe to remove cataracts. He wrote:

*I saw this being used in India and brought the idea to Karanda. The device was a sterile, disposable syringe with a fat, soft copper wire extending out the bottom about 1/8 inch.*

*After making the incision through the cornea, I would hold the large end of the syringe for the nurse to squirt some ethyl chloride into it to freeze the wire inside the barrel. Then, as I touched the lens with this exposed end of the fat wire, it would freeze onto the lens and stick. I would then carefully work it out of the eye.*

*We used this instrument for years by cold sterilizing it between patients. Later, it became available commercially as a disposable unit.*

Dave was also grateful for the "home-brewed" silver sulfadiazine cream that Rick Froese, the pharmacist, made for use on burn victims of all ages. This helped to reduce mortality considerably.

When Wilma Gardziella's parents came to Karanda as associate missionaries during the war for independence, her father, Walter, made wooden peg legs out of old broomsticks for the many amputees resulting from land mine explosions. Dr. Dave Drake said, "When we did an amputation, we put these peg legs on immediately in surgery."

Over time, equipment gradually improved at the hospital. This usually occurred as hospitals in the States updated and donated their "old versions" to Karanda. Su Bowler Everswick gave her impression of the hospital in the 1980s when it had reopened after the war:

*We only had two incubators, which were glass and warm but very rudimentary. We had many premies, especially during malaria season. The moment another was born and needed an incubator, the baby who had been in one the longest had to go out to Mom.*

*I remember that in the year I was there, we only lost one premie. This amazed me with so little technology! These babies were fed breast milk from Mom through an NG tube and had a scalp IV. Oxygen came in via a funnel in the corner of the incubator. There were no monitors of any kind! Most of these babies were well under five pounds and did incredibly well!*

Su was also impressed with the low post-op infection rate at the hospital. She said it was the lowest she had ever observed, and she credited it to the good post-op cleaning of the operating rooms.

In 2004, Dr. Dan Stephens wrote that the hospital had standard incubators by this time. However, the medical staff still used the sun, rather than UV lights, to decrease elevated bilirubin levels in newborns, when needed, as well as to dry up skin grafts on other patients.

Kiersten Hutchinson told how they use a bicycle pump, when needed, to pump up the thigh cuff that reduces blood flow to the leg for surgery. They also recycle IV bags as urine bags and use old magazines to sterilize and reuse "disposable" gloves.

Wilma Gardziella Riddell explained that recyled gloves were usually used only for non-surgical purposes. The magazines made them much easier to sterilize and use than if they had to be individually wrapped. She described the procedure:

*After being washed, tested for holes, and powdered, the gloves are put between the pages of a magazine, which is then wrapped and sterilized. When a glove is needed, the magazine is unwrapped, and the first page of the magazine opened to expose a sterile glove. As additional gloves are needed through the day, further pages are turned. These gloves are usually all right hand gloves. If a left hand glove is also needed, a right hand glove is turned inside out and used for the left hand.*

Dr. Roland Stephens, still practicing medicine at Karanda Hospital in his retirement years, told of how the Lord supplied a flexible bronchoscope for the hospital and how he adapted it to save a young child's life:

*The hospital's old flexible bronchoscope finally wore out a few years ago. In May 2004, while in the States, I was able to purchase a replacement for $100 at International Aid. (A new scope of this nature normally runs between $6,000-8,000.) I sent it to MedServe in Maryland, and they refurbished it at no charge. Then my son Brian brought it to Karanda in August when he came with a short-term missions group from the Blue Ridge Bible Church in Round Hill, VA.*

*We have been able to use the scope several times already. Yesterday a five-year-old came in with symptoms of a foreign body lodged in his trachea. I used the scope and visualized the foreign body, a large seed, which was occluding the right main stem bronchus.*

*The problem I was faced with was how to get it out. I tried a tiny catheter with a balloon on its end, but the balloon broke. Finally, I used a stone basket made for going through a cystoscope to remove stones out of ureters. The wire basket slipped easily through the bronchoscope and enclosed the seed, enabling us to pull it out of the bronchus, literally saving the child's life. The Lord does provide.*

Dr. Dan Stephens, Roland's son, indicated that he had adapted to the absence of modern technology at Karanda Hospital and really did not feel deprived in his practice of medicine. "We simply use our hands and brains to diagnose instead of lab tests and machines," he explained.

## Roller Bandages

One thing that has remained constant at Karanda is the dependence upon roller bandages made by faithful ladies' missionary societies throughout the United States and Canada. These ladies collect used sheets and cut them into strips two to four inches wide. Then they sew the strips together to make a long strip that is rolled up in spool fashion. From the beginning of the medical work in Zimbabwe, these bandages have been invaluable, not only in their primary purpose of bandaging wounds but also for the many other adaptive uses they have served over the years.

Myrtle Finsaas described how she used them to bandage tropical ulcers and other wounds in schoolchildren at Kapfundi:

*During the rainy season, especially, the students had lots of tropical ulcers as well as ax cuts and other sores that needed to be treated. At recess every day at least a dozen of them would come to the clinic. I had them line up and put their affected arm or leg on a long bench. Then I came along to apply medicine and wrap their wounds with roller bandage I had received from the States.*

*The children liked the nice clean bandage and came back to be treated often. It took a lot of bandages, and we were so*

*thankful for those faithful women who wanted to have a part
in our missionary work and supplied them for us.*

"When the bandages were made from colored, striped, or flowered sheets," Wilma added, "they were worn with even more pride by the recipient!"

Wilma also wrote of their use in the nursing school at Karanda:

*Unlike ace bandages, roller bandages have no give to them.
Therefore, we had to teach the students how to wrap fingers,
limbs, and heads in such a way that the bandage conformed
to the shape of the body part being wrapped and couldn't
fall off. We used lots of roller bandages in our First Aid
classes, especially when teaching the "reverse spiral" and
"cappaline."*

Dr. Dave Drake shared about a time when he and Judy Gudeman were blessed not only by the availability of the bandages themselves but by something special tucked inside one of the rolls:

*Judy and I had had a long day working together in the oper-
ating room, and both of us were really exhausted. We were
finishing up a burn case at the end of day, and Judy handed
a neatly rolled bandage to me. As I started unrolling it onto
the child's leg, a piece of paper dropped out of it. Judy
picked it up and read it: "Our God shall supply all your
needs according to His riches in glory by Christ Jesus." We
looked at each other, and with tears in our eyes we stopped
and gave thanks to God for giving us the grace and strength
to carry on in spite of our exhaustion.*

In addition to being used as bandages, these handy rolled strips of cotton cloth were used to make slings, to tie sterilization packs, to hang IV's, to provide traction, and to wipe off thermometers on the wards and pipettes in the lab.

Dottie Larsen used roller bandages, along with large soft sponges she also received from her home church in the States, to make shoes for an elderly woman with leprosy. She had difficulty walking because of her missing toes, and these soft, hand-crafted shoes enabled her to walk to the clinic for treatment.

How faithful God was in providing the resourcefulness that enabled the missionaries to adapt to so many situations in which they lacked the resources to which they had been accustomed in their homelands! Their resilient attitudes that were so willing to "make do" with what was available, no matter what the need, were a rich testimony to His all-sufficient grace.

## Ministry Adaptations

Adaptations had to be made in the area of ministry as well. Churches in the rural areas were often started under a shady tree with people sitting on logs, cement blocks, or just on the ground. The next step was usually a shelter constructed with poles and a thatched roof. Eventually churches were built with mud bricks or burned bricks. Backless pews were made with a brick foundation topped off with a smooth cement surface.

Baptisms were held in rivers and streams. Because of the concern for parasites, Chuck and Verna Knapp added copper sulfate to a spring-fed pond before using it for a baptism. Later, as ministries developed in urban centers, swimming pools were used.

Having the proper elements for communion was also a challenge in the early years, with any available kind of juice and bread or crackers being used. Most commonly raisins were boiled and the water used for the juice.

Dottie Larsen wrote of her first village communion service in the early 1960s:

> *Wilfred Strom and I were going out that Sunday, and I was to prepare the bread and juice. Usually the missionaries boiled up raisins to use for juice. However, I did not have any raisins; neither did anyone else on the station; nor were there any corner stores.*
>
> *However, on the Friday before the service I received a package from home, and in it was one of the new "fizzies" that were popular in the States at the time. By God's provi-*

*dence the flavor was grape. You guessed it! I prepared it in a covered Tupperware glass and served it along with crackers.*

Diane Powell Hawkins remembers using kool-aid for communion at the Karanda church in the 1970s. After the war, grape juice was difficult to obtain even in urban areas. Chris and Joyce Goppert recalled one of the ladies at Chisipiti Baptist Church using Fortris concentrate, a syrup from which children's drinks were made.

Missionaries had to be adaptive in creating visual aids to use in ministry as well. Marg Jackson recalled using the Wordless Book a lot, which was also helpful for the early evangelists, who often didn't know how to read. Chuck and Verna Knapp made their own flannelgraph materials.

Dick McCloy described his efforts to duplicate the limited visual aids available for teaching Scripture classes in the public schools so they could be used by more teachers:

*While we were in Mabelreign from 1975 until 1980, we were anxious to take advantage of the opportunities we had for teaching Scripture in the schools. I even asked another young man to help me. He was willing, but since he had never done anything like this, I took it upon myself to supply a lesson with pictures for him.*

*I had been using "Footsteps of Faith" flannelgraph figures stuck to sheets of colored paper. By motorcycling across the city, I could have a duplicate made on that now obsolete, shiny photo copy paper. This worked so well that I began supplying four or five new teachers I recruited with these materials.*

*I soon discovered, however, that many of the Scripture teachers from other churches had no visual aids at all, and I wondered how I might be able to help them too. About that time I had a friend, Rob Wilkins, who was in charge of printing at the YMCA. When I explained my desire to have coloring book-style pictures to teach the Scripture classes, he became excited and showed me how we could do it. By drawing or tracing our pictures on a paper master, we could print 50 copies at a time. These teaching aids were so popu-*

*lar that we soon began printing 100 at a time and then 200.*
    *Later, when Rob's assistance was no longer available,
we tried another method. Joyce Goppert would look at our
flannelgraph layout and draw the pictures on purple ditto
masters. They were messy but easy to work with and had
such an intoxicating smell to them!*

While in language school at Chironga, Diane Powell made a
hand puppet, complete with several changes of clothes, from left-
over scraps of material she had. She named the puppet Uyai (Shona
for "come") and carried him in a small cosmetic suitcase. Then at
after-school programs she and Bonnie Lanegan presented on the
station, she would use him to invite the schoolchildren to come to
Sunday school and other youth activities. Uyai was also a "special
attraction" at the area youth rallies she organized.

Diane's pastor, Forrest Williams from Calvary Memorial
Church in Racine, Wisconsin, inspired her to begin a Bible camp
for the children in the Karanda area as a "sister camp" to her home
church's Camp Life. This was held each year Diane was on the field
and continued afterwards under the leadership of Lorraine Waite
until missionaries had to leave the area during the war.

Many adaptations were necessary in putting together a Bible
camp in the bush. Diane was grateful to have the help of local workmen to build grass-walled sleeping shelters and latrines. Camp was
always held during the dry season, so roofs were unnecessary.

A cook was hired to set up an outdoor kitchen. One or more
goats, along with vegetables and milk, were purchased from local
villagers. Beans, bread, margarine, oil, tea, and Cokes, for a special
treat, were purchased in town. The children each brought a large
bucket of corn to be ground into corn meal for *sadza*, the staple
food of the Shona diet. A home-made gong was set up to summon
the campers for meals and other activities. Meals were generally
eaten outside and meetings held in a nearby church building.

For recreation simple American games, such as "Drop the
Hanky," "Steal the Bacon," and "Dodge Ball" were great hits with
the campers along with their more traditional net ball and soccer.
Diane also constructed a home-made "pin-the-tail-on-the-donkey"
game and a cardboard replica of a leaping frog game she had

observed on a cruise. Walter and Wilma Gardziella were recruited to make a bean bag game that provided lots of fun as well.

Perhaps the most creative event Diane designed was an obstacle course, using empty barrels, a ladder, a hose, and other common items she could find around the mission station. The campers thoroughly enjoyed being timed as they raced through the various requirements of the course. For a craft project one year the campers made papier-mâché animals.

In addition to their recreational activities, the campers also attended Bible classes, Christian living discussion groups, and heard stirring messages given by local pastors at the evening services. Many received Christ as Savior or rededicated their lives to the Lord. Several of the young men went on to Bible school and into the ministry. For Diane, the reward of listening to the testimonies given at the last campfire made all the planning and improvising well worth the effort.

## CHAPTER 6

# God Gave Grace to Persevere

*"Let us run with perseverance*
*the race marked out for us."*
(Hebrews 12:1c)

God never promised that working in His harvest field would be easy or without opposition by Satan, but He did promise to accompany those who answered His call every step of the way (Matthew 28:20). He would also provide the grace they needed to persevere through whatever challenges they faced (2 Corinthians 12:9-10).

Again and again the Zimbabwe missionaries drank deeply of this grace as adversities of many kinds befell them, sometimes even before they reached the field. At times they wondered if they could continue. In most cases, however, the constraining love of God in their hearts made them unwilling to turn back if God's will was for them to persevere. They did not take their calling lightly.

The grim circumstances they faced and surmounted through God's grace strengthened their faith for battles yet to come. As God gave them the inner fortitude to persevere through these difficult times, His dynamic presence in their lives became all the more real. Their perseverance also dealt a resounding blow of defeat to Satan's efforts to stop them.

# The Early Pioneers

Learning how to survive in a totally unfamiliar environment was not easy for the Danielsons and Dunkelds as they embarked upon their new lives on the Msengedzi mission station. Helen Dunkeld described some of their discouragements:

*The first year down in the Valley was really difficult. We were so green. We took potatoes and many other food supplies with us, but we had only built a house for the Danielsons and a temporary shelter for ourselves and had no storeroom. The rains caught us unexpectedly early. They don't usually start until the middle of November, but that year they began in October. We put a tarp over the potatoes, but it didn't keep the dampness out, and they all rotted in the first month.*

*Our flour got so wormy that if you took a handful of it, you could feel it wiggling. No one had told us about putting carbon disulphide in our flour drums. Instead, we hired a woman to come and sift all of our flour once a week to get at least the big intruders out. The little ones went right through the sieve.*

*At that time we were also trying to make our own yeast. We either didn't have the procedure down, or the climate was too hot because it didn't work very well. Our bread would only rise a little bit and came out looking gray. So our bread was kind of solid, grayish in color, and not too appetizing, but it was full of protein and we thanked God for it.*

While these fledgling missionaries could blame their own ignorance for these initial disappointments with their food supply, greater crises lay ahead that were totally out of their control. In a manner reminiscent of Satan's assault on Job, they would hardly recover from one blow before being hit by another.

To help supply fresh milk for their children, the two couples got a number of goats. They would each give up to a cup of milk a day during certain seasons. In some seasons they were completely dry.

Then one morning the goat herder rushed over to tell them that the goats were all dead! Desperately hoping it wasn't true, they ran to the goat house, only to find its floor covered with dead goats. A leopard had broken in through the grass roof and, with a single bite on the throat or back of the neck of each goat, had decimated their flock, leaving only two babies.

The missionaries also tried hard to raise a garden to get some fresh vegetables. Lacking any farm experience, they had one difficulty after another. Helen reported:

> *We had planted the garden where the local people had told us was a good place, only to have the river come up and flood it when the rains started. Most of our first planting was rotted out. A few things survived, but the second time it flooded, everything was lost.*
>
> *The third time the river came up so high that we stood outside in the night to watch it, wondering if we were going to have to leave our house, and we had built it on a high spot. Never since have we ever seen the rains so heavy or the river so high as it was that first year.*

In a letter dated April 1, 1943, Rudy and Mary Danielson wrote:

> *This year we have had a record rainfall here in the Valley . . . . We had quite a surprise one morning to see a huge lake just below our house. The heavy rains had brought such a volume of water down from the mountains and from the various smaller streams which drain into the Msengedzi that the banks could not contain it all. It came higher and higher till we wondered if even our houses were safe, although they are on quite a rise. We were surrounded on three sides. Our gardens, which had been threatened by two previous floods, now were under ten to fifteen feet of water. We were just about to reap the results of many months of waiting for vegetables when everything was wiped out. Now that it has dried out a bit, we are busy getting another garden started.*

What resilience! Seemingly undaunted, they just turned around and started all over again! Certainly God was providing His grace to enable these couples to persevere through yet another blow to their food supply. Their unshaken faith in His presence, though shaken, was evident as Mary wrote, "But God had not forgotten us. The people brought us tomatoes, green mealies [corn], squash, and rice."

They recognized the hand of the enemy working against them, however. "Satan had tried our little missionary band in every possible way that first year in the Valley," Mary wrote. Undoubtedly, he wanted to destroy this brave young group of missionaries who were invading a region of the world he had held tightly in his grasp for many generations with virtually no challenge.

Satan's next attack came in the form of illness. As the rainy season arrived and the Msengedzi River rose, blocking their only exit from the Valley, Rudy, Helen, and one of the children all came down with malaria. Rudy was hit the hardest, and as the others watched him suffer week after week, they seriously wondered how much longer his tired body could hold on.

They had sent word up to Peter Lind at Mavuradonha that Rudy was seriously ill and they needed to get him out of the Valley. Apparently they also told him of the other trials they had endured, as Peter responded by sending some chickens and other food supplies back with the messenger. Then he began working on the road from his end, trying to make it passable for them.

The missionaries were overjoyed to receive the food and hear that Peter was working on the road. Helen reported, "That night we had the best meal we had had in a long time."

Finally in early April, after Rudy had suffered for six long weeks, they were able to get him across the river and up to the Mavuradonha station with its higher elevation and healthier climate. With adequate medical care and rest, Rudy recovered and gradually regained his strength. The two couples were then able to take a holiday trip and replenish their supplies in Harare.

As June came with its cooler temperatures, they returned once again to Msengedzi. Their trials were not over, however. When the hot, humid weather arrived in October, Rudy again became ill. They thought he was having another bout with malaria, but he didn't respond to quinine, the normal treatment for malaria. Instead, his fever continued to climb higher each day.

When it stayed at 104° for a whole day, the others decided they had to get him to the nearest hospital, which was 160 miles away in Bindura. It was October 23rd, and the rains had not yet started, so they were still able to get out of the Valley.

They left that very evening, feeling that the somewhat cooler night air would be more tolerable for Rudy. When they reached Mavuradonha, Helen and the boys remained there while Peter Lind and Orv drove Rudy, Mary, and Muriel on to Bindura.

When they arrived at the hospital, the staff initially agreed with their diagnosis of malaria, although one of the nurses suspected that Rudy might possibly have typhoid fever. Two days later another doctor came out from Harare to fill in for the Bindura doctor, who was sick. This man agreed with the nurse and changed Rudy's diagnosis to typhoid fever.

Although no treatment was available, Rudy seemingly began to improve. Mary was even considering returning to Msengedzi to start packing their things so they could leave for furlough as soon as Rudy was able to travel.

The doctor encouraged her to wait, however, because of the possibility of a relapse. As it turned out, Rudy's ordeal was far from over. Mary continued to stay at his side, watching and praying as wave after wave of the disease slowly sapped the strength from his body.

Two men from Bindura drove out to Msengedzi to tell the Dunkelds of the seriousness of Rudy's condition. When the car drove into the station, Orv and Helen at first thought the Danielsons were returning, as they were still under the impression that Rudy just had a bad case of malaria.

Upon learning the new diagnosis, Helen returned with the men immediately. Orv and the boys came a few days later after closing up the station. The days that followed were grim. Helen sat with Rudy through the night and Mary during the day. Despite their discouragement, the doctor never gave up hope.

Then, on November 21st Rudy's bowel perforated and he began hemorrhaging. An urgent call went out for blood donors, and a surgeon drove out from Harare to operate on him. Rudy never regained consciousness, however, and on November 25th, Thanksgiving Day 1943, this brave pioneer met His Savior in glory.

Mary wrote:

*Much prayer was made on his behalf both here and over-seas with groups in [Harare] praying as well, but his work was finished. He had been so keen to see the work opened up across the Valley, and we were planning after our furlough to open work on the Hunyani [River]. This has now been left to others, but how wonderful that God makes no mistakes, and when He calls one home, He sends others to take his place.*

Mary's words once again reflected the grace that God was pouring out to her at this time of heartbreaking loss. Just as she stated so strongly by faith, God did send others to take Rudy's place. Following his death, Irl McAllister of the South African field wrote a pamphlet entitled "Rudy So Loved." This tract about Rudy's untimely death concluded with the challenge, "Who will take Rudy's place?"

Several years later Russ and Marg Jackson felt God was leading them into missionary service with TEAM. When Russ picked up and read this tract at a missions conference, its message pierced his heart, and he felt for sure that God wanted him and Marg to apply for missionary service in Zimbabwe—to take Rudy's place.

A funeral service was held for Rudy in Bindura and he was laid to rest in the cemetery there. The remaining three grief-stricken missionaries then returned to Msengedzi so Mary could pack up her things to go on furlough. Helen Dunkeld shared their feelings:

*We found Rudy's death very difficult to take. We wondered what God had in store for us now. Rudy was the one who knew the most about building and was quickest with the language. If we had chosen ourselves, we would have said that he was the one who was most necessary. Yet for some reason God chose to leave us and take Rudy.*

The local people were also stunned and deeply sobered upon hearing the news of Rudy's death. That Sunday, as the group held their usual church service, several responded to the message of salvation that these missionaries had come to share with them, risking their very lives in a climate that had harshly claimed one of them. Once again, God revealed to this persevering little group that He had not deserted them as He began to reap a harvest from the costly seed that had been sown.

One of the converts that Sunday was a young man named Shikiravau Chasaya, known at that time as "Scaval." This young man had been the Danielsons' gardener and had frequently gone up the escarpment to get the station's mail bag. Before his salvation he frequently came to work drunk, but God had His hand on this man, turned his life around, and used him as a dedicated evangelist and hospital chaplain for nearly 60 years.

The Zimbabwe missionaries were still under South Africa's Field Council at the time of Rudy's death. Being concerned that typhoid might still be in the area, they sent word to the Dunkelds that they should not stay at Msengedzi but go up to Mavuradonha for the duration of the rainy season. With heavy hearts and bereft of their only co-workers, they obeyed. Satan's latest blow had hit hard, but they were not ready to give up.

Unfortunately, this was not the last time that serious illness, and even death, would strike the missionaries as they continued their efforts to bring the Gospel to the Zambezi Valley. Each time, however, God continued to give them the grace to persevere and remain true to their calling.

The Dunkelds were not alone for long. In April 1944, as the rainy season ended, they happily welcomed Eunice Ott as a new missionary to help them in the work at Msengedzi. Over the next four years Norman and Thelma Everswick, Orla and Marguerite Blair, Russ and Marg Jackson, and Lillian Nelson also arrived, and Mary Danielson returned as well. With its growing missionary force, Zimbabwe was established as a separate field from South Africa in 1947.

The arrival of these new recruits provided the opportunity to expand into new areas in spreading the Gospel. By 1948, progress was being made toward opening new mission stations at Rukomechi and Hunyani, also located on the Mozambique border, when illness struck again. Satan was seemingly not going to allow this further invasion into his territory to occur without opposition.

One after another, six of the adults came down with hepatitis. Thelma Everswick became so sick that she had to be taken to the hospital in Harare.

Seven-year-old Dick Dunkeld also became severely ill, and everyone assumed that he too had hepatitis. Because he was so sick, Helen didn't want to force the otherwise routine, but bitter, malaria prophylactic down him. She reported:

> *His fever would go way up to 106°, and I would put cold compresses on him. Then his temperature would plunge to below normal and he would go into shock. Because Orv and so many of the other adults were sick, we couldn't get him to Harare to the hospital.*
>
> *Finally, Orv began feeling a little better, and we were able to make the trip. At the hospital Dick was diagnosed with malaria, not hepatitis, and I felt so badly that I had not given him his malaria medicine. He was in the hospital for quite awhile but gradually recovered.*

Other discouragements came that year as well. A severe famine hit the area and drove many people from the Valley. The missionaries were also troubled by the frequent "beer drinks" occurring in the surrounding villages, which hindered their visitation outreach.

In spite of these trials, however, God enabled them to carry on, and by the end of 1948, both the Rukomechi and the Hunyani stations were opened. How delighted they were that the local people in these new areas were beginning to receive a Gospel witness!

Each year God continued to bring more recruits to the field. Martin Uppendahl arrived in 1950 with Winifred Roeper, Effie Byrd, Warren and Lois Bruton, Marian Wilterdink, and Betty Mason following in 1951. This enabled even further expansion. When the Zambezi Mission was having staffing difficulties and asked if TEAM could take over their stations at Mavuradonha and Rusambo, TEAM had the personnel available to do this.

With missionaries now scattered in numerous locations, including Harare, coming together for an annual conference became even more important. These were always greatly anticipated events for both their business and social opportunities.

Lillian Nelson and Les Austin decided that the annual conference to be held at Hunyani in April 1951 would be a perfect time for them to get married. This was the first wedding in the missionary family, and it was a joyous time for all.

Before the conference ended, however, their hearts were turned to sorrow as Helen Dunkeld unexpectedly gave birth to a baby boy, Leonard Willard, nearly a month early. With no medical capabilities to care for this tiny infant's special needs, the child died 10 hours later en route to Harare.

Returning to Hunyani, the grieving family was joined by their co-workers in committing him to the Lord and burying him near the church being built on the station. This was only the first of five missionary babies and two toddlers to be laid to rest on Zimbabwean soil over the next decade.

More devastation struck in 1952, when a cyclone swept through the Zambezi Valley, completely leveling the Msengedzi school and leaving the partially completed church building in ruins. Thankfully, the missionaries' houses were untouched and no one was hurt, but this was another major loss. The damaged buildings, so central to their work, would now have to be rebuilt.

Eunice Ott had been deeply invested in teaching the school children at Msengedzi to read and write and obtain at least an elementary education. This was the only way they would be able to read the Bible for themselves and the only way the missionaries could hope to develop Christian leaders who would eventually be equipped to teach others.

When Eunice returned from her first furlough in 1951, TEAM had just acquired the Mavuradonha mission station, which included a boarding school. She was assigned to teach there rather than returning to Msengedzi. She would also help Thelma Everswick in the dispensary.

When Norman Everswick started a Bible school on the station, Eunice began teaching the wives of these students as well. She loved this work, but she was also concerned about raising the standards of teaching in the mission schools, which she viewed as the "spearheads of our evangelistic work."

In order to accomplish this goal, the missionaries established a Teacher Training Institute at Chironga in 1955. Although Eunice was due for another furlough by then, she stayed on the field because of the shortage of staff and moved to Chironga to teach at the new TTI.

Completely unaware of what lay ahead, she embraced her new assignment with enthusiasm.

Then, on April 12, 1956, a leopard clawed the grass thatch off of her chicken house during the night and killed three of her chickens. The next morning as she was talking to Carol Olsen at the clinic, she heard a terrific racket in her chicken house again. Her first thought was, "The leopard is back!!"

Bravely grabbing a broom, she ran to drive it away. It wasn't a leopard, however. It was a mad dog! As soon as it saw her, it lunged at her and clamped its teeth into her right leg and wouldn't let go. Carol and the men at the clinic heard her scream and came running. As soon as they approached, Eunice yelled, "Run! It's a mad dog!"

Upon seeing Carol, the dog let go of Eunice's leg and started running towards Carol. Carol's little dog, Prince, courageously came between them, however, and the dog bit Prince instead of Carol.

The missionaries were able to find the dog's owner in a nearby village, and he immediately killed it. Later, a smear was taken from its brain and sent to the lab in Harare. The results came back positive for rabies.

Eunice was given a series of 14 rabies injections and was still taking them as the missionaries gathered for their annual field conference at Kapfundi, another new mission station. Although most people suffer a reaction from this grueling set of shots, Eunice said she felt fine except for having a cold.

On April 28, the Saturday evening of conference, the missionary family had a special dinner for Les and Lil Austin's 5th anniversary and everyone was supposed to wear their best "bib and tucker." Les later wrote to Eunice's family:

*Eunice entered in a very stylish dress, white knitted stole, and sparkling necklace. Wow! She did a graceful bow as everyone sang, "Stand up, Eunice, Stand up!!" She was the queen of the conference that night!*

Marie Schober continued the story:

*Conference closed on May 7, and after four days of shopping in [Harare], Eunice and the rest of the Chironga staff*

*left for their station on May 11 to prepare for school. The
days were busy as all of the Teacher Training students and
staff would be leaving shortly to go to Mavuradonha for the
dedication of the church built in memory of Eunice's father
[who had donated money to build it].*

Marian Wilterdink wrote:

*On Tuesday, May 15, Eunice was not feeling well, so she
went to bed quite early that evening. During the night she
became worse, and by morning she was really in pain when
Carol came to check on her. The leg that had been bitten
was hurting as well as her back and chest.*

She obviously needed to go back to the doctor, so Clarence
Cedarholm took her to Harare the next day. On the long journey
into town she cried with pain. Upon reaching the hospital, she was
treated for malaria, and released. In spite of her recent bite by a
rabid dog, her having rabies was deemed impossible because she
had had the necessary shots.

That night at the cottage on the Plot she was very restless, but
she still thought that she would be able to go to Mavuradonha on
Saturday for the dedication of the church. Wanting her to be present
if at all possible, the field council decided to change the dedication
from Saturday to Sunday.

The blood slides made at the hospital did not reveal malaria, so
that treatment was cancelled. On Friday two doctors came to see
her at the cottage. They diagnosed her with polio, called an ambulance, and sent her to the isolation hospital.

Saturday morning she was unable to swallow and had to have a
tracheotomy. A few hours later, on May 19, 1956, she too met her
Savior in glory.

An autopsy was performed, which ruled out polio. The official
cause of death was given as "an unknown virus." Several weeks
later test results showed that she had indeed had rabies, a new strain
not covered by the series of shots she had taken.

Meanwhile at Mavuradonha the church dedication began as
planned. The missionaries were delighted that even more local

people had come from the surrounding villages than they had anticipated. Stirring messages were given on Saturday morning, but no one responded to the Gospel message. In the evening Norman Everswick preached a powerful message on heaven from John 14. Still no one responded.

At midnight a messenger arrived with the sad news that Eunice had passed away that morning. After much prayer the missionaries felt led to go ahead with the dedication on Sunday as planned, but instead of naming the church after Eunice's father, they would call it the Ott Memorial Church in honor of both Eunice and her father. The two were now together in heaven.

In the morning service both the Mavuradonha and the Chironga School choirs sang. An informal message was preached on the brevity of life and the urgency to preach the Gospel. Out of the approximately 1000 people who attended, four stood to their feet to accept Christ. Many who were Christians publicly confessed sins.

That afternoon 50 believers followed the Lord though the waters of baptism, and 100 took part in the Lord's supper with the missionaries. In the evening the local people conducted their own service while the missionaries spent time in prayer.

On Monday evening Eunice's body arrived at Mavuradonha for burial. A large group of teachers and students helped to dig the grave and offered to serve as pall bearers, a thrilling response.

At the funeral service held the next day, Warren Bruton spoke in English and Norman Everswick in Shona, both emphasizing the victorious nature of Christian death. The Mavuradonha school girls, Cliff Ratzlaff, and Ken and June Munger all sang special numbers.

A government official who had known Eunice for some time made a special trip out to Mavuradonha to attend her funeral. He also gave an impromptu talk to the local people in Shona about why missionaries come—not for wealth or fame but because of the love of God.

In their letter to the family Les and Lil Austin wrote:

*From the church the entire group walked slowly up toward the mountain to a spot where two other graves are. There under the peaceful shade of a beautiful tree at the foot of the mountains, Eunice's earthly body was laid to rest. But how vividly God's assurance was and still is—that she is not in her body but is present with Jesus.*

At the graveside service both Russ Jackson and Orla Blair spoke.

The Austins continued, testifying of the effect of Eunice's life and her death:

*We do believe that her life was a living epistle that glorified God. The following Saturday a school lad who had committed a sin confessed it before the entire school group. The headman of this area, hardened for years, came voluntarily on Sunday to ask God's forgiveness and grace. We trust that this is only the beginning of a chain of spiritual awakenings and blessings.*

One of Eunice's last letters to her supporters closed with these appropriate words:

*We are not on the losing side; we are on the Lord's side and the victory is His. So we press on as victors, regardless of how things look.*

## Difficult Beginnings

Following God's call to Zimbabwe required the missionaries to take many brave steps out of their comfort zones. Even navigating the logistics of international travel for the first time was potentially intimidating, let alone confronting the huge changes in environment and lifestyle awaiting them on the field. Each one had to draw upon God's grace to persevere through the anxieties and discomforts of this "launching out" phase of their missionary service.

During this time they were particularly vulnerable to Satan's arrows of doubt, discouragement, and defeat. As he witnessed the growing number of recruits coming to wage spiritual warfare in the Zambezi Valley, he would certainly not stand idly by. Some of the extra complications experienced during this period may well have originated with him.

Whatever the source or nature of the challenges they faced, most of these new missionaries prevailed by once again drawing upon God's sufficient grace. Being assured of their call, they successfully weathered the storms of their initiation process and "graduated" into fruitful ministers of the Gospel in a country ripe for harvesting.

Orla and Marguerite Blair were prime examples of this as they persevered through a difficult beginning and went on to serve the Lord for 30 years in Zimbabwe. Marguerite wrote:

> *Trusting wholly upon our Lord and Savior, Jesus Christ, who had called us to serve Him in [Zimbabwe], we boarded a freighter, "The Marine Carp," on August 30, 1946. David was three years old and Bonnalyn seven months. World War II had just ended, and transportation to Africa was difficult to obtain.*
>
> *After two weeks we landed in Haifa, Palestine, and took a train to Cairo, Egypt. We had to stay in Cairo for a whole month before we were able to get air transport to Beira, [Mozambique]. This was by means of a sea-plane that landed on the water. It was very humble, noisy, and far from comfortable. On top of that, I became very ill with food poisoning en route.*
>
> *When we landed on an ocean bay at Beira, a doctor met the plane while we were still on the water. He examined me and prescribed some huge pills, almost the size of American quarters. I was so weak that I had to be carried in a chair to the hotel. We stayed there only one night, as a train was going to [Harare, Zimbabwe] the very next day and when there would be another one was uncertain.*
>
> *I was still feeling extremely weak when we boarded the train. A kind lady saw our predicament and offered to care for David and Bonnalyn en route. What a blessing that was!*
>
> *We arrived in [Harare] on October 21st, 1946. The cable we had sent to Norman Everswick never reached him at Msengedzi, so no one had come to meet us.*
>
> *Feeling alone in a strange place, Orla was finally able*

to contact a Dutch Reformed pastor, who took us to a nearby hotel. We were only able to get accommodations for one night, however.

The next morning Orla went to the post office to try to locate a Mr. Siebert, who they were told was a friend of the TEAM missionaries. In the meantime a woman came to clean the hotel room, so the children and I had to vacate it. With much struggle I was able to move us and our luggage to the lobby.

When Orla returned, he found us there with another lady watching the children while I was fast asleep on a couch. Mrs. Siebert, an angel from the Lord, awakened me with the words, "I'm here to take you to our home."

The Sieberts were so gracious and kind to help us in our time of great need. We stayed with them for two weeks before departing for Mavuradonha Mission Station.

At Mavuradonha the children and I stayed with Mary Danielson and her daughter, Muriel, while I regained my strength. Mary was also an angel of mercy to us. In the meantime Orla went down to Msengedzi with Norman Everswick to help prepare for our move there.

We moved just before America's Thanksgiving into the Danielsons' old home that Rudy had built before going home to meet the Lord. Eunice Ott lived next door to us, and the Everswicks were living in the Dunkelds' house at the entrance to the station.

Our trunks, crates, and fridge did not arrive for a whole year. Clinton Brown, a member of our main supporting church, the Evangelical Congregational Church in Stamford, Connecticut, had given us 24 cartons of Gerber's baby food and 24 boxes of Rinso laundry detergent. When our crates finally arrived, we discovered that the Rinso had been stolen en route. Many of the bottles of baby food and some dishes were broken. Rubber toys had melted into misshapen masses.

In all honesty, we did not have an easy beginning. We fretted and felt discouraged, but the Lord comforted us and gave us the strength to continue. We had come to do a work for

*Him. A lovely Christian lady in [Harare] told me, "For every circumstance, you have the Lord." We never forgot that.*

Marian Wilterdink also had to persevere through a difficult beginning in fulfilling God's call upon her life. For her, it began much earlier in the process. She wrote:

*Knowing that God had clearly called me to be a missionary to Africa, I asked Him to direct me in finding the right mission with which to serve. When I heard that the mission board of my own denomination was planning to meet in Grand Rapids, I went to the meeting and told the board members that God had called me to go to Africa.*

*One of their first questions was whether I was married. When I said I wasn't, they informed me that they only accepted couples and advised me to look for a husband. I replied that I felt I could devote more time to the Lord's service by being single.*

*Later, at another of their meetings, when I told them that God had called me to show the children in Africa the way to heaven, they said that I needed a degree in order to do that and should go to college and seminary. I told them that if I did that, I would be over 30 years old, which was their age limit for new recruits.*

*Hearing the board's response, my pastor told me I should accept that the door to Africa was closed. I informed him that I intended to put forth every effort to go to Africa and would apply to other mission boards.*

*Knowing my deep sense of call to Africa, a friend suggested that I apply to The Evangelical Alliance Mission. After I had graduated from Bible school and completed two years of nurses' training, they accepted me. I was so grateful and have thanked the Lord almost daily for leading me to this mission board.*

*TEAM asked me to go to Zimbabwe. I had to raise enough money to cover my transportation, supplies, and support. All of this money came in quickly, for which I thanked the Lord. I left for Zimbabwe in November 1951, without knowing anything about the country.*

Marian succeeded in overcoming the initial obstacles in her path so she could follow the call of God upon her life. Once she was in Zimbabwe, she again had to persevere in pursuing her goal of teaching the Gospel to the Shona children, which was a very specific part of God's call to her. Marian continued:

*Because of a shortage of missionaries at that time in Zimbabwe, I was assigned to many different kinds of ministries, including caring for the missionary children at the hostel, running clinics, taking patient histories and perform-ing anesthesia at the hospital, teaching Shona to new missionaries, directing the Homecraft School, serving as field secretary, playing the piano in schools and church services, beginning an AWANA program, teaching Bible classes in government schools, and caring for two tiny orphans.*

*During my fourth furlough, TEAM asked me to be princi-pal of the Homecraft School again. This time I reminded them that God had specifically asked me to present the Gospel to the children. For my first 19 years in Zimbabwe, I hadn't had the opportunity to carry out this part of God's call.*

*Instead of sending me to the Homecraft School, TEAM responded by releasing me to teach Bible classes in the government schools on a full-time basis. I was so delighted and happily did this for the next 32 years. Through most of this time I also had a group of national teachers working with me so that together we could reach even more children in more classes and more schools.*

*Before teaching each new class, I would ask the students to write down what they believed was the way to heaven. Only a few would know it. Then, each week as I taught them a lesson, I would have them memorize a new Bible verse, including John 14:6.*

*At the end of each school term I would ask how many knew they would go to heaven when they died. I was always thrilled to see so many hands go up! And their faces were radiant, indicating that they really understood. Even some of the Muslims in these classes were born again.*

*God richly blessed this ministry with approximately 100 children being saved every year in each of the five schools where I taught. During the 51 years that I served God in Africa, He gave me a constant inner peace, joy, and contentment, showing me that I was in the center of His will.*

George and Pat Dee also persevered through considerable discomforts as they began their 38-year career as missionaries in Zimbabwe. Pat wrote:

*When we arrived in New York City on November 9, 1953, to sail for Africa, we had never even seen the ocean before. We were driving a truck we had bought for use on the field, which had to be loaded onto the ship along with our other baggage.*

*The ship we traveled on was a freighter with only about 12 passengers. One of them didn't like "religious people" and noticeably avoided us while two Afrikaans ladies were quite taken with our "accents." The crew did very well in caring for us, although the captain couldn't understand why we turned down his offer of wine. The food was wonderful, but George got seasick and had to take pills for the entire 25-day voyage.*

*When we approached Cape Town, South Africa, we hit the "Cape Rollers." These are huge swells generated by the meeting of the Atlantic and Indian oceans. In the midst of this stretch of water, all of the dishes and glasses slid off the tables and many people got quite sick.*

*After disembarking in Cape Town, we took a cab to the missionary home where we were to stay for a few days. The driver really frightened us by driving fast on what we thought was the wrong side of the street.*

*When we picked up our truck from the ship, we still had a 2000-mile trip to make up to Harare, Zimbabwe. Since we had almost no money, we slept in the back of the truck. Everything we encountered was so new and different to us.*

*We found it very difficult to adjust to so much all at once and all on our own.*

*We arrived at "the Plot" in Harare in the middle of the night. Ken and June Munger, who were in charge of the children's hostel at the time, got out of their bed and graciously let us sleep in it, as we were so tired. The next day we were instructed to pitch the tent we had brought with us, as this was the only available place for us to sleep while we waited to go to language school.*

After only three months of language study at Msengedzi, George and Pat were sent to the Hunyani station, once again on their own. They continued:

*This was a very difficult time for us. It took awhile even to be able to communicate with the people. Nobody knew English, and hardly anyone could read and write as they had no school. White people were foreign to them. We also didn't know much about their culture, which was very primitive with a lot of superstition and demon-possession.*

God's grace enabled George and Pat to persevere through these initial challenges to become excellent Shona speakers and church planters.

Donna Hendrickson also suffered from seasickness as she and Carl sailed to Africa, with other difficulties confronting her after they arrived. She wrote:

*Carl and I both grew up in the city of Los Angeles. We arrived in Zimbabwe in September 1954 with our daughters, two-year-old Janet and one-year-old Nancy. I was also pregnant with our third daughter, Julie. While we had sort of imagined what living in Africa would be like, we could not possibly have been prepared for the mammoth lifestyle changes that we encountered.*

*During language study we lived in a small, condemned, two-room storage building on "the Plot" in Harare. It had no bathroom or running water, which was quite inconve-*

*nient with a baby in cloth diapers. We had to share a bathroom with the many families who came to town for supplies and stayed in the guest cottage. They, in turn, shared our refrigerator for their milk and ice cream.*

*Our single bedroom was only about 12' by 12.' In it was squeezed a double bed for Carl and myself, a screened-in crib for Nancy, and a cot for Janet. The walls were lined with boxes, which contained all our earthly goods. Each week the boxes had to be removed, and the walls and floor cleared of termite tunnels.*

*In November we were sent to Chironga for several weeks so that Carl could help Russ Jackson and Merle Bloom put up the first building on that new station. Shortly after returning, although we had faithfully taken our malaria prophylactic since we arrived in September, I came down with a raging case of malaria, followed by Carl and Jan. While in bed with malaria, I was unable to move the boxes lining our bedroom with the result that the clothes and fabric inside came out with huge holes and ragged edges where the termites had had their meals!!*

*Then Nancy, still in cloth diapers, came down with a severe case of diarrhea. So here I was in language school, five months pregnant, doing all my own cooking and cleaning, and now running back and forth to the guest cottage numerous times during the day and night to rinse out diapers!*

*It was a rough beginning, but we felt the hand of God on our lives. This was where He called us. He put a pioneering spirit within us and we would persevere! We actually grew through the many challenges we faced.*

Don Hoyt was also unprepared for the drastic change in lifestyle that confronted him as he and Lynn arrived at Msengedzi in 1960 for language studies. He candidly revealed his intense inner struggle from that traumatic period of his missionary career:

*First of all, I felt quite isolated way out in the bush with my family, which at that time included two young children with a third on the way. This was in spite of having the*

*Sherwoods, Clemengers, Christiansens, Dunkelds, and Shirley Bradford on the station with us.*

*The news on the radio from Harare was also filled with political tension. Hearing about riots and destruction occurring in the townships and the streets being patrolled by the military was quite unsettling to me. This was the beginning of political unrest in the country, although I realized later that the severity of the problem at that time was greatly exaggerated in my mind.*

*Creating equal anxiety for me was the weekly language assignment to ride my bike to outlying villages where I was to engage in very rudimentary Shona conversations. Helen Dunkeld would give each student a specific set of questions to ask. The nights before these excursions I would literally lie in bed sweating, knowing I had to do this in the morning.*

*The sights, sounds, smells, and culture of village life were so drastically different. I did not like that environment at all and had a difficult time being thrown into it "cold turkey." I seriously entertained the thought that I was perhaps not cut out for this kind of life and pressure. In fact, if I could have found a way to have "saved face" and returned home at that point, I would have welcomed the opportunity.*

*In one sense my silent suffering was made worse by the contrasting experience of my wife, Lynn, who threw herself into each new challenge with great enthusiasm, obviously enjoying every minute. In retrospect, however, I can see how her example served as a stabilizing influence for me during that time, along with the positive attitudes exhibited by the other missionaries on the station.*

*In spite of all my inner turmoil, however, I knew God had called me to be there. He gave me the grace to persevere and eventually to experience a 180 degree turn-around in perspective. I thank Him for that as it has led to lifelong relationships with many Shona brothers and sisters and ministry opportunities I could never have imagined at that time.*

Don went on to have a very fruitful ministry on the field. He also had an exceptional sensitivity in relating to other new missionaries as they became acclimated to the field. What a breath of fresh air he was to Diane Powell when she visited Mavuradonha on a clinic trip shortly after arriving on the field in 1971! Being able to connect with someone who remembered what it was like to be thrown into such a drastically different environment was so encouraging to her.

Culture shock was definitely lessened for those second-generation missionaries who had grown up in Zimbabwe as MKs. Their return to the field was not without challenges, however. Joyce Everswick Goppert described those she and Chris faced when they arrived as missionaries in 1973:

> *As Chris and I look back over the many years of serving in Zimbabwe, we stand in awe of God's faithfulness and His loving perseverance with us, His all-too-human and frail servants. He brought us to Zimbabwe in January 1973, as a newly-married couple. The war of independence was just beginning.*
>
> *In the plane as we were flying over, we read in a British newspaper that a town called Mount Darwin had been attacked and a rural store burned down by the "freedom fighters." As we traveled by road out to Chironga, where we were to have our language studies, not only did we see the pock-marks on the walls of the club in Mt. Darwin that had been attacked, but we discovered that the rural store that was burned down was only a mile or so from Chironga!*
>
> *"Uncle" Orv and "Aunty" Helen Dunkeld welcomed us warmly, but to me Chironga was a spooky place to live at that time. It was no longer the thriving hub of activity it had been when the Teacher Training Institute was operating. It looked more like a ghost town with its string of abandoned, dilapidated homes from those bygone "glory days."*
>
> *As we settled into the house that would be our home for the next nine months, we discovered that the double bed in our room had also seen better days as it sloped precipitously down to the center. To make matters worse, a family of screech owls had established themselves outside our window.*
>
> *At night we would often hear trucks crowded with soldiers*

*roaring through the station, or the screech owls would shriek at our window as though some poor soul were being decapitated! Sometimes we heard helicopters flying overhead as they brought the wounded war victims to Karanda.*

*It was an adjustment, to say the least. Only the grace that God gave brought us through it all and kept us from bolting!*

Rita Ibbotson faced other difficulties as she arrived in Zimbabwe in 1988. The war of independence was over, but a major crisis had arisen between the mission and the Evangelical Church, the official organization of churches planted by the TEAM missionaries. Coming as a new missionary into the midst of this unsettling situation with no advance preparation was very traumatic for her.

Then, after only two months she received word that her father was in Intensive Care and on a ventilator. Suddenly she was faced with the difficult decision of whether to stay in Zimbabwe or to return home to see him. She decided to go home and was able to be a big help to her mother in caring for her father for six weeks. Returning to Zimbabwe, this time with the knowledge of the major problems occurring there, was not easy, but she did return.

Rita spent 10 months in language school in Chinhoyi, but her experience in working with the church there was very distressing. Her entire language course was overshadowed by her uncertainty over whether the mission would be able to continue its work in the country. "As a result, my language course was not as effective as it could have been," she acknowledged.

Things did not improve when she moved to Karanda. She wrote:

*My first two years were awful. Out of necessity I was thrown into my teaching role at the nursing school way before I was ready. With no time for adequate preparation, I had a nightmare putting together my lessons to teach in this vastly different medical environment.*

*I was also teaching a Sunday school class and being pulled in too many directions. Feeling overloaded, I wondered how I could possibly have an effective ministry in this country to which I believed God had called me.*

God had indeed called her there and would never desert her. He faithfully provided His grace, enabling her to persevere through this difficult introduction to the mission field. The crisis with the Evangelical Church was satisfactorily resolved, and Rita is still serving at Karanda today. She looks back at her initial struggles and trusts they have made her more understanding of other new missionaries coming to the field.

The difficulties that Carol Eagles faced in inaugurating her missionary service were primarily centered on the logistics of getting to Zimbabwe. She too was temporarily affected by the crisis occurring on the field.

Having served for a number of years as a missionary in the public schools of Ontario, Canada, she learned from the McCloys that Zimbabwe had the same open door for teaching Bible classes in their schools. When very clear signals were given that Canada's policy was about to change, she began praying about what God wanted her to do next. Within months she felt the Lord was leading her to continue her Bible teaching ministry in Zimbabwe.

In an article entitled "When the Lord Wants You in Africa, You Go," she described how she persevered through a series of obstacles confronting her:

> . . . *To see what teaching in Zimbabwe was like, at Mary Ann [McCloy]'s prompting I applied for a short-term summer ministry with TEAM. Ironically, I was turned down. I am small boned and don't weigh much—off the charts, according to the "average" weight for my height. Without a medical (not required for short-term missionaries) TEAM had no way of knowing whether I was healthy enough to endure life overseas.*
>
> *TEAM's Canadian representative, Nelson Bezanson, was not easily deterred when he sensed the Lord's leading in someone's life. He called me with a proposal: Would I consider going long-term with TEAM, where a required medical could confirm I was actually able-bodied and healthy?*
>
> *Unknown to him, his call came just weeks after Ontario*

*courts struck down the provision that allowed Bible classes during school hours. By March break of 1990, this door would close forever, and six-and-a-half years of full-time teaching the Bible ended for me.*

*Talk about the Lord clearing your schedule! I needed a new ministry. Not only was I willing to consider full-time service with TEAM, I was also free to attend their three-week Candidate School as well.*

*So, in June 1990, I arrived in Wheaton, Illinois, USA, as a TEAM candidate for teaching Bible in the public schools in Harare, Zimbabwe, Africa. I soon learned that one of the staff, Don Hoyt, spoke Shona, one of Zimbabwe's main languages. He promptly started teaching me Shona greetings and even loaned me his Shona language book. I asked a Zimbabwe representative, Tom Jackson, to start going over lessons with me.*

*But before Tom began Lesson One, all candidates for Zimbabwe were given devastating news. Unless a problem involving TEAM's Karanda Hospital in Zimbabwe was resolved, TEAM would not accept any new candidates for the Zimbabwe field. My whole future ministry was in jeopardy.*

*"Do you still want to proceed with Shona lessons under those circumstances?" Tom asked me.*

*"I sure do," was my reply. God had called me to Zimbabwe, and He would get me there somehow.*

*The next day TEAM's restriction was relaxed. Candidates already being considered for ministries other than Karanda Hospital would be allowed to proceed. I was in! Thank you, Lord!*

*So, in April 1991, less than a year later, I was on the plane heading for Zimbabwe via South Africa. A TEAM missionary (George Dee) was scheduled to pick me up at the South African airport, help me buy a car, and drive me up to Zimbabwe.*

*I spent a wonderful stopover in Portugal visiting Canadian missionary friends. That evening they dropped me off at the Lisbon airport, and I checked in for my final, after-midnight flight to South Africa.*

*"Where is your visa for South Africa?" the ticket agent asked.*

*"Visa? What visa?"*

*"You need a South African visa to stop in South Africa."*

*"Isn't my ticket good enough?"*

*"No, it is not."*

*After an anxious hour of debate, concerned airport personnel finally advised me what to do: Since I couldn't stop in South Africa and be driven to Zimbabwe, I would buy a ticket and fly ahead to Zimbabwe, where I had a valid work permit to get me into the country.*

*All international calls from the airport ceased at 12:00 midnight, so with little time to arrange flight details, I hurriedly placed a call to Zimbabwe's field chairman, Ray Williams, at 11:45 p.m. (12:45 a.m. by his clock). Ray sleepily concluded our call by asking when he should expect my arrival.*

*"I don't know yet. I'll call when I get there."*

*By God's perfect timing I arrived the following evening. Of course, no one knew I'd come (except the Lord). So after collecting my luggage, I once again phoned Ray (at a much more respectable hour), and he came to the airport to pick me up. God in His faithfulness had brought me to His desired destination.*

*Thus began 5 wonderful years teaching Bible classes in Zimbabwe's public schools. Yes, when God wants you in Africa, He gets you there.*

## Discouraging Events

While the first months of missionary service almost always presented challenging hurdles requiring God-given perseverance, major discouragements could occur at any time in one's career. Some were precipitated by sudden, unexpected tragedies. Others developed over time as the result of a steady continuation of disappointing or trying circumstances. Some made continuing on the field impossible. Many caused missionaries to reassess their call. Those able and willing to stay the course again drew upon God's grace to persevere.

With the relatively young missionary force that God called to Zimbabwe, many children were born on the field. While these were usually joyous celebrations, they occasionally turned into times of great sorrow. In addition to the Dunkelds, the Brutons, Prescotts, Stroms, Austins, Uppendahls, and Ratzlaffs all lost precious infants or young children on the field.

Dorothy Strom told of the all-too-brief life of their little daughter Valarie:

*Valerie Judith was born at Central Hospital in Harare on July 27, 1956. As was common in those days, I stayed in the hospital with her for just over a week. Then, after a few days in the old cottage on the Plot, our family drove back to Kapfundi.*

*Valerie was not a fussy baby, but when napping, she would sometimes cry out. By the time I would get to her, however, I would invariably find her sleeping soundly.*

*When she was about three months old, Valerie developed diarrhea and was given appropriate medication by Thelma Everswick, our nurse on the station. Wilfred was scheduled to make a supply trip into Harare for the Bible school about that time, and we discussed whether I should go with him to take Valerie to the doctor. We decided, however, that the hot trip in the truck over bumpy roads might be hard on her and actually hinder her recovery. Besides, she had started to respond to the medicine. As he left for Harare, Wilfred said he hated to leave me when she was fussier than usual, but I wasn't worried as I had had worse days with Gloria and Brenda when they were ill.*

*The day passed, and I remember Valerie drinking her bottle well and giving the girls and me some nice smiles. I tucked her in for the night without any undue concern.*

*She was sleeping through the nights, so when I got up at 5:30 a.m., I peeked under her mosquito net to check on her. She lay very still. As I touched her, she didn't respond, and her body felt cooler than normal. My first thought was that she was dead, but in my shock I felt it could not be true.*

*I immediately sent Gloria with a note to Norman and Thelma Everswick asking them to come at once. After examining Valerie's body, Thelma told me that Valerie had probably been with the Lord for quite a few hours. The shock and grief was deep as I attempted to accept the reality and to seek grace and strength from the Lord.*

*Norman drove to a police outstation 18 miles away so he could phone Russ Jackson in Harare where he and Marg were serving as hostel parents to the MKs. Although Wilfred was in the city doing his necessary business and shopping, Russ assured Norman that he would find him.*

*According to the law of the land, bodies that were not embalmed had to be buried the same day as the death. While the Bible school men kindly dug a grave on the station, Norman made a box coffin which we lined with a sheet. Thelma kindly prepared Valerie's body and dressed her in a sweet little dress her auntie had sent her.*

*Just as we were about to leave for the gravesite, Wilfred drove into the station. We took a little time to grieve together privately and pray. He had stopped on his way out of town and purchased flowers from the venders by Central Park which we lovingly laid on her grave. It was October 27. She was with us for exactly three months.*

*News of Valerie's death traveled quickly to the surrounding villages, and all through the day I had several local Christian women and others sitting with me, singing and quoting Scripture. They would come and go as their duties demanded and I did the same. Although we were far away from our families, we had the love and concern of our Shona friends, many of whom had buried babies of their own. Our peace came from knowing that God was in control.*

Carol Austin told a similar story of the baby she and Reg lost at Chironga. After what Carol described as a "very easy" pregnancy, little Barbara Grace was born April 22, 1958, at the Lady Chancellor Maternity Home in Harare under the care of an obstetrician. While she weighed only five-and-a-half pounds, she appeared very healthy, and Reg and Carol were delighted when they received permission to take her back out to Chironga.

Once again, however, great joy turned to deep sorrow. Carol wrote:

> *At the age of five weeks Barbara died practically in my arms. I remember my whole body going numb. Since the Stroms never knew why their baby had died so suddenly, we decided to take Barbara's body to Harare for an autopsy. Cliff and Jeanette Ratzlaff drove us in their car.*
>
> *On the way we had to stop at the police station in Mt. Darwin to report Barbara's death. There we met Dr. Wall and his family driving out from Harare. We informed him of our tragedy, and he asked to see Barbara. After feeling her abdomen, he told us that something was wrong inside. All her organs were pushed over to one side. We were relieved to learn that her death was not caused by anything we had done or not done for her.*
>
> *The government doctor in Harare who did the autopsy discovered that Barbara had a deformity of the aorta. Her heart had grown very large trying to push blood through an area of the aorta that was no bigger than a thread. It had finally just given up.*
>
> *It was a very sad time. . . . The missionaries arranged to have a little funeral on the Mavuradonha Mission Station as there was already a small cemetery plot there with four graves: one for Eunice Ott and three for other infants who had died.*
>
> *Dad Austin living in Harare was not a believer at this time. Orla Blair drove Reg's folks out to the funeral and witnessed to Dad on the way. As they returned home, Dad told him that he wanted to go where that baby had gone, so Orla led him to the Lord!*
>
> *Later that night when Reg and I got to his folks' house to stay for a few days, we heard that Dad had become a Christian. Right then and there I knew why we had lost Barbara. She came to win her grandpa to the Lord. Reg and I were comforted by this.*

Roy and Lydia Eichner suffered tragedies of a different kind. They were in their second term of service when they were literally "tried by fire." Their dual catastrophes began in 1963, when they were left alone with Dottie Larsen on the Kapfundi station while the other missionaries went to Harare for committee meetings.

On Friday evening the Eichners invited Dottie over for supper before they were scheduled to chaperone a social activity at the Bible school. Roy wrote:

*We really enjoyed the meal and fellowship with Dottie, but the time slipped by so quickly. All too soon it was time for Lydia and me to go to the Bible school. I made a quick decision and whispered to Lydia that I would go on up myself and she could continue visiting with Dottie a little longer.*

*As the two women finished talking, Dottie asked to borrow a can of fruit. Lydia graciously went to get it from the pantry, which lay between the dining room and kitchen. Seeing a bright light coming from the kitchen, she went to investigate its source. To her horror, the thatched roof over the kitchen was in flames!*

*By this time I was at the Bible school having a great time playing games with the students. Suddenly, however, we were interrupted by the repeated, loud blowing of a horn. It sounded like the horn of our car, but I couldn't imagine who would be doing this or why. I rushed to the door, and just as I opened it, Lydia arrived in the car, screaming, "Fire"!*

*As my eyes scanned the dark sky over the station, I quickly spotted what looked like a huge torch burning— right where our house was located! Without saying a word to anyone, I started running to the house. The students, recognizing the crisis, followed right behind.*

*As I ran, I had one question consuming my mind: "Where is our 18-month-old daughter, Debbie?" I hadn't had the presence of mind to check whether she was with Lydia in the car. Now all I could think was, "Could she possibly have been left in her crib?"*

*Upon reaching the house, I went straight to Debbie's*

*bedroom. Her crib was empty! The relief I felt was inexpressible! I knew she had to be safe with Lydia in the car. Knowing Lydia's love for her, I never should have questioned the possibility of her leaving Debbie behind.*

*Meanwhile Dottie had been frantically trying to fight the fire in any way she could. Being near the end of the dry season, the station's water tank had very little water in it, and the pressure was so low that water from the hose couldn't possibly reach the burning roof.*

*With no hope of putting the fire out, the students immediately started rescuing our belongings from the house. Standing in the living room of our L-shaped house, I looked in one direction and saw several students carrying out our paraffin refrigerator. They hadn't even stopped to turn it off. Others followed with the stove. Looking in the other direction, I saw a relay of students passing out stacks of books from the shelves in our bedroom. The teamwork was unbelievable.*

*Then Baba Jeke, with his big handlebar moustache, came to ask where my ax was. With the huge upheaval taking place, I had no idea but wondered why he wanted it. My curiosity was soon dispelled when I saw him pushing the bathroom sink, cupboard and all, out the side door.*

*The cooperation and speed of the students was outstanding. Everything was rescued from the house except for the food in our pantry. We had just returned from town the week before, replenishing our food supply for the next three months. However, the burning thatch was now falling quite badly, and I insisted that we leave the building.*

*We could do nothing more except to stand and watch as the fire began consuming the entire inside of our house. Burning mats of thatch were also sliding down from the roof and falling in heaps on the outside.*

*Then the explosion of our three months' supply of canned goods began. We never expected a fireworks display in Africa, but we sure had one that night. As we watched empty cans fly over the walls of the house going in every direction, we laughed at the sight. Isn't it wonderful how in the most serious situations God can make you smile—and even laugh? Our laughter that evening helped to release the tension of our adrenaline-charged bodies.*

*When the fire finally died down, we had to make sure that all the embers were completely out lest the wind lift them up and start more fires. Lacking a good supply of water, we had to beat them out by hand, a process that seemed to take forever.*

*When we were satisfied that the last ember was out, we looked at the bulk of our "worldly goods" lying all jumbled together in a huge pile in the backyard. With Lydia being such a tidy housekeeper, I momentarily wondered how she would react to seeing all of our things in such disarray. My concern was very short-lived, however. She was as thrilled as I that that heap of goods did not go up in flames as well.*

*As we walked around to the front of the house, a very different scene greeted our eyes. There in our front yard stood our dining room table, still fully set with table cloth, dishes, tea cups, and everything just as Lydia and Dottie had left it when the fire was discovered. The students had carefully removed it "as is." God again made us smile, as it looked like we were planning a special dinner party in our front yard under the stars.*

*Our attention was quickly diverted, however, to the job that still lay before us. What were we to do with all of our rescued belongings? Thankfully, there was an empty house on the station not too far away. This seemed to be the most logical place to become our new home.*

*Realizing that the students were very tired by now, we hesitated to ask them to help us yet again in carrying every-thing to the empty house. They were only too willing, however, and before we knew it, a brigade of wheel barrows heaped with clothes, books, dishes, unwinding 5-inch reel tapes, towels, and "you name it" all mixed together was on its way to this house.*

*Lydia and I remained in the backyard of our burned house through this process to make sure nothing was left behind. When we finally made our way to the other house, we saw that here too everything had just been dumped from the wheel barrows into a five-foot high pile in the middle of the living room. What a disastrous sight it was!*

*We were thoroughly exhausted as we set up our beds in this new house, but we also experienced an overwhelming joy that night that God had spared the lives of Dottie, Lydia, Debbie, and Steve, with whom Lydia was pregnant at the time. The preservation of our possessions was an extra blessing. We were also amazed at how the students to whom we had come to minister were used by God to minister so greatly to us.*

Eighteen months later the Eichners had just returned from another shopping trip to Harare, once again bringing with them a three-month supply of food for their family as well as numerous supplies for the Bible school. The next morning Roy drove the car down to the Bible school, unloaded the supplies, and proceeded to teach his morning classes.

He wrote:

*We had just started our second class at 9:00 a.m. when I happened to look out of the window. I could not believe my eyes as I saw a huge fire and billows of black smoke filling the sky over our station. I immediately had a deep, sinking feeling in the pit of my stomach. I quickly discerned that the fire was on the left side of the dirt road—and our house was the only building on that side of the road! Certainly it couldn't be happening again!!!*

*I jumped into my car and headed for home thinking only of finding my family. I had left Lydia, Debbie, and Steve in the living room when I drove up to the school that morning. My only thought was, "Where are they now?"*

*Figuring that they must have gone to one of the other missionary homes, I started to look for them there. No one was home at the first house. I ran to the second shouting, "Have you seen Lydia and the children?"*

*"No!" came the concerned and fearful reply.*

*I started making my way across the road toward our house. By that time the wind had blown burning grass onto the thatch of the mission storeroom, igniting that roof as well. I kept running, frantically searching for my family.*

*My heart was pounding as I circled our burning house. There in the backyard, away from the smoke and heat of the fire, I found Lydia trying to comfort the children. I shall never forget the hugs and kisses, mixed with tears, as we held each other, so glad to be safely together.*

*Little did we know then that at that exact time, which was the middle of the night in Pennsylvania, one of our prayer partners could not go to sleep because of a heavy burden God had placed on her heart for our family. She knew that we must be having a serious need and, without knowing what it was, she felt compelled to get out of bed and have a prayer meeting all by herself for us. God in His grace heard and answered her prayer in saving the lives of our family.*

*The fire had apparently started in the thatched roof over our bedroom, but we never knew how or why. This time it spread so quickly that none of our belongings could be rescued. In the midst of our tremendous loss, however, we realized anew the value of life in comparison to possessions. Though all our "things" were gone, because of God's grace and mercy the lives of our family were spared.*

*As we continued to watch our house go up in smoke once again, Bud and Lolly Fritz, joined us. Having lost many of their own possessions in a fire a few years earlier, their hearts could readily empathize with ours at that moment.*

*After some time, however, they said, "Standing here watching until the fire goes out won't accomplish anything. Why don't you come to our house for a cup of tea?" We knew they were right and readily accepted the invitation.*

*Up until this time Carl and Donna Hendrickson had continued with their responsibilities at the Bible school and the Light of Life office completely oblivious to what had happened. When they learned of the fire, they were shocked and immediately came to join us at the Fritz's.*

*I don't remember much about that tea time except for how stunned I felt as we sat in their living room. Bit by bit the reality of our loss was sinking in as Lydia and I began to think of specific things that were now gone. I mentioned my file containing all of my Bible college and seminary notes and other teaching and preaching materials I had collected over 17 years, which could never be replaced.*

*Lydia piped up, "Honey, just think, all our pictures are gone—our wedding pictures and all the children's albums."*

*Then, looking down, she suddenly gasped, "Oh no! When I washed my hands this morning, I put my wedding and engagement rings on the shelf over the bathroom sink. I don't even have my rings anymore!" This really impacted her!*

*Sensing her pain, I promised, "As soon as the house cools off and I can get in, I'll go and look for the rings." Bud and Carl quickly assured us that they would help too. In all honesty, having seen the intensity of the fire and felt its extreme heat, I thought we had little hope of finding those rings.*

*Around 4:00 that afternoon we were finally able to enter the charred remains of our house. The heat had indeed been intense, destroying even our pots and pans and melting our Pyrex jars. We found only two items that could be salvaged from the ashes: a cast iron frying pan in the kitchen and a cast iron wedding gift still hanging on the cracked, sooty wall of what used to be our living room. It read, "As for me and my house, we will serve the Lord." As Lydia and I held each other there in the burned ruins of our home, we said, "Yes, Lord, we said that when we got married, and we still mean it."*

*After convincing ourselves that nothing else could be salvaged, Bud, Carl, and myself started looking for Lydia's rings. Using a window screen, we began sifting through the knee-deep ashes in the bathroom. In my heart I felt it was a hopeless task, but we would at least fulfill our promise.*

*You can imagine our astonishment when suddenly there on the screen appeared two tarnished rings! We couldn't believe our eyes! They hadn't even lost their shape. We were so excited and Lydia was thrilled! Thanks to God and a great job done by a Harare jeweler, Lydia still wears her treasured rings today, and the only remaining wedding gift that we have—"As for me and my house, we will serve the Lord"— still hangs on our kitchen wall where we see it every day.*

*With Lydia's rings retrieved, our attention turned to the inevitable "what now?" Where do you start when you suddenly have nothing—no furniture, no food, no basic living supplies, no toys for the children—not even a change of clothing or diapers for your baby? Obviously, we had to return to Harare for another shopping trip.*

*In the meantime our co-workers were wonderful and immediately chipped in to lend us clothing to wear to town. Lolly Fritz went through a drum of stored supplies and found some new dish towels for us to use as diapers for Steve. Then she sat down at her sewing machine and quickly produced a beautiful new dress for Debbie.*

*The next morning we headed back to Harare with the Fritzes and Hendricksons accompanying us in separate cars. Upon arriving at the cottage on "the Plot" the next day, a big surprise was waiting for us.*

*When our Field Chairman, Orla Blair, had heard about our fire on the wireless radio, he immediately called the pastor of Mabelreign Baptist Church to request that they pray for us at their prayer meeting that night. The pastor not only agreed to have the church pray for us, but he also contacted all the members, asking them to bring any household items they could spare to give to us. Their generous contributions filled many boxes and were there to greet us at the cottage. What an encouragement that was to us!*

*This outpouring of love towards us was only the beginning. In the weeks to come, when the MAF plane made its usual trips to Kapfundi, it brought donations from other TEAM missionaries as well, including some toys for our children. We were deeply humbled as we recognized the love of God's family for us.*

*Orla and Marguerite Blair graciously looked after Debbie and Steve while we spent long days in Harare trying to purchase everything we would need to set up housekeeping again, using money borrowed from TEAM. Three-year-*

*old Debbie was such a blessing and encouragement to us during those days. Whenever she sensed our concern over the many decisions needing to be made, she would say, "Jesus is going to give us another house."*

*The question of where we were going to live when we returned to Kapfundi was indeed a major one we had to confront. Every house on the station was being used. The only place we could think of was the storeroom behind our carport where we kept our tools, etc. It was only about 12' by 12' and would have to serve as a bedroom for all four of us—as well as our kitchen. Actually, it would have to serve as our entire living space. By going outside and into our old house, we could use the bathroom there as it was still intact except for the roof.*

*As we were considering all of this, we also came to grips with the reality that the rainy season would arrive soon. That meant the children would have to stay indoors more. While I would be at the Bible school most of the day, Lydia and the children would have to stay in that one crowded room.*

*I had to ask Lydia if she felt that this would be too diffi- cult for her. I knew that our hearts were deeply committed to the Bible school ministry and we were needed there. However, with all that we had been through, I wondered if the added stress of living in the storeroom would be too much for her.*

*I will never forget the sincerity in Lydia's voice when she said, "If God does not make another way, then He will give us grace for this situation." Instead of giving up, we both felt a renewed commitment to the work that God had given us to do.*

*Little did we know that God had been working to fulfill what little Debbie had been telling us all along! When we arrived back at the station, Carl and Donna Hendrickson, who had returned earlier, flagged us down and invited us in for dinner after our long day. As we ate, they told us that they had decided that since their four children were all in the hostel, the two of them could live in the storeroom much easier than our family of four, especially during the rainy*

*season. Therefore, they had already moved into the store-
room, which they dubbed "Camp Carlonna," and were
offering their house to us. They had even left most of their
furniture there for us.*

*We were overwhelmed by their act of love and willing-
ness to sacrifice on our behalf. Everyone on the station and
in the surrounding area was also impacted by their actions,
which were worth a thousand messages. Such living sermons
are not soon forgotten by those involved or those watching.*

Donna described a bit about living at "Camp Carlonna":

*It was a challenge, but we had fun seeing how creative
and innovative we could be. The storeroom had to serve as
our living room, dining room, bedroom, and kitchen all in
one. We set up our washing machine in the kitchen of
Eichner's burned house.*

*We used the bathroom in their house as well. Being roof-
less, the floor flooded whenever it rained, so we had to walk
on bricks to the corner where the "throne" was located. We
also felt uneasy whenever we took a bath, fearing the MAF
plane might happen to fly overhead. We told Dave Voetmann
to veer off to the east when he approached Kapfundi or just
to close his eyes.*

*In time, we built up the walls of the carport that was
attached to the storeroom, making it into a second room.
This gave us a little more breathing room. Also, as the
Eichners purchased their own furniture, refrigerator, and
other necessities, we were able to bring more of our things
to "Camp Carlonna."*

*When our kids came home for their Christmas holiday,
we had to make some adjustments to accommodate all six of
us. The Eichners graciously moved out of their bedroom in
our home and into a smaller one. Our family then used the
vacated room for sleeping while we continued to cook, eat,
and live at "Camp Carlonna." We also took a family vacation away from the station during part of that school holiday.*

*We lived in our makeshift house for about eight months*

*until we went on furlough in May 1966. God's grace enabled us to be adaptable in this time of need on the station. We praise Him for being so sufficient in every circumstance.*

The Hendrickson children also showed remarkable adaptability in adjusting to a very different version of "home" during this time, largely due to the attitude of their parents. Daughter Nancy wrote:

*I was so impressed with the way Mom and Dad had adapted. Mom always made a game of adapting to circumstances that might otherwise be discouraging, so I had fun finding creative ways to adapt to this situation too.*

*Things were not as convenient, especially with the roofless bathroom being a ways off and our needing to go through quite a maze to get to it. Then I realized how spoiled we had gotten with the luxuries of indoor bathrooms for a few years. We had had outhouses to start with, and this bathroom was more airy, comfortable, and clean than the original outhouses. This helped my attitude about that.*

*Mom and Dad calling their temporary home "Camp Carlonna" really helped me adapt mentally too. Camping was always a special family time that bonded us together in various ways, so thinking of spending the holidays on a luxurious "camp-out" versus "home" became fun.*

*We kids also enjoyed climbing through and exploring the burned ruins of the Eichner's home. The way the walls sat created neat new places to have our "club meetings."*

Major adversities such as these definitely had a disheartening effect on those involved. Perhaps more common sources of discouragement, however, were the lesser disappointments that were compounded by their ongoing extension over a period of time. These included more insidious health problems, insufficient financial support, frequent moves and changes in ministries, inadequate staffing, philosophical disagreements, personality clashes, the daily monotony of unchallenging work assignments, and unfulfilled ministry expectations.

No matter what role they played, the missionaries' primary

objective for being in Zimbabwe was to see souls saved, churches planted, and Christian leaders developed. Often this did not happen as quickly as anticipated. Sometimes converts who showed great promise or were already in positions of church leadership backslid into sin, causing great disappointment to both the church leaders and the missionaries, especially those who had invested deeply in their discipleship.

Mary Danielson expressed her dismay at the spiritual indifference of the ladies she was attempting to reach with the Gospel in a 1947 prayer letter:

*Some of the old grannies with snow white hair just haven't the slightest concern that any day they may be swept into a life of everlasting suffering. Won't you [pray] that God will break down this wall of indifference and give them a real conviction of sin and their need of a Savior?*

Phyllis Rilling had similar feelings as she witnessed the Word being preached over and over at the Rusambo clinic with so little response.

Mothers with young children were often discouraged by the amount of time they had to spend in the home when they longed to be more involved in active ministry. While fulfilling an important God-given role, their spirits could easily get bogged down in the often repetitive and seemingly mundane duties of tending to the needs of their children. Watching their husbands or other women being much more fulfilled in ministry-related activities was sometimes hard.

The overextended work schedule required of the often inadequate number of doctors and nurses at Karanda Hospital became discouraging for some on that station. Coping with the seemingly unrelenting stress and fatigue was difficult at times. For many, the diminished opportunity for spiritual ministry under such conditions was also a major disappointment.

The magnitude of the AIDS crisis that struck the continent in the 1980s often took a further toll on the emotions of the medical staff. With energy levels already taxed, confronting the futility of treating so many patients with such life-threatening illnesses could be even more draining.

How infrequently God seemed to intervene and bring supernatural healing was another potential source of discouragement. In a 1994 article entitled "God, Heal that Baby!" Dr. Dan Stephens expressed the despair he frequently feels in these situations as well as the way in which God has encouraged him to persevere:

*Each time God gives you a blessing, you have to build a little monument to it. Then, when you're surrounded by floods of despair and frustration, you can see those monuments standing above the flood waters and remember those blessings.*

*I'm a doctor at Karanda Mission Hospital in Zimbabwe. When I walk the wards of the hospital, I see about one-third of our patients suffering from AIDS.*

*Of those dying from AIDS, we have babies. We have 15 year-old girls who were just beginning their lives. We have grandmothers 75 and 80 years old. We have 4 year-olds and all ages in between. All of them are dying.*

*I struggle for months over a little baby, thinking perhaps it has AIDS, maybe malnutrition. I don't know. The child dies, and the test comes back. It's probably AIDS. The father has it and the mother has it—the infection at least.*

*Sometimes I'm called to the hospital three or four times in one day about a baby who I know is going to die. I think, Don't call me anymore...the baby is going to die. It's bad enough having to see the baby...just leave me alone...But they call me back down again.*

*On the way to the hospital, I say, "God, if it's your will, you can heal that baby. I know you can. Just show me one time that you're going to heal that baby." The infant dies a few hours later, and I say, "Well, I knew it."*

*You really get discouraged if you think about what you would do if you were God. That's when you have to remember that God never asks you to understand Him. He asks you to trust Him.*

*"Trust in the Lord with all your heart and lean not on your own understanding; in all your ways acknowledge Him, and He will make your paths straight" (Proverbs 3:5-6, NIV).*

*I've known these verses since I was a child. The message is so obvious, but I hardly ever think about it. God doesn't expect me to understand Him, and I shouldn't try to. I know this much: God does use the diagnosis of AIDS to bring many to Himself.*

*But mostly I just keep my eyes on those monuments standing above the floodwaters.[1]*

In addition to the personal discouragements experienced by various individuals, other catastrophes occurred on the field that shook the entire missionary family. As political unrest spread through the country, they often felt great dismay as they witnessed their dear Christian brothers and sisters suffer great harm and personal loss. In 1974, two beloved national Christian leaders serving at the Mavuradonha High School were brutally murdered, devastating the entire Church and missionary community. With the violence of the war penetrating this mission station, both the school and the station were shut down.

In 1978, as the safety of the Karanda Hospital staff and students seemed to be jeopardized, this station was also shut down. Terminating the operation of these two key ministries dealt a major blow of discouragement to the field and especially to the missionaries who were deeply committed to them. Their grief was compounded as they considered the loss that the students and local people would suffer by the closing of these institutions. By God's grace both were reopened after the war ended, but whether that would ever be possible was unknown at the time.

Another heartache to the missionary family occurred as the national Church body they had helped to birth moved into maturity. The conflicts that occurred between the mission and the Evangelical Church during this time caused painful feelings of rejection for both sides. Only through God-given patience and perseverance were these crises resolved in a way that allowed both organizations to proceed intact with separate, but cooperating, ongoing ministries in the country.

While God truly did give grace to persevere through many discouraging situations, the missionaries were not invincible. These traumatic experiences left emotional "bruises" on many.

Stew Georgia was coerced to witness the murder of his two Shona co-workers at Mavuradonha. This was something he relived in his mind for a long time afterwards. Eventually he and Marlene transferred to minister on TEAM's Pakistan field. Here they were finally able to put the trauma of that horrific night behind them, remembering it only on its anniversary every year. When political upheaval began erupting in Pakistan, however, the memories and emotions of what Stew had experienced in Zimbabwe were unexpectedly stirred again.

Chris and Joyce Goppert were also emotionally affected by their experiences in Zimbabwe. Arriving on the field during the early stages of the country's war for independence, they were present for each of the disheartening blows mentioned above.

The community in which they ministered from 1993 to 2003 was greatly impacted by the often traumatic transfer of ownership that took place in the country's farmlands some years after independence. In their role of offering pastoral care to the wider community in general and to the church family in particular, Chris and Joyce agonized alongside one displaced family after another, while their fervent prayers for God to intervene seemingly went unanswered.

Finally, after several years of sharing in the devastating tragedies of these people, Chris and Joyce's strength began to falter. In their emotionally depleted state, they sensed God gently leading them to withdraw from the situation and bring to a close their thirty years of missionary service in the country they so loved.

Grieved and disillusioned, they returned to the States and entered a structured Christian community to receive professional counseling for post-traumatic stress disorder and clinical depression. Here they worked through their emotional responses to the overwhelming events they witnessed and grappled with their shaken view of God's compassion and justice.

In this setting Chris began to understand that his emotional exhaustion had come from striving to understand the "why" of God's actions rather than resting in the assurance of His integrity and the truths of His Word he had always known. This enabled him to see with greater clarity the big picture of God's sovereignty.

He was further impacted by the pattern he saw as he read the Scriptures and some of the writings of C.S. Lewis and Charles

Spurgeon in which focusing on what one knows to be true of God in the past fortifies one with strength and grace to endure present hardships. He now sees this as the key to sustaining a Christian through the worst trials and disillusionments. Strengthened by these insights, Chris has launched into a new ministry in the States.

Sometimes God does not deliver us out of trials because He wants to use them to teach us greater truths about Himself. The more we understand of His unchangeable nature, character, and love, the more we have to draw upon to help us persevere when the going gets tough.

---

[1] Dan Stephens, "God, Heal that Baby!" *TEAM Horizons* (July-August 1994), 15.

# CHAPTER 7

# God Gave Grace to Sacrifice

*" 'Everyone who has left houses or brothers or sisters*
*or father or mother or children or fields for my sake*
*will receive a hundred times as much*
*and will inherit eternal life.' "*
(Matthew 19:29)

Personal sacrifice is generally inherent to being a missionary. Serving in a foreign country usually entails extended separation from home and family. It may also mean living with diminished material comforts and financial security as well as facing potential perils to health and life. Many of these sacrifices, however, are more notable to outsiders than to the missionaries themselves. For many, the commitment to God's call on their lives significantly obscures the sense of sacrifice in carrying it out. This is once again evidence of the grace God faithfully provides to His servants in fulfilling the role He has chosen for them.

## The Early Pioneers

### Standard of Living

The living accommodations of the early pioneers were quite austere, to say the least, but this was a reality they willingly embraced in the goal of bringing the Gospel into the Zambezi

Valley. The Dunkelds considered the one-room, mud hut they moved into during their first year at Msengedzi a "palace" after living for several months in their temporary shelter, which was essentially a tent with grass walls.

The early missionaries' focus was much more on the people to whom they had come to minister than on their own material comforts. They were delighted to find the Shona people in the area friendly, happy, and very interested in them—even if that compromised their privacy. Orv and Helen described some of their early experiences with them:

> *They would come early in the morning and plaster their faces against the screens on the windows, asking each other, "What are they doing now?" We would salt our food, and they would say, "Sugar, sugar." They thought that we put sugar on everything.*
>
> *With their curious faces constantly at our windows, we had to wait until after dark to take our baths. Being winter when we first arrived, the temperature would drop considerably in the evening, often into the '50s. We didn't have a bathtub in the beginning, so we could only take a sponge bath with a basin of water on those chilly evenings.*

When questioned about their sacrifices, Helen's response was: "We didn't feel as if we were sacrificing. We felt we had a good life because we knew God was leading us in it."

John Wolfe, who was introduced to the TEAM missionaries while working for a farmer in rural Zimbabwe in the early '50s, was quite impacted by the sacrificial conditions under which they lived. He described the first time he visited Les and Lil Austin at Hunyani:

> *One of my first observations of this dear couple was their material poverty. They were so short of food and supplies. About all they had lots of was Ovaltine. They just about lived on Ovaltine until they could get back into town for supplies.*

This initial visit with the Austins eventually led to John's becoming a Christian and joining TEAM as a missionary himself. He continued to recount his early observations:

*Having to wait a year before I was able to go to Bible school, I spent the interim helping Russ and Marg Jackson at Rusambo. They were also living in very primitive conditions in those days. Water was critically rationed as they were hauling drums of water from the Mazoe River many miles away over treacherous tracks. One basin of water for washing our hands was used for almost a week with Dettol, a disinfectant, being added every day.*

While John was at Rusambo, he eventually had to make a very difficult sacrifice that pained him deeply. He wrote:

*I had taken my dog, Jock, along with me to Rusambo. Russ was trying to raise turkeys, and unfortunately Jock developed a taste for turkeys. I don't remember just how many turkeys he killed, but inevitably the only solution was to kill Jock. This was one of the hardest things I ever had to do. Russ and I remained friends, though.*

## Travel

Travel was not easy in those days either. Wes Hendrickson recalled the potential difficulties his parents, Carl and Donna, and the other missionaries experienced in getting to the sites where they were planting churches:

*They often had to drive miles over rough, dusty, gravel roads and ford rivers, risking the possibility of getting stuck in mud from torrential, tropical rainstorms. Yet I never heard a word of complaint from any of them.*

Marian Wilterdink wrote about a particularly difficult and uncomfortable trip she made by motorcycle with Chuck Pruitt in order to minister to needy people in an outlying area:

One day the District Commissioner came to the *Kapfundi Mission Station* to let us know that many people in the Zvipani and Rengwe areas were in need of medical assistance. He asked if we could help them. After he left, we discussed the matter and decided to make a medical trip there.

Since each of these places was about 30 miles from the station, we felt that going by truck would be too costly, so Wilf Strom offered the use of his motorcycle. Chuck Pruitt was designated to drive it, and I offered to go with him as the nurse. What was never told to me until after the trip was that the motorcycle had no brakes.

To prepare for the trip, I made some dark purple culottes, which were very wide at the bottom. Then I realized that they could get caught in the spokes of the wheel, so using two large safety pins, I pinned them tightly around the bottom of each leg, making them look like oversized bloomers.

A heavy wooden box was attached to the left side of the motorcycle to carry our medical supplies. Since we would be gone for a full day, I also put in some dishes, silver, glasses, a can of spaghetti, and a can of fruit.

When it was time to leave, I got on the back of the cycle, sitting on a square frame made up of four pipes each about nine inches long. This was the only thing I had to hold onto during the trip. With the big wooden box positioned up against the left pedal where my foot was supposed to rest, my leg had no alternative but just to hang out to the side or bend backwards. I quickly realized that this was not going to be a comfortable ride.

Then, looking down, I saw that the rear tire was flat. So I got off the cycle while the tire was pumped up. Recognizing the uncomfortable nature of what I had to sit on, Chuck's wife, Scotty, got two small cushions to cover the pipes.

As I remounted the cycle, I looked up and saw dark clouds moving our way. Now I really began to dread this trip.

Not wanting the village people to recognize me riding by with another woman's husband, I tied a large kerchief around my head so that it covered much of my face as well. I

*was so surprised when everyone who saw us called out:*
*"Mangwanani Sista!" ["Good morning, Nurse!"].*

*The dirt road was very rough and stony. It also had long*
*stretches of corrugations when it felt as though each section*
*of my brain was rubbing against the others. I had to grit my*
*teeth to keep them from clattering. How I envied Chuck as*
*he sat on a comfortable seat with his arms stretched out*
*holding on to the handle bars while I was sitting on my*
*hands as they clutched the small frame under me with one*
*leg hanging in the air. (After the trip, I was told that some of*
*these bars were broken!)*

*At one point I warned Chuck that around the next curve*
*would be a vicious dog. Sure enough, it heard us coming*
*and came running toward us, snarling and growling. Chuck*
*tried kicking it, but each time he did, the cycle almost tipped*
*over. I told him to keep his foot on the pedal and I would*
*kick the dog. I didn't want to fall with that dog so close.*

*Then Chuck said the front wheel was up in the air so I*
*must move forward. This he ordered all along the way. He*
*wasn't aware that only a few inches separated us. He was*
*the one who should have moved forward, not me!*

*His other constant command was: "Lean way to the*
*right!" This was to balance the cycle with the heavy box on*
*the left. One time as I leaned way over, the cushions and I*
*were about to fall off, so I asked Chuck to stop. He said he*
*would as soon as we got to the top of the hill. When we*
*reached it, he came to a stop right at the edge of a deep*
*ravine. As the cycle tipped towards it, I could just picture us*
*rolling down it.*

*To make matters worse, my bare leg touched the red hot*
*exhaust pipe as I dismounted. This did not help my comfort*
*level at all. As we continued down the road, the burn*
*became even more painful, possibly from the sand and dirt*
*which settled on it. I again asked Chuck to stop so I could*
*bandage it. Then, as I bent over the cycle to get some roller*
*bandage from the box to wrap around it, my other leg*
*touched the exhaust pipe! So I bandaged it too.*

*On we went. "Move forward!" "Lean to the right!" The*

*bottom of my right foot was so sore from pressing hard on the pedal, which had no rubber on it. My left leg was so tired from holding it out and away from the cycle with no support whatsoever. By this time I was very sorry that I had offered to make this trip.*

*Then we came to a rocky spruit with lots of water flowing over it. I didn't want to get my shoes wet, and my feet were too tender to wade through without them. Besides, I was afraid of getting bilharzia [parasites]. After explaining this to Chuck, he told me to stay on the cycle and he would push it across the river with me on it.*

*On the other side was a steep hill with deep rivulets crossing it. Chuck said the cycle didn't have enough power to climb the hill, so we would have to walk up it. As I made my way up the difficult terrain, I became quite concerned about encountering this spot going downhill on the return trip.*

*At times Chuck would speed up and go very fast. When I asked him why, he explained that he had to get enough momentum to climb the next hill. Then to my horror, as we sped down the other side of one of these hills, I saw a huge puddle surrounded by black muck in the middle of the road at the bottom. We hit it much too fast, and the cycle swerved, discharging the two of us in the middle of the puddle.*

*As I lay there, I saw that the cycle had hit a tree and come to a stop. I also saw Chuck's shoe lying there but wondered, "Where is he?" I decided I must get up quickly and find out how he was. I couldn't, however, because I was being held down by a heavy weight. Then it moved, and I realized that it was Chuck.*

*He stood up and said, "Where were you? I looked all over for you. Are you hurt?"*

*I told him I wasn't because I landed on the black muck. He was surprised that he didn't get hurt either. I said that was because he landed on me. He gave me his handkerchief and told me to wipe the black muck off my face, arm, and white blouse.*

*Then I noticed that my hand was turning purple and beginning to swell. My thumb was sore and evidently sprained, so I had to bandage it.*

*Chuck managed to straighten the wheel of the motorcycle enough so it could go around. Then I saw petrol streaming from the tank and quickly found a stick to plug the hole. The cycle had no petrol gauge, so we hoped we had enough left to get us home, as there were no petrol stations along the way.*

*When we arrived at the village, we ate a bit of our food before the people came. As they gathered, they stared at me with the bandages on my legs and hand. Needless to say, I had some explaining to do.*

*After treating the people, we began our hazardous ride back home. At one point we hit some deep loose sand, and the cycle began swerving back and forth. Rather than staying on until it fell over, I jumped off.*

*As I did, the stitching at the top of the large pleat of my culottes tore wide open. I immediately closed the large gap with my hands before Chuck stopped the cycle. How he laughed when he saw me! And how he wished he had taken his camera! I had no choice except to take the two large safety pins from the bottom of my culottes and use them to close the gaping hole I now had at the top.*

*When we reached the village of Four Wire, about three miles from Kapfundi, I could take my discomfort no longer. I told Chuck to stop; I had to get off that thing. Because my legs had been bent for such a long time, I stood in a sitting position.*

*How I longed for someone to come by on a bicycle so that I could go the rest of the way on it! But no one came, and after a brief rest I had to get back on the cycle.*

*Finally, we reached home and I was so glad to be there. I was most dismayed, however, when I recounted all that had happened and all that I had suffered, and no one showed me any sympathy. They just laughed!*

## Isolation

The site chosen for the first mission station was on the far side of the Msengedzi River. With the river in flood nearly four months of the year during the rainy season, the missionaries were stranded and unable to get out of the Valley for that period of time every year.

When asked why they didn't build the station on the near side of the river, Orv replied, "Most of the Shona population we wanted to reach was on the far side of the river. We didn't want to be separated from them." Once again they sacrificed their own convenience for the sake of the people they had come to reach.

In this precarious location the early missionaries had to entrust their well-being entirely to God during the months they had no way out of the Valley. This was tested on numerous occasions. In just their second rainy season Muriel Danielson, then two years old, fell and bit completely through her tongue, leaving it attached only on the sides. Because of the impossibility of getting a vehicle across the river at that time of year, her parents and the Dunkelds instructed little Muriel to keep her mouth shut, praying that it would begin to heal on its own. They were greatly encouraged when, after just a few days, they could see good signs of healing.

Muriel continued to keep her mouth shut, eating and drinking through a straw, until it completely healed! She wrote:

> *I have the scar across my tongue to this day. The Dunkelds still tease me, saying I have the longest tongue they've ever seen because I can actually touch my chin with it. What a claim to fame!*

Paul and Helen Smith recalled the time when their son Fielding fell off his bike at Msengedzi when he was six or seven years old. He was knocked unconscious for a day or two with no way to get him to a doctor. Lorraine Waite, the nurse on the station then, was the only source of medical care available for him. "Knowing that we couldn't get out of the Valley, no matter what, was the hard part," they said. We prayed and God answered. Fielding made a good recovery.

Living on their isolated stations, the early missionaries were also cut off from nearly all forms of communication. Orv Dunkeld described their difficulties in even getting mail:

> *In the beginning the closest the mail came to us was Mt. Darwin. We then had to find a way to get it from there to us.*

*We were always anxious to have visitors come down into the Valley, as they would also pick up our mail for us and take our out-going mail as well. If the game ranger came down, he would do the same. We never knew when we would get our mail. We might go for a month without getting anything at all and then get a whole month's mail all at once.*

*If no one came into the Valley for awhile, we had to send a rider on a bike to make a mail run. With our first riders we never knew when they would get back, so the arrival of mail was still unpredictable.*

*After awhile, however, we got more reliable men who would go up one day and come back the next. We also set up a routine for getting the mail each week, if possible. One young man who made this trip for us would come back so hot and tired that he would tell us he was quitting. When the next Tuesday came, however, he would always show up and be ready to go again.*

*During the rainy season we could only get mail when the river was low enough to get a bicycle across. Sometimes we had to wait a long time for this.*

*When bigger loads or parcels came in, we would be notified and have to go in and get those ourselves, either by car or motorcycle. I remember one time when Paul Smith and I made the run on our motorcycles to collect Christmas parcels that had been sent early enough to reach us before the rains began. We had to tie parcels to every conceivable part of our cycles. What a sight we were as we rode along with these parcels sticking out in every direction!*

When Russ and Marg Jackson and their family lived on the Rukomechi station, they sent two Shona men on foot to get their mail bag, which was dropped off by a bus about 20 miles from the station. Russ wrote:

*The men would always go in twos. They said it took two people to watch in both directions for wild animals, such as lions, which might attack them.*

# Sacrifices of Health and Life

For decades the Zambezi Valley had been considered uninhabitable by white people because of its unhealthy climate. Malaria was rampant, especially during the rainy season. Lying about 1000 feet above sea level, the region was also plagued by the tsetse fly, carrier of sleeping sickness.

When the early missionaries sought permission from the government to move into this area, they were warned of the dangers in doing so. Nevertheless, they received the permission they needed and proceeded with their plans. Others viewed them with both admiration and apprehension—admiration for their willingness to penetrate an area which white people had avoided for so long but apprehension about their welfare.[1]

### Loss of Life

Certainly that apprehension was warranted. The Valley's climate did take a significant toll on the health of the missionaries and their children. Some made the ultimate sacrifice of life itself. Most stunning was the early death of Rudy Danielson from typhoid fever in November 1943.

Twenty years later the malaria parasites that had infected Ken Munger during his time of service in Zimbabwe brought his premature death as well. His wife, June, wrote:

*During our time back in the States, Ken and I both returned to college to get secondary education degrees. One day in December 1963, after teaching music at Balaton, Minnesota, Ken became ill with a severe attack of malaria. We rushed him to the hospital, but appropriate medication was not available. The malaria triggered a coronary thrombosis and in five short hours he died.*

Although unrelated to the climate of the Zambezi Valley, Eunice Ott also sacrificed her life on the field, dying from an unrecognized strain of rabies that was not included in the rabies shots she received after being bitten by an infected dog at Chironga. Eunice may not have considered this a sacrifice at all. When asked, "What happens if the shots don't work?" she very matter-of-factly answered, "Well, then I guess I'll just go to heaven."

Unfortunately, the vulnerability of the missionaries in Zimbabwe also extended to their children. Several parents experienced the heart-rending pain of having a son or daughter's life snatched away because of the inaccessibility of adequate medical care or other circumstances related to life on the mission field.

Orv and Helen Dunkeld's son Leonard and Cliff and Jeannette Ratzlaff's son Timmy were born prematurely out on the rural stations and died while being transported to the hospital in Harare. Warren and Lois Bruton's daughter Martha was also born prematurely. Even though Lois was in the hospital for the birth, Martha lived just 39 hours. She was buried at Mavuradonha alongside Reg and Carol Austin's daughter Barbara and Eunice Ott.

Just a few months later, as the missionaries gathered at Mavuradonha for their annual conference, 13-month-old Jimmy Prescott would be laid to rest in the same little cemetery after an illness of less than 48 hours. With Jean Schmidt and Wilbur Beach's wedding already scheduled to conclude the week, the missionaries would once again *"weep with those who weep"* and *"rejoice with those who rejoice"* (Romans 12:15; KJV) at the same conference.

When Jimmy began running a fever, the nurses at the conference felt he was probably getting the deep chest cold that had been going around amongst the missionaries. He was given penicillin, but his condition worsened in the night and his parents called Thelma Everswick to examine him. By morning his fever was soaring and blood was oozing from his ear. Recognizing the seriousness of his illness, an effort was made to try to get him to a doctor.

In a letter dated May 28, 1955, Mary Danielson wrote:

> . . . *We hardly realized that he was ill until they were getting ready to take him to the nearest doctor a hundred miles away.*
>
> *We spent considerable time in special prayer for them as they got ready and drove off. Late in the afternoon we heard the cars coming back, and we felt that the little life must have been taken to his Heavenly Home. They only got about forty miles when he passed away.*

> *We gathered around them on a little hillside in front of their tent, watching the setting sun as we sang choruses of comfort [and recited] Scripture verses accompanied with thoughts that had been our comfort at a time like this.*
>
> *It was marvelous the way the Lord gave the parents such peace. As they told their little four-year-old girl [of Jimmy's death], we could hear her pleading, "But I want my Jimmy." "But Jesus wanted him too" was the reply.*

That night a coffin was made for Jimmy, and the following morning the missionary family gathered at the little Mavuradonha cemetery for another funeral. Jimmy's death was later thought to have possibly been from viral meningitis.

Martin and Wyn Uppendahl also had to lay a dear child of theirs to rest in Zimbabwe. Martin wrote:

> *Timothy Gale Uppendahl was a miracle baby from the day he arrived. We were on furlough, living in Grand Rapids, Michigan (Wyn's birthplace and childhood home), when he was born on January 2, 1956. Dr. Johns, the attending doctor, announced his birth as a miracle because his umbilical cord was around his neck and became detached during the birth process. The potential problem never bothered little Timothy. He was the picture of health, and in a few months he went with his parents back to Africa via a large new freighter sailing directly from New York to Cape Town in 21 days. . . .*
>
> *Back in Zimbabwe we were living and working at the Chirundu mission station located next to the Chirundu Sugar Estates. Here Timothy grew into a very active, healthy, bright, and curious little boy. He was always running and chattering, trying to keep up with older brother Dan and sister Maryjean.*
>
> *On two separate occasions several weeks apart, well before he was two years old, for no apparent reason Timmy, who was speaking very well, made the emphatic statement, "Daddy, I have a home in heaven and someday Jesus will take me there!" As I tried to ponder how a less than two-*

*year-old could absorb that much theology, I shuttered in wondering if it was a possible premonition. It obviously was.*

*On January 2ⁿᵈ we all celebrated Timmy's 2ⁿᵈ birthday at the Chirundu mission station . . . situated on a bluff 200 yards from the Zambezi River. It was an abnormally heavy rainy season. The Zambezi River remained in high flood and backed up the small stream that separated us from the sugar plantation, effectively cutting us off by road from the rest of the world.*

*On Sunday morning, February 23, 1958, we had breakfast together as a family. A part of every breakfast was to pry open, with some effort, a tin of tasteless, anti-malarial tablets and give one to each person. The tin was then tightly closed.*

*After breakfast the Shona pastor and I crossed our small flooded stream by boat and walked ¼ mile to the church. Our wives and children stayed behind.*

*As Wyn and the children carried the dishes to the kitchen, two-year-old Timmy climbed up to get the tin of anti-malarial pills. When Wyn and the older children returned to finish clearing the table, Timmy had used his spoon handle to pry open the tin and was already ingesting handfuls of the pills.*

*In just a few moments Timothy went into convulsions. Wyn sent a Shona boy running to call me at once. I arrived a few minutes later, and Wyn placed Timothy's convulsing body in my arms while she tried to work with him. Suddenly he relaxed, took a deep breath, and was in the arms of Jesus. We were stunned and devastated! A few minutes later a neighbor from the sugar plantation, who was also a nurse, arrived, but Timmy was already gone.*

*We all loved and adored our little Timmy, but somehow the Spirit of God gave Wyn and me a peace and comfort that is beyond description. Oh, we had tears, but the visiting neighbor was baffled by our calm composure and the inner comfort we received in our submission to God.*

*Using my boat to cross the flooded stream, I went to the Sugar Estates to call Orla Blair in Hatfield and inform him of the tragedy. Orla's immediate response was, "We're coming out." The difficulty he and Marguerite would have in getting to us did not seem to deter him.*

*Since they would be arriving late at night, I drove my jeep, which I had been leaving on the other side of the stream separating us from the main road into the Sugar Estates. This road was flooded by another stream, but it was only knee to thigh deep while the one in front of our house sometimes rose to a depth of 10 feet with quite a current. The party coming could park their car and wade across the first stream to get to the jeep. I left the keys in it and a note instructing them to drive it to the stream in front of our house. Then they could take the boat, which was attached to a cable, to get across.*

*As it turned out, when they arrived at this second stream sometime after midnight, it was a raging torrent of water, and they had great difficulty in crossing it. But God was good, and the Blairs, along with newly arrived Dr. Wall, eventually made it through to be our comforters and to bring a small white casket for the funeral we had the next day.*

*It was, and still is, hard to recall that tragic day, but nothing can match the reassuring, uplifting arms of God and the confident knowledge that HE is still in control of all things. Isaiah 43:1-2 [NLT] says, "Do not be afraid, for I have ransomed you. I have called you by my name; you are Mine. When you go through deep waters and great troubles, I will be with you." Surely He was with us.*

The missionaries and their children who laid down their lives on Zimbabwe soil made the ultimate sacrifice from a human standpoint. Were we able to pull back the curtain of heaven, however, the word "sacrifice" would hardly apply. These individuals just reached their heavenly reward on the "fast track." They now welcome each co-worker and family member whom God calls home one-by-one at His appointed time.

## Health Risks

Many other missionaries succumbed to the threatening diseases of the area but by God's grace recovered. Some developed other medical conditions that either terminated their service on the field or left them with lifelong effects.

Malaria was virtually inescapable in the early days. Helen Dunkeld had her first bout while still in South Africa, and it continued to plague her throughout her life. Fred Dunkeld also became infected with malaria in South Africa when he was only six months old. Later, when he was found to be deaf in one ear, the doctor informed his parents that this could have been caused by his having been given quinine at such a young age.

Tommy Jackson also contracted a serious case of malaria as an infant. His father, Russ, described this experience and the concern that he and Marg had for all of their children:

*Malaria was a constant threat and needed to be treated early. When the children were young, Margaret and I developed a habit before going to bed each night of reaching under their mosquito nets and placing our hand on the forehead of each child to check for signs of fever.*

*Tommy was only a few months old when he did develop a fever. We had been told, however, that as long as Margaret was taking malaria prophylactics and breastfeeding him, he would be protected too. Therefore, we thought that his fever was most likely a sign of cutting his first tooth.*

*When his fever continued to rise over the next several days, however, Margaret and I became very concerned. Although we were in the midst of the rainy season, when the bush roads and rivers were very treacherous between Rusambo and Harare, we decided we had to get Tommy into Harare to the hospital.*

*There tests quickly revealed that he did have malaria, which had developed into cerebral malaria. This was very serious and his life was in danger. How we rejoiced when he began responding to the medications and we knew he was going to recover!*

*Through those difficult days, we were comforted by Mathew 18:10 [KJV], where Jesus said: "Take heed that ye despise not one of these little ones; for I say unto you, that in heaven, THEIR ANGELS do always behold the face of my*

*Father which is in heaven." Many occasions through the early years caused us to praise the Lord that indeed our precious children had "THEIR ANGELS" constantly caring for their safety.*

Ray Finsaas had a close call with malaria while he and his family were stationed at Mavuradonha. His wife, Myrtle, wrote:

*I treated him with the full course of chloroquine, but his temperature stayed at 104.6° for many days with his whole body aching badly. After a grim station meeting Dick Regier offered to take Ray, myself, and our two children to Harare in his big truck with dual wheels on the back. No plane service was available back then.*

*The rivers were up and hard to cross. All five of us were crowded into the front of the truck. Ray was very sick and uncomfortable all the way, but the Lord undertook and Dick succeeded in getting us there.*

*When we arrived in Harare, Dr. Wall, our own TEAM doctor, happened to be there and took Ray under his care. Blood tests revealed that he had two strains of malaria as well as a touch of Black Water Fever [a complication of malaria involving kidney failure that usually leads to death].*

*We thanked God for Dr. Wall and his good work. He gave Ray an intravenous medication and another one, Camaquin, which helped him recover fairly soon. When Ray asked Dr. Wall why he had had such a difficult time breathing during his illness, Dr. Wall explained that it was due to the strain put on his heart. If it had not been strong, he would have died.*

*We stayed in Harare about a month while Ray got well and regained his strength. . . . By God's grace he never had malaria again.*

John Wolfe came down with malaria as his family was moving to Hunyani. Their vehicle got stuck about eight miles from the station, but by that time John was too sick to care. Betty wrote:

*He lay down right in the middle of the road and stayed there
. . . . Teacher Temani was also being moved from Msengedzi
to Hunyani, so he helped me get the children to the house
and then went back with a spare bicycle for John.*

Dick and Mary Ann McCloy's daughter Debbie was infected
with malaria while in Zimbabwe but did not become sick until
years later when she was in college and became "run down." This
often enables the disease to take hold if one is carrying the parasite.

Bilharzia, or schistosomiasis, was as endemic in Zimbabwe as
malaria. Many of the missionaries and their children contracted this
disease and experienced varying degrees of distress from it. The
only way to prevent it was to stay out of virtually any body of water
in the country.

Helen Dunkeld told of her family's first experience with
bilharzia in their son Fred:

*In October 1945, after returning from the annual
conference in South Africa, we noticed that the impish luster
had gone out of Fred's eyes. He had also gotten very pot-
bellied and was throwing up all of his meals. Before that,
when he was listless, we would look for a place to go on
holiday to get him out of the heat of the Valley. This time we
realized something was physically wrong, so we made a trip
into Harare to see the doctor.*

*The doctor looked at him and immediately knew it was
bilharzia, a parasitic disease you can get from the water. The
parasites penetrate through your skin, enter your blood
stream, and then lodge either in the bladder or in the intestine.*

*We had known about this possibility, but we understood
from others that as long as the water was clear and running,
there was no danger. We had carefully boiled all of our
drinking water, but in the hot weather we would go down and
bathe in the river. When we were out on trek, we would do
the same. It was wonderfully refreshing in that hot weather.*

*When the doctor found it in Fred, he tested the rest of us
and found that we all had it. This was very discouraging to
us because it meant a long treatment in town—six or seven*

*weeks of intravenous injections. Because we wanted to get back to Msengedzi before the rains started, the doctor said that he would give us an intra-muscular type instead of the intravenous type so that we could finish it at home.*

*We stayed with the Sieberts and started treatments on October 29th. We remained there until December 4th. This was as long as we felt we could stay and still get home before the Msengedzi River flooded. Once we were home, we continued to give ourselves three intra-muscular injections a week until the course of treatment was finished.*

*After that we all felt much better. Later we found out, however, that Orv still had it. He had to take about four different treatments before he was totally clear of the parasites.*

Russ and Marg Jackson's son Bud gave his perspective of the bilharzia treatment:

*Bilharzia was the #1 most feared "nasty" of all for us MKs! Streams and rivers were definitely out of bounds for us as kids. Getting too near water got a lot of us into trouble, and some kids maintained an almost religious respect for the dreaded "nasty."*

*When I was 15, my appendix almost burst but fortunately was removed in time. When the doctor sent it to the lab for examination, it was found to be full of bilharzia. This was the first indication that I had contracted the parasite.*

*Today, bilharzia infection can be treated with a one-time treatment in tablet form. The old treatment was a course of twenty-four intravenous injections. I had my treatments in a doctor's office above a cafe. I had to go there every other day. My first stop, however, was the cafe where I bought a piece of Bazooka bubble gum. The doctor told me to chew gum during the injection as it helped fight the rising taste of the medicine in my throat. Each injection took five minutes to administer. I'll never forget that experience, having to go through the ordeal every other day for over a month!*

*The only upside to my experience was that our family*

*went on holiday to Lake MacIlwaine just before my treatment. Only I was able to fish that holiday—since I was already infected! That was hard for my brother, Tom, to take as he was a very keen fisherman.*

Other kinds of parasitic infections occasionally affected the missionaries and their children too. Norman and Thelma Everswick both tested positive for filariasis on their first furlough. Norman had the type that affected the nervous system. As a result, he experienced an unusual degree of nervousness, which disappeared after he was successfully treated. Phyllis Rilling and her son Art were also treated for this parasite on furlough.

June Munger also tested positive for it when she and Ken returned to the States in 1961. She never felt any symptoms until two years later when she began feeling a constant sense of movement in her eye. She would ask friends if they could see any foreign matter in it, but they couldn't. Eventually she returned to the Chicago hospital where her previous testing had been done. Here they confirmed that the filaria parasites had infested her eye.

The medication used to treat her made June quite sick with a high fever and swollen glands. This prevented her from immediately responding to the invitation she received after her husband's death to come back to Zimbabwe and teach at Mavuradonha. In this interim period, while she was recovering from her eye treatments, June met and became engaged to Pastor Waldo Wiebe. The call she felt to go back to Zimbabwe was so strong, however, that they both agreed she should return for a year before they got married.

June spent a wonderful year at Mavuradonha but returned to the States with prism vision and joint pain. Once again she returned to the hospital in Chicago. This time the treatment they gave her for the filariasis was completely successful, and she has never had a reoccurrence of it. She praises God for this, as she is well aware that once you have this disease, it rarely goes completely away.

In addition to parasitic infections, the missionaries suffered many other illnesses on the field, some of them life-threatening. Dysentery took its toll on Helen Dunkeld and her sons when they returned to South Africa for their annual field conference in 1945. Helen wrote:

*It was great to be at the conference and to meet again with the missionaries that we had worked with before we had gone up to Zimbabwe. We received a hearty welcome from them and the local people as well.*

*Then dysentery hit me and our two boys. We lay in bed and got weaker and weaker. When the conference ended, the missionaries took us in to a doctor, who put us on an antibiotic.*

*We got better after that, but getting our strength back took a long time. We stayed in Swaziland longer than we had planned in order for us to rebuild enough strength to come back home again.*

*We made the trip back up to Zimbabwe by train and had only been home a short time when we went out on trek. It was very difficult to sit at home and realize that all these people were around us who had never heard God's message of salvation. I soon discovered, however, that I still didn't have my normal strength back. When we came to little dips in the road or little hills, I found that I couldn't get the bike up by myself and had to have Orv or one of the Shona people help me with it.*

Hepatitis also struck the missionary family from time to time. Thelma Everswick had it so severely in 1947 that she almost died. When she recovered, the doctor impressed upon her that she must do everything possible to avoid getting it again. This meant that as others came down with it, she could have no contact with them.

Gladys Cedarholm wrote about one of the times that hepatitis spread through the missionary family:

*At the 1957 field conference we were asked to go to Harare as the new hostel was ready for its roof. In the process of packing up, Clarence was feeling "yucky." He would pack some and then rest some, pack some and then rest some, trying his best to keep going, but he barely made it. Upon arrival in Harare, Clarence was too ill to think about a building project. The doctor diagnosed him with hepatitis, and he was confined to bed for six weeks.*

*I was pregnant with Ruth at the time, and the doctor was particularly concerned that I might contract it too. Instead, I came down with pneumonia. This was not surprising as we were living in the hostel parents' apartment with the roof not yet completed during one of Harare's coldest winters on record.*

*While Clarence was recuperating, another TEAM missionary came down with hepatitis. Next to be infected were Cecyl and Bessie Till, who faithfully came to our conferences to care for the children and youth. There may have been others too.*

Emil Rilling became very sick with hepatitis a few years later. His wife, Phyllis, wrote:

*In 1960, we went on a trip with other TEAM families to the Hot Springs. Here Emil got very sick, so we returned to Harare. Soon he turned quite yellow, and Dr. Clemenger, who was in town, diagnosed him with hepatitis and sent him to Central Hospital.*

*Soon I became very sick with it as well and was taken to the Wilkinson's Infectious Disease Hospital. About a week later Emil was brought over to the same hospital and put in my room, so we were together. Shortly after this our son Bill was brought from the hostel with hepatitis too. He was put in a room across the hall from Emil and me.*

*When we got out of the hospital, Len and Effie Byrd Baillie were going to be gone for a few weeks and offered us their home. What a haven this was to us at that time! We sent for our cook from Rusambo and told him how to cook fat-free for us. We were also very grateful for all that Norman and Thelma Everswick did for us during this time when they were so fearful of Thelma ever getting hepatitis again.*

Mildred Rogers became very sick at Hunyani with what the doctors finally decided was typhoid fever, the same disease from which Rudy Danielson died. She had an atypical rash the doctors could not explain, however, which led her to believe that she may have had measles at the same time. John Wolfe took her to Harare for medical treatment. She stayed with the Blairs for several weeks under the care of Dr. Wall, Dr. Gelfand, and dear Marguerite.

Russ and Marg Jackson's four-year-old daughter, Lynnette, also came down with what was initially thought to be typhoid fever when they were living at Msengedzi. Russ wrote:

*Our little girl, Lynnette, suddenly began running a very high fever. When she didn't respond to the malaria treatment Margaret had given her, we both realized we needed to make an emergency trip to the hospital in Harare.*

*When we arrived in Harare, the doctor who examined her put her in the isolation wing of the hospital, fearing she might have typhoid fever. We will never forget the feeling of utter helplessness we felt as we said good-bye to our little girl and left her in the care of total strangers.*

*The next day when we went to see her, we were informed that we were not allowed into the isolation ward. The head nurse told us that Lynnette had been told that her mother and daddy could not come to see her, as they had gone back to the mission station. They would return when she was well again. This was most upsetting to us, as I had assured Lynnette that we would come to see her every day and would not return to the mission station until she was with us.*

*Margaret and I knew the nurse's words would have been very troubling to her, so we went to the hospital office and shared our concern about the situation. I told the head nurse that if I could just talk to Lynnette, I could explain to her in a manner that she could understand why we couldn't come into her room. We were told, "If your little girl sees you, she will be even more upset and unsettled."*

*Not knowing what to do, we noticed that Lynnette's room opened onto the veranda and that there was a window in the wall of her room. I went back to the office and asked if I would be allowed to go to the window and explain to Lynnette what was happening, assuring her that her mom and I would come to the window to see her and talk with her every day until she was all better. I was given this permission.*

*While I talked to Lynnette, she was holding her doll in her arms and crying. I told her, "If you cry and make a fuss and don't settle down and be a good little girl, we won't be able to come to see you." As I explained the situation clearly to her, she stopped crying, and I could see that she understood.*

*The nurse shared with us the next day that after I had talked to Lynnette, they had had no more trouble with her. How we praised the Lord a few days later when the reports from tests taken proved that she did not have typhoid fever but glandular fever [mononucleosis]. A few days later she was moved into a general ward where we could visit her while she slowly recovered. . . . Lynnette had recurrences of this disease well into her adolescence.*

Dick Regier became extremely ill the day of his wedding. He got up in the morning with a painful neck. At first he thought he had probably just slept on it funny, but it continued to linger. By the time the wedding started, he was not feeling well at all. Ruth saw how pale he looked as he entered the church and immediately knew something was wrong. As they stood together at the altar, Dick almost fainted. Nevertheless, the wedding proceeded. After the recessional Dick breathed a huge sigh of relief that he could finally sit down. He was too sick to eat a thing at the reception.

The couple traveled to the Eastern Highlands for their honeymoon, but Dick was very sick the entire time. They found some malaria medicine up there but had to guess at how much he should take. Afterwards they learned he had taken too much, which had caused his skin to turn quite yellow. He also did not respond to this treatment.

When they got back to Harare and he was finally able to see a doctor, he told them that he had seen Dick's symptoms often in North Africa during the war. He didn't know exactly what caused them but that it was some unknown tropical disease. He said that all he could do was to try to keep Dick alive while it ran its course, so he put him in the hospital for a few days, Thankfully, Dick survived.

Rusty and Jo Sherwood had a close call with their two-year-old son Paul when they were living at Rusambo. Rusty wrote:

*Many children in the area were coming down with severe cases of a form of bronchitis following measles. Paul got it too, but whatever we did to try to help him didn't seem to be enough. We were exhausted. One night we tried making a homemade croup tent for him, but that didn't work either.*

*In the middle of the night we decided we needed to take him to Karanda Hospital. By the time we had driven two and a half hours in the truck to get there, his breathing was labored and he was turning a shade of blue.*

*Dr. Roland Stephens immediately put him in an oxygen tent, which was set up in the operating room. Jo was able to lie beside him on the operating table and try to get a little sleep herself.*

*Waking up as soon as she heard Paul cry, she put her hand in the tent to check the temperature. She then suggested that the nurse put some more ice on top of the tent. After that he settled down and began the process of getting well.*

*Dorothy Strom and everybody at Karanda were so good to us while we were there. We especially appreciated Dorothy's apple pie, which we took home with us along with our precious son Paul, who was a skinny runt but ALIVE!*

Reg and Carol Austin's son, David, also became quite ill while they were serving at Mavuradonha during the war. Reg was head-master of the mission high school there, and David was living at the hostel in Harare. Reg reported:

*It was a very traumatic experience for him. He had ulcers in his mouth and all through his digestive system to his anus. We took him to the ear, nose, and throat specialist in Harare and also down to Johannesburg in South Africa. Nothing helped him.*

*The explanation for his condition came months later during our furlough when we took him to a psychologist in Wheaton, IL, who had been recommended to us. Through figure drawings that he made, we discovered that the source of his illness was his fear that I would be murdered at*

*Mavuradonha, as other headmasters in the area had been.*

*I felt so badly that we never realized this on the field, but he had never been able to verbalize this. It came out only in his drawings under the skilled direction of the psychologist. The ulcers cleared up after he was separated from the traumatic situation on the field, but he developed Crohn's Disease as a result of it.*

The missionaries were also vulnerable to accidents and other injuries to their bodies because of the conditions under which they lived and worked. Clarence Cedarholm developed a slipped disc in his back from bouncing on his motor scooter over rough roads to visit outlying villages. While he was able to have successful surgery when he returned to the States, his doctor emphasized that he should not subject himself to any further driving on the bush roads. The Cedarholms were then assigned to work in the bookstore and developing the literature ministry on the field.

Carol Austin developed thrombophlebitis in her leg. She wrote:

*Over the years this leg has continued to give me a lot of pain. Had I had proper treatment then with a blood thinner, I perhaps would not have the swelling and discomfort I experience today.*

Bob Medaris had a most unfortunate accident while he was working on the new hostel. He wrote:

*We were sent to Hatfield to help build furniture for the hostel dorm. They were using orange crates and whatever, so the need was certainly there. In doing this, I got my hand in the way of the table saw, partially severing two fingers.*

*This was very difficult for both Fran and me. I had worked many years with no accidents, and here we were on the mission field and this happens. I really had a lot of questions on my heart as I went to surgery.*

*When I woke up from surgery, I felt I could hear a voice saying, "Bob, I did this for you, aren't you willing to do this for Me?" In my mind I could see two hands with nail prints in them!*

*Before, Fran and I both struggled with wondering if we were in the wrong place. After that experience you couldn't get us off the mission field. It was difficult getting used to two missing fingers, especially when typing, but it could have been a lot worse. Isn't our Lord wonderful?*

While some of the potential health risks of the earlier decades diminished over time, a grave new danger arose as the AIDS epidemic swept through the continent of Africa, beginning in the 1980's and rapidly accelerating in subsequent years. As a result, the entire medical staff at Karanda Hospital now works with the constant threat of exposure to the deadly HIV/AIDS virus. Dr. Dan Stephens wrote:

*We do not have the equipment we need for proper protection from this disease affecting over 60% of our patients. Our reliance is entirely on God.*

What has remained constant over all the years is the prevailing presence of God's grace and the strength of His calling that has made His dedicated servants willing to risk their very lives for the sake of the people to whom they came to minister! They too will hear, *"Well done, good and faithful servant"* as they enter heaven's splendor (Matthew 25:21).

# Financial Sacrifices

Being a missionary usually entails financial sacrifices as well. TEAM missionaries raise their own financial support and live by faith that this money will be supplied month by month. The amount of support is determined by the mission, according to the cost of living in the particular country in which they serve. It is designed to provide an adequate, but not plush, standard of living for them.

Relying on God and the faithfulness of others for all their financial needs puts missionaries in an often precarious position. They never know when circumstances might change for one of their supporters or supporting churches, making them unable to continue in that role.

When Betty Mason first went out to the field in 1951, the pastor of her home church told her that she did not have to do any deputation. She would be "their missionary" and they would fully support her. They generously helped her get the supplies she needed to take with her. The ladies even made her some dresses and a beautiful quilt. Several years later, when she married John Wolfe, they took on his support as well. When their first two children were born, they also covered them. They even raised the money to send them a one-ton, International pick-up truck.

When the couple returned to the States on their first furlough, however, the attitude of the church had changed completely. A new pastor had been called, and he informed them that they would receive no more support from the church.

This put John and Betty in a very difficult situation, as they had landed in the States virtually penniless, expecting to receive the church's latest support checks upon arrival. Because this church had taken on their *entire* support, John and Betty had no other supporters to take up even part of the slack.

Thankfully, TEAM was willing to advance them money so they could get a second-hand car to use while on furlough. They were also able to meet with the board of Betty's church to explain the desperate situation the abruptly ended support had created for them. This resulted in the church agreeing to provide a trailer in which they could live. They also offered to pay John $25.00 a week if he would serve as a visitation pastor for them.

Having a car and a place to live helped but fell far short of covering all of their financial needs. Betty wrote, "Times were really tough, and I had a hard time just finding food we could afford."

Then, just before they were due to return to Zimbabwe, the church board prevailed and the church took on their full support again. While grateful for the change, John and Betty were even more thankful to culminate what had been a very trying furlough and return to the country to which God had called them.

While in most cases God graciously and faithfully cared for the missionaries' basic financial needs both at home and on the field, this was never guaranteed. Some families lived under great uncertainty with consistent shortfalls in their support. Whether this was due to human inadequacies, spiritual dynamics, or a combination was often difficult to ascertain. As missionaries battle for the Kingdom in foreign lands, they certainly are not exempt from Satan's strategies to undermine their endeavors or God's desires to hone their spiritual development through hardships (James 1:2-4; Romans 5:3-5). Fluctuating economic dynamics in the country and the world also affected the financial stability of the missionaries.

Regardless of the level of support reaching their pockets, virtually all of the missionaries had to learn to "tighten the belt" and make their dollars stretch. Recycling in as many ways as possible was an accepted reality long before it became popular in the States.

Overall, however, the Zimbabwe missionaries were content with the standard of living they had on the field, and their focus was much more on ministry than on finances. The only time their financial sacrifices seemingly impacted them was when their ability to provide for their children and spouses was affected.

Ray Williams was somewhat disappointed that, as missionaries, he and Marti were limited in what they were able to give their children. Most MKs on the field did not have the abundance of toys they might have had in their homelands. Those they did have were often cherished, as Nancy Hendrickson Snyder revealed:

> *When the Eichner's house burned down, I remember feeling so badly for their kids losing what few toys they had. Then the Lord spoke to my heart, asking me if I loved Him enough to give up my special doll, Debbie, if He should ask me to do so.*
>
> *Debbie was a doll I loved and planned to keep with me always. I spent a lot of time playing with her. I could feed her a bottle of water and she would wet and I could change her diapers, etc. This doll also had really nice hair that I loved to wash and style, so giving her up was not an easy thing for me to do. When I did give her to Debbie Eichner, however, I had such a spirit of joy that made giving up my dreams for that doll's future well worth it.*

Dr. Dan Stephens wished he could have provided more financial help for his children when they were ready for college. Instead, however, he has had the joy of watching God provide for them. After all, they are His children too.

Carl Hendrickson was often concerned about his limitations in providing for his wife in their retirement or having any kind of an inheritance to pass on to her and his children when he died. Carl suffered an untimely, sudden death in London, England, as he and his wife, Donna, were returning to the States in 1983, after serving for a time on TEAM's South Africa field. Though deeply bereaved, Donna was not abandoned. She was safe in the hands of her loving Father, who would never leave her nor forsake her. She wrote:

> *God had given me Jeremiah 29:11-13 [about God having a plan to prosper me and give me a hope and a future] just four weeks before Carl's death. I knew He would provide for me in His own perfect way. Though feeling I could never marry again, God had His plan for me. I met and married Bert Abuhl in December 1986, and we had the joy of serving a short term together in Zimbabwe as dorm grandparents to my four grandsons there. We then moved into a retirement community. Bert died there in December 1995.*
>
> *I then transferred into a sister retirement community in California. After three years God so clearly led Carroll Robinson and me together. We were married in Zimbabwe while involved in a short term service in 1999. God has so graciously met my needs in His own perfect way.*

Carl's children also feel abundantly blessed. They look far beyond the dollar and cents value of what their father left behind and cherish the rich, intangible gifts they received from him. Daughter Jan Catron wrote:

> *We feel he has left us the greatest inheritance a family could ever want: memories of many happy times together; a loving, godly example of self-sacrifice, obedience to the Lord, and ministry to others; a faith that trusts God to provide our needs; and a hope and assurance that our inheritance is eternal and that we will all be reunited one*

*day with him before Christ. What more could we want? We*
*are blessed. We are rich.[1]*

Many of the missionaries could certainly have earned consider-ably more money and provided a much more comfortable lifestyle for themselves and their families had they used their particular skills and training in their homelands. When God's call came on their lives, however, this was rarely a consideration. Dr. Roland Stephens expressed that for him the financial sacrifices he accepted in being a missionary doctor were more than compensated for by the satisfaction he gained through using his skills in ministry and knowing He was serving God with them.

## Family Sacrifices

For many missionaries, the only sacrifices they acknowledged pertained to family issues. Being separated from their loved ones at home for such extended periods of time understandably brought a certain degree of sadness and loss. Chris Goppert wrote:

*Perhaps the one significant sacrifice we have had to make is*
*in having to say good-bye not only to the stability and secu-*
*rity of life in America but more so to the love and support of*
*having family close at hand. At the end of the day, however,*
*considering all that Jesus has done for us, this short-term*
*sacrifice is no real sacrifice. Without question, it is an honor*
*and a joy to serve the Lord in Zimbabwe.*

Holidays were times when separation from loved ones at home was felt more acutely. Carol Olsen Austin described an incident that occurred as she and Donna Kahlstorf were facing their first Christmas in Zimbabwe:

*It was the rainy season, and we experienced water seep-*
*ing through our grass roof in various places in our home.*
*Donna Kahlstorf, my housemate, was a teacher in the*
*Teacher Training Institute on our station for young Shona*
*men. Our house was a mud and brick, grass-roofed duplex.*

*She had one side, and I had the other, sharing the kitchen in the middle of the house.*

*I stepped into the kitchen one day and found Donna whipping up some cookie dough to make Christmas cookies. Her tears were dropping into her cookie dough along with the rain drops from the roof above. She was lonely and so was I as we thought of Christmas at home.*

*However, I had an invitation to go to the city of [Harare] to spend Christmas with Reg (home for the holidays from Bible school) and his parents in their home. I was joyfully looking forward to the visit. I don't think my joy went over too well with Donna just then. I should have reached out to her more.*

*I can't remember having any Christmas decorations in our house that year. Even in Reg's home there was very little to remind us of an American Christmas. They had found a small fir tree and decorated it as best they could, for my sake, I'm sure.*

Thanksgivings were when Judy Everswick felt the pangs of separation from her family. While she considered life in Zimbabwe much more the fulfillment of a dream than a sacrifice, she acknowledged feeling a sense of loss as she thought about her family being all gathered at her mother's house for what was the highlight of her family's traditions and not being able to be with them.

Another time that separation from family tugged on the missionaries' hearts was when major family milestones or crises occurred and they were unable to be present. For Marti Winchell Williams this included her brother's wedding and her dad's retirement. Most difficult of all, however, was not being able to be with her mother when her father unexpectedly died.

Not knowing what would transpire in the lives of their loved ones before they would see them again compounded the difficulties of the already painful good-byes the missionaries had to say so frequently. Many left aging parents behind and did not know if they were possibly saying a final good-bye. In the early days, before air travel became more available, returning home for crises that occurred there was virtually impossible.

Helen Smith remembers very clearly the day that friends with the Post and Telecommunications Service in Zimbabwe came to the Chirundu station, where she and Paul were living in 1959, and gave them the message to call the hostel immediately. Their son Fielding was in the hostel at that time, and they were afraid that something was wrong with him. Instead, they learned that a cablegram had been received with the word that Helen's father had passed away.

Helen said:

> *That was hard news to receive. I can remember going back to our mud brick, thatched-roofed house and sitting down by the kerosene lamp and reading Daddy's favorite passage of Scripture, 1 Thessalonians 4:13-18, about the resurrection and rapture when we would all be together again with the Lord. Then Paul and I prayed together.*
>
> *That was all I could do to mark his passing. In those days you never gave going home a thought, but the Lord did give comfort, knowing that Daddy was with Him. I had always hoped that Daddy would come and visit us in Africa, but that was not going to be. Still the Lord gave grace.*

Welton and Betty White went to the field after their family was grown, so they left behind not only their aging parents but also their children and a three-year-old grandson. This was hard and they certainly missed these loved ones. Then, during their second year on the field Welton's father died, and they were unable to return to be with his family at this time. Nevertheless, God comforted them through this difficult time.

When Bud and Mandy Jackson answered the call of God to become missionaries, they were already in Zimbabwe. Mandy had grown up there and Bud had been working for the government. A week before their departure to the States to attend Bible college, Mandy's father suffered a massive heart attack. Mandy wrote:

> *It was so hard to say good-bye to him in the intensive care unit, knowing that he had not accepted the Lord yet and that I would probably not see him again. The Lord impressed on us at that time the importance of our obedience to, and trust*

*in, Him. What a joy it was when a month later I received word that my father had accepted the Lord!*

John and Kelley Ulrich's concern as they left home also centered on the spiritual well-being of the relatives they left behind. They had to entrust those who were unsaved totally to the Lord. God graciously encouraged them after they were in Zimbabwe with the salvation of Kelley's step-grandmother, who had been an atheist. This was very affirming to them and their sense of God's call on their lives.

Being separated from family at home also meant that the missionaries were not able to see their nieces and nephews, and in some cases their grandchildren, grow up. By the same token MKs missed developing strong relationships with their grandparents, aunts, uncles, and cousins. Julie Hendrickson Stephens wrote:

*I met my grandparents and other relatives for the first time when my parents went home on their first furlough. I was four and a half years old. I met them a couple more times during my childhood on subsequent furloughs but never really knew any of them well.*

Lynn and Judy Everswick expressed the same situation with their children but also noted how God made up for this loss:

*Our children really do not know their relatives in the States very well, but the missionary "aunties" and "uncles" they had in Zimbabwe were very much family for them.*

Some of the MKs shared what a blessing their substituted "relatives" in Zimbabwe were. Janine Driedger Richmond wrote:

*The missionaries were family to us. I have great memories of our get-togethers. Some of these "aunties" and "uncles" became very special. Uncle Orla Blair called all of us MKs "chickadees" as we climbed over his fence to come and visit him. I used to have tea with Auntie Marguerite Blair as she taught me to crochet. They were like a grandpa and grandma to me. Uncle Carl and Auntie Donna Hendrickson were also very special. They always took note of us kids.*

Wes Hendrickson expressed similar feelings:

*No other family on earth could have as many uncles and aunties, brothers and sisters as the TEAM family. . . . The uncles and aunties mostly made up for the lack of blood relatives, although a real grandpa and grandma can't be beat. Regardless of their physical family role, the missionary uncles and aunties were wonderful encouragers and role models and great to be around. We also learned a variety of skills from them.*

The missionaries, too, felt that their separation from family back home was compensated for by the new "family" they entered on the mission field. The Zimbabwe field was particularly noted for the closeness that the missionaries felt to each other. These bonds truly did become as strong or stronger than their family bonds, but this is exactly what God promised to those who leave family for the sake of the Gospel (Mark 10:29-30).

Another sacrifice inherent to the transient lifestyle of the missionaries was the lack of a clear sense of "home." Not only did they move between homeland and mission field every four years or so, they usually had to do extensive traveling when on their furloughs, or "home assignments." Even on the field many moved frequently from station to station as their job assignments changed. As George and Pat Dee pointed out, this meant constantly adjusting to change and never being able to put deep down roots anywhere.

Julie Hendrickson Stephens expressed her perspective of this situation:

*As an MK and now as a missionary, my life has been a series of comings and goings. I have lived in four different countries and in four different states in the United States. As far as I can recall, I have never lived in any one house for more than four years without moving. In fact, the number of times I have moved averages out to a move about every 2 to*

*2½ years. I think when I retire and have some extra time on my hands, I'm going to write a book entitled "Packing for Dummies."*

*The hardest question for me to answer, however, is one I am asked countless times: "Where do you consider 'home' to be, here or over there?" For a long time I answered this question differently depending on how I felt at the time. You see, neither place truly feels like home. In Africa I am always looked upon as a foreigner, and in the United States I feel like a foreigner. I see America and Americans through the eyes of a foreigner.*

*So, where is "home"? Though there are downsides to living such a nomadic lifestyle (and on a bad attitude day I would be happy to inform you of each of them in full detail), the positive aspect, if one chooses to see it and accept it, is that you are forced to acknowledge where your real "home" is. When I'm asked if my home is America or Africa, I now answer, "Neither. My home is in Heaven."*

Bud and Mandy Jackson noted the effect that this frequent moving had on their children's education. They felt their only sacrifice was what Erin and Heath missed because of the interruptions and adjustment challenges they experienced due to having to change schools at critical times in their education process. They wrote:

*Our home assignments happened to come at times that, in retrospect, we see were not most conducive to their needs. The resultant educational, social, and cultural adjustments they had to make were very difficult and had a profound impact.*

For parents, the only sacrifice that surpassed that of being separated from family back home was being separated from their own children for extended periods of time when they went to school. Betty Wolfe wrote:

*The mission policy was for our children to go into the hostel in Hatfield the school term that they turned seven. That time came all too soon, and I felt as if I were cutting off my right arm when we had to leave Mary at the hostel the first time.*

*The children lived at the hostel under the care of a missionary couple and attended public schools, which . . . had very good reputations. The situation sounded ideal, but every new term when we had to take Mary back to school, I shed many tears and so did she. We talked once a week by radio and wrote letters, but when she or the others had a hard time, we just weren't there to help them through it.*

Donna Hendrickson Robinson expressed similar feelings:

*Saying good-bye to our children at the age of seven and eight, knowing we wouldn't see each other for several weeks or months was heart-wrenching. Not being involved in their everyday life or being there for their "open days" at school, their sports days, and special musical programs was difficult. I call this a "Price" we pay as missionary parents. Yet, I would do it again because Carl and I knew we were following God's will for us.*

*Perhaps the times we felt the separation most was when one of the children was sick. When Wes came down with measles, it tore me up inside to be unable to have him at home or to be with him when he was so sick.*

*Later, Nancy needed an appendectomy, and Carl and I were at Hunyani, having driven the Bible school students there for their practical work week. We just had to commit her to the Lord and dear Thelma Everswick, who lived on the Plot at that time as the field chairman's wife. As soon as we returned home to Chinhoyi, I drove to Harare to spend time with her in the hospital and then in the hostel after she was released.*

Their son, Wes, shared his perspective about living at the hostel away from his parents as a child:

*I have painful memories of days far from home during the school term as a young child. It was difficult not to have*

*Mom or Dad's lap and loving arms to crawl into when feeling sad or rejected by life.*

*However, I also claim many fond memories from my hostel days as highlights in my life. The activities and opportunities for fun seemed limitless. I also built lifelong friendships and priceless extended family members while there. The "communal" living style taught me to be tolerant of others and sensitive to their needs, putting the needs of others before my own.*

Their daughter, Jan, wrote, "The separation proved harder for our parents than for us kids."[2]

Barb Christiansen described the inner turmoil she felt in observing how leaving home to go to the hostel affected her children:

*I think the biggest sacrifice for me was having to let my children go to the hostel. They were young enough when we first arrived on the field that they had the opportunity to observe the older children from the station going to the hostel before they had to go themselves. Initially, it sounded like a lot of fun to them, and they actually looked forward to going. When that time came, they gave us no trouble at all.*

*Once our oldest, Steven, had been there awhile, however, the newness wore off, and he began to realize that he missed Mom and Dad and being at home. After that he would lie awake the night before going back to the hostel and be very concerned about it. He would also talk about it quite a bit. One time I asked him, "Steven, you know that we love you, don't you?" and he said, "Yes, but I can't feel it."*

*When he was seven, eight, and nine at home, he was giving me hugs every time he turned around. When he was at the hostel, he wasn't getting those hugs. I had a hard time seeing him have to readjust every time to that separation.*

*I think that each of our children struggled a bit in their own personal ways, though maybe not as much as Steven. The hardest part for me was observing these struggles. If I didn't sense that they were feeling these stresses, I think I could have accepted it better.*

As would be expected, the experience of living in the hostel was unique for every child, differing even among siblings. Some readily adapted to hostel life and enjoyed it very much while others felt the painful separation from home and parents more acutely.

Don and Lynn Hoyt felt that all of their kids loved the hostel and none of them felt deprived in having to be there. They expressed their great appreciation for the field's provision of such an excellent option for their children's care and education:

> . . . *Rich went there from the time he was in kindergarten. Paul and Helen Smith were the hostel parents at that time, and Helen was as much of a mommy to him as to her own son Billie, who was the same age and shared a room with Rich. We have always felt that we could parent remotely. The longest we ever went without seeing our kids was 10 weeks.*
>
> *While recognizing that many others might disagree, our philosophy was if the Lord has called you to missionary service, and you have a good facility in which you feel confident to put your children, this is the way to go. After all, the kids are owned by the Lord rather than us.*
>
> *We thank God that we were serving in Zimbabwe where God had led the field to do the right thing for their MKs in building the hostel and establishing principles by which it was operated. One of those was not putting just anybody in the position of hostel parents but picking out the people they thought could do the job. We believe that Zimbabwe had an extraordinary situation for the MKs.*

Joyce Everswick Goppert was one of those who thoroughly enjoyed living at the hostel. She wrote:

> *I loved every minute of the time I was in the hostel. I had TONS of friends to play with! It was a wonderful place to get to know the opposite sex and feel comfortable with them. I learned discipline there and never resented it. I also learned the discipline of having a quiet time in the hostel, and how I thank God for that wonderful training and gift! . .*

*. They were great days! I feel so incredibly blessed to have had some time in the hostel.*

Other MKs, such as Ruth Finsaas Kojetin, Jan Hendrickson Catron, and Dan Stephens, echoed similar thoughts. Faye Rilling Kobus wrote, "The great times we had in the hostel could not be captured in these pages." Bud Jackson agreed. He wrote:

*My years in the hostel are a definite highlight in my life. I still value the friendships that were made during those years. I also recall many details of the daily "family devotions" we enjoyed as well as some of the specific challenges that visiting missionaries would present to us. . . . I identify the years of my hostel experience as a time when I began to understand and model the practical dynamics of Christian living.*

When Lynn and Judy Everswick were ministering in Bindura, their children were able to live at home while attending school there—until high school. With the hostel no longer in operation in Hatfield, their oldest child, Kim, chose to go to a government boarding school in Chinhoyi for high school. Judy wrote about her feelings when this occurred:

*Sending Kim away to a government boarding school when she was ready to start high school was very difficult. I don't think that Kim ever resented that time because all of her friends on the farms were also going away to school since there was no high school in Bindura. It was harder for US to leave her, and I can remember the feeling that my heart was literally going to break as we drove out of Chinhoyi and stopped to mail some letters so that she would hear from us the next day.*

*The price of fuel was unbelievably high. Because of the political instability in the country at that time, there were 6 p.m. to 4 a.m. road curfews, making it hard to get to Chinhoyi for her all of her games and sporting events, which was a disappointment.*

*Lynn had encouraged her to "hang her banner" the first day of school and let people know that she was a child of the King. He reminded her of the words his father had said to him, "This will be what you make it. You have choices before you. Just be all that God made you to be."*

*Kim did "hang her banner." She got a Bible study started almost immediately and made awesome friends. She played sports, was a great student, and had the privilege of being a light for Jesus there. She was also encompassed with love from other "aunties" and "uncles" living nearby.*

*As an adult, Kim is still starting Bible studies. She started one over a year ago with seekers in her town and is now teaching at her church. She just led her church's first short-term missions team to South Africa to work with AIDS children. It has been such a blessing to us to see her deep passion for God and sharing His love. We don't see any scars from those two years in boarding school.*

The pangs of separation between parents and children grew even stronger when the time came for them to enter college, especially before era of electronic communications. Russ Jackson described the emotions he and Marg felt when they faced this time with their children:

*As we look back, Margaret and I feel that the separation from our children was by far the most difficult experience of our missionary career. We felt this was really the only sacrifice we were called to make while on the field.*

*In 1961, Lynnette, our only daughter, was 16 and needed to make a decision concerning her future education. She expressed a keen desire to train as a nurse at the Nightingale School of Nursing in Toronto. To be accepted, she needed the equivalent of grade 13 in the British system. After much prayer and many inquiries we decided that Lynnette should leave home in Zimbabwe and get this additional year at Briercrest in Saskatchewan.*

*On August 15th, her mother's birthday, we said goodbye to her at the Harare airport, along with two other MKs*

*[Bonnalyn Blair and Lynn Everswick] who were also leaving to complete their education in North America. We can never forget how torn our hearts were to be so separated from our only daughter.*

*Two years later we had to make another major decision to send our two boys, Paul (Buddy) and Tom, overseas as well. Because our furlough was coming up in the spring of 1965, we felt it wise to send them ahead to begin the school year at Ben Lippen High School, a fine Christian school in Asheville, North Carolina. As we bid them farewell at the Harare airport, we looked forward with great anticipation to being reunited the following spring.*

*What a joyous day that was! We were able to settle in Asheville near the school so that we could have them with us as much as possible. When summer arrived, we purchased a 19-foot Winnebago trailer so that we would be able to travel together as a family. Lynnette also joined us for those summer months.*

*When our furlough was over, we again had such mixed feelings as we left Paul at Ben Lippen to complete his high school education. We brought Tom back with us as we felt that at 14 he was too young to be left for the rest of his high school education, even though the adjustment back into the Zimbabwean system of schooling would be difficult. It was not easy to separate the boys on two sides of the ocean either.*

Bob and Betty Endicott agreed that the most difficult thing they ever did was seeing their daughter Linda off at the airport to go to college, knowing it would be 22 months before they would see her again. Donna Hendrickson Robinson also expressed how hard it was for Carl and her to be 10,000 miles away while their children made all the difficult adjustments from living in a 3$^{rd}$ world country to college life in the States on their own. Many others echoed these feelings as well. Only by the grace of God were they able to go through these difficult separations.

Their children were never abandoned, however. They were always in God's hands. Joy Finsaas Lindgren described how God faithfully met her needs and took what was a very difficult experience and used it for good in her life:

> *As MKs, leaving home at a young age to go to the hostel as well as going to the States for college was difficult. We became independent at a young age and often had to "punt" for ourselves. These times of "aloneness" spurred me toward a closer walk with God and dependence on Him—to know His will for my life and to depend on Him financially for college and everyday living.*
>
> *Dad often speaks about "the sovereignty of God." During difficult times God has always been sovereign. . . . Growing up in Zimbabwe, I may have been away from home a lot, but I had adopted uncles, aunts, and hostel friends who, along with my parents, encouraged, prayed, and were examples for me. I appreciate all of them and what they did for me.*

While every MK naturally responded in his or her unique way to the experience of living on a mission field, the vast majority fell in love with the country and the extended TEAM Zimbabwe "family." Twelve of them returned to Zimbabwe as full-time missionaries and fourteen others on a short-term basis.

These children grew up with a host of godly role models, which resulted in an unusually high number of them entering Christian ministry themselves. In addition to those who returned either short-term or long-term to Zimbabwe, ten are serving full-time on other foreign fields, and at least four others are involved in full-time mission endeavors in the States. Many others have become full-time pastors, youth leaders, and music directors or are active in lay ministries in their local churches.

While being a parent on the mission field certainly entailed significant sacrifices, the joys greatly surpassed them. A greater sacrifice was perhaps made by those for whom going to the mission field meant giving up their desire for children and a family.

Joe and Olga Reimer were told that they would have to give up their desire to adopt a child and have a family if they went to Zimbabwe. This was a hard decision for them to make, Olga shared, but they chose to be obedient to God's call.

Kiersten Hutchinson also felt that she perhaps sacrificed having children by being in Zimbabwe. Had she stayed in the States, she believed she would have been more likely to have gotten married. However, this was a sacrifice God helped her to make, and she trusted in the fact that He knows what is best for her. She is happy being in Zimbabwe because she knows it is where God wants her.

This is the assurance that enabled God's servants to draw deeply from the well of God's grace and move forward through the difficult sacrifices they were sometimes called upon to make. One day they will be welcomed into God's eternal kingdom with the words, *"Well done, thou good and faithful servant"* (Mat. 25:21).

[1] Vernon Mortenson, *God Made it Grow* (Pasadena: William Carey Library, 1994), p. 193.

[2] Jan Catron, *TEAM Horizons* (Nov./Dec. 1985), p. 7.

[3] Ibid., p. 6.

# CHAPTER 8

# God Enabled

*"The one who calls you is faithful*
*and he will do it."*
(1 Thessalonians 5:24)

As the missionaries obediently followed God's call to Zimbabwe, most went with the assurance that He would enable them to fulfill the purposes for which He had called them to this far-away country. How grateful they were that their success would not depend solely on their own skills and wisdom!

Over and over again, as these brave ambassadors faced challenges that seemed totally beyond their own capabilities, God indeed proved Himself faithful. He never required them to do anything for which He did not also provide the enablement they needed. This applied to everything from building houses and surviving in a totally new environment to raising up indigenous church leadership.

The unknown author of an early history of the Zimbabwe field wrote:

*From the beginning there was a complete dependence on God in everything. It was true for the physical, but how much more was it true for the spiritual. Could that barrier of distrust of the white man be broken down? Would the Gospel light penetrate the prevailing darkness of heathenism and ignorance? Only God, by the Holy Spirit, could work a work of grace in their midst, and He did.*

# The Early Days

Perhaps the most daunting physical challenge of the whole missionary endeavor occurred as the Danielsons and Dunkelds arrived at Msengedzi to set up their first mission station. In this totally new and unfamiliar environment they had to learn how to get water, how to get food, how to prepare food, and how to build a home that would be safe from the elements and wild animals. These two couples willingly approached this formidable task only because of their confidence in God. He had called them there. He had successfully brought them there. Surely, He would enable them to conquer whatever challenges they encountered in fulfilling His will there.

As the missionary force increased and new stations were established, they too had to be "started from scratch." The only advantage the builders of the new stations had was the ability to draw upon the knowledge gained from those who had set up previous stations.

The unknown author went on to describe the work involved when Norman Everswick and Orla Blair began building the Rukomechi Station:

*When the work started on the Rukomechi Mission Station in July 1948, there was a real consciousness of complete dependence upon God. Recruiting local laborers, clearing the land, making bricks, securing and transporting building materials, and getting the work done before the rains set in again all combined to make problems which, outside of His care, could not have been solved. But God was faithful, and in November 1948, the Everswick family moved in to occupy the station in that needy area.*

In 1954, Russ and Marg Jackson were assigned to open a station at Chirundu, just outside the large sugar estates located there. Marg wrote of the major expectations placed upon them in this endeavor:

*We had to be able to do anything and everything. Russ had never built a house, but he had to learn to make mud bricks so he could teach other men from the local villages to do so, and together they could build our home.*

*I had to tend to the medical needs of the local people, even helping women in childbirth, though I was not a qualified nurse. We learned a lot by trial and error, but we also believe that God gave us the wisdom we needed to do that which was necessary.*

The new stations enabled the teaching of the Word to expand to ever-broadening areas. Usually a missionary couple, and perhaps a single person, were assigned to the new stations. When they went on furlough, replacements were needed in order for the work there to continue. This sometimes resulted in new missionaries being sent out on their own before they really felt ready.

In 1953, George and Pat Dee were sent to Hunyani to replace the Blairs after having had only three months of language study. That same year Chuck and Verna Knapp were sent to Rusambo to replace the Jacksons. They wrote:

*Can you believe that after two months of language study, a lion hunt, and a cross-country trek to Mavuradonha, we were left on our own at Rusambo with just Ruth Ebbern and Teacher Mandas White knowing English? We were just learning to read the Shona Bible and beginning to understand it, but God soon enabled us to do rudimentary witnessing.*

God was faithful to these fledgling missionaries who were thrust into situations that initially stretched them beyond their comfort zones. Experience became their teachers, and they learned directly from the people they had come to serve. With God's enabling presence they prevailed.

## Stretching Job Assignments

Another time that missionaries had to trust in God's enablement was when they were given job assignments for which they felt inadequate. Often these proved to be special opportunities for them to learn and grow and see the grace of God working in their lives in new ways.

## Replacing Furloughing Missionaries

Again, these stretching job assignments frequently occurred as replacements were needed for individuals going on furlough. Most ministries, once they were established, needed to continue operating even though key individuals had to leave for various reasons.

Effie Byrd was called upon to fill such gaps numerous times. She was able to recognize the hand of God in each one, however, and claimed John 10:4: *"When HE puts forth HIS own sheep, HE goes before them."* She testified:

> *. . . It was the LORD's direction that Effie and Marian Wilterdink were temporarily put in charge of the children's home at Hatfield.*
> *. . . It was the LORD who gave Mary Danielson a furlough, and a replacement was needed at Mavuradonha for a year. Effie was taught by the Great Helper and Eunice Ott, who was a tremendous blessing. . . .*
> *It was the LORD who, through another field council decision, sent Effie to take the leadership of the Rusambo School as it grew. With the help of Teacher Mandas White many were confronted with the claims of Christ through the school, village visitation, and the giving out of the Word in the area.*
> *It was the LORD who, after furlough (1956), gave yet another appointment for Effie to become a helper at the TEAM headquarters in Hatfield. Another duty came in living as "aunty" at the girls' hostel until her marriage to Leonard Baillie of the Baptist Union.*
> *It was the LORD who directed the Byrd-Baillie union. Together they worked in other fields, including Zambia, and later back in Zimbabwe. . . .*
> *TO GOD BE ANY GLORY!*

Roy and Lydia Eichner faced their greatest challenges in job assignments when they were sent to Kapfundi to help out in the ministries that had been established on that station. Roy recounted how God faithfully enabled them to do what initially seemed beyond their capabilities:

> *Later on that first term we were assigned to Kapfundi, where Lydia was to take charge of the Light of Life Correspondence School, which was still in its beginning stages of development. Lydia would have to organize the development of new courses and update office procedures. In addition, she was given [teaching responsibilities] in the women's department of the Evangelical Bible School.*
>
> *I'll never forget the day we arrived at the station. The same truck that brought our few personal belongings took away the personal effects of the previous Light of Life director, Marian Wilterdink. As I helped to unload and reload the truck, Marian explained office procedures to Lydia.*
>
> *With less than eight hours of training, Lydia had to assume the directorship of the correspondence school. No one was to blame for so little overlap; sufficient staff was simply not available. Nevertheless, the situation seemed impossible to Lydia. How could she carry such heavy responsibility with so little training?*
>
> *Then, within a few weeks of our arrival, I was made principal of the Bible school and was asked to set up an English Bible course. I had never taught in a Bible school before. Although I had the training for this, I had no practical experience at all. What a challenge this was to me! It, too, seemed impossible!*
>
> *What Lydia and I lacked, however, God faithfully supplied. He gave both of us the ability to fulfill our assignments. Today Lydia and I rejoice in [hearing of] so many students whom we taught being used by the Lord in His service.*
>
> *Light of Life has also grown immensely; some 80,000 people [had] enrolled since the courses started. Many have received Christ as Savior; others have grown in the faith. The courses have reached into many institutions that missionaries cannot enter as well as geographical areas too*

*distant for us to visit. We are reminded of Matthew 19:26 (RSV): "With men this is impossible, but with God all things are possible."[1]*

Don and Lynn Hoyt felt similarly stretched when they were asked to take Bud and Lolly Fritz's teaching responsibilities at Mavuradonha Christian High School in 1963. Lynn had a Master's degree in education and some practice teaching experience, but Don had been trained in business, not education. However, they accepted the assignment trusting that God would go before them.

Don was assigned to teach first and second year general science, math, geography, and Bible. He hadn't studied general science since high school and felt insecure with math and geography. Lynn was to teach both years of English, home economics, and Bible. To add to the challenge, they had to walk into their classrooms in the middle of a term.

For the rest of the school year they experienced the challenge of keeping up with the daily requirements for all these classes. Don still marvels at how this turned out to be a very successful experience. He stated:

> *It was very definitely a tribute to the Lord. He brought forth skills and abilities we did not know we had and enabled us to use them in the classroom to His glory.*
>
> *This experience deeply impacted us with what God can do with human inadequacy. We are also grateful for His giving us this opportunity to discover we had a love for young people and gifts for teaching. This brought a huge change in our lives. From that point on God has continued to open doors to working with young people.*

Don and Lynn continued teaching at Mavuradonha for two more years until they were replaced by Stew and Marlene Georgia in 1965. They returned to fill in again from 1970-71. The last year Don took on even more responsibility as he became principal, taking over from Reg Austin, who went on furlough.

Bob and Betty Endicott were equally amazed at how God enabled them, as a printer and a housewife, to do tasks for which they had no previous experience. Bob expected to work as a printer at Word of Life Publications, but he was eventually made Director.

He was also asked to serve on TEAM's Literature Committee and Building Committee. He was even elected to be secretary of the Evangelical Fellowship of Zimbabwe's Literature Committee. "He never writes letters!" his wife exclaimed, but here he was taking minutes and writing letters for this organization of evangelical churches and missions who had joined together to develop literature that would be mutually beneficial to them.

Betty's opportunity to be stretched came when Dick and Pat Dunkeld had to leave the field for health reasons. With no experience as a typist, Betty had to take over Pat's responsibilities in the financial office. This included operating a bookkeeping machine she had never even seen before.

Once again, God faithfully enabled both Bob and Betty to fill each of these unexpected positions. Many others placed in similar "pinch hitting" roles could join them in testifying that their success was due to the marvelous "Coach" who accompanied them to the "plate."

## Setting Up New Institutions

Another time when missionaries felt a critical need for God's enablement was when the field moved forward to establish new ministries or to extend existing ones. Many had to assume roles in setting up, directing, or carrying out the new ministry that stretched them beyond any previous experience they had had. As they yielded themselves to the Lord, however, He was always more than able to fulfill the visions He inspired. He only needed willing servants who would trust in Him.

The two ministries that became an integral part of the early mission stations right from the beginning were education and medicine. Not only was permission to penetrate the Zambezi Valley contingent upon the missionaries opening schools and clinics, but these services also proved to be extremely effective spearheads for evangelism. As local people came to the schools and clinics, they would also hear the Gospel. In time, those responding became the nucleus for starting a church, which was the true goal of the missionaries' efforts.

All went well with this strategy until 1954, when the government raised its standards for teachers. Having an eighth grade education was no longer sufficient. They would now be required to have two years of formal teacher training.

The crisis precipitated by this sudden change left the field with only two options. They would either have to shut down all their primary schools or build a Christian teacher training facility themselves. They chose to do the latter, in spite of the immense undertaking that would entail.

Nine months later, with the help of local headmen who did not want to lose the schools established in their areas, Chironga was chosen as the site to build the new Teacher Training Institute (TTI). Merle and Kay Bloom were initially sent to open the station and begin the spiritual outreach to the people.

The Cedarholms, Rillings, and Bill Warner soon followed to begin the massive building project. The plan included not only building the teacher training school itself but also a large primary school where the teachers-in-training could "practice teach" while being observed and supervised.

In all, 27 buildings were needed for the two schools, dormitories, and staff housing. Some of the smaller ones would be simple pole, mud, and grass structures. Others would be built of mud bricks with thatched roofs. The Teacher Training Institute itself would be a more substantial building constructed of burned brick with a metal roof.

Reminiscing on this huge endeavor, Gladys Cedarholm wrote:

*When they started in 1955, Clarence and the other workers couldn't help but feel overwhelmed with all that needed to be done and wonder how it was all going to come together. I'm sure they felt inadequate for the task. In their own strength they never would have succeeded, but God was indeed faithful in providing what they needed, including some good local workmen to assist them.*

With God's help the station went up very quickly. Twenty-four buildings were completed during the first dry season, and the schools were formally opened in January 1956.

By this time God had also brought together a wonderful team of missionaries to staff the new, all-male training institute, some of whom also felt stretched in their assignments. Donna Kahlstorf, for instance, was a new missionary who had taught 4th and 5th grade students in the United States. She had assumed that she would teach at this same level in Zimbabwe. Never did she expect to be training *teachers*!

As she moved forward by faith into this position, she praised God for the gifted co-workers she could rely on for assistance in areas in which she felt inadequate. The high regard with which she esteemed them was evident in her descriptions:

*Cliff Ratzlaff was the first principal and extremely intelligent. He excelled at everything he touched. He was a gifted musician who could pick up almost any instrument and play it. He formed and led a wonderful choir at the institute. He was also good at sports and had a significant spiritual ministry to the students. Bill Warner was also a very competent teacher I could rely on for help when I needed it.*

*Eunice Ott was a capable and practical person who had a lot to offer as well. I appreciated her because she understood the Shona people. She had taught at Mavuradonha before coming to Chironga and was a real help to the rest of us, who were new on the field. Unfortunately, she taught only one term before her life tragically ended from a rabid dog bite on the station.*

*Mary Danielson came to take her place. She too was a trained teacher and brought a lot of maturity, wisdom, experience, and much solid spiritual depth to the staff. All of the Shona people appreciated her as a wise and experienced missionary.*

*I usually taught subjects like Methods and Principles of Teaching. I helped the students learn how to use the blackboard effectively and how to make teaching aids, such as charts, posters, relief maps, globes, etc., out of nothing but papier-mâché and shirt boxes. We produced some beautiful*

*creations that proved to be valuable teaching aids, which
the teachers used for many years.*

*We began every class with prayer, and the men attended
chapel and a Bible class daily. On the week-ends we often
took a group of students out to do village visitation and
teach Sunday school classes. I really enjoyed reaching out
to the people in the villages on these occasions.*

In 1959, the Teacher Training Institute had to be closed due to a
lack of staff. It reopened in 1962 but was permanently shut down in
1967, when the government raised its standards for teachers again.
Training students to this higher level was too costly for the mission
to consider.

During the time that TTI was temporarily suspended, the
mission made good use of its buildings for another major undertaking. With Dr. Sam Wall, the field's first medical doctor, arriving in
1958, TEAM was ready to take its medical ministry a step further
and launch a hospital program. While the search was conducted for
a good site on which to build the envisioned hospital, the field voted
to have Dr. Wall set up a temporary hospital at Chironga, using the
TTI dormitories.

The vision for a hospital ministry had gained significant
momentum in 1952, when TEAM board members Carl Gundersen
and Joseph Horness visited the field. God deeply impressed upon
them the need for a hospital to support the clinic ministries being
carried on at the various out-stations. Upon returning home, they
followed the Lord's leading in making generous financial donations
to make this possible.

The hospital project was perhaps the most ambitious endeavor
the field ever undertook. Not only would it involve another massive
building project, but the setting up process would also stretch the
medical personnel beyond any previous experience they had had.

This "stretching" began as Dr. Wall, Carol Austin, and newly
arrived missionary nurse Jo Sherwood began the job of transform-
ing the TTI dorms into a temporary hospital. Carol wrote:

*Dr. Wall put me in charge of setting up the operating
room. Now, how do you go about doing that 175 miles from*

*the city? I sent a letter back to Miss Clara Olson (assistant supervisor of nurses) at the Swedish Covenant Hospital in Chicago, where I trained, telling her my predicament. She came through, sending me a book on all that was needed to set up an operating room. I read that book from cover to cover. It also explained all the operating drapes and glove wrappers and [other supplies] I would need.*

*[I went to Harare] and ordered a couple or more bolts of green material conducive for using in surgery. I had to measure and cut it all out. [Then] I hired a young [Shona man who came] daily to sit on my verandah and sew. My [hand-operated] Singer machine was put to good use. . . . He worked for weeks, hemming drapes, etc. I could never have done it by myself, although I did sew the plastic glove wrappers . . . .*

On April 6, 1959, the temporary hospital opened. An official dedication was held with Field Chairman Orla Blair, District Commissioner Radamacher and his wife as well as the national teachers, students, and missionaries in the area.

By this time George and Pat Dee, Glenn and Dorothy Hotchkiss, Ruth Ebbern, Marian Wilterdink, and Lorraine Waite had joined the team of missionaries at Chironga. This added four more nurses to the hospital staff. Dr. Al and Donna Clemenger and Phil and Barb Christiansen would arrive within the next year, adding another doctor, nurse, and laboratory technologist. Since the medical staff lacked an anesthetist, Marian Wilterdink, with only two years of nurse's training, was sent to Harare Hospital for two weeks to learn this skill.

By all standards of comparison, the Chironga Hospital was very crude with its mud brick, grass-roofed structure, small wards, and a vastly under-equipped operating room (OR) and laboratory. Phil Christiansen described the "lab" as consisting of an about six by ten foot room with a bench along one side. On it sat a few chemicals, books, microscope, and a hand-cranked centrifuge.

The hospital had no electricity. Phil had to rely on sunlight for his microscope. Coleman lanterns, supplemented with hand-held flashlights, provided light in the OR.

Emily Wall wrote:

*Somewhere along the line we got an old generator. Trying to get it to kick in before surgeries was extremely exasperating, however, and rarely left Doc with the calm spirit and steady hands he needed for surgery.*

*I also remember the time of year when the white ants came out to mate. It was impossible to keep them out of the OR—if you want to call it that.*

While Dr. Wall was pleased that the hospital program had been launched, rudimentary as it was at this stage, he described the inner struggle with which he sometimes wrestled:

*It was our conviction that medicine was an effective means of evangelism in Africa for a number of reasons. Nevertheless, we felt there were more important and effective ministries, such as the Bible school.*

*Without a doubt, the medical ministry was the most expensive, which became very apparent to me. Early in our service, as we worked with limited funds, limited facilities, and limited personnel, I had to struggle at times as to whether the use of certain medicines would most likely save a life and thus justify their expense.*

*The Lord answered my perplexity in an unusual way. One Sunday one of our evangelists came to our home with a gift of eggs, and a visit ensued. Without mentioning my problem or at that time even having it in mind, I asked him, "What keeps your people from Christ?"*

*His clear reply was "Superstition."*

*I then asked him what, if anything, could be done about this.*

*He said, "Your medical ministry. When the people see their pagan measures fail, and then healing occurs at your hospital, it breaks down their unbelief, and they become receptive to the Gospel."*

*Wow! As important as saving a life was, it was of greater value in that it made penetration of the Gospel more effective! That gave me a much needed shot in the arm!*

During its first year alone, 35,000 local people attended the daily Gospel preaching services conducted at the Chironga Hospital.[2]

Meanwhile, Dr. Wall and Orla Blair found an ideal location for the permanent hospital five miles down the road. They were able to gain the necessary permission from both the government and the local chiefs and officially leased 50 acres of land for 99 years for a dollar.

The site seemed to promise an excellent supply of water, which was critical. Furthermore, the confidence of the local people had already been built through the medical ministry that had been operating at Chironga for nearly five years.

Reg Austin worked with Dr. Wall and an architect from Harare to draw up the plans for the hospital. The cement block structure was designed with a long, open main corridor from which any number of separate wings could be built. It began with only two wings, although one was built with an exposed basement, making it essentially two stories. One wing was for women and children. The lower portion of the other wing served as the men's ward with the upper level devoted to a surgical suite, delivery room, and pharmacy. Across the corridor from the main ward were a small lab and the out-patient department.

On February 6-7, 1961, the hospital moved from its temporary quarters at Chironga into its permanent home. What a great improvement this was! In addition to being constructed of durable materials with fiber-board ceilings and providing much more space, the hospital had running water and the capacity for electricity—at least for short periods of time.

The 65-bed hospital (which eventually grew to 150 beds) was formally dedicated on April 21st. This grand event was attended by all the local tribal chiefs, the District Commissioner, the American Ambassador, and their families as well as TEAM board member Mr. Carl Gundersen and his wife. Hundreds of families also came from the local villages and joined in a feast of typical Shona food afterwards.

The hospital was initially staffed by two doctors, Dr. Sam Wall and Dr. Al Clemenger, and five missionary nurses: Lorraine Waite, Donna Clemenger, Ruth Ebbern, Barbara Christiansen, and Pat Dee. Phil Christiansen was the medical (lab) technologist, Marian

Wilterdink the anesthetist and out-patient supervisor, Emily Wall the bookkeeper, and George Dee the hospital chaplain. They would soon be joined by Rick Froese, the pharmacist, and nurses Joanne Froese and Wilma Gardziella, who were completing their language study at Chironga.

Ten Shona staff members, hired from the local area, served alongside these missionaries. Phil Christiansen wrote:

> *They received on-the-job training in whatever area they were needed and did well at their jobs. They were also most gracious in putting up with our poor attempts to speak their language. We had lots of good times together.*

The goal of the entire hospital staff was stated well in the dedication brochure:

> *It is the prayer of all the staff that many more [Shona people] will learn to know the Love of Christ in an intimate and personal way because years ago God laid the plan for a hospital which today is becoming a reality.*[3]

In order to provide adequate staff for the hospital, plans were to begin a nursing school along with it. Wilma Gardziella had been guided by the Lord to accept the assignment of setting up the school, even though she felt very inadequate for the task. She described some of the major challenges she faced:

> *The syllabus provided by the Medical Council for training what were called "Medical Assistants" in Zimbabwe had minimal information concerning the content of the material to be taught. This basically left me on my own to determine what was important.*
>
> *I decided to visit several other hospitals with nursing schools to see what I could learn from them. I went first to the government hospital in Harare and was pleased to receive some teaching notes from them. I then visited a couple other mission hospitals with established training schools. Seeing what kinds of things they were teaching was*

*helpful too.*

*As I inquired about textbooks for the students, I was rather disheartened, however, to learn that no appropriate texts had been written in simple enough English for students to understand at that time. Other teachers seemingly developed their own teaching notes and required students to take whatever notes they could as they listened. They had nothing to hand out to them.*

After two years of preparation the Karanda Nursing School began in July 1963, with eight students. They were joined six months later by a second class. The students lived temporarily in staff housing until the nursing school building was completed in early 1964. The single building housed the students, classrooms, dining room, and kitchen. Later, a separate boys' dorm and classroom block were added.

Wilma continued:

*Since many of the early students had only an eighth grade education, I quickly discovered that teaching slowly enough for them to take sufficient notes was much too difficult and time-consuming. I finally ended up writing the text and drawing the diagrams I believed were important for them to know on purple ditto masters and duplicating them.*

*The first three years were rather stretching with the teaching staff barely keeping up with writing notes for the next day's classes. Since newly arrived Dr. Roland Stephens, who taught the Medicine and Surgery course, had no time to put his notes into printed form for the students, one of us would have to sit in his lectures, take notes, and then edit, type, and duplicate them for the students as well. Whenever we left the station for any reason, we had to prepare our notes ahead of time for all of the classes that we would be missing so they were ready for those who would be teaching in our absence.*

*As I look back, I wonder how I ever thought I could possibly succeed in starting a nursing school, even with the Lord's help. That is how I know that He was the one giving me what I needed at the very times I needed it. This included some very good help from others through the years, many of whom had lots more expertise than I had.*

*With God's help in so many ways, our nursing school had one of the best programs in all of Zimbabwe. In the early years almost every student passed all their exams the first time, and Karanda had a good reputation in the medical community.*

Soon after the nursing school began, the hospital staff recognized the need to start a midwifery training program as well. Cherith Till, a new missionary nurse ready to join the field, was targeted for this task. Before she began language school, she was asked to take a midwifery course in South Africa.

In 1968, when she was finally ready to join the Karanda staff and launch the midwifery course, she felt as inadequate for the task as Wilma had. She wrote:

*With only a half-page syllabus provided by the government, I attempted to convert my city training to the bush situation. I developed my own set of goals, which were to train the students:*

- *To look after a woman from the beginning of pregnancy through delivery,*
- *To recognize when a problem arose that needed more skilled medical help,*
- *To teach the mother proper feeding of her baby and other aspects of well-baby care,*
- *To teach the mother emotional and physical health, including hygiene and nutrition,*
- *To have a caring spirit and to be able to give spiritual counseling when possible or needed,*
- *To recognize that each birth was a miracle of God in which they had had a part.*

*The first year was particularly challenging as I could only guess at what would be covered on the final govern-*

*ment exams. This left me constantly wondering if I was teaching what was required.*

*I was also the only trained midwife on staff, and I had students who were on duty 24 hours a day. This meant I had to work long hours supervising them as well as being on call every night. Thankfully, when this schedule became too much for me, one of the other nurses would take over so I could get some rest. Eventually both Wilma Gardziella and Ann-Britt Byrmo obtained midwifery training too so that I was not the only one.*

*I was so amazed that in spite of doing poorly in my own early schooling, the Lord enabled me to set up this training program and successfully teach the midwifery students. I even taught anatomy one year, something for which I was definitely not trained. I credit all of this to the Lord's goodness and the helpful support of my co-workers.*

When Gordon and Jean Marshall arrived at Karanda in 1974 to take the place of Dave and Marilee Voetmann's place as the resident MAF couple, they were quite impressed with what they saw as the hand of God putting together all aspects of the hospital ministry. Jean wrote:

*When we stayed at the Southern Baptist mission station at Sessami for a few months before coming to Karanda, the two nurses there were graduates of the Karanda Nursing School. Once I saw the hospital and nursing school programs that had been established at Karanda, I wasn't surprised to learn that graduates could get jobs anywhere in Zimbabwe. Considering that the training was all done out in the bush with little or no contact with other nursing schools or seminars, such as most city schools have, the achievement was even more remarkable.*

*What sticks in my mind the most was the way one and all fit together to make a successful whole: Diane Powell in the lab, Dr. Stephens, Dr. Drake, and Bev Asa in surgery, Wilma Gardziella, Ann-Britt Byrmo, and Karen Drake in the nursing school, Thelma Everswick in the TB ward, Cherith Till in the maternity ward, Ruth Ebbern on the wards and Out-Patient Department, and that quiet, but most effective, Judy Gudeman directing the whole orchestra as Matron.*

*Then there were Chaplains Chasaya, Jeke, Sibindi, and Norman Everswick, who would spend many hours preaching in the wards, reading Scriptures to the patients, and praying with them. Their presence took away the feeling so often felt in medical institutions that the staff only had time to care for the bodies.*

*Out on the station Olga Riemer and Mrs. Gardziella [Wilma's mother] were making uniforms while Joe Reimer, the Rillings, and Dunkelds were keeping the station supplied with water and electricity, maintaining all the buildings, and managing the general upkeep of the entire station. Up in my radio room I sat and watched it all take place—and, of course, listened for radio messages from the other stations and Gordon as he flew to and fro between them!*

Bud Jackson also recognized the outstanding quality of the work that God raised up at Karanda:

*What the medical staff there accomplished over the years is part of Zimbabwean legend, particularly during the war years. Some of the best nurses in the country are trained at Karanda before spreading throughout Zimbabwe to serve. The extent of the lives touched by God through the various facets of the medical work at Karanda will only be fully realized in heaven.*

Raising up one of the best equipped mission hospitals in the country with a nation-wide reputation for excellence in treatment and training can only be credited to God and the excellence of His handiwork. To Him belongs all the glory!

During the war for independence Karanda Hospital truly did serve a crucial role as a frontline medical facility. Land-mine and gun-shot victims were ferried in by helicopter, often just as dusk was falling. Somehow God gave the staff the stamina to work through many a night with extraordinary teamwork to stabilize critical patients and save lives.

The hospital continued to operate in this capacity as long as possible. Located as it was in the middle of the war zone, however, safety was constantly being monitored. When missionaries were targeted and killed at several hospitals in the country, this was seen as a clear signal that the lives of the Karanda staff and students might also be in jeopardy. Therefore, in August 1978 the hospital was closed and the station was evacuated.

When the war ended two years later, the mission decided to work towards re-opening the medical work at Karanda. Much repair had to be done on all of the trashed and looted buildings. During this time of physical rebuilding, the hospital was operated by Friday Chimukangara, a 1976 Karanda graduate, as an outpatient clinic. The initial missionary staff, consisting of Dr. Dave and Karen Drake, Lorraine Waite, and George Smazik, commuted by MAF plane from its new base in Harare. A year later it was finally ready to be opened once more as a hospital with a resident staff.

With "free health care" being offered by the new government in 1982, the number of patients soared. Up to 400 out-patients a day were being seen and the 150 in-patient beds almost always occupied. The burgeoning AIDS crisis filled more and more of these with AIDS patients. Sixty to seventy-five babies were also being delivered each month. Although the free health care soon ended, the patient load remained high. Several full-time chaplains ministered to the patients and their families on a daily basis, reaping the spiritual fruit of this valuable ministry.

## Stretching Medical Challenges

God's hand was also evident in enabling missionaries, both at the hospital and the rural outstations, to execute critical medical interventions that were well beyond their scope of training. Sometimes missionaries who had no medical training were called on to do some major "pinch hitting," and God wondrously enabled them.

Betty Mason Wolfe told about an early experience of hers at Msengedzi:

*One day a little boy was carried in who must have been about 10 years old. He was unconscious and his eyes were rolled back in his head. He was gasping for air and convulsing with each painful breath.*

*I had no idea what was wrong with him, so I took a blood smear and stained it. When I looked at it under the microscope, every red cell had a ring formation in it, which was a manifestation of malaria. Normally you were doing well to find one ring formation after examining two or three slides. This child had no healthy red blood cells left!*

*My distilled water consisted of rain water that I had collected in a glass bowl and then filtered and boiled. I dissolved a tablet of quinine in a syringe of this "distilled" water and managed to get a little bit of it into his vein before it collapsed. I injected the rest into his muscle, and that was all that I could do for him.*

*I went to the Dunkelds' for lunch and waited to hear the death wail. Later, I returned to the dispensary to see if perhaps his family had carried him back to the village to die. I couldn't believe my eyes when I saw this same child conscious, sitting up, and visiting with the others! God had miraculously intervened.*

Phyllis Rilling told of a time when she and Emil were serving at Rusambo and took a severely injured man to the hospital. On the way they met another man who begged them to pick up his wife, who was in labor and "just a little ways off the road." It was rainy and turned out to be quite a distance off the road, but they nevertheless did pick up the woman.

The baby was born en route to the hospital but wasn't breathing. Phyllis immediately started doing mouth-to-mouth resuscitation while the mother, in great distress, was outside the car giving a death wail. Phyllis wouldn't give up, however, and soon the baby started to breathe and cry.

Phyllis held the baby the rest of the way to the hospital to make sure it kept breathing. When they arrived, Dr. Stephens checked the baby over and pronounced it perfectly fine. God had marvelously enabled Phyllis to save this tiny baby's life.

Carol Olsen Austin told of a most unusual challenge she faced one day at the Chironga clinic:

*One afternoon I heard "go-go-goi" out in the front yard. I went out to see who it was. A village man was standing there, calling for me to come to the clinic. The Shona people did not knock on doors but would call out to inform others you were there and wanted to see you.*

*As far as I could make out the man's words, somebody was ill and needed help, so I went with him. Approaching the clinic, I saw a cow standing there by a tree. It didn't take long to see that the cow needed treatment, as it had a large, gaping wound on its side. I found out later that the village man had taken his cows to the river for a drink, and while there a crocodile jumped up and bit this particular cow, taking a good portion to eat.*

*Now, cows to the Shona people are their wealth, and this man was not going to let this cow die. So he walked it up from the river to our station and straight to the clinic. As I had been treating patients for a few weeks, he evidently thought I could help his cow recover.*

*Taken by surprise at such a task, I had to think for few minutes about what to do. First of all, I needed help, as I was not about to treat a cow by myself. I was able to locate Emil Rilling, and he agreed to come and see my predicament with this cow.*

*We agreed the cow needed to be tied down, which he did while I prepared some disinfectant water to wash out the wound. I gingerly approached the animal and splashed the water onto the wound.*

*The only other thing I thought of to do was to get penicillin ointment into that deep wound, but how? I put a big wad of gauze on a long pair of forceps, dipped it into the ointment, and then put it against the wound.*

*Now, what could we do to keep the gauze in place? I foolishly tried to wrap a bandage around the cow's middle, but when she took her first step, it all fell off. I really didn't know what to do and Emil had no suggestions either, so I told the village man I was done and that he owed me a shilling (about twelve cents). He didn't like that very much, but I argued I had used more medicine on his cow than I would on a person. He paid me and was off with his precious cow.*

*I went back to my house and wondered what I was getting into out here in the "bush." A few weeks or a month later the man came to tell me his cow healed and thanked me. That made me feel good.*

*Later in the year the same man began working for the mission under the guidance of Clarence Cedarholm, who held devotional times early each day when the men gathered to work. He heard the Gospel daily and eventually gave his heart to the Lord. I couldn't help but think that perhaps my willingness to treat his cow had just a little part in bringing that man to salvation.*

Dr. Dave Drake told about a time when God enabled him to perform a critical surgical procedure he had never done before:

*Rick Froese was out camping with his boys near Pulpit Rock when a woman carrying a baby on her back flagged them down on the road after dark. The baby had been tragically injured when her husband came home drunk. In his rage he had thrown a brick at his wife. She ducked and avoided getting struck but the brick hit the child's head.*

*When Rick examined the baby, she was not breathing very well and seemed to be in a life-threatening situation. Medical intervention was needed as quickly as possible, and Rick offered to take the mother and child to the hospital immediately.*

*The baby survived the nearly one hour trip to the hospital. I was at home on a Saturday evening when the group came to my door and apprised me of the situation. I quickly ran down to the hospital with them.*

*I examined the child, took her vital signs, and realized I had to act quickly. The baby's skull was deeply creased into the brain tissue, causing pressure and moderate bleeding. I knew the correct intervention was to make several burr holes into her skull to relieve the pressure on her brain, but I had never done such a procedure on my own, let alone on such a young child.*

*We gathered the surgical team. Then we prayed and I clearly asked the Lord to guide me in the operation. After praying, I made two small burr holes, one on each side of the crease. Then I inserted an instrument through each of the holes and literally snapped the bone upward.*

*Bev Asa, our anesthetist, immediately reported that the child had begun breathing normally. We all praised the Lord as one of the nurses led in thanking Him for answering our prayers. We then closed up the surgical sites and put a big bandage on the child's head.*

*The next morning as I came on rounds, the little girl was standing up in her crib and looking around. Her life had been saved by the grace of God. I am not a brain surgeon; yet the Lord guided my hands through the entire procedure.*

Cherith Till also told of a time when God allowed her to perform beyond her experience in saving the lives of a mother and baby:

*I was called one night to a patient in labor who had had a previous Cesarean Section for a small pelvis. Our only doctor was away from the station, taking a break.*

*After praying and discussing the situation with Judy Gudeman, I gave the woman a combined sedation and relaxation injection in an attempt to try to slow things down, even though she was quite far along in labor. The result was that she relaxed and we delivered the baby. The baby, however, was not breathing well due to the sedation I had given the mother.*

*The Lord enabled me to intubate the baby and provide artificial respiration while at the same time giving medication to counteract the sedation. I had never intubated a baby on my own and could not have succeeded in this without God's help. The end result was that we had a healthy mother and baby.*

Dottie Chick came to Karanda in 1970 as a nurse on loan from the South Africa field to help fill a staffing shortage at the hospital. She too felt the hand of the Lord helping her as she faced challenging midwifery cases, as she had never received any training in this area. She also appreciated the help she got from Judy Gudeman.

Mary Ann McCloy was even less prepared to handle midwifery cases. Having had no medical training at all, she told about a time at Rusambo when she and her husband, Dick, had to deliver a baby when no nurse was around:

*One day I heard a voice calling, "Sister! Sister! [British term for "nurse"] My wife is ready to have a baby!" Lavonne Kinney, the station nurse, was away in town, however. What were we to do?*

*Well, Dick went with the car and brought the lady to our clinic. She had been in labor for three days, and it was her first baby. Since she was young and very small, both Mary Danielson and the matron of the Homecraft School, who had delivered babies in the past, felt there were too many dangers in trying to deliver her at the clinic. We tried to get the MAF plane to come to take her to Karanda Hospital, but we were told it was down for inspection.*

*Rather than just watch her die, Dick and I decided to do what we could. I figured that I had at least been awake for the births of most of my own children.*

*We got to the clinic and found a* Good Housekeeping *magazine article that Lavonne had there on "How to Do Home Deliveries." Thank you, God! Dick stayed in the middle room reading the instructions from the magazine to me.*

*The gal was fantastic. I could give her nothing for pain except verbal encouragement, but she did well trying to push during the contractions and relax between them. The Lord kept us all calm.*

*Just as the baby was making its appearance, a knock came at the door. "Hold on a minute!" I called. "It's a girl! Okay, come in." There was our six-year-old daughter, Debbie, to announce that the plane could now fly. We no longer needed it, however, as the Lord had helped us safely deliver the baby after all.*

*Mary Danielson also appeared just then in time to tie and cut the cord. What rejoicing there was for the Lord's watch care over this new young mother and baby!*

## Empowerment for Ministry

The area in which the missionaries probably felt most compelled to rely on God's enablement was in their various ministry endeavors. They fully recognized that building the Church in northeast Zimbabwe would only be accomplished by the power of the Holy Spirit working through them. As they committed their efforts to Him, He faithfully enabled them to accomplish the primary purpose for which He had called them, in whatever niche of service that was.

In an article entitled "Sixteen Years of Progress in Southern Rhodesia" the 67 missionaries on the field at that time (1958) reviewed some of what God had enabled them to accomplish thus far in the field's history, giving all the glory to Him:

*Now, 16 years later, we look backward and exclaim, "What God hath wrought!" ...*

*Ten organized churches and regular Sunday services held in some fifty widely separated places represent some of the accomplishments. ...*

*Medical care has played an important part in helping the people. Until this year, our seven clinics were manned entirely by nurses (who often did the work of a doctor).*

*Education has its share in reaching [the lost] with the Gospel and in strengthening the convert.*

*From the small beginning of one school taught by one missionary, TEAM's education program in [Zimbabwe] has grown to 1812 students in 19 schools, taught by 40 [national] teachers and eight missionaries. Three more school blocks have been built for future expansion in the densely populated Karoi area.*

*As Christians become literate, they need more Bible training. Out of this need has come the Evangelical Bible*

*School where men and women are carefully trained in the Bible.*

*During the past year, three men completed the evangelist's course (two years of classroom instruction and one year of internship). Several women have completed one year's Bible training. Trained evangelists are few in number, but their value to the Lord has been strengthened by their Bible school background.*

*Three-month Bible courses are being added on the local level to train villagers as lay evangelists, so sorely needed in these early days of the indigenous church.*

*For a long time TEAM missionaries have had a burden for training [national] women who have had little opportunity for education. This coming year, construction will begin on a Homecraft School at Rusambo for teaching them in the Word of God as well as in the domestic sciences. . . .*

*With the rapid increase of literacy among the [nationals], Christian literature is a must. False cults as well as Communism have advanced their causes alarmingly with their use of this medium.*

*The few tracts translated in the Shona dialect have been much in demand. The Light of Life correspondence course on the Gospel of John, offered in the [national] languages and English, has a large enrollment of over 4000 students. . . .*

*Radio has been the latest venture of evangelism in [Zimbabwe]. Recorded programs in the Shona dialect have been broadcast periodically over the African Broadcasting Station in Lusaka, across the border in [Zambia], reaching thousands. . . . The [Shona people] themselves supply the music, give testimonies, sing Gospel songs, and preach. . . .*

*In light of what the Lord has done in the past, we of TEAM in [Zimbabwe] are looking to the King of Kings for great blessings in the coming months. May we advance by His Spirit as we take root downward and bear fruit upward.*

In the years that followed God was indeed faithful in enabling every one of the budding ministries mentioned in this article (reviewed by Marie Schober) to grow further, reaching even more individuals for Christ and training as many as possible in the knowledge of the Word. Countless lives were changed among not only the Shona people but also the white, colored, and Indian races living in the country.

As God worked through the missionaries' lives, they usually had to take His enabling presence by faith, recognizing it primarily by the fruit that was produced. Bill Warner recounted an incident when he thought he had failed miserably in his attempts to share the Gospel, only to discover that God had indeed worked through his fumbling words:

> *Before I had really learned Shona, I tried to witness to three national men under the garage light at TEAM headquarters in Hatfield. I was using Shona song titles and verses and whatever I could think of, along with plenty of prayer. At one point all three men left me alone under the light and went off in different directions.*
>
> *I felt I had failed until they began to speak from their distanced positions, "Ini ndinoda kutevera Jesu; kunyangwe ndoga ndichatevera." ["I want to follow Jesus; although alone I will follow."] I had used that song in my stumbling witness, and they had physically separated themselves from me to indicate their desire to "follow" the Lord. I never forgot the joyous, fulfilling feeling I had of God's using my humble efforts for Him.*

Mildred Carnall described times when she was extremely conscious of God's anointing on the words she spoke:

> *There were a few times when leading the service at the dispensary that I particularly felt the touch of God. As I taught the Scriptures, I felt a sort of chill go over my body, and I knew I was standing on holy ground.*

For missionaries such as Bob Endicott, who had come to the field as a printer, becoming involved in any kind of more direct spiritual ministry took them outside of their normal comfort zones. This created an even greater reliance on God's enablement. Bob described two instances in which God gave Him the ability to fulfill unexpected roles for which he did not feel qualified.

The first was when Dick and Pat Dunkeld returned to the States in 1970 and he was asked to take over responsibility for the Tafara Church, which was meeting under a tree in one of the Harare townships. With the help of some of his staff at Word of Life Publications (WLP), he fulfilled this assignment as best he could until another missionary with greater skill in the Shona language became available to replace him.

The time he felt God's enablement most of all was when Boarding Master Richard Tsinakwadi and Pastor Frank Kakunguwo were tragically murdered at Mavuradonha Christian High School during the war, one of the most tragic days in TEAM Zimbabwe history. With virtually all of the other TEAM staff in Harare being occupied with Easter week-end activities, Bob was sent to the airport to pick up Mr. Tsinakwadi's body and his widow, Nancy. He will never forget how, as she stepped off the MAF plane, she knelt and prayed, "Father, forgive them for they know not what they do."

With the help of MAF pilot David Voetmann, Bob loaded the blanket-wrapped body into a borrowed, metal police box and secured it to the top of his Peugeot station wagon. Accompanied by a Shona nurse (to testify concerning the nature of the death) and another Shona staff member of WLP, Bob started off with Mrs. Tsinakwadi to the village where her husband would be buried.

On the way they stopped at the boarding school where the Tsinakwadi children attended. Bob had to tell their eight-year-old daughter and even younger son that their father was with Jesus and his body was in the box on top of the car. As soon as this word was out, much wailing erupted at the school.

When the party neared the village, however, the atmosphere was totally different. The Christians came out to meet them and walked alongside the car singing hymns.

Once in the village, Bob suffered a printer's worst nightmare—he was asked on the spot to preach the funeral service! From a human perspective Bob felt grossly inadequate, but with the help of an interpreter, God enabled him to fulfill this divinely given assignment.

Missionaries serving in ministries that were not directly

involved in evangelism, discipleship, or church planting often needed the most faith to believe that God was indeed working through them for the advancement of the Kingdom. Lorraine Waite was delighted when she saw God clearly use her community health work to plant new churches.

This new outreach was launched as Karanda Hospital endeavored to place a stronger emphasis on preventive medicine after the war. Lorraine took charge of the project and began by setting up a model "Nutrition Village" behind the hospital. She described some of its features and how her work gradually expanded to neighboring communities:

> *The purpose of the village was to give mothers of malnourished children a place where they could learn about nutrition while their children were brought to a better state of health. Then, when they returned to their own villages, they would be better equipped to keep them healthy.*
>
> *We had a large garden as well as an area where we raised chickens, ducks, goats, and rabbits. Because we liked to give eggs to all of our malnourished patients, both in the hospital and the Nutrition Village, I always had lots of good laying hens.*
>
> *We used the goats to provide an alternate source of milk for newborns that reacted to their mother's milk. They could generally handle the goat milk, and we used that to get them over the hump until they could tolerate their mother's milk.*
>
> *I also got into making soy milk. In earlier days people used to raise soybeans in the Karanda area, so I got a lot of them to start doing that again and taught them how to make the soy milk.*
>
> *I also experimented with other ways to use the soybeans and found a recipe for making soybean bread. In order for them to be able to bake the bread, I taught them how to make ovens, first out of five-gallon cans and then out of clay and sand.*
>
> *I also taught them recipes for making bread, cakes, pies, biscuits, and all kinds of things. It went over real well, and the women would tell me, "These classes are really helping*

*us. Now our husbands love us more than they used to."*

*A lot of those who were malnourished had zero income. . . . We used the rabbits we had in the Village to develop an excellent self-help project for them. We would teach them how to make a safe rabbit hutch, what to feed the rabbits, and how to properly take care of them. Then we gave them a pair of rabbits so they could start raising their own.*

*The Nutrition Village became a springboard for going out to other villages to do what we called a "community analysis" and to teach the people healthier ways of living. . . .*

Before going into a community, Lorraine would get permission from all the political and village leaders and invite them to join the team, which many did. She would also take up to 15 student nurses with her. She continued:

*When I went out to a new area, I would tell the people, "We're coming to see what your needs are. We want to hear from you what you think your needs are, and we want to look and see what we feel your needs are. Then we want to get together and see what we can do about it." . . .*

*We were especially anxious to teach them a healthier latrine system and how to make Blair toilets. These are ventilated toilets that trap and kill disease-carrying flies and mosquitoes. Of course, we told them not to drink river water and taught them to dig safe wells in their villages.*

In the process of doing this work, Lorraine had opportunities to share the Gospel. She reported:

*One of my happiest experiences was when we went to Munyapere in the Date area. Mr. Munyapera, who was the sub-chief, was having a meeting with all his people the day we went to talk to him, so he invited us to come to the meeting and share with the whole group. . . . My student nurse talked about the advantages of family spacing so as not to wear the mother out or have a dead mother and a bunch of little children.*

*When she finished, both the men and the women did a lot of discussing between themselves. Then the men came up with a question. "Why is it," they asked, "that women once they're married don't keep themselves or their children or houses as clean and neat and nice as they did before they were married?" In attempting to answer that question, I took them to Ephesians and shared what Paul had to say about the relationship between husbands and wives.*

*When I finished, they closed the meeting, and everyone went off to eat. I didn't get to eat, however, because so many of the women hung around to ask their questions. Many of them came and said, "Sister, I want to talk to you privately." Then they would ask me about this or that female problem.*

*The last woman started the same way, "Sister, I want to talk to you privately." Then after we found a place to sit on some stones, she surprised me by saying, "My husband and I were talking it over, and we don't know the Lord. Would you teach us to know the Lord?" Of course, I was delighted.*

*Then as we began visiting the people from house to house, I mentioned what this lady had said, and without exception the folks said, "If this woman is going to get a church started, I'm going to be part of it." So I got permission for that too, and I began taking some of the teen-agers from the Karanda church, and we started meeting at the sub-chief's home on Sunday afternoons.*

*People started coming to the Lord, and they didn't come one by one but family by family. The husband and wife and all their children who were old enough to understand would come together. I would then explain the way of salvation, using Campus Crusade's Four Spiritual Laws booklet in Shona.*

*As I did this, I always worked with the student nurses and other young people I had brought with me. Soon they began saying, "I want to do that. Let me talk to the next one." So they started leading these people to Christ, and all I had to do was to sit back and watch. It was so rewarding for me to watch God work in their lives in this way and actually lay the foundation for a new church.*

*Once we had begun doing this community work, I was receiving requests from as far away as Mukumbura and many other places asking, "When are you coming to our village?" I knew I couldn't get to all of them, but I continued to work with and train the student and graduate nurses and the church people, and now many of them are carrying on with the ministry even since I've come home. As a result there are a lot more churches in that area—all as an outreach from the community health program.*

What Lorraine developed in the Karanda area has now spread beyond the borders of Zimbabwe. Dr. Muriel Elmer, daughter of pioneer missionaries Rudy and Mary Danielson, came out with her husband to visit and observe Lorraine's project. She was so impressed that she went back and started teaching these concepts to her students at Wheaton College. Many of these graduates are adapting and using Lorraine's model in many other countries. Muriel has continued to spread these concepts even more broadly in her ongoing role as a cross-cultural specialist.

As a fitting capstone for many years of labor and her major contribution to medical missions, Muriel nominated Lorraine to receive the "Alumnus of the Year" award from her alma mater, Wheaton College, in 1991. Her fellow missionaries even paid her way to receive it in person. Today Lorraine cherishes both the plaque and the rocking chair that she received at that time. She says that her last twelve years on the field working with the community health project were her most rewarding years.

Kim and Sean Doyle also experienced extraordinary enablement when they took over the ministry in Mvuri while Kim's parents, Chris and Joyce Goppert, went on furlough. Joyce wrote:

*What an experience they had! And how God used them! As if stepping into this role was not challenging enough, suddenly the socio-political instability of the country started to escalate. Through it all, however, God gave Sean and Kim strength, wisdom beyond their years, and grace to minister to a ravaged, desperate community.*

*We returned after our furlough to witness further*

*erosion of national life. And through this entire painful time, Jesus Christ was WITH us in our boat (as He was with the disciples in the storm), and He whispered peace to our hearts.*

*How grateful we are to have been given the great privilege of being His representative to this hurting part of the world during those years! We reminded ourselves again and again of what TEAM's general director, Charlie Davis, told us before we left to return to Zimbabwe that term: "Don't try to change the situation. Just minister [God's] Grace to the people's hearts in the midst of the turmoil." That's what we endeavored to do with God's enablement.*

---

[1] Roy Eichner, "God of the Impossible," *TEAM Horizons* (no date), 10 (slightly modified).

[2] Gunderson-Horness Mission Hospital Dedication Program, 1961.

[3] Ibid.

# CHAPTER 9

# God Provided

*"And my God will meet all your needs
according to his glorious riches in Christ Jesus."*
(Philippians 4:19)

As God led His faithful servants into missionary service, He was their Master Supplier. Whether their need was physical, emotional, spiritual, or financial, all they had to do was call to Him for help. While often allowing them to live under circumstances that would test their faith, He never disappointed them. He faithfully supplied all that they needed in order to fulfill His call on their lives and often added special blessings just because He loved them.

Chris Goppert wrote:

*The Scriptures tell us, "Faithful is He who calls you, who will also do it" (1 Thessalonians 5:24; KJV). As Joyce and I look back over our years as missionaries, we can say that God has been so very faithful to our family. He has always been there for us and met our needs, even in times of recession and war. We have seen His good hand provide in so many different ways (finances, medical care, wise counselors, quality education for our girls, protection from harm during the war, and safety in the air over tens of thousands of miles flown). The Lord has been our faithful provider and defender, just as He said He would be."*

# Finances

Finances were a major need the missionaries depended on God to supply, usually commencing with their college years and extending throughout their entire missionary careers and into their retirement. God's faithfulness to His servants, who had followed Him into a sacrificial life of service, often demonstrated the special favor with which He esteemed them.

## Educational Needs

While she was at Bible college, God taught Mildred Rogers Carnall both the principle of tithing and His faithfulness in supplying her needs. She wrote:

> *In my Old Testament survey class Mr. Sells explained how even the Levites had given a tithe to the Lord. Therefore, those of us who had given our lives to the Lord to learn His Word and serve Him wherever He directs should be doing the same.*
>
> *I began right there in class to figure up how much tithe I had not paid since coming to Columbia Bible College. It came to $18. When the class broke up at 10:00, I went to the mailbox and found a letter from a girl whom I hardly knew with $20 in it. This covered the $18.00 I owed plus the $2.00 tithe on this gift!*
>
> *I went through four years of college completely on faith, working in the dining room and elsewhere and tithing the entire time. The Lord supplied everything that I needed all the way through, which was so amazing to me. At graduation time I went to settle up with the financial office and was even given a refund from my work in the kitchen!*
>
> *Then as I prepared to leave for the field, God also provided financial and prayer support from many relatives and friends. All of this served to confirm to me that God had truly called me. When the going got tough on the field and I*

*wondered if I was really in the right place, I would remember how wondrously God had provided for my financial needs in preparing to come. This would give me the reaffirmation in my heart that I needed. I knew that I had been called of God and was in His will. That settled all doubt.*

Roy Carnall also learned lessons about God and finances at Bible school. For him, God very poignantly demonstrated His concern for even seemingly small, mundane needs as well as His creativity in supplying the money to purchase them. Roy reported:

*While I was at Bible school in Cape Town, I shared a room with another man, Tom. We were both relying on a monthly check for living expenses, and one month the checks never arrived. We were so financially strapped that we were even sharing toothpaste and shaving cream.*

*The college was quite near the beach, and I would go down there for my morning devotions. One day I put my hand on the sand, and there was a "two and six" coin. I said, "This is as good as it gets. I must come to this place again." Then I kind of rubbed around in the sand some more, and I found over eight shillings. That was enough to buy toothpaste and shaving cream and apple pie for both of us! The next day our checks arrived.*

Phil and Barb Christiansen experienced the same kind of divine intervention in providing their needs while they attended Columbia Bible College (CBC). Phil wrote:

*When we started out at CBC, we had a little financial buffer, but that was soon gone. Once when we were flat broke and needed milk and bread, Barb's former roommate at Wheaton College followed the Lord's prompting and sent us a note with a $5 bill. She did this each week for three weeks. It was just enough to buy bread, milk, and a few other staples. Then our income tax refund came, and the $5 notes ended.*

*Another time a fuel truck stopped and filled our tank on the Friday of the coldest weekend of that year—even though we hadn't ordered it, nor could we have paid for it if we had ordered it, as my paycheck would not arrive until after the weekend. They put 250 gallons of fuel into our 250-gallon tank. We did not realize we were so low and were, in fact, poised to run out in the middle of that cold week-end, which would not have been good for small kids! But God took care of our need in an unexplainable, but remarkable, way!*

Bud and Mandy Jackson also began learning about God's faithfulness in supplying their needs when they ran out of money at the end of their first year of Bible college. By faith they started out on an overland journey from New Jersey to a summer ministry lined up for them in Canada with only $70.00 in their pocket. They wrote:

*God provided all our needs throughout the summer, for four more years of study in South Carolina, and over two decades of exciting ministry.*

## Support Needs

Except for a few retirees who were able to finance themselves, all of the TEAM Zimbabwe missionaries had to raise their financial support. A few had home churches that committed themselves to covering the entire amount, but this was the exception rather than the rule. Most had to build their support base from churches and interested individuals, an objective that was accomplished in a matter of months for some and several years for others. Single missionaries were often able to raise their required support more quickly than families simply because they only needed to cover the needs of one person.

Betty Mason Wolfe was one of those whose home church, Fort Wayne Gospel Temple, took on her entire support and helped in getting her needed outfit as well. She wrote:

*The quilting circle made me a lovely quilt. Several of the ladies made dresses for me, and various ones supplied other items that I would need, including a kerosene refrigerator.*

Carol Olsen's church, Kimball Avenue Evangelical Congregational Church of Chicago, also took on her entire support and paid for her transportation to the field as well. When she returned on her first furlough as Mrs. Reg Austin, another church pledged Reg's full support. As their children were born, a group of 22 Evangelical Congregational Churches pledged the support needed for them.

Wilma Gardziella also saw God provide her support in one fell swoop, even though that was not necessarily her desire. She wrote:

> *Because I really did not want to go to the field single, I thought that one of the ways I could delay my departure would be if God didn't bring in my support. At that time, however, four of TEAM's board members belonged to my home church, Wheaton Evangelical Free Church. When TEAM accepted me as a missionary, a board member spoke to our church missions committee, and I soon received a letter saying that the church would fully support me. They would be giving me $2,000 a year when my support at that time was set as $1850 a year!! So—off I went.*

God also supplied Phil and Barb Christiansen's support from a single church. They shared:

> *The first missions conference in which we were scheduled to participate, as we began preparing for the field, was at the First Baptist Church of Pontiac, Michigan, which was Barb's home church. Mary Danielson and George and Pat Dee were also there, but we were the new missionaries being presented at their conference that year.*
>
> *This church's policy for missionaries initially going out to the field was to appeal to the people, whether in Sunday school classes or individually, to take on part of their support—so many dollars a week or month, etc. Whatever money was raised in this manner basically set the support level that would come from the church. If the people who had pledged their support were unable to continue for whatever reason, the church would guarantee those funds.*
>
> *In the Sunday morning service on the last day of the*

*conference, Pastor Henry Savage put the sign-up sheets for pledging our support (which we had informed them was $4020/yr.) on a table at the front of the church. He then invited those who were interested in supporting us to come up and sign them following the service.*

*During our trip home that noon we realized that in the figure we had given them, we had forgotten to include the support needed for our third child, whom we were expecting in a few months. This would have raised the amount by $20/mo.*

*When we returned for the evening service, at which time the total figure was to be announced, the secretary excitedly told us, "Guess what? You have $20/mo. over." God was so faithful! When the pastor announced that all of our support had been provided, the choir very appropriately sang "To God be the glory, great things He has done."*

While these were exceptional examples of God's providing hand, those whose support came in bit by bit considered God just as faithful. In the end they were often grateful for the broadened prayer support they gained through their extensive support-raising trips.

Russ and Marg Jackson told of how God brought in the remaining support they needed just before they were ready to sail for Zimbabwe. After going through the usual deputation procedures, they had succeeded in raising most, but not all, of their support. Nevertheless, they decided to go ahead by faith and book their passage on a ship leaving New York for Zimbabwe in April 1948. As they headed to the east coast in preparation for departure, TEAM headquarters advised them to go through Toronto and meet Dr. Oswald J. Smith of the People's Church. Russ wrote of their experience there:

*When we arrived, Dr. Smith asked us to share our testimonies at the mid-week service. Then, immediately afterwards he came to us with two questions. "When do you leave for the field?" and "Do you have all of your financial support?"*

*At that time we did not yet have the full amount required*

*by TEAM. When he heard this, he responded, "Russell and Margaret, you leave on schedule, and let your mission know that we here at the People's Church will be fully responsible for any lack in your support requirements."*

Emil Rilling, another Canadian, was also supported by the People's Church in Toronto, but they were reluctant to take on his wife Phyllis' support since she was an American. Phyllis described how God worked things out for her to receive support as well:

*As we were approaching another furlough and needed more support, I told Emil, "We get support from several parts of Canada and many places in the United States, but the one part of the States we have never visited, or even passed through, is the Southeast. Wouldn't it be nice if we would get some support from somewhere in that region?"*

*Before long we received a letter from a church in St. Petersburg, Florida, saying that Dr. Oswald J. Smith had spoken at their first, week-long missionary conference in which they had introduced faith promise pledges. By the end of the week the pledges they received surpassed the needs of the missionaries they knew at that time.*

*They had written to Dr. Smith about this situation, and he told them that was no problem. He would just transfer several couples or missionaries being supported by his church to them because People's Church was always receiving new applications from missionaries needing support. Emil was among those chosen for the transfer. Seeing that I also needed more support, this church in Florida took me on too. That doubled what we had been receiving from the People's Church. To us, that was a real answer to prayer— and also provided the opportunity for us to travel into the southeastern part of the United States.*

*Support from each and every church was, and still is, a provision from the Lord in a wonderful way! Many have dropped us—one by one—in our retirement, but some are still with us. Many of these are miracle stories for sure!*

People had predicted that Bob and Betty Endicott would have a difficult time raising their support because of having two teenage daughters, but this was not the case at all. They testified:

*With God all things are possible. He had no difficulty rais-ing over 40 supporters, including 10 churches, to share in our ministry through their finances and prayers. The amaz-ing thing was that none of this resulted from our own efforts. God did it all.*

Lynn and Judy Everswick also saw God bring in their support much more quickly than they had anticipated. They told of one of their interesting experiences in this process:

*We were invited to a church (that was not supporting us) whose youth group wanted a missionary speaker one evening. We bonded quickly with the kids, and although they were in Staten Island, over an hour's drive away, they invited us back several times.*

*One night before we were to speak, several announce-ments were made that "Ellsworth was coming." We had no idea who Ellsworth was but we were finally introduced! He was a HUGE papier-mâché elephant the kids had made. As a group, they had decided to raise the $1150 that was needed at that time to get the three of us to the field. They had earned the money through "slave days," babysitting, and doing many chores. The check for the full amount was given to us four weeks before we left for Africa.*

Kiersten Hutchinson had raised her support and necessary trans-portation expenses, but when she arrived at the airport to check in for her flight, she was assessed $1200 for excess baggage. She described what happened when she gave her credit card to the agent:

*As the agent tried to swipe my credit card through his machine, it didn't work. After repeated tries also failed, he finally said, "If they can't give me a machine that works, I'm not going to charge you!" and he let me proceed.*

Many missionaries testified of God's faithful provision for their financial needs throughout their missionary careers. Lynne Hawkins shared, "I have had times when my support was short, but the Lord always supplied my needs." Karen Longnecker reported the same thing: "I always had just enough for what I needed. When supporters died or were unable to continue giving, the Lord raised up others."

Chuck and Scotty Pruitt once had one of their largest supporting churches drop out in mid-term. They responded by expectantly putting their trust in the Lord to meet their needs. Scotty testified, "God did just that. We received an abundance of money from unanticipated sources."

Dr. Roland and Kathy Stephens had a similar experience when they had a major financial need. A doctor, whose brother had worked with Roland but who had not even met the Stephens personally, sold some stock market shares and gave the money to the Stephens. The amount came to $4,000, even more than the donor expected, and was a gracious provision of the Lord for them at a very needy time.

Dick and Mary Ann McCloy's support needs increased during their second term on the field after they added two more children to their family. Although they had no committed supporters to cover this increase, the Lord graciously took care of their needs too. Mary Ann described the lesson she learned from Him one Christmas:

*One Sunday morning just after we had received our quarterly financial report and saw that it was in the "red," I was having my devotions and complaining to the Lord that our support was insufficient, and it was almost Christmas and we wouldn't even be able to buy a turkey.*

*As I waited before Him, I felt Him impress upon me the question of whether I was trusting in my supporters or in Him to meet our needs. After reaffirming my belief in His adequacy as our Provider, I dressed and we headed for church.*

*After the service one of the deacons handed us an envelope, which he said had come in the offering. It had our name on it, and when we opened it, money fell out!*

*God had moved on someone's heart to minister to our*

*need that very day! Not only that, but at Christmas we were GIVEN two turkeys! God had certainly proven that He is able to supply our needs in a superabundant fashion.*

God's financial provision for His obedient servants extended far beyond their daily living needs on the field. Tom and Lois Jackson testified:

*God has been so faithful in providing for us and our children financially, including the educational funds needed at every level of their schooling, whether in public or private schools. Three of our four children have now graduated from college debt-free!*

George and Pat Dee praised God for the wonderful way He has taken care of their needs, even in their retirement. When they wanted to build a retirement home for themselves on a farm that George and his brother owned, they experienced a tremendous outpouring of love from their supporters and other Christian friends. Through their generous donations of materials and labor, George and Pat now live in a lovely, three-bedroom, three-bath, full basement home *with no mortgage.*

Many other retirees could echo this same praise as they too have experienced God's faithful provision for their needs. God never forsakes His own; nor does He forget their sacrificial lives of service for Him. Every year they have invested in the Kingdom of God has resulted in abundant treasures being laid up for them in God's eternal storehouse. They will fully appropriate these when they step triumphantly into His presence. However, it often seems that God has allowed some of the dividends to trickle down as special blessings in their retirement years. How good He is!

## Special Needs on the Field

Trusting God for their financial needs was an ongoing lifestyle for the missionaries. Often on the field special needs would arise that lay outside the parameters of what their normal support was intended to cover. When these came up, the missionaries were responsible for raising whatever additional funds were needed, once again trusting God to supply.

When Orla and Marguerite Blair joined Eunice Ott and Norman and Thelma Everswick on the Msengedzi station in 1946, the three households shared a single, half-ton Chevy truck. As they contemplated opening new stations, they quickly realized that they would need another vehicle. In anticipation of this they all wrote to their supporters to appeal for funds to purchase a five-ton, Dodge truck. God raised the necessary money, and when Orv and Helen Dunkeld returned from furlough in 1948, they brought the new vehicle back with them.

Russ and Marg Jackson told of a similar situation when they moved to Bindura to begin a ministry in this community, only their need was for a house to live in. While initially camping out in their van, they prayed and trusted God to supply their need. Russ wrote:

*In a very wonderful and remarkable manner funds were provided by one of our godly supporters living in Saskatchewan, Canada. . . . We were able to purchase a piece of land at a very low price and continued to camp in our van while the house was built.*

Tom and Lois Jackson reported how God worked to supply the funds for purchasing a large house suitable for a hostel in 1990, when the field once again needed one. (During the war years most of the rural stations were shut down and TEAM's ministry became more focused in farming communities where children could live with their parents and attend local schools. Therefore, the large hostel on the Plot was no longer needed and was converted to a campus for the Harare Theological College.)

Tom wrote:

*On our morning walks Lois and I often greeted an elderly man who was usually out for a walk at the same time. One day we stopped and introduced ourselves, and he invited us to tea. He and his wife lived alone in a large house on a very large piece of property.*

*As we sat in their beautiful enclosed veranda and enjoyed our tea, the man asked if the mission might possibly be interested in the house, as they had decided to sell it. I was a bit taken aback by this unexpected question and told him I would get back to him with an answer.*

*When I shared the situation with the Field Council, they decided that we really had no need for a property and house of that size. Therefore, I called the man back and thanked him for thinking of us but informed him that the mission was not in the market for such a property.*

*Shortly after that I went to Wheaton to attend a TEAM consultation. Since Candidate School was also going on at that time, I was asked to speak with the potential candidates for Zimbabwe. This included Dr. Dan and Julie Stephens, who wanted to know what options would be available for their children's schooling if they were to go to Karanda.*

*That evening I called Field Chairman Doug Everswick back in Zimbabwe and told him about the Stephens' concern. I reminded him of the house that had been offered to us and asked him if we should reconsider purchasing it to use as a hostel. An excellent Christian school had recently opened in the area, making its location ideal for this purpose. Doug agreed and told me I could promise the Stephens that the field would provide care for their children.*

*When we contacted the elderly couple again, we learned that they had a buyer, but the sale was not going well. They reiterated their desire to sell it to TEAM and said we could have it for US$62,000. This was far more than the field had ever spent on a house before.*

*In order to help raise some of the money, we decided to sell another house owned by the mission in an Asian area of town. In anticipation of this income we then took out a short-term loan from a local bank, informing the bank manager of our plans to finance repayment of the loan through the sale of this other house.*

*We put the house on the market at a price we were prepared to come down on, if necessary. A week or two later, however, the real estate agent called to tell us that two Asian brothers each wanted the house and were bidding against each other for it. This pushed the selling price substantially above our listing price, bringing it much closer to the amount that we needed for purchasing the house we envisioned for the new hostel.*

*When I shared what had happened with the bank manager, he said, "Someone is looking after you!" I agreed wholeheartedly! Twenty-seven Marlborough Drive has been an incredible provision and blessing from the Lord!*

God was just as faithful in providing finances for needed equipment on the field and often did it in a way that clearly indicated that His hand was involved. This was certainly true when Word of Life Publications (WLP) needed a power stapler. With only two used ones available in the country, the staff began praying for funds to purchase one of these.

God's response was clearly evident when Bob and Betty Endicott's next quarterly support remittance included a gift specifically designated for WLP. When converted to Zimbabwe currency, the amount of the gift equaled the exact price of the particular stapler they wanted, right down to the penny!

Noël and Ann Liddle shared the surprising way in which God provided the money needed to buy a new transformer for the Bible college. While on furlough Noël preached a sermon at Ann's home church in which he used an illustration about the great improbability of anyone ever presenting him with a $1,000 gift. He wrote:

*As I spoke of this unlikely gift, a peculiar ripple of amusement went across the audience. The explanation came at the end of the service when the congregation presented Ann and me with a $2,000 check for our ministry in Zimbabwe!*

*About 50 of Ann's relatives had attended the service as part of a family reunion to celebrate Ann's homecoming and first furlough from the mission field. . . . All 50 then met at one of Ann's brothers' house for lunch that afternoon. Imagine my surprise, when just before saying "grace" for the meal, another of Ann's brothers, who was proprietor of Fehrman Tool and Die, presented me with a check for $2,000 specifically for the purchase of a transformer for the* *college in Zimbabwe. This was the second miracle of the day and another evidence of God's love and concern for His work through us in Zimbabwe.[1]*

Dr. Dan and Julie Stephens were similarly surprised when they went on furlough in 1996 with a list of all the things they needed on the Karanda station. This included a new guest house, an internal telephone system, a washer and drier for the hospital, and endoscopic instruments for surgery. By the time they were ready to return to the field, God had spectacularly provided for each of these items!

Sometimes instead of supplying the finances to buy a needed item, God arranged for someone to provide it as an outright donation. Karanda Hospital received many such gifts, which were greatly appreciated by the staff there.

Back in the fifties Dorothy Cook worked as a surgical supervisor and manager of Central Supply Services at the same California hospital in which Dr. Sam Wall did his residency. Through him, she learned about the hospital to be built in Zimbabwe.

Inspired to do what she could to help, she began to collect and repair medical equipment that was no longer useful at her hospital but would be much appreciated in a bush setting. She also talked about the hospital and its needs to the sales reps who visited her. Soon God moved in their hearts to donate sutures and other wonderful, new supplies, which she also packed up and sent to Zimbabwe. (After her retirement, she and her husband, Sam, served as associate missionaries at Karanda for three years.)

Joseph Horness was another generous benefactor for the hospital. In addition to serving as a TEAM board member for many years, he was head of a manufacturing plant for laboratory and office furnishings. Having already contributed a substantial amount of the funds needed to build the hospital, he offered to supply all of the furnishings for the laboratory as well.

Phil Christiansen, who was preparing to become the hospital's first medical technologist running the laboratory, wrote:

*I sent Mr. Horness my dream plans for the 10' X 12' room that was initially designated for the lab and subsequently received all of the equipment I requested: steel-case cabinetry, sinks, counter tops, electrical outlets, gas and air fittings, and all the material that was necessary for installation. All I had to do was provide the labor. What a pleasurable job that was!*

*Later, when the new out-patient wing was added to the hospital and the lab was relocated to a much larger room (12' X 25'), Mr. Horness donated more equipment. When this was combined with the equipment from the old lab, we had a very efficient, modern-looking facility. All of the equipment was "first class." The countertops were top-of-the-line, 1¼" plywood topped with black, laboratory-grade Formica. Each section was bonded together with black epoxy, making a seamless counter top.*

*Again, it was a pleasure to assemble the cabinetry. None of the labs in which I've worked in the States have had cabinetry of the quality that was given to Karanda Hospital. When God supplies, He does it very well.*

What amazed Phil even more was how God supplied the microscope for the laboratory. He wrote:

*Back in 1958, Barbara and I attended a TEAM fellowship gathering in Williams Bay, WI, where we met Dr. Sam Wall. I will never forget the awe-inspiring words he spoke at that time: "You can take anything you want for the lab, but you will have to raise the funds for those items yourself." That was truly a challenge, as we were just then beginning to realize the magnitude of raising support for a family of five, to say nothing of funds for a laboratory.*

*Nevertheless, I began going through laboratory supply catalogs, drooling and dreaming, while at the same time recognizing that most of the items that grabbed my attention would remain purely a fantasy. One item was high on my priority list, however. That was a quality microscope.*

*Because of the central role a microscope plays in laboratory work, I felt it was essential that we have a quality piece of equipment. The ultimate at that time was a Bausch and Lomb binocular scope. This was a sturdy instrument with high quality optics and would certainly be a good choice for long-term use at Karanda.*

*Funds to purchase such a microscope did not come in, however. Instead, I was given a couple of ancient, monocular scopes. Somehow they did not seem adequate to me, and I continued to "lust after" the B & L one.*

*The following year on a visit to TEAM headquarters we had the opportunity to meet Dr. Alan Clemenger, who with his wife, Donna, was also preparing to serve at Karanda. He invited us to come up to the apartment where they were staying to see the microscope he had acquired for the hospital.*

*As I graciously followed him, I was rather upset internally, as I felt I was the one who was supposed to choose what lab equipment we would take. Then, when we arrived at the apartment and he opened the microscope case, I could not believe my eyes! There was the B & L binocular scope which had been my dream!*

*Al then told us the story of how he had acquired the scope. A man had been fishing in the Mississippi River when he snagged an inanimate object. As he brought it to the surface, he discovered that it was a microscope. Realizing the value of the item, he tried through all means possible to find the owner. In spite of advertising, serial number checks, etc., he received no response to his inquiries.*

*The man's brother "happened" to be a TEAM missionary in South America, who knew of the hospital being built in Zimbabwe. He suggested that the microscope be donated for it. When TEAM received the microscope, they had it completely refurbished, and it was now in the case that Al was showing me. For all practical purposes it was in mint condition: no scratches, flaws, or any sign of wear.*

*The rest of the story did not unfold until over a decade later. . . . Upon returning to Wisconsin after two terms of service at Karanda, I took a job in Stoughton, WI. My boss there had been a medical technologist in Iowa in the late 50's and told me that the labs at that time had been plagued by microscope thefts to the extent that they had to chain their scopes to the bench tops.*

*Suddenly my thoughts turned to the B & L microscope we had acquired for the Karanda lab at about that time. Very possibly it was a hot item and landed in the Mississippi River when someone needed to get rid of evidence quickly! Obviously, God knew where it was all the time and where it was needed.*

*THE microscope was used well into the 80's before being replaced by newer equipment. Nevertheless, it is still at Karanda, serving as a reminder of God's faithfulness and His care for the details in our lives.*

God's care was also demonstrated in restoring articles that He had provided for ministry in Zimbabwe. Tom Jackson described how the Lord enabled him to recover a guitar and sound system that was stolen out of a church where he and Lois had been holding youth meetings:

*About four months later I "happened" to go into a used instrument shop, and I saw the guitar. I was able to use photos to identify it as belonging to us, and we received it back. We also got the sound system back when it "happened" to be taken to a particular repair shop where the owner knew that we had lost a system like it!*

## Food

Food was one of the missionaries' most basic needs of all, yet something they could not always take for granted on the field. God never intends His children to go hungry, however. While situations sometimes arose in which they came to the end of their own resources to provide food for themselves or those for whom they were responsible, God always came through for them—sometimes in remarkable ways.

The first rainy season the Danielsons and Dunkelds spent at Msengedzi was an especially challenging one as disaster after disaster occurred to wipe out more and more of their food supply. Helen described the situation and how God took care of them:

*We were rained in; we couldn't get out of the Valley and our food supply was pretty low. Our garden had been flooded out, our potatoes had rotted, the rice was finished, and our flour was full of worms.*

*We weren't allowed to have any cattle as we were in a tsetse fly area, and tsetse flies live on cattle. Orv was also having difficulty at that time hunting game. He wasn't too used to it, and that was our only source for meat.*

*God provided for us, however, because in the middle of the rains the local people started bringing us green mealies—that is, corn on the cob. They couldn't understand our eating it when it was so soft and tender. They said we ate it like the baboons did. The Shona people always waited until it got hard. They also brought us tomatoes and squash from their gardens, so we were able to get along quite well.*

Orla and Marguerite Blair shared how God took care of their immediate need for food when they left Msengdzi in 1948 to open a new station in the Hunyani area:

*En route we encountered a small dyker [type of antelope] standing broadside in the middle of the road, a perfect shot for Orla. Pastor Yotamu, the evangelist at Msengedzi, had also given us a chicken as a parting gift, and upon our arrival that chicken laid an egg in the corner on the stones. Here was God's provision of food for us: fresh meat and an egg. We were fully aware of God's care accompanying us in this new undertaking.*

Chuck and Scotty Pruitt saw God's hand of care supply their needs in a special way when they ran out of money for food while serving as hostel parents in Harare. Scotty described how she wrestled with the Lord about this situation and His response:

*I can remember one day when we had no money to buy food for the kids. In those days the kids paid five pounds per term. When that money was gone, we had to take personal responsibility for their needs from our own support.*

*I had told the Lord when I was saved that I would never pray for money for myself. Now here we were in Africa and I was still a young Christian, and we had no coins to put out for milk the next day. It was also the day I was supposed to buy meat for the week. So I said to the Lord, "I really don't want to pray for money, but we're responsible for these kids, so what do I do?"*

*Then at mid-morning the mail arrived. Two letters came for us with checks in them. One was from a lady friend I had met at a conference when I was in college. I had never seen her again and don't know how she got my address, but she sent a $30 check. The other letter was from a childhood friend of Chuck's who was unsaved but sent a $50 check. We never heard from either of these people again, but God had provided the money we needed just when we needed it. And He kept doing it. We lived on faith all the time.*

Lynn and Judy Everswick also described a time when their pantry became nearly bare, and God intervened to bring them food in an unexpected manner:

*Christmas 1980 had come and gone. With all the extra entertaining we had to do over the holidays, our finances were quite depleted. We were greatly anticipating our quarterly support that was due in mid-January.*

*When it had not arrived by the end of January, we were informed that TEAM was changing over its financial system and computers, so support would be late. We ended up having to wait almost until March for it to arrive. In other words, we had to stretch our previous quarter's support to last nearly five months—a time period that included Christmas and the beginning of the new school year for which three of our five children needed new uniforms, to say nothing about the food needed each day to feed a hungry family of seven.*

*By February we were literally at the end of all of our resources. We had $3.00 in our checking account and no savings. We had eaten just about everything in the cupboards* *and were down to some vegetables in our garden and five little doves at the bottom of our freezer, which Lynn had shot on a hunting trip with our oldest son, Ricky.*

*I had just taken the doves out to thaw and was cleaning the deep freeze when I heard a knock at the door. Garth Snook, one of the local farmers, had come by to say that he had just been slaughtering sheep and was wondering if our family ate lamb. He brought us a WHOLE sheep! About two hours later another farmer, Johannes Steyl, came by and said, "We have just been slaughtering sheep and were wondering . . . ."*

*Nobody in the Bindura area knew about our delayed support—but God! We had come to the end of our human resources, and He provided "king's meat" for His children!*

*For our last few months in Zimbabwe before leaving on furlough, I prepared lamb dishes from virtually every recipe I could find. In fact, with furlough coming, we reminded our five children that if we were visiting in a supporter's home, and they served leg of lamb—which is still our all-time favorite meal—they were not to say, "Oh, no, not lamb again!" because in the States it is very expensive and people don't fix it every day like we had, thanks to the Lord's provision.*

Bob and Betty Endicott also had a time when they ran out of money for food. They had just sent their daughter Linda home to college and had given her a little extra money so she could do a bit of sightseeing en route. Betty shared how God intervened for them at that time:

*Our greatest need at the time was for margarine. In order for Bob to go to the store to buy some, I counted out the smallest change left in my wallet and wished it had been enough for some tomatoes too.*

*After Bob left, I cried out to God in prayer, "Lord, don't You know about our needs?" Immediately, I noticed a car slowing down in the street as it passed our house. It went by and then slowly backed up. A woman got out and came up the walk to the door. She explained that she had been instructed to go to every third house. This would have been the Regiers' house, but they were not home, so she decided to back up and come to our house instead. In her hand was a sample bar of a new margarine. She asked if we would try it and then answer several questions about it two weeks later.*

*She never came back, and during the remainder of our term we never saw any new brand of margarine come out on the market. Free samples also seemed to be unheard of in Zimbabwe.*

*After receiving the margarine, I walked to the TEAM office to get our mail. There in our box was a bag of tomatoes—a thoughtful gift from another missionary's garden!*

*When we received our statement for our next quarterly support remittance, we noted that a $100.00 gift was listed as coming in at just about that time. It was from someone who was not even on our mailing list and had never shown any interest in us before we left for Zimbabwe. We asked Linda to find out for which ministry the gift had been intended. She learned that it was meant to be for personal use and not used for any ministry.*

*At our time of deepest need the Lord had given us margarine, tomatoes, and money! What a valuable, lifetime lesson I learned about God's care for us!*

God also extended His hand to enable the Karanda missionaries to supply food for the Shona people in their area during a time of great drought. Many had their crops fail in 1989 due to inadequate rainfall and came to the Karanda Hospital asking for food. The missionaries didn't know how to respond. If they gave to one, they would have to give to all, and how could they possibly do that?

They began praying about the situation, and very shortly they received a generous financial donation from Drs. Duane and Muriel (Danielson) Elmer's church for drought relief. This gave them the ability to start supplying food and developing programs to do so equitably. George Smazik was given oversight of the effort. George wrote:

*We began distributing food on a "first come, first served" basis but quickly recognized that this was not the best way to give to the needy. Therefore, taking the biblical example of "gleaning," we came up with two programs. One was a "Food for Work" program in which we paid a worker a tin of corn meal for a day's work.*

*The other program was a "Self-Help Scheme" that was laid on our hearts by the Lord. Because of their massive crop failure in 1989, many villagers had no money or credit to be able to purchase maize seed and fertilizer to try to raise a crop the following year. This program provided these things in exchange for labor.*

*To participate in the Scheme, the head of the family would tell us how much seed and fertilizer he needed for the next growing season. The government controlled the price of these things, so we knew in advance how much what they needed would cost. We then put these people to work around the hospital, slashing grass, digging Blair latrines, clearing a new road, digging for water in the river bed, etc. For each day's work, they accrued $6.00 towards the price of their seed and fertilizer, which was substantially more than what the government was paying for their work program. When they had earned enough to pay for a 50 kg. bag of maize seed, they would be given the seed. They would then work on a similar basis for their fertilizer.*

*The program was well-received, and those who participated retained their self-respect and didn't become dependent on Karanda. We operated the Self-Help Scheme for three years. The first year we helped 125 families. This decreased to 70 families for the next two years. The Lord supplied the money and food for these programs from many different sources.*

In 1991, the Karanda missionaries were confronted with another need. Several headmasters from primary schools in the area came to them regarding the serious problem they were experiencing. Students were failing to show up, falling asleep during class, or fainting during sports activities because of their lack of food.

Again the missionaries sought guidance from the Lord as to what they should do. As a result, they began a "High Protein Porridge" program for the schools. George described how it worked:

*To begin with, we had several of our Shona staff members visit each school that requested assistance to assess the legitimacy of their need. Then on their recommendation the school would be added to our distribution list. We ended up with 27 schools serving 17,000 students.*

*Because we had access to hard currency (US dollars), we were able to purchase all the high protein porridge mix we needed. Sugar was in short supply, however, but after working our way up the chain of command at the sugar distributor, we were finally granted as much sugar as we needed too.*

*We supplied each school with a clean 44-gallon drum and a large, long-handled paddle for cooking the porridge. The children would bring their own dishes. Our Nutritional Village leader, Mrs. Nyamande, determined how much porridge and sugar mix was needed to feed the number of students at each school for a day. We mixed the ingredients at Karanda and put this amount in separate bags for each day of the week. Then once a week our truck would drop off a week's supply at each school.*

*A different village in the area which the school served was in charge of preparing the porridge daily for a week. Mrs. Nyamande had a system in which she would train five "cooks," and they, in turn, would train five more. In this way each of the neighboring villages were also involved.*

*The funds for the program came from the United States, Europe, Taiwan, and Korea. Periodically we would have local pastors speak at school assemblies, reminding the children that the food was an evidence of God's love for them, that He had laid the need on the hearts of His people throughout the world, and they had responded to support the program.*

*One day while I was in Harare picking up supplies, the*

*field treasurer informed me that our fund was Z$90,000 in the red. I assured him that this was the Lord's work, and somehow He would supply the needed funds. Three and half hours later, when I arrived back at Karanda, Dr. Dan Stephens told me that he had just received a letter from his uncle, Rev. Billy Kim, in Korea. They were donating US$20,000 to the porridge program. At that time this was equivalent to Z$100,000! We were constantly amazed at the Lord's provision.*

*Many of the villages in the areas where the high protein porridge was distributed began requesting that Karanda Fellowship Churches be planted in their area. Through our food programs we had the privilege of sowing the seeds of the Gospel; others have watered that seed and are now harvesting the fruit. PRAISE THE LORD!*

# Furlough Needs

Every time the missionaries returned for furlough (or what is now called "home assignment") they faced a new set of needs, and God was just as faithful in meeting these needs for them. Russ Jackson wrote:

*When we went on our first furlough, the winter in Manitoba was unusually severe and cold. . . . I said to Margaret, "There just must be a warmer place to live in North America than Minnedosa." I also mentioned the correspondence we had had with our TEAM office about the church in Greensboro, North Carolina, who had taken on some of our support and was eager to have us visit them.*

*We decided to contact their pastor. What a surprise it was to hear that the church was expecting word from us and that they, in fact, had a home all ready for us to stay in! They said we could live there as long as we desired during our furlough year . . .*

*When we arrived at the home they had prepared for us, we found that a large deepfreeze had been filled with a great variety of frozen foods. The refrigerator was also full of the necessary supplies for our immediate use. As the church welcomed us so warmly, they assured us that the Lord had put our family upon their hearts and that they wanted to stand by us financially too.*

*Now after over forty years, while in retirement, this lovely body of people still takes responsibility, together with TEAM, in providing us with a quarterly retirement supplement. Without a doubt the Greensboro Westover Church was the Lord's special, loving provision for Margaret and me and our ministry over the past 46 years.*

Phyllis Rilling also told of God's faithfulness in supplying the needs of her family on furlough:

*Each term on the field and each furlough we saw the Lord provide us with just the right kind of vehicle. The same was true about places to stay on furlough. Occasionally one of these may not have been our first choice, but it was always a roof over our heads and often came at great sacrifice to some of God's choice servants. Some places were perfectly ideal for us. We also saw God provide for our clothing needs and just everything we really needed!*

Lynn and Judy Everswick described how God supplied their need for a car and a place to live on one of their furloughs:

*Whenever a missionary goes on furlough, where they will live and what they will drive to get to all of their meetings is a HUGE challenge—especially if you have children. One time we had sent out feelers but had neither of these big questions answered when we left our remote Kapfundi station just three days before our departure from Zimbabwe.*

*On our way out, having just checked the mail two days before, we decided to stop in at the post office and see if anything else had possibly come for us. When Lynn came out with the large canvas mail bag, there were two pieces of mail in it. That's all.*

*One was a telegram from Mel Mathisen saying, "There*

*is a fuel crisis going on in America. Big cars are going for a song. I bought a car in great shape for only $900. We will meet you at the airport, and it is yours for the year."*

*The other was a small, blue airform from Bethany Church in West Orange, NJ, saying, "Our pastor has recently resigned and the parsonage is sitting empty. We don't like to leave it like that in that part of town. Would you be willing to 'house sit' for us? It is fully furnished. God had once again abundantly supplied our needs!*

Dr. Dan Stephens is grateful to God for providing the Southwestern Medical Clinic in Berrien Springs, MI, as a place where he has the opportunity to work on furloughs and get updated on advances in the medical field. Being able to return to this area for each home assignment has also given his family a consistent home base in the States.

## Special Favors

As a loving Father, God delighted not only in supplying the needs of His obedient servants but also in granting them special favors. A number of missionaries reported times when they received special treatment that they felt came from His hand.

Mary Danielson experienced this several times on her exceptionally difficult trip home from Zimbabwe after her husband, Rudy, had passed away in late 1943. She and little Muriel started out by traveling down to Cape Town, South Africa, hoping to find a ship to take them back to the United States. When they arrived, they found over 200 missionaries from many other organizations and countries seeking the same thing.

With World War II still in progress and the ocean filled with warships and submarines, very few passenger ships were venturing out. Mary's only option was to add her name to the long waiting list. As random places became available on other ships, they would be allotted according to the order of the names on the list. All of this translated into the reality that Mary and Muriel were in for a long wait.

During this time they were befriended by another couple who

had a little girl Muriel's age. (Muriel had her third birthday there in Cape Town.) Since their older son had gone home by troop ship, they asked if Mary (and Muriel) could take his place when their family's name came up. This was granted, and eight months later they were all able to depart on what was called a "blackout ship." All the portholes were covered with black fabric blinds, everyone had to wear black clothes, and no lights were permitted to show at night.

After spotting a submarine en route and running from it for three days, the ship eventually docked at Rio de Janeiro, Brazil. Mary then had to find a plane to take her and Muriel to the United States, which again was no small feat during wartime.

When she finally found one, they hadn't gone far before they were bumped off of it because of military priorities. This happened twice. However, in each of these strange places in which they were essentially stranded, God provided a Christian to take them in and care for them during the several weeks they had to wait to get on another plane. Muriel wrote, "My mother was so amazed at how carefully God watched over us and brought us people to meet our needs during those days." Eventually, they were able to get on a plane that took them to Miami.

John and Betty Wolfe definitely felt God bless them with special favor as they returned home for furlough one year. With their tickets allowing them two stopovers, they decided to visit Israel and Austria, as John's sister lived in Israel, and neighbors they had while stationed at Maquadzi owned a cottage in Austria, which they offered to let them use.

In each place they were shown hospitality that went far beyond their expectations. Betty described all that the Lord had in store for them, beginning in Israel:

> *We were virtually penniless but managed to have a great time and found Israel the most interesting place in the world. Every step we took, we were walking on the ground of biblical history. John's sister even treated us to a bus tour of the Sea of Galilee.*
>
> *After spending time with her in Haifa and hearing her play as a cellist in the Haifa Symphony Orchestra, we went by train down to the Jerusalem area and stayed in Bethlehem*

*with a Mrs. Lambey, the widow of a missionary to the Arabs. This lady would not quote us a price for our stay and treated us royally, giving us full room and board and arranging for us to be taken into Jerusalem with a guide. She even had a birthday cake for Margaret's sixth birthday. At the end of our stay she told us to pay whatever we could. We were embarrassed by the small amount of money we had available to give her, but she was quite gracious about it.*

*When we arrived in Austria, we had no idea that our neighbor would ask his brother and his wife to look after us while we were there. They also treated us royally. We roamed the hills and picked mushrooms and blueberries and went into the little village of Graz to see the armory and the elaborate clock, etc. that were there. We were very spoiled, indeed.*

Bob and Betty Endicott were also treated in an extremely unexpected manner when they arrived at the Johannesburg airport on their first trip to Zimbabwe. They wrote:

*We arrived in Johannesburg just after noon. Our flight to Zimbabwe would not depart until evening, so we anticipated a long, tiring wait in the airport. Almost immediately, however, a tall, slender man with white hair stepped out of the crowd at customs and came towards us, calling out, "Endicott." He offered to help Bob claim our luggage, then exchange some of our money, and also confirm our flight up to Zimbabwe.*

*He then asked if we were tired and needed a place to rest while we waited for our flight. He called two men to carry our luggage upstairs. We were then led to two rooms, each with two double beds and a private bath. Before he left us, he gave us meal tickets, as he knew we would be hungry. (It's unbelievable to us that we never asked any questions. This is not at all like us!)*

*After settling into our accommodations, we wondered how we would ever pay the bill. At suppertime we looked at the menu and ordered the cheapest thing, bowls of soup. When we checked out before boarding the plane to*

*Zimbabwe, Bob went to the window to ask what we owed. He was told that everything was taken care of and we owed nothing. When we inquired as to who had paid our bill, no one could tell us.*

*We were inexperienced travelers and had no idea what was to be expected. Had our travel agency arranged this? Had the TEAM South Africa field sent someone to help us? We thought we surely would get an explanation when we arrived in Zimbabwe.*

*This was not the case, however. Nobody to whom we recounted our story had ever had such an experience; nor could they offer any explanation. How did the white-haired man know our name? Or know that we had a long wait for our next flight? Had he gotten our name on the passenger list confused with some other VIP family he was supposed to meet? Or was it possible, as some dared to suggest, that he was an angel?*

Years later when it came time for Linda Endicott to fly back to the States for college, Bob and Betty were once again grateful for the special people God graciously placed in her path the entire way. They wrote:

*God's care for her was evident each step of the way. On her first flight a Zimbabwean couple (named Bob and Betty!) took her under their wing. When she had to stay overnight in Johannesburg, the Christensen family, who had spoken at Zimbabwe's annual field conference in 1972, came to her hotel and took her out for the evening.*

*She then flew to Israel since she would miss visiting there with us when we returned to the States. As she was eating dinner at St. Andrew's Hospice the first night, she met three young women sitting across the table from her. One of them was a cousin of Marilyn Traynor—a Karanda nurse! Since it was their last night in Israel, they invited Linda to join them as they viewed Jerusalem for one last time.*

*Her next stop was Austria where she stayed with TEAM missionaries.*

*TEAM's general director, Dick Winchell and his wife, Marge, happened to be visiting at the same time, and they included her in their dinner and entertainment plans.*

*The Lord then provided an older, single girl from our home church to accompany her on the rest of her journey. She flew out to meet Linda in Vienna. Together, they toured Amsterdam and England, where they had accommodations provided for them at the home of the girl's English cousin, whom she had never met before.*

Dick and Ruth Regier also saw God's hand in the preferential treatment they received on several occasions when they returned to Zimbabwe in March 1999 to supervise the construction of a three-classroom block for the Harare Theological College. In the last correspondence they received from the field before leaving, they were given the impression that everything was ready to go, and because prices were expected to go up on the first of April, they needed to get there quickly.

When they arrived, they found that the plans for the new building had not even been completed or a building permit obtained. Their first task, therefore, was to find the draftsman whose name and address was written on the plans. This was no small feat in an unfamiliar suburb. When they finally located his house, Dick used the best Shona he could muster to tell the elderly couple living there for whom they were looking. The couple informed him that the man was their son, but he had died nine months ago.

After returning to the college, Dick consulted with TEAM co-worker David Rousseau concerning finding another draftsman. The new man was able to complete the plans so they could be submitted for a building permit. Meanwhile Dick began scrambling to gather materials, as he now had less than a week before April 1.

During this time the Regiers received a phone call from a lady who identified herself as the older sister of the young man who had died. Her parents had told her about the visit they had had from two Shona-speaking foreigners with a mission organization, and she wanted to know if the Regiers had ever lived in Chinhoyi. When they informed her that they had, she continued asking questions:

"Was Mr. Regier a 'priest' [stumbling for a word] in the Evangelical Church?"

"Y-e-s" [also hesitantly].

"The church on the corner?"

"Yes, the one with a fence around it."

Then came the surprising announcement: "I was one of the little girls in your Sunday school!"

The woman was now Mrs. Majoni, and she wanted to know how they were coming with their plans for the new building. She asked lots of questions and then informed them that she was an administrator in the office of city planning. She also knew the draftsman who had completed the plans for the classroom block, as he was a building inspector for the city.

Because she knew all of the people involved, this divinely-sent woman was able to expedite the mission's request for a building permit through the necessary departments, acquiring the six or seven signatures needed for approval. As a result, the building permit was received in less than eight weeks rather than the four to five months the university reported routinely waiting for approval of their building plans.

After receiving their permit, Dick and Ruth invited Mrs. Majoni and her husband out to a hotel for dinner. They described the evening:

*For three hours we talked about Chinhoyi. We laughed, we cried, and we ate, but the most memorable part of the evening was when Mrs. Majoni told us, "The things you taught us in Sunday school, I live by them!"*

The preferential treatment that God was orchestrating for the Regiers didn't end there. When they wanted to get their visas extended for another three months, they were told that this would involve many hours of waiting in the immigration office. In fact, they might even want to bring a lunch with them.

The morning they walked in, Ruth noticed a small object on the outside of the lady's booth that said, "I love Jesus." Ruth immediately exclaimed, "Oh, I like that! That's good!" The lady just beamed, took their passports, went in the back room, and stamped them. They were back to Hatfield in time for morning tea at 10:00.

Sometimes the favors God did for the missionaries came in the form of special gifts or compensations. John and Betty Wolfe described such a situation when they brought a camper back to the field with them. They had purchased it while on furlough because they had seen how handy a camper had been for Orla and Marguerite Blair when they went out to do evangelism on various farms. Betty told the story:

> When our furlough was over, we packed the camper full of things that we were taking back with us. This included an electric sewing machine plus my mother's good china, which she had given to me. I had packed all of it in used clothing which we could later distribute to the Shona people.
>
> When we sailed from Savannah, GA, it was apparently not adequately secured in the hold of the ship, as it was badly damaged when we reached Cape Town. Thankfully, it was insured and all of the contents were okay.
>
> We were absolutely stunned when the insurance company replaced it with a much superior, 6-berth caravan! What a gracious gift from the Lord! When we drove it up to Zimbabwe, we became the envy of all the missionaries. In addition to using it for ministry outreach, we enjoyed traveling in it for holidays. It also came in handy on trips to Harare when the guest cottage was full.

Lynn and Judy Everswick also received a special gift from the Lord. Although it was quite different in nature, it too was very useful to them in their ministry. Judy explained:

> We did a lot of entertaining during our seven years of ministry in Bindura, a mining and farming town located midway between Harare and Karanda. This meant that we frequently had the privilege of having Karanda missionaries stop by for lunch or a cold drink on their way in or out of town.
>
> An integral part of our church planting ministry there was also entertaining farmers, miners, and many other

*people who would stop by throughout the day, especially on Mondays, which was our designated day off. On a typical Monday we would easily have eight to ten different groups of people stop by. Some would come as early as breakfast, others for early coffee around 8:00, more for tea time at 10:00, etc., continuing throughout the entire day. They would invariably say, "We knew we would catch you home today, because it is your day off."*

*Ben Van Slot owned the Coach House Inn in Bindura, and when he accepted Christ, his life perspective totally changed. One day he came by bringing us 10 cases of Coke. He told us that he ordered 100 cases at a time for the motel, and because of all of the visitors that came through our house each week, he wanted to bring us his "tithe" of 10 cases. What a blessing that was!*

## Personnel Needs

God's provisions also included the personnel needed for each ministry on the field. The care He took in sending out individuals with just the right qualifications at just the time they were needed was often remarkable, though sometimes recognized only in retrospect. Only He had the divine foresight to know what lay ahead and the expertise that would be needed for each situation.

Dr. Roland Stephens noted this in regard to the timing of the doctors God sent to Karanda Hospital:

*Dr. Sam Wall, the first doctor, was far better equipped for finding a place for the hospital, making the plans, and getting everything built than I would have been. Even though Dr. Al Clemenger was only there a short time, he also had particular skills that were necessary for opening the new facility.*

When Roland arrived, the basic physical plant was in place, and the hospital was ready to make use of his tremendous expertise as an internist and surgeon. Phil Christiansen observed that Dr. David Drake arrived as the hospital began receiving more specialized orthopedic cases, which were his area of strength.

The same timely deployment of specially gifted personnel was also seen in the hospital laboratory. Phil Christiansen initially set up the lab, securing and improvising equipment, establishing contacts for purchasing reagents and supplies, writing procedures, etc.

Then, after two terms of service at Karanda, the Lord led Phil and his wife, Barb, back to the United States so they could be together as a family during their children's high school years. Diane Powell was God's provision of a replacement for Phil in the lab. While initially undergoing culture shock at the scarcity of equipment and the outdated nature of what *was* there, she was extremely glad for all that Phil had put in place so that she could just step in and carry on the work. Setting it all up would have been totally out of her skill and comfort zone.

Before coming to the field, Diane's favorite area of lab work had been blood banking. She loved working in a large hospital and having three medical emergencies going on at the same time, each requiring blood transfusions as quickly as possible. Little did she know what lay ahead for her at Karanda during the war of independence.

Diane later had an opportunity to share with Phil what those years were like:

> *During this time we worked all day doing our normal work, and then quite frequently just after dusk the army helicopters would bring in landmine victims and other wartime casualties. By this time my lab help had gone home and could not return because of the curfew. So I was it! Most of the time they would bring a group of three to five severely injured landmine victims, each with multiple, compound fractures and massive bleeding.*
>
> *Dr. Roland Stephens would triage them, but they usually all needed x-rays before they could go to surgery and blood transfusions as quickly as I could possibly get them. So I had to take x-rays, develop x-rays, type and cross-match blood, and draw blood donors for several people at once.*
>
> *Those were really challenging times. We all worked through the night and then had to pick up our normal duties the next day, not knowing what would happen that evening.*

Diane was astounded when Phil told her that he didn't see how he could have possibly handled that. Barb agreed that he was not a multi-tasking person and could never have survived under such demands. Suddenly Diane realized that God had specifically prepared her and put her in the Karanda lab at that time to meet this need. What an encouragement this was to her after feeling so greatly overshadowed by Phil's superior expertise in setting up the lab!

In 1998, when a new, freestanding building had been constructed for the lab, Phil was asked to come back to the field for two months to do again what he had done so well the first time—set it up. When he arrived, however, he discovered that what God had really brought him there to do was quite different. The lab wasn't anywhere near being ready to set up, but the hospital desperately needed someone to rebuild an autoclave (sterilizer). Several of the staff had already tried and failed.

After a few weeks of work Phil finally succeeded in getting it running again as well as teaching the staff how to clean out the lines and traps so it wouldn't happen again. He had hardly finished this when the other autoclave broke down with the same problem. This time he was able to get it fixed in just a few hours. In the process he again did something he was adept at doing in writing up the procedure he had gone through in fixing these autoclaves so that anyone could walk in and fix them should they go down again. (Phil also did other things around the station too, including putting in the 110 volt electrical lines need for hooking up the transformer in the lab and addressing some personality clashes occurring among the lab staff.)

Short-term workers, such as Phil was at that time, have played a crucial role in meeting specific needs on the field through the years. Some filled in for personnel going on furlough or provided a particular skill needed for only a short time. Others helped ministries catch up on tasks continually put aside because of higher priorities or enabled a ministry to have a greater outreach. Usually participating in a firsthand missions experience also had a significant impact on the lives of those who came.

At Karanda, Anne Watson took charge of the nursing school while Wilma Gardziella took a midwifery course in Harare in 1971. Cynthia Sander assisted in the nursing school when Wilma went on furlough in 1976, taking charge for several months when Karen

Drake also went on furlough. While she originally came for a year, Cynthia felt led to stay for two, continuing to help out with needs both at the hospital and the nursing school.

She shared the impact that this experience had on her life:

> *I strongly believe that the Lord used my time at Karanda to heighten my awareness of missions, and that this was the primary reason He sent me there. I came from a missions-minded church and family, but this experience gave me a depth of awareness I would not otherwise have had.*
>
> *Since returning from Karanda, I have been consistently involved in missions-related activities at my church. I also feel privileged to pray regularly for a number of missionaries, including those with whom I worked in Zimbabwe.*
>
> *As a nursing school instructor, I have used my experience at Karanda extensively, both formally and informally. One of the classes I taught was on nursing in the developing world—with an emphasis on missions. This was particularly enriched by my personal experience.*

Susan Goldsmith brought her skills as a physiotherapist to Karanda for two years. During this time she was able to enhance the treatment given to patients with muscle or joint problems. She was a blessing to all in the way she reached out to children and adults alike with her friendly personality. She also extended her services to a number of grateful missionaries.

Sonja Goppert, daughter of Chris and Joyce Goppert, took Julie Stephen's place at Karanda teaching first and second grade to children of the hospital staff while Julie went on home assignment in 2000. She wrote:

> *Being so far away from family and friends and so isolated on the station was hard, but it was the best year of my life. I think that short-termers at Karanda added energy and enthusiasm to the work, but we all came away with so much more than we gave.*

When Donna Hendrickson Abuhl came to help out at Karanda in 1997, she was able to update surgical records and teach a simple computer course to the head nurses so they could write business letters. Since she could speak Shona, she also did visitation on the wards.

Judy Gudeman returned to Karanda as a short-termer in 2001 and spent many hours cleaning and organizing various storerooms, getting accumulated supplies sorted and out for use or processed to become useful. This included putting together new baby packs, altering sheets to fit hospital beds, and sewing surgical wrappers.

Dr. Dan Stephens told of the impressive accomplishments of a team of short-term workers from the Blue Ridge Bible Church in Purcellville, VA, who came to help out at Karanda in 2004:

*In the space of 10 days they built a playground for the station, met with a number of the local Shona leaders, and with the assistance of the Karanda pastor and youth did evangelism on the wards, conducted marriage and pastoral seminars, special church services, and a two-day evangelistic outreach using the Jesus film. During these services over 300 came forward for salvation. (Afterward the team also enjoyed a fabulous trip to the Wankie Game Park and Victoria Falls.)*

Dan also expressed his great appreciation of short-term workers in general:

*Short-termers have definitely been a provision of the Lord for the Karanda station. We have had many of them come over the years, and each one fits a special niche. We find them both helpful and a lot of fun to have around. They challenge us, keep us on our toes, and stimulate us to new efforts. We often talk about them and their impact for years. Many provide significant prayer and financial support after they return home, and some go on to become career missionaries.*

His father, Roland, whole-heartedly agreed with this assessment. He recalled the major spiritual effect Dr. Chester Scott had during his short-term service because of his enthusiasm and exceptional ability to reach out to others. Another short-term doctor played a significant role in giving funds for the chapel on the station.

Short-term workers were just as valuable in other areas of the field. Goldye Gustafson, secretary to TEAM's general director in the home office, and Shirley Bradford, secretary for the TEAM Zimbabwe field chairman, switched places when Shirley went on furlough in 1971. During this year they both found husbands on their particular side of the ocean. Shirley continued her secretarial position in the home office, but a replacement was needed for Goldye in Zimbabwe after she became Mrs. Cecyl Till.

To meet this need, God sent another short-termer, Jan Hendrickson, daughter of Carl and Donna Hendrickson, who was office secretary from 1973-74. She wrote:

> *They needed someone who was familiar with the country and mission to fill Goldye's spot quickly. I had just graduated from business college, and the field invited me to come and fill the vacancy. Since I grew up in Zimbabwe, they felt I could adjust more quickly.*
>
> *It was a very busy and profitable time for me spiritually and in service to the field. The Hatfield office served as the hub of all the various aspects of missionary activity on the field as well as the liaison with local government officials and the home office in the United States. I helped to keep communication flowing in all directions.*
>
> *It was enlightening and enriching for me to see the mission field from an adult and missionary perspective. Later, my husband, Mick Catron, and I served as church planters for four years with TEAM in Venezuela. We are currently church planters with Calvary Chapel, and my husband is senior pastor of a Calvary Chapel in the California desert. Our years of missionary experience have helped us know how to pray for and support missionaries better and to keep the vision alive here in the States.*

Grace Archer, a TEAM MK from Japan, came as a short-termer to take over the financial office for a year in 1983, when Helen

Smith had to return to the States because of family health concerns. Then, in 1988, when the field urgently needed to fill the position of office secretary again, the Lord sent Betty Stermer, a retiree from TEAM's Japan field. She recalls being welcomed with the words "You are the living, walking, breathing answer to our prayers!" Obviously, this made her feel very wanted and appreciated.

Burt and Donna Hendrickson Abuhl came as short-termers in 1993 to fill in as hostel parents for the four Stephens' boys (their grandsons) while Tom and Lois Jackson went on furlough. Donna also served as guesthouse hostess and worked part-time in the office.

Marilyn Larson came for six weeks to organize the Bible college library. Kathy McKamey helped type up teaching notes for the college. Other short-termers have helped with construction projects, taught Scripture classes in schools, or assisted in church and youth ministries.

Sherrie Rhodie was only 16 when she came to Zimbabwe to help Dick and Mary Ann McCloy. They reported how well she was able to bond with the youth at their church and help with many of their activities. She also put together a PowerPoint presentation with drawings she made to illustrate Dick's ABC Bible Study Method. Dick and Mary Ann were able to add to this and use it in their presentations to churches on furlough. They were very grateful for Sherrie's contribution to their ministry.

Tom Jackson told how the AWANA ministry in Zimbabwe was launched through the assistance of a short-term, summer worker in 1983:

> *Lois and I were working with the Southside Evangelical Church in Waterfalls, along with Marian Wilterdink, and we wanted to start a children's program. We decided to ask TEAM to assign a summer worker to us for this purpose.*
>
> *We were soon connected with Susan Schneider, a nursing student who wanted to come for a summer ministry. She asked us how she could best prepare for this and what materials to bring with her. At that point we hadn't decided on either the structure or the materials we wanted to use for the program.*
>
> *However, Petros Kapurura, an Evangelical Church*

*member who had been in the States for further education, returned to Zimbabwe at about that time with a suitcase full of promotional materials for AWANA. His children had been in an AWANA club in the States, and he had been asked by the leadership to introduce the program to people in Zimbabwe.*

*In order to do this, he announced a meeting at the Harare Evangelical Church one evening. Here he showed a film strip of the AWANA ministry and shared AWANA's vision to see clubs started in other parts of the world. Only about five or six people attended the meeting, but Lois, Marian, and I left very fired up about the program.*

*We immediately called Sue Schneider to tell her that we had decided on what materials she should bring. When we asked her if she knew anything about AWANA, she exclaimed, "Know anything? I grew up in AWANA, and my dad is a full-time AWANA missionary!" Obviously, God had connected us with just the right person to help us get this program started in our church.*

*Susan arrived with a couple of suitcases full of AWANA handbooks, T-shirts, game circle lay-outs, training materials, etc. She began by holding a training course for leaders at the Southside church. We then launched the program, and it was a huge success, growing dramatically to over 200 children being involved each week, most of whom made decisions for Christ. The leaders were primarily young people of the church, who also grew by leaps and bounds as they became involved in ministry themselves.*

While the AWANA program was initiated in English, the handbooks were soon translated into Shona as well. Now both English and Shona handbooks are produced locally. The uniform was also redesigned so that it could be produced and purchased locally. In Zimbabwe different colored t-shirts, screen-printed with the AWANA logo, are used to designate the various ranks through which the children progress.

The program spread quickly to other cities and churches, both TEAM-related and not. Today AWANA is a thriving ministry in Zimbabwe. A local board has been formed, and three full-time, local, AWANA missionaries now serve in the country, supported by the Stateside AWANA organization. What a fruitful forest grew from the seed planted by a short-term worker!

# Help

Another critical area in which God provided for His servants was in bringing the right kind of assistance at the right time when they were in difficult situations. Many of God's timely "rescues" seemed almost miraculous in nature. Once again He proved Himself faithful to those who had confidently entrusted their welfare to Him in the country to which He had called them.

## Being Lost

Shortly after Russ and Marg Jackson arrived at Msengedzi in 1948, Russ was asked to go out hunting for meat. Being anxious for an opportunity to cross into Mozambique and see that part of the Valley, he eagerly embraced this challenge. He had no difficulty getting two Shona men to accompany him, as they were hungry for meat too.

Russ described what transpired on this first hunting trip:

*I drove eight miles to the Kadzi River, which marked the border into Mozambique. There I set up camp for the night and planned to cross into Mozambique as early in the morning as possible. I not only wanted to shoot some meat, but I had a keen desire to see the Zambezi River, which I knew lay to the north.*

*As we ventured further away from the Kadzi, I was surprised to see no signs of villages. The bush country that lay ahead was totally unmarked, without any sign of human habitation. The further north we trekked, the wilder the country became with a great abundance of wild animal life. I could have shot several types of animals nearer the border, but I was determined to reach the Zambezi.*

*Finally, I realized that we could go no further and still have time to return to our camp on the Kadzi, so I shot three impala. This delighted the two Shona men accompanying me. They quickly cut a long pole, and after tying all the impala to it, we started back to where we had left the truck at the Kadzi. . . .*

*I followed the men carrying the impala for a short distance, but they were walking so slowly that I decided to leave them to bring the meat and to take what I was sure would be a shortcut back to the camp. This was a big mistake. Once I was on my own, I had absolutely no landmarks to orient me. The bush country around me all looked the same. . . .*

*After I had walked for some time, I found that I had been going in a huge circle. This was very alarming, as I realized I was lost. I will never forget the hopeless, fearful feeling of knowing I was really lost—with no water, no food, and darkness fast approaching.*

*After walking for some time in what I hoped was the right direction, I heard a faint sound that I felt sure was not made by a wild animal. As I hurried toward the sound, it gradually became clearer. Soon I came upon a man chopping a hole in a tree with a wild bee hive in it. I walked up to the man, startling him. He turned and looked at me, and I will never forget the shocked expression on his face when he found himself looking into the face of a white man.*

*The fact that I was lost must have been obvious to him. . . . Without a word he reached over and lifted my rifle from my shoulder and placed it on his. Then he turned and started to walk quickly away in the opposite direction from that which I had been walking. After some time we came to a well-defined path made over the years by wild animals going to and from the river. Still without saying a word, my heaven-sent guide pointed in the direction I was to go. Then he placed my rifle back on my shoulder and turned and disappeared back into the bush.*

*By this time the sun had gone down, and it was beginning to get dark. You can be sure that without a moment's hesitation, I followed the game path in the direction the man had pointed. Long before I reached the river, I could see the glow of a campfire that my men had made, hoping that it would guide me back to camp.*

Feeling the helplessness and hopelessness of being lost and then the huge relief at being found had a major impact on Russ's life and ministry. Through this harrowing experience God had given him a powerful, firsthand experience that he was able to use in the exercise of his gift of evangelism.

## Needing Medical Assistance

Some time later, while the Jacksons were still living at Msengedzi, Marg was the one who urgently needed help. Russ had gone to open a new station about 50 miles away at Hunyani. Norman Everswick and Orla Blair had also gone to prepare for opening a new station at Rukomechi. This left Eunice Ott and the three wives at Msengedzi alone.

Marg was about three months pregnant at the time, and while the men were gone, she became extremely ill, vomiting violently. The other women knew she needed to get to a hospital but were unable to get her there on their own.

At this time of her great need and with no other means of communication available, God Himself summoned Russ to return to Msengedzi. Russ described how he received this call:

> *Several nights after my arrival at Hunyani, while lying in my bedroll, I began to sense a deep feeling of uneasiness concerning Marg. This feeling lasted through the night. Each time I would wake up, the feeling of concern was greater. I began to feel quite sure that the Lord was speaking to me concerning Marg's need for help and that I must go to her immediately.*
>
> *In those days when going any distance by truck, we always carried a 44-gallon drum of petrol [gasoline] and a bicycle in case of emergencies. I felt that I could make a cross-country shortcut back to Msengedzi by following the foot paths on my bicycle. By this time all the rivers were dry, so they would not be a problem.*

When he arrived back at Msengedzi, the women were so relieved to see him, informing him of Marg's condition. Russ quickly made a pallet of straw in the back of the mission's old

Chevy truck and with the ladies' help carried Marg, by now semi-comatose, out of the house and laid her on it. Thelma Everswick graciously offered to ride with Marg in the back of the truck, and they started out immediately for the long trip to Harare.

The truck's brakes were not working well, and the road up the escarpment out of the Zambezi Valley was steep and treacherous with many hairpin turns in it. When they got to the base of it, Thelma positioned herself on the tailgate of the truck with a big stone beside her. Every time the truck stalled or had to stop, she would jump off and place the stone behind the rear wheel to keep it from rolling backwards.

When they arrived at the emergency room, the doctor admitted Marg, telling Russ that she was very dehydrated and would need several days of intravenous fluids to regain her strength. Under the doctor's care she made a remarkable recovery, and in a few days they returned to the Valley. Marg had no further problems during her pregnancy.

Rusty Sherwood recalled the time God sent very timely help to save the life of Baba Soda, one of the early Shona evangelists. He had been traveling with Rusty, and Rusty had left him to watch the truck at some point. During this time he was bitten by a poisonous snake. He probably would have died had the Lord not intervened and sent along a government ambulance *at just that time!*

Mary Ann McCloy told about a time God had the right help in place for her when she and her family were at Mana Pools, their favorite animal preserve:

*The tsetse flies were taking over more and more terri-tory, and when we were out game driving, I got at least two bites, one on my wrist and one near my elbow. I had been bitten by these flies before, and apart from the pain of the bite, that was it. This time, however, my body responded with a major allergic reaction. My whole arm between the two bites became very swollen and red.*

*I went in to the park office to see if I could get any help there. The Lord had obviously gone before me because in the office at that very moment was a DOCTOR who was doing TSETSE FLY RESEARCH! He, of course, wanted*

*pictures of my arm, but he also had some antihistamine!!*
*Thank you, Lord!*

## Needing Help on the Road

Another time when God often chose to send special assistance was when the missionaries' vehicles broke down on the bush roads. This was usually a very disheartening situation, as resources for obtaining help were generally pretty slim. When the right kind of help arrived at the right time without being summoned, they knew that God was looking after them.

Helen Smith told of a time when she had to finish packing up her household and move it from Chirundu to Kapfundi before leaving on furlough, as the mission was no longer going to post missionaries at Chirundu. Her husband, Paul, couldn't help her because he was in Harare having just been released from the hospital with acute phlebitis and needed to continue keeping his leg up. Upon hearing of her need, Marguerite Blair graciously offered to help Helen.

When the two ladies finally had everything packed up, dusk was falling, but since Marguerite wanted to get back for classes at the Bible school the next day if at all possible, they set off for Kapfundi. When they were just five miles from their destination, they had a flat tire. It was now midnight or later. Helen pulled off to the side of the road, and the exhausted women contemplated the task they were going to have to undertake by themselves.

Just then they heard another vehicle coming around the bend, an unusual occurrence on bush roads at night. It was a large truck and, seeing their predicament, the driver stopped and changed the tire for them. How they praised God for coming to their rescue when they were so tired so late at night!

As a single lady, Rita Ibbotson testified that God had faithfully cared for her in similar ways every time she had a vehicle problem. Whether it was to change a tire or to charge her battery when her alarm system had drained it, someone would always "happen" along to help her take care of the problem, even when she was traveling on very isolated roads.

Barb Christiansen told about the time she and Phil needed rescuing on their first trip out to the Msengedzi station. They were traveling with the Sherwoods and the Beaches and got stuck in the mud in the Sapa River bed at about 7:00 in the evening. When, even after drafting the help of three local villagers, they failed to get the vehicles unstuck, Phil and Wilbur Beach began walking the 14 miles to the station while the rest of them spent the night in the two vehicles.

The next morning the "rescuers" were delayed in getting back to them because of more rain. Finally, around mid-morning they heard Orv Dunkeld's truck arrive. Barb wrote:

> *The men unloaded the Sherwood's truck, hooked a chain onto it, and in a short time pulled it out. Then they unloaded ours and pulled it across. What a relief that was!*
>
> *Next they began carrying the unloaded equipment across. Just when they were about to pick up the last piece, someone yelled, "The Sapa is filling!"*
>
> *We all ran to look. Sure enough, water was beginning to flow. It was most likely a backflow from a larger river. The Lord's timing is always perfect! Had Orv come just fifteen minutes later, we would not have gotten through for days.*

She also told of the time God came to their rescue when she and Phil were returning to Karanda from Harare with a truckload of hospital equipment, along with their own supplies:

> *We went down in a spruit and broke the rear axle-shaft of our vehicle. So there we were—stuck between Mt. Darwin and the hospital. It was about 7:00 at night, dark and a bad time for mosquitoes. Ron was still a very small baby.*
>
> *As we were sitting in the truck waiting to see how God was going to work this out, along came an empty truck that had just made a delivery at the Chironga store. When the driver saw our predicament, he unloaded all of our essential stuff onto his truck and took us 25 miles back to Karanda. The next day George Dee and Phil drove back to our disabled truck and towed it to Karanda. There they removed the rear axle and sent it to Harare for repair. We were very happy when we once again had wheels.*

Lynne Hawkins also had an experience on the road when she greatly appreciated the timely arrival of help. She wrote:

*During the Easter holiday in 1973, I was driving some of the Evangelical Bible College students to Rusambo. One of them was to be dropped off at Chironga. Coming to a spruit, I tried to slow down, but because of the slope and the sand, my car skidded into a boulder at the bottom of the spruit. My face hit the windshield, and I thought I had broken my nose.*

*To make matters worse, the car would no longer go forward, so I had to back out, turn around, and then back through the spruit again. I then started driving backwards down the road towards Chironga with a sore face and neck.*

*Pretty soon I saw another car approaching. Then it pulled over onto the side of the road and stopped. When we got there, I discovered it was Helen Dunkeld and the female language students from Chironga. She said something about wanting to get out of the way of some crazy person driving backwards down the road.*

*We left the car there, and after dropping the language students off at the Kudyanyemba Church, she took me to Karanda to have my nose checked by the doctor. It wasn't broken. Meanwhile Orv Dunkeld fixed my car so it could be driven properly, and after spending the night at Chironga, we continued on our way to Rusambo.*

Dottie Larsen recalled a time when she got stuck in a riverbed, and God not only provided the help she needed to get on her way again but the means to pay these men as well. She wrote:

*I was coming back to Kapfundi from Harare and had picked up my post [mail], which included several packages from the United States. I then ended up getting stuck in a riverbed. Since I always had a couple of young Shona men along, they walked to the nearest village to get more help.*

*Quite a few men arrived to push and pull my vehicle up the riverbank. They worked very hard for quite awhile, and I had no money to pay them. Then, I decided to open one of the boxes from home. Lo and behold, the women from my home church had felt led to collect a bunch of neckties to send. They made the perfect payment that I needed at that moment, and the men couldn't have appreciated them more. Of course, this was also an opportunity to tell them of God's love and care.*

God also had in place just what Diane Powell and Anne Watson needed when they failed in their attempt to ride their newly purchased horses from Mt. Darwin to Karanda. Diane had ridden on a 300-mile horseback trip with Youth for Christ, so she felt quite confident in being able to ride these 30 miles to Karanda.

She soon learned that riding two unfamiliar horses through the African countryside with its many rivers and spruits was a completely different situation. It took them hours to cover the first few miles, mainly because the horses refused to cross a bridge. When they finally conquered this hurdle and stopped for brief rest, the horses spooked and took off without them into the bush.

Now what were they to do? They committed the situation to the Lord, and soon they saw two Shona boys emerging from the bush, leading their horses back to them. What a joyful sight that was! Then a bus that was headed for Karanda came by, and they were able to send a message to the hospital that they would not be able to make it to Karanda by nightfall.

They still didn't know what they were going to do for the night but continued plodding down the road. Anne's horse had lost a stirrup in its dash through the bush, so they were now moving very slowly. They were extremely happy when an approaching vehicle arriving almost at dusk contained the familiar faces of their Karanda co-workers, who had received their message and were bringing food and sleeping bags.

However, at the very point at which the two parties met, they could see an empty corral just off the road. It was the perfect place to leave their horses for the night, which meant they would not have to camp out in the bush with them. Instead, they rode back to the station, had Walter Gardziella, the station's "Mr. Fix It," construct a new stirrup for Anne's saddle, got a good night's sleep, and then were driven back to their horses in the morning. The remainder of the ride back to Karanda was uneventful.

Tom and Lois Jackson experienced a different kind of timely intervention by the Lord. They had had a serious car accident while returning from a holiday in South Africa. None of their family was hurt but their car was totaled. A gracious TEAM missionary in Johannesburg loaned them his car to drive back up to Zimbabwe.

When they got to the border, however, they learned that they could not bring the South African car into Zimbabwe. Just at that time a carload of missionaries from another mission, whom they knew, arrived from the other direction. When they learned of the Jackson's problem, one of them offered to drive the borrowed car back to Johannesburg while Bud Jackson was summoned to pick up Tom and his family.

# Peace

Sometimes God's most powerful interventions were not physical in nature. Bringing supernatural peace into the hearts of His servants during deeply troubling circumstances was another remarkable provision of the Lord. Often this was the only way they could courageously continue on the path He had chosen for them.

## In War Time

By the early '70s, Zimbabwe's war of independence was having a significant impact on life in the outlying areas. No longer could missionaries walk freely to visit in the villages. In many areas the people were forced to leave their homes and live in large, crowded "protected villages," or "keeps," established by the government. Travel on the roads became extremely risky because of the danger of land mines. Curfews were set to prohibit the movement of people after dark, and a large security fence was erected around the Karanda station to monitor all who went in and out.

Nights were frequently interrupted with the sounds of gunfire and mortar attack at varying distances from the rural stations. The tensions and uncertainties of the situation left no one unaffected. These were unprecedented times in everyone's lives. They were times of learning to trust God in brand new ways—and finding Him so faithful once again, providing not only safety but a peace that defied human understanding.

Several missionaries shared how God personally ministered to their fears in the midst of this precarious situation. In each case they testified of the comfort and assurance they received from His Word and the supernatural peace that took hold in their lives, enabling them to go forward with what God had called them to do in this increasingly dangerous country.

Pat Dunkeld Christensen recalled many nights when she went to sleep at Karanda with the reassurance of Psalm 4:8: *"I will both lay me down in peace, and sleep: for thou, Lord, only makest me dwell in safety"* (KJV). The verse God used to minister to Mary Ann McCloy when she awoke to the sounds of gunshots or barking dogs at Rusambo was Psalm 34:7: *"The angel of the Lord encamps all around those who fear him, and delivers them"(NKJV).* She wrote:

> *I would ask the Lord to put His angels at each door and window around our house, and then I could go back to sleep. He was on duty, so I didn't need to be awake and worrying. Thank you, Lord.*

In an article entitled "In Nothing Terrified," Norman Everswick wrote about the peace that God gave to him and Thelma through His Word in the midst of the war tensions:

> *"And in nothing terrified by your adversaries" (Philippians 1:28a; KJV); "For He shall give His angels charge over thee, to keep thee in all thy ways" (Psalm 91:11; KJV).*
>
> *These and many other precious promises from God's Word have been priceless to my wife and me in the comfort and strength they have given us during these last five years of service as missionaries in Zimbabwe. It is now 32 years since we first came here to preach the Gospel to Shona people who had never before heard it. We lived under very primitive conditions . . . and had many opportunities to witness God's protective and loving care. Never before, however, have we leaned so heavily upon God's Word, and*

*witnessed so clearly His undertaking in protecting His own.*

*For four years of our last five-year term of service, we found ourselves serving the Lord at our Karanda station, surrounded with the horrors of war. Two of our Shona Christian leaders were murdered on one of our stations while a missionary was made to watch. Murders were taking place all about us . . . . What will happen, we asked ourselves, when we are visited and the animosity is vented against us?*

*One day tensions were particularly high on our station. We heard rumors that the station was about to be attacked. My wife was home alone. When she began hearing shooting, she [was overcome] with fear. In desperation she took her Bible into the bedroom and opened it upon the bed as she knelt there. "I'm only a woman, Lord. I can't stand this!" she cried. "You've got to help me!" And, as if in immediate reply, her eyes became fixed on the words of a verse from her open Bible lying before her: "And in nothing terrified by your adversaries." A miracle took place. She got up from her knees a new person. Fear was gone!*

*Some time later we were "visited." I was home alone at about 6:30 p.m. It was dark outside. I was sitting, drinking a cup of tea, when I heard a knock on the back door. . . . When I opened the door, two men with automatic weapons in their hands greeted me, saying, "We have come. . . . We want to speak with you, let us in."*

*Knowing that the house was surrounded, I opened the door and let the two men in. Immediately a third man came around the corner with a fixed bayonet, following me into the house. They assured me that they wouldn't kill me. Inside, they made me sit between them.*

*Fifteen minutes later [Dr. Drake], passing by our house and realizing what was taking place, came to the door and joined me inside. The ["visitors"] stayed for 1½ hours. They talked mainly about their political aspirations, and we talked about the love of God. Finally, we were asked for medicines, and the doctor was permitted to go to the hospital for them.*

*When he left, they said to me, "Preach for us." I opened my Shona Bible to Psalm 125:1-2 and spoke as God gave me utterance. As I spoke, my eyes were opened. I [saw them as men] for whom Jesus had died and who desperately needed Him as their Saviour that they might know the peace and security that He had already given to us. This was unbelievable! We prayed for them that they might know Christ and asked if they would be willing to take Gospels of John with them and also give to each of the men with them. They did, and after the doctor returned with the medicine, they left.*

*Needless to say, after that we spent much time in apprehension—and in claiming the precious promises of the Word of God and in prayer. Nights in particular were difficult when we'd hear a strange noise outside; yet how priceless were these sleepless moments in sweet communion with God when He drew near to comfort and speak peace to our hearts!*

Diane Powell also wrote an article, entitled "Faithful Promises," that recounted how God used His Word to bring peace to her heart during those troubled times:

*Because the war was fought primarily under the cover of darkness, we never knew what a given night would bring. Our ears were quickly tuned to discern the critical sounds: the rhythmic whirr of helicopters bearing casualties, the distant lobbing of mortar shells, the sharp bursts of artillery fire, or the dreaded rustling of grass signaling the approach of an unknown being—friend, foe, or animal.*

*Many times as I lay on my bed wrestling with inner tinges of fear, I reached for a card from one of the promise boxes I kept by my bedside. On every single occasion that I needed a word of encouragement from God, the verse I pulled from the box spoke of safety or protection. His faithfulness in ministering to me in this way made His presence seem almost palpable. Oh, how He loved and cared for me!*

*One night it seemed that the military activity was exceptionally near. When I reached for a promise card, it again contained the reassuring words of God. This time it was: "A thousand shall fall at thy side, and ten thousand at thy right hand, but it shall not come nigh thee" (Psalm 91:7; KJV). In the darkness I whispered, "Thank you, God."*

*As time crawled forward and the barrage of gunfire continued, I reached for another card from the other box. To my amazement it contained the exact same verse as the previous card! It was as if God were saying to me, "I told you once, but if you need it, I'll tell you again, 'You are going to be safe.'" What a God!*

*A time of heightened fear for me during the war years occurred when my turn came to fill in for the matron of the female nurses' dormitory when she went to town. This meant spending the night in her apartment, which was located at perhaps the most isolated corner of the mission station. How I dreaded that assignment! Nevertheless, my turn would come, and when it did, I would postpone the inevitable and stay in my own home as long as I could. Then just before bedtime I would finally make the dark, lonely trek down to her apartment.*

*As I did this one night, fear gripped my heart, and I found myself pondering, "How is God going to speak to me when I don't even have my promise boxes with me?" With my heart pounding, I finally reached her porch and managed to unlock the door. As I quickly entered and locked it behind me, my eyes rested on a plaque just inside the door that read, "What time I am afraid, I will trust in Thee" (Psalm 56:3; KJV). "Oh, God," I exclaimed, "You did it again—even without my promise boxes!"*

*When I returned home to the United States in 1976 and prepared to tell of God's faithfulness to me during those challenging years, I wanted to see how extraordinary it was for me to receive a promise of safety or protection every time I reached for a verse from my promise boxes. So I took all of the cards and sorted them by subject. Only one-third of them had to do with protection. What a blessing to have such tangible proof for what I already knew without a doubt in my heart! God was indeed faithfully intervening to provide what I needed during those fearful nights.*

God also brought the reassurance that Lydia Eichner needed on a very disturbing day in Hatfield. The routine radio contact with all the stations that morning had just brought the horrifying word that the boarding master and the chaplain at the Mavuradonha High School had both been murdered during the night. As field chairman, her husband, Roy, made immediate plans to have the MAF plane fly him out there.

Lydia described what went on in her own heart that morning:

*As we said good-bye at the airport, I held him just a bit longer with the horrible thought in my mind of whether we would see each other again on earth. While Roy was at Mavuradonha, the decision was made that the entire station would be evacuated. The Shona staff and students would leave immediately. Then the MAF plane would fly the missionary ladies and children to Harare.*

*After hearing this news, I began to prepare for the folks coming into the cottage. My thoughts were filled with concern about the safety of the missionary men who would remain longer at Mavuradonha. Then there was a question about the future of the national students who had been sent home. Would TEAM have to evacuate other stations soon? How long would we be able to work in this troubled country? What did the future hold? Yes, my mind was full of questions concerning our tomorrows.*

*That day I received a tape in the mail from our home church. On it was a song I had never heard before. The Lord used this song to encourage my heart during that difficult week: "Because He lives, I can face tomorrow; Because He lives, all fear is gone. Because I know He holds the future, And life is worth the living just because He lives."*

*When the Mavuradonha ladies arrived, we had a meal together, and then I was able to share this song with them. We all were blessed and encouraged by it. How gracious of the Lord to allow this tape to arrive that very day! His timing is always perfect.*

Lynn and Judy Everswick will never forget the evening that God provided His peace to their children in a very supernatural way. As parents, they were attending a PTA function at the Bindura school. Judy had, in fact, been in charge of the dinner. She described what happened that night:

> *We left our five children at home in bed with Baba Friday sleeping outside in his home. Kim was 11, Rick 9, Brad 4, and the twins Tim and Brendon 2.*
>
> *We were never ones to over-dramatize the war situation with our children. Some threats on the town of Bindura had been recently uttered, however, so as we left that evening, Lynn told Kim that if she heard any loud bangs or noises, she should wake the four boys and put them in the hallway and close all of the doors (in order to avoid the possibility of being hit by broken glass from the windows).*
>
> *Around 10 p.m., just as our dinner ended, the mortars and exchange of rifle fire started. Our first reaction was to get to the children. We were instead made to get on the floor under the small tables in the gym. As we gathered together, we prayed for peace in the hearts of our little ones. We were not as concerned about the mortars actually hitting the house as much as five frightened children trying to comfort each other and Kim being the "little Mom" all alone.*
>
> *After about 20 minutes an army vehicle took Lynn to the house. As he opened the door into the passageway, he saw all of the children sound asleep with their pillows on the floor in the hallway. Kim looked up when she heard her dad, rubbed her eyes, and said, "Daddy, can we get up and go to bed now?" God had protected the children, but more importantly, He had answered our prayer and given those five children HIS PEACE.*

## In Sorrow and Loss

God's supernatural provision of peace is available not only in times of fear and anxiety but also in times of grief and sorrow. Donna Hendrickson shared how God ministered to her needs as she walked through the "valley of the shadow of death," bidding a very sudden and unexpected farewell to her husband of almost 33 years.

Having essentially worked themselves out of a job at the Evangelical Bible College in Zimbabwe, Carl and Donna were invited to continue in Bible college ministry on the TEAM South Africa field. After five years of service there they were on their way home for furlough in 1983, when tragedy struck.

As a gentle Shepherd, God had lovingly gone ahead to prepare Donna's heart for the major changes that lay ahead for her. She shared:

*On several occasions during 1983, Carl had preached on Isaiah 26:3 [NLT]: "You will keep in PERFECT PEACE all who TRUST in you. . . ." While I didn't realize it at the time, I now recognize this as Carl's and God's message preparing me for December 4, 1983.*

*As I spent time alone with the Lord on November 5th, He gave me the special verses of Jeremiah 29:11-13 (NASB): "'For I know the plans that I have for you,' declares the LORD, 'plans for welfare and not for calamity to give you a future and a hope. Then you will call upon Me and come and pray to Me, and I will listen to you. And you will seek Me and find Me when you search for Me with all your heart.'" At our annual end-of-the-year banquet at Durban Bible College I was able to quote these verses that God had so poignantly laid on my heart.*

*On Sunday, November 27, Carl, as college principal, presided over the beautiful and very meaningful graduation service. . . . On Tuesday, the 29th, we left for furlough, flying to Amsterdam for a few days and then on to London for R & R before arriving in the States.*

*Sunday morning in London was beautiful but very cold. . . . After dinner we walked in Hyde Park and then took a two-hour tour through London on the upper deck of a red, double-decker bus. . . . Arriving back at Hyde Park at 5:00 p.m. in pitch darkness, we walked hand-in-hand through the unlit park on the way to our holiday flat, planning to attend a concert that evening. . . .*

*Then very suddenly Carl turned to me and said: "I feel dizzy." Immediately, he slumped to the ground and gradu-*

*ated into the presence of the Lord. I went to the ground with him, holding his dear head tenderly in my hands. I gently spoke into his ear telling him I loved him and prayed for God's help, all the while knowing he was totally lifeless.*

An ambulance came and took them to the hospital where he was pronounced dead after an unsuccessful, 30-minute attempt to resuscitate him. Donna continued:

*I met with the doctor, who explained that Carl had had a massive heart attack. As we spoke, he commented that I was a very strong lady. I told him it was not me but God Who gave me His strength. . . .*

*Before leaving the hospital, I wanted to settle my account for the ambulance, ER, and doctors—but there was no bill. God had provided free service! The nurse then directed me to the front desk where a gentleman called a taxi for me. The taxi driver was a very kind and sympathetic Arab, who drove me directly to my holiday flat.*

*As I entered the flat alone and began taking Carl's clothes out of the hospital bag piece by piece, I burst into tears. Very quickly, however, I knew I had to pull myself together and make some phone calls. . . .*

After several tries Donna was able to contact her daughter Nancy and Gordon, one of Carl's brothers. They then spread the news of Carl's passing to other family members and informed TEAM headquarters. One by one these loved ones began calling Donna back, sharing in the great sorrow of the moment. She recounted her feelings as her son, Wes, phoned:

*As we heard each other's voice, neither of us could verbalize any words. Finally, I simply asked, "Can you come?"*

*He said, "Yes, I'm leaving tomorrow and will arrive Tuesday morning in London.". . .*

*After talking to Wes, I opened my Bible to where I had been reading in the Amplified New Testament, which was Colossians 1:2b: "Grace to you and HEART PEACE from*

*God our Father." As I read those words, an instantaneous
and very tangible PEACE began at the top of my head and
ran down through my arms and fingers and the entire trunk
of my body, then down my legs to the very tips of my toes.
This was my Heavenly Father pouring His sweet and
PERFECT PEACE through my body, which was in shock.*

Dick Winchell, TEAM's general director at that time, also
called to inform her of the arrangements being made for returning
Carl's body to the States. He also told her that he had made contact
with a couple, Keith and Ann Donald, serving under another
mission in London, and had asked them to connect with Donna so
she didn't have to be alone at this difficult time.

When they called and offered to take Donna home with them
for the night, she initially expressed her need to stay where she was
to await an important call from Carl's brother. She continued:

> *Shortly after Harry called, the Donald's phoned again.
> It was about 1:30 a.m. They were in bed praying for me and
> couldn't go to sleep. They asked again if they could come to
> get me. My response this time was "Yes, thank you so much.
> I'd be very pleased."*
>
> *About 45 minutes later Keith called from his cell phone,
> telling me he was across the street. I said I would meet him
> in my lobby.*
>
> *We had never met before, but after we introduced
> ourselves, his first words were, "Do you need a hug?" I
> gratefully accepted. He then took me into their home where
> they lovingly welcomed me. . . .*
>
> *As phone calls came in the next morning from friends
> expressing their devastation at Carl's death, I told them that
> I felt surrounded with a loving blanket of prayer.*

On Tuesday Donna went to the airport, eagerly anticipating
Wes's arrival. She continued her story:

> *It felt so good to receive his very special and wonderful
> bear hugs. Even as we traveled home on the plane, he had a*

*sense of knowing when my hand needed to be held or I needed his arm around my shoulder. God was so good to send him to accompany me home. . . .*

*We celebrated Carl's memory at the First Covenant Church in Los Angeles, our home church where we both grew up and were married on June 8, 1951. One great joy was having Onesimus Ngundu participate in the service. He was sent by two of his professors at Dallas Theological Seminary. He had been mentored by Carl for four years as a student at the Evangelical Bible College in Chinhoyi. Also participating were Rev. Dick Winchell from TEAM, Rev. Orla Blair from Zimbabwe, and Rev. Dean Erickson, the current pastor.*

*Special memorial services were also held at the Evangelical Bible College in Zimbabwe, Durban Bible College in South Africa, and at both the Zimbabwe and South Africa Annual Conferences. Carl was loved and well-remembered by all his friends and co-workers.*

*The days ahead were spent traveling between my families. . . . The year was filled with making new and big decisions on my own. . . . Carl was not only my husband, my lover, but also my best friend, my mentor, my decision-maker, my co-worker. We worked together all through our lives, and I was his lifelong secretary. I now had to find out who I was without him.*

*So I searched the Scriptures daily and communed with God. Much time was spent in the Psalm with the recurring assurance of God's lovingkindness. I was living in God's loving "Waiting Room" as over and over again I read the words, "Wait upon the Lord." In my heart I just wanted to go to heaven to be with the Lord and with Carl.*

*Then, on Carl's birthday, November 3, 1984, I had a horrendous headache. I remember standing over the sink thinking it must be a brain tumor, BUT also thinking that I really didn't want to die. After all those months of grieving I now wanted to live to serve God and be there for my family and grandchildren.*

*God lovingly walked with me through that year of heart*

*searching and loneliness. I knew of a certainty that if it hadn't been for His love, His strength, His lovingkindness, and the caring prayer support of family and friends, I would have been devastated. Praise God for those "Footprints in the Sand." Jesus had lovingly carried me through those overwhelming months. It was only after that that I began to experience the reality of Jeremiah 29:11-13, which God had so poignantly given to me just a month before welcoming Carl to his eternal reward.*

---

[1] Slightly modified from Noël Liddle, *A Million Miles of Miracles* (Bulawayo, Zimbabwe: Baptist Publication House, 1995), p. 68.

# CHAPTER 10

# God Protected

*"'Because he loves me,' says the Lord,*
*'I will rescue him; I will protect him,*
*for he acknowledges my name.'"*
(Psalm 91:14)

Becoming a missionary in Zimbabwe definitely meant accepting a lifestyle of increased dangers. Like the Apostle Paul, these brave men and women could list the many perils they encountered in fulfilling God's call upon their lives: perils from wild animals; perils from poisonous snakes, perils of health; perils in travel; perils of war in the country and turmoil in the city. Like Paul, they held tightly to God's promise to be with them always and willingly subjected themselves to these risks because of the urgency of presenting the Gospel to those living in darkness.

The stories of God's protection in the midst of all these perils abound, but they are probably exceeded by the many strategic interventions that God made without the missionaries even knowing they were in danger. Those who ministered year after year without suffering any significant trauma in their lives bear just as great a witness to God's gracious and faithful protection as those who saw it occur in more overtly dramatic ways.

# Perils of Wild Animals

One can hardly think of Africa without envisioning the exotic, wild animals that typically inhabit this continent. While they no longer roam as freely as in bygone days, the Zambezi Valley was indeed home to many of these when the early missionaries came to bring the Gospel to this region.

## Naïve Experiences

Because ministering to the spiritual needs of the people was paramount in their minds, these early pioneers were often naïve about the dangers these beasts presented and how to protect themselves from them. Helen Dunkeld told of an experience she and Orv had on one of their exploratory camping trips out from Msengedzi, trying to make contact with the people in the surrounding areas:

> *We set up our camp and got bundles of long grass, which we laid out on the floor of the tent. Then we put the sleeping bags that I had made on top of the grass. We had one sleeping bag for us and another for the boys.*
>
> *In the middle of the night I heard a strange noise and woke up with a start. I was immediately aware of a rather large animal sniffing at our tent. I wondered if Orv was awake. Then I realized I could hear his heart beating, so I knew he was.*
>
> *"What is it?" I whispered.*
>
> *"It's a lion," he responded.*
>
> *"Where's the gun?"*
>
> *"Out under the tree."*
>
> *We always traveled with a gun, mostly to shoot meat for ourselves on the trip. With it sitting outside under the tree, all we could do was lie there and pray. We did reach under the kids' bed and pull out a bunch of grass, which we stuck outside the tent and lit, as wild animals don't like fire.*
>
> *Shortly after that we heard the lion roaring as it slowly retreated down the path away from our tent. We were so relieved to hear it go.*

> *The next morning we told the local people that a lion had been outside of our tent during the night and asked them, "It wouldn't come inside the tent, would it?"*
>
> *They looked at the tent and said, "That tent is like paper to a lion. It comes by here every night looking for chickens or anything it can find."*
>
> *The next night we prepared ourselves for its return. We had a fire burning outside the tent with a heap of firewood piled beside it. We also had our gun in the tent with us. That night we never heard the lion come, however, and slept straight through the night.*
>
> *After that incident 1 Peter 5:8, which speaks of Satan walking about like a roaring lion "seeking whom he may devour" became very real to us. We realized that when we are strong in the Lord and prepared for Satan, he doesn't come, but when we are not expecting him or looking for him, that is when he comes. We thanked God not only for protecting us from the lion that night but also for using that frightening experience to give us a good illustration, which we were able to use many times after that.*

Gradually the missionaries learned about the behavioral traits of the various wild animals living around them and how to respect them. When they gathered at Hunyani in December 1951 for the field's second annual conference, they still had had little experience with buffalo, however.

Soon after arriving for this highly anticipated event, the ladies informed the men that they did not have enough fresh meat to feed the group. Russ Jackson, Martin Uppendahl, and Les Austin volunteered to take care of that problem.

The next morning at daybreak they headed out into Mozambique where they knew they would find plenty of game. Soon they were on the trail of a large herd of buffalo. After an hour or so of tracking these animals, they finally came to a small clearing where they were able to make visual contact with two large buffalo.

Both Russ and Les took aim and shot at them, but none of the men were prepared for what happened next. Russ wrote:

*We were soon to find out that the African buffalo can be a very dangerous animal to hunt. As Les and I shot, both bulls vanished into the bush. In our inexperienced foolishness we dashed after them, hoping to get another shot.*

*We had only gone a short distance when I caught a glimpse of the wounded buffalo. I immediately shot several more shots at him in quick succession. Instead of taking him down, however, my shots only incited him. From a very close range he turned and charged, bellowing angrily and holding his head and immense horns high.*

*At that very moment, to my utter horror, I found my gun was empty! I immediately shouted, "Every man for himself!" dropped my rifle, and dashed for a tree.*

Les reported:

*Russ and I got to this small tree, and he went up first. I was helping push him up, as this "mack truck" was coming right at us. We got up in the tree, and then it changed course from us to where Martin had disappeared. Soon we heard this awful noise, and I thought for sure that it had gotten Martin.*

Martin was not the source of the anguished outcry, however. He had not even seen what had transpired. He had only heard the shots and Russell's yell. At that point, however, he quickly loaded his gun with some special, "armor-piercing" ammunition, which a hunting buddy had given him before he left home. While it was illegal in the States, his friend thought Martin might find it useful for hunting big game in Africa.

Martin described what he did next:

*I bravely stepped out from the brush to see what was happening. There about 40-50 yards away was a charging bull with its head held high. I took one quick shot at it and then headed for the only tree I could see. I quickly climbed up in it, followed by one of the Shona trackers, who climbed right past me in his zeal to get to an even higher position.*

*In reality, neither of us would have survived had the*

*buffalo truly taken after us. We wouldn't have made it to the tree in time, nor would the six-or-seven-inch thick tree we climbed have withstood the fury of an angry, 2000+ pound buffalo bull. Thankfully, as we waited in the tree, the buffalo never arrived.*

*After about five minutes of silence my Shona companion slowly slipped down from the tree to check things out. Just a few yards away he found the buffalo dead.*

The men were certainly delighted with their success but also recognized the very close brush with death they had had. Russ wrote:

*Our first reaction, after the intense excitement had settled somewhat, was to sit down together on the huge carcass and have a very emotional time of prayer and praise to God for His very obvious protection of three inexperienced buffalo hunters.*

Martin continued the story:

*We sent for the mission truck and hauled the carcass back to Hunyani, but we were greatly perplexed by the fact that we could see no sign of a fatal bullet wound on the buffalo. As the Shona workers skinned and butchered it, we told them to look carefully for the fatal bullet wound. They, too, could find none—until late at night when they retrieved a bullet and brought it to us. It was an armor-piercing slug that had entered the buffalo's eye and lodged in its brain. I truly believe an angel of God was sent to direct that bullet to a vital place so that we three men could continue to praise and serve Him in Zimbabwe (Psalm 34:7; Hebrews 1:14).*

## Hunting for Meat

Hunting for meat was a necessity for the early missionaries, but one that was never devoid of potential danger. Many times God's hand of protection was evident on these excursions. Russ Jackson told of one of his experiences:

*This time Margaret decided she would come along and help me shoot some fresh meat. We also took Lynnette and Buddy, much to their delight. Lynnette rode with Margaret in the cab of the truck, but Buddy stayed with me in the back, helping me look for eyes in the gleam of my head lamp.*

*Margaret was following a faint trail off into the bush when Buddy and I spotted the unmistakable gleam of the eyes of an animal. I immediately tapped gently on the roof of the truck cab, which was the signal for Marg to stop.*

*I was sure the animal was a bush buck and took a shot at it. We then heard the thrashing sounds of a wounded animal only a few yards off to the side of the truck. I quickly jumped down and started to rush towards it before it could get away. I had taken only a few hurried steps, however, when Marg called out "Russ, stop! I heard a leopard grunting."*

*I knew that to follow up on a wounded leopard in the tall African grass would be fatal. I came back and climbed onto the truck, instructing Marg to back the truck slowly to where we had last heard the sound.*

*When we reached the place where the animal had fallen, . . . we were shocked to find the beautiful body of a huge male leopard. After loading the leopard into the truck, we all gathered around for a time of praise and thanksgiving to God, who had so graciously and unmistakenly saved us from what could have been a very serious tragedy.*

Wilf Strom told of the time when he, Russ Jackson, and Merle Bloom joined George Dee at the Hunyani station to hunt for meat for the Bible school. When they arrived, George had his truck packed with the essentials they needed and had also arranged for some proven Shona guides to accompany them.

Once again the party headed into Mozambique. After driving for a few hours, they set out on foot. Only on the second day of walking, after spending the night sleeping in the bush, did they finally come upon a herd of buffalo.

When they shot into the herd, the buffalo took off at great speed in different directions. The men noticed that the leaves and grass in one direction had smears of blood on them, however, indicating that at least one of the buffalo had been injured. They took off running in this direction with Wilf out in front.

Then all of a sudden the wounded buffalo emerged from the tall grass and charged. While the others ran in retreat, Wilf quickly realized that his legs were too exhausted to run, and the best option for him was to stand and shoot as the buffalo came for him. If it didn't fall, then he would have to devise another plan to protect himself.

He made his first shot, and the buffalo stumbled but kept charging. Then he shot again, and the buffalo fell to the ground about 20 feet in front of him. God protected his life and the men finally had their meat!

## Killing for Protection

Sometimes missionaries had to hunt down wild animals that were jeopardizing their safety, their pets, or their food supply. They would also help the local Shona people when they were being bothered by these problems in their villages.

Russ Jackson told of a time when he was summoned to help a village man who reported that lions had attacked his cattle the night before and killed one of his cows:

> *Since I had learned that lions almost always come back to their kill, I told the man to go back to his village and tie the carcass of the cow securely to a tree. Then just before dark I would come and wait for the lion's return.*
>
> *When I arrived, I found that the village men had built a small platform in a large tree a few yards from where they had tied the carcass of the cow. As the sun was beginning to set, one of them joined me in climbing up to the platform to wait for the lion. . . .*
>
> *Before long we saw two lions, a huge male and his mate, coming towards us. I wanted to shoot the male lion, but just a few yards from the tree in which we were sitting, he stopped in a clump of bush. He had seemingly become suspicious of danger and was not coming any further. The female, however, continued walking confidently right up to the carcass. She looked so dignified and beautiful as she stood just a few yards from me.*

*I shot the female lion, but because darkness was falling, I left the body in the village and walked about two miles to where I had left the truck. The next morning, when I returned to pick up the lioness, I saw the tracks of the male lion following my trail all the way back to the truck. Once again I was aware of God's protection.*

Another time a leopard that had mauled the Jackson's dog and plundered many villages in the Rusambo area had to be killed. Russ described the situation and how he addressed it:

*Early one morning while we were living at Rusambo, our Alsatian dog, Pal, came to the house with horrible wounds. He had obviously been mauled by a leopard and yet had miraculously managed to survive.*

*In the days that followed, we could often hear a leopard coughing around our yard, even in the daytime, which was very unusual. I was quite sure it was after Pal.*

*Hunting the leopard at that time of year with the grass tall and thick was impossible. Therefore, I decided to try building a trap for it. I enlisted the help of several local men, who were only too pleased to assist because the leopard was molesting their villages as well.*

*Together we built a small, round, pole pen to enclose a goat for bait. Then we built a narrow, log passageway leading up to the pen. The trap was so constructed that the leopard could not reach the bait but would squeeze into the narrow passageway trying.*

*Much to the delight of the villagers and ourselves, the trap worked perfectly. Early the next morning the men came excitedly to our house to announce that the leopard, a huge male, was in the trap.*

*I quickly took my rifle and rushed down to the river where we had made the trap. The leopard was indeed captured. I remember how impacted I was by the fierce, angry sounds it was making and the way its eyes looked like balls of fire. To think that for several weeks the children had been playing in the yard with this fierce animal stalking around was very frightening. Once again Margaret and I were so thankful for the guardian angels that had obviously watched over them.*

## Close Encounters in Daily Life

While hunting for wild animals always involved a known risk, many close encounters occurred even in the everyday lives of the early missionaries. Each time they were grateful for the Lord's faithful hand of protection.

Les and Lillian Austin had such an encounter on their wedding night. They had had a wonderful ceremony at the end of the annual field conference held at Hunyani in 1951 and had made a happy get-away for their honeymoon in the mission truck. Halfway up the escarpment, however, they severely damaged one of their tires. Unfortunately, the spare was chained up, and they had not been given the key to unlock the chain. Consequently, they had to spend their first night of marriage in the truck, stranded in the bush.

When morning came and others began leaving the conference, they discovered the newlyweds on the road. The needed key was obtained and the tire changed, but in the process someone noted fresh lion tracks around the vehicle. Considering that no modern restrooms were available, the Austins thanked the Lord for His protection.

Russ Jackson also had a close encounter one day as he was walking back to his house after working in the garden at Msengedzi. He was quite startled when a huge leopard leapt from a limb of a wild fig tree overhanging the path. Fortunately, it just took a good look at him and then walked indifferently off into the tall grass.

Russ and Marg were appalled, however, to think that their young children had run up and down that path several times that day. Again, they were mindful of the guardian angels looking after them, not only that day but every day!

Martin Uppendahl once walked within five feet of a crouching leopard when he was out surveying the Zambezi Valley for future ministry sites. On another occasion he ran head on into a herd of elephant as he was returning to the station in his pick-up truck just after dark. A large male rolled up his trunk, let out a very loud trumpet, and charged. Martin wrote:

*At the last moment he must have seen an angel or something because he suddenly veered aside, breaking off a six-or-seven-inch mupani tree that was only two feet from the truck's front, passenger-side fender as he passed.*

Martin and his wife, Wyn, were aware of God's protection on many other occasions as well. They testified:

*The Lord truly takes care of His own. Time and time again we have seen Him protect us from disease; accident; discouragement; and harm from lions, rhinos, hippos, and snakes.*

June Munger told about a time during language study at Msengedzi when she and Jean Schmidt went out to visit in a village:

*We were on bicycle, and as the sun was soon to set, we decided to start home. The grass was very tall along the road, and when we came to a place where the road split, I couldn't see which way Jean had gone. I called out for her but heard no answer.*

*Left on my own, I checked the sandy path and chose to go in the direction that I thought had the freshest tire marks. As I rode and rode, darkness fell, and I could just see the white sand on the path. Then I heard drums beating and knew I was nearing a local beer drink. I was so afraid of meeting a drunk person on the road in the dark.*

*Finally, I took courage and asked a man, "Missioni kupiko?" ["Where is the mission?"] He pointed in the opposite direction that I was going. As I headed back, I was so relieved to see two headlights of a car, which turned out to be my co-workers coming to look for me.*

*The next morning we were told that elephants had gone on a rampage through the same area that night, uprooting trees and destroying fields. I definitely thanked the Lord for protecting me from being in harm's way that night.*

Joy Finsaas told how the fear she felt one night as an MK when her family's car broke down on a pitch dark, moonless night in elephant territory led to her salvation. The car's radiator had over-heated, and her father, Ray, had set off on foot in search of water. He ended up walking 11 miles, staying on the road only by the feel of the grass on either side and trusting God for his safety.

As Joy sat in the car that night waiting for his return, she expressed her fears to her mother. Myrtle talked to her about trusting Jesus to protect them and led her to accept Jesus as her Savior. God not only watched over them that night, but He also brought a precious child into His family.

## Perils of Snakes

Perhaps more perilous for the missionaries was the large variety of poisonous snakes in the country. Their smaller size enabled them to move about less conspicuously, even through relatively short grass. They could also hide in much smaller places, which meant an unsuspecting person could encounter them almost anywhere, outdoors or in.

Mary Danielson described a time in 1970 when snakes were particularly prevalent at Rusambo:

*We thank the Lord for protection from snakes in the past month. Just in our immediate area we have seen seven quite large ones and all in the dangerous group. The other day a huge one slithered up the big tree just beside the house. . . . Another was killed on the bougainvillea by the side of the house and another behind the water tank. It may be because of the drought that we have had in the past two months that they [have come] looking for water. The greenness around the houses probably attracts them. One does walk with care, especially at night. We keep all the grass cut short.*

When Dr. T.J. Bach, TEAM's General Director, came out for the first field conference in 1947, he did what Founder Fredrick Franson had done earlier in India. He prayed that no missionary would ever be bitten by a poisonous snake in Zimbabwe—and no one was. This is not to say there were no close encounters. These abounded, making God's supernatural protection all the more real.

Lynne Hawkins probably had the most intimate, physical contact with one of these potentially deadly creatures when she inadvertently stepped on one barefooted behind her house. The unidentified green snake coiled itself around her leg but miraculously did not bite her.

Several others were spat at by spitting cobras but suffered no lasting injury. Shirley Bradford Bennett described her experience, which occurred while she was serving at Karanda for two years:

*Someone broke into my duplex while I was attending our Sunday evening church service at another missionary's home. The intruder gained access through a window and left my window screens open when he departed.*

*After the service I returned to my house, entering my back door with only the light of my flashlight. In its faint gleam I caught sight of a snake slithering across my kitchen floor. At first I was frozen in place, but then I gathered my wits about me enough to close the kitchen door and stuff a rug under it.*

*I then called several men to come and kill the snake. They came but could not find it anywhere. Needless to say, I wasn't about to sleep at home that night, so Bob and Fran Medaris kindly let me stay with them.*

*Rick Froese was sure the snake had made its home under my kitchen cupboards, so he put some strong* muti *[medicine] under them to kill it. Several times a day he would come and check my house, but he never located any sign of the snake, dead or alive. By Thursday he was pretty certain it had to be dead, so I moved back home.*

*Just before crawling into bed that night, I went to put some papers in my bottom dresser drawer. As I bent over and opened the drawer, there was the snake!! It immediately reared its hooded head and started spitting at me. By God's grace I had not yet taken off my glasses, so the venom covered the left lens of my glasses rather than my eye!!*

*Once again, when I recovered sufficiently, I called Rick*

*on the phone to inform him of my surprise encounter. He incredulously retorted, "You're kidding!" When I convinced him that I was indeed serious, he rode down on his motorbike to address the situation.*

*He began by dragging the dresser drawer out of my bedroom and onto my back porch using broom handles. The snake then crawled out and hid behind my petrol drum. In his haste to come to my rescue, however, Rick had forgotten to bring his gun. Therefore, I was commissioned to "watch" the snake while he went to get it. When he returned and killed the snake, we measured it to be about 5 ½ feet long.*

*For several nights after that episode, all I could see when I went to bed and closed my eyes was that snake rearing its ugly head at me!! How grateful I was that the Lord had protected me from harm from this most unwelcome house guest!*

Five-year-old Lorne Strom unexpectedly encountered a spitting cobra at Kapfundi when he bent down to pick up his bicycle that was lying beside a bush near his home. In this instance the cobra succeeded in spitting its venom right into Lorne's eye. Crying out in pain, he quickly found his parents, who took him to Dottie Larsen, the station nurse. She washed it out with milk, which greatly relieved the severe stinging pain in his eye. While it was bloodshot for a day or two, he suffered no lasting effects from the incident.

Puff adders were another species of poisonous snakes frequently encountered by the missionaries. Orv Dunkeld was folding up his tent after an exploratory trek out from Msengedzi in the early days and was quite startled to discover a large puff adder had crept under the floor of the tent and curled up in a depression beneath where his feet had been all night. He said:

*I'm amazed I didn't step on him at night. I'm sure he couldn't have bitten me through the canvas floor, but . . . . I don't know whether I would have slept so comfortably night if I had known he was under there.*

Betty Wolfe discovered a puff adder asleep between the back benches of the Hunyani church just after a women's class was dismissed. Bob Endicott encountered one in the high grass along-side the path between two houses at Chironga. Had he not been alerted by a group of birds circling over it, he would have walked dangerously close to it.

Dorothy Strom once found the path of a large python leading into the window of her outside kitchen and then out the doorway. She wrote: "I really kept my eyes open in there after that. It was such a dark, little room."

Encounters with snakes were particularly alarming when they were found *inside* the missionaries' homes. Phyllis Rilling discovered one on top of a corn flakes box in her pantry. Chris Goppert found a six-foot, banded cobra curled up on the kerosene tank of his deepfreeze when he went to adjust the flame. He wrote:

> *I had obviously disturbed it, and it wriggled just past where I was kneeling. When I saw it, I froze in position, knowing that if I moved, it might have struck me—but the Lord protected me.*

Betty Wolfe told about a time she encountered a cobra in her house at Hunyani:

> *John was away, and I had put the children to bed. I was pregnant with Margaret at the time and was really feeling the heat that night. We had a rollaway bed in the little passage between the living room and the bedroom section of the house, so I decided to lie down there for a little while before going to bed. It was getting dark, but I hadn't lit the lamps.*
>
> *After a little awhile I heard something plop on the floor by the screen door and thought that the cat was probably chasing insects. Eventually I decided I should go to bed, so I picked up the flashlight I had on the floor and turned it on. There, not more than four feet away, was a large cobra staring me in the face. It had fallen down between the sheets of asbestos on the roof. Thankfully, it moved faster than I did and hid under a chair in the living room.*
>
> *I immediately checked that all the nets around the children were securely tucked in and stuffed towels under their*

*door. Then I lit a lamp and pulled everything away from that chair. I got out the shotgun and loaded it, then called for Zhuwaki, who was assigned to sleep in one of the outbuildings while John was away. He came to the door, and I sent him for Lameki, who was a hunter and knew how to handle guns.*

*Lameki came and I told him where the snake was. Neither of these men seemed quite sure whether to believe me or not. Nevertheless, since Lameki didn't want to shoot in the house, they dragged the chair over to the door and up over a step that had been built to keep snakes out. After they had it several feet away from the house, they tipped it onto its back. They were on the wrong side to see the snake, so I told Lameki to come over to where I was standing. When he did, he immediately saw it, and putting one hand around the wrist of his other arm, he gasped, "It's this big!" The Shona people never talked about the length of a snake, but how big around it was.*

*Zhuwaki had a spear in his hand with a spike on the end of it. Lameki instructed him to pin the snake to the strut of the chair with his spear. As he did, the snake shot its head out, and I shouted, "Shoot, shoot!" Lameki waited, however, until the snake put its head out for the third time and kept it there. Then he shot and killed it.*

Several missionaries described a form of supernatural communication from God to warn them when poisonous snakes were in their homes. Chuck Pruitt woke up one night with a strong feeling that he needed to check on his son, Charles. Just as he walked barefooted out into the hall, a snake slithered by him. He immediately went for his hatchet and was able to kill it, a deadly boomslang, while it was coiled under the kitchen door.

He went back to bed but awoke again several hours later with the same uncomfortable feeling. He got up and found another snake in the house and killed it too. The family was very grateful that God had awakened Chuck at just the right time to confront these dangerous intruders.

God warned Lorraine Waite at a critical moment of danger in an even stronger manner one night at Karanda. She described what happened after she returned to her house from assisting in an emergency C-section at the hospital:

*Like the five foolish virgins, I had let my lamp burn out of kerosene. The batteries in my flashlight were also dead. I managed to feel my way around my house in the darkness and get into bed. I then heard a strange noise, however, that I thought sounded somewhat like an animal drinking water.*

*Hyenas had been killing some of the cows of the local people, so George Dee put strychnine in the carcass of one of the heifers they had killed. The hyenas would then come and feed on that meat, but the strychnine would make them real thirsty, so they would then go down to the Ruia River and drink lots of water. As they did, crocodiles pulled some of them into the water and made a meal out of them.*

*Being the rainy season, I had a galvanized tub set outside under the eaves of my house to catch rainwater from my roof, so I thought that the noise I heard was most likely hyenas drinking from the tub. Wanting to put my mind at ease, I got up, thinking the light of the moon might be sufficient to enable me to verify this.*

*As I got over to the window to look out, something rubbed against my foot. My neighbors, the Ratzlaffs, had a little puppy, so I thought it might be that puppy—or possibly a snake.*

*I had a chair right by the window, so I climbed up on it. Then I heard an audible voice say to me, "Whatever you do, don't step down on the floor again." Well, it was midnight, and I didn't particularly want to be standing on the chair all night with some unknown, live creature on the floor, so I pushed the screen up and climbed out the window.*

*I then went next door and knocked on the Ratzlaff's bedroom window. They were like the five wise virgins and had kerosene in their lamps, so they came over to check things out with me. Cliff went in the back door, and Jeannette and I went in the front door. As we did, we saw a cobra just under the sofa. It then went into the kitchen.*

*We all crept cautiously into the kitchen but couldn't find the snake anywhere. Finally, we saw it curled up behind a little portable oven I had. We took a piece of tin and dropped it on the snake. Then, as it came out hissing, we killed it with some flat brooms. It was over four feet long.*

Any close encounter with a poisonous snake was frightening. Those involving children, however, were particularly heart-stopping. While parents did their best to protect their children with mosquito nets or screened-in beds while they slept, during the day they generally had full run of the various mission stations, often under the care of a Shona nanny during their younger years. With no way to assure their protection around the clock, the parents' only option was to trust God and His guardian angels to look after their children.

Both outdoors and indoors, snakes did come precariously close to many children. Mary and Ruth Wolfe both remember having a snake run between the wheels of their tricycles as they were riding them on the station.

Myrtle Finsaas and her six-year old daughter, Nadynne, had an extremely frightening experience as they rode their bicycles home from the dispensary one evening at Hunyani during the rainy season. They had to ride across the airstrip, which was surrounded by grass six to eight feet high, and Nadynne's bicycle had no brakes. Myrtle wrote:

*Out from the tall grass onto the airstrip right in front of us came a large mamba snake, traveling as fast as a galloping horse. It was black, and its head was raised up about three feet high as it moved along. It is a very dangerous snake and will strike at anything that moves into its path. Striking at the jugular vein in the neck area, it injects its venom into the blood stream. Unless antivenin is given quickly, the victim will die in 5 to 20 minutes.*

*The snake came into our path so quickly that we were totally helpless to do anything to avoid it, especially with Nadynne's bike having no brakes. God sent a guardian angel, we are sure, as Nadynne turned quickly off to the side, just missing this huge snake.*

*We quickly rode to the house, hollering "Snake, snake!"*
*Ray came with a gun, but the snake was traveling so fast*
*that only a few workmen saw it go by the church. They said*
*it was the biggest snake they had ever seen.*

*God protected Nadynne and me from terrible tragedy*
*that day. I believe He lets these things happen to make us*
*realize He is watching over us, and our lives are in His*
*hands. We marveled at God's protection over our six-year-*
*old daughter Nadynne, who so happily played and rode her*
*bike all over Hunyani station, along with her [Shona]*
*nanny. . . .*

*This experience also made us aware that people in the*
*homeland had been praying for us, and God had protected*
*us just as He promised in His Great Commission: "Go ye*
*into all the world and preach the Gospel...and lo, I am with*
*you always, even to the end of the world" (Mark 16:15;*
*Mathew 28:30 ).*

Sometimes God used cats to draw attention to threatening
snakes. Phil and Barb Christiansen had a part-Siamese cat, Puss-in-
Boots, that was a constant companion to their son Ron whenever he
was outside.

One Saturday afternoon when Ron was just a toddler, Phil
"happened" to notice that the cat, with Ron right beside him, was
acting strangely at the base of the one of the hibiscus bushes in their
back yard. When he checked on what was going on, he saw a puff
adder partially hidden by the bush and was able to remove little Ron
quickly from the dangerous situation.

John and Betty Wolfe also had a cat that would point out snakes
by staring at them until someone came and dealt with them. Betty
told of a time that this occurred while John was away and one-year-
old Mary was napping in her crib on the verandah:

*This day I saw the cat staring at a tub of ironing sitting*
*on the step of the verandah. When I looked, I saw a big*
*cobra coiled under the tub.*

*We had Mary's crib out on the verandah where it was*
*cooler, and she was having her mid-day nap. "Rescuing"*

*her would mean going past the snake both to and from her crib. Since her crib was screened in on all sides with a loose net over the top, she seemed quite safe to me.*

*John had gone to repair the crossing at the Sapa River, so I sent for Orv Dunkeld to come and shoot the snake for me. He didn't want to use a shotgun, as it would ruin the tub, so he shot it with a .22 rifle. He injured the snake but did not kill it.*

*Instead of escaping out into the garden, the cobra made a beeline for the corner of the verandah where Mary's crib was. It then started climbing the wall until its head was even with the top of Mary's crib. Orv could not possibly shoot it in this position, so all we could do was to stand and watch.*

*Finally, it fell beneath the crib, and Orv shot it again, as the mattress would protect Mary. By that time Orv was quite white, and so was I. Later, John found a whole nest of cobras in a French drain about 10 feet from the house. He was able to kill them all.*

In spite of the missionaries' best efforts to protect their homes from opportunities for snakes to enter, they occasionally found their way in. Martin and Wyn Uppendahl told of the time a six-foot cobra slid through a hole that had somehow been punched in the screen door to their enclosed verandah. All three of their children were playing on the verandah at the time. Timmy, their youngest, was only 18-20 months old. As the snake hissed at them, they ran into the house calling for Martin to come and kill it. He quickly did that and they all thanked the Lord for His protection.

Emil and Phyllis Rilling recounted a time when a snake came into their kitchen through a hole that their cat had made in the screen door. Phyllis "happened" to enter the room as the snake headed straight for 18-month-old Arthur. She was able to grab him very quickly and call for Emil to come and shoot it.

Snakes are also attracted to water and were sometimes encountered in bathrooms. Phyllis Rilling told of another time at Rukomechi when she had just bathed the boys and taken them out of the bathtub:

*Emil heard a noise in the bath water, which had not yet been let out of our cement bathtub. He went in to see what it was, and a spitting cobra came up out of the bathtub and hooded at Emil, who quickly went for his gun and shot it. It must have been in the room as I bathed the boys—but God protected us!*

Donna Hendrickson Robinson told about a time when her children encountered a snake in their bathroom at Mavuradonha:

*The bathroom consisted of an oblong, red brick bathtub plastered with cement on the inside. We didn't have running water, but holes were made in the wall above the front of the tub with the hopes that one day pipes would bring water flowing through them into the tub.*

*We would put a wash bowl with water, soap, and a towel at the end of the tub for the children to clean up before meals. One day when they went in to wash up, they yelled, "Nyoka!" ["Snake"]. We dashed into the room and saw that a cobra had found its way through one of the holes and was sitting on the edge of the tub with its head up and fangs extended.*

*We told the children to back slowly out of the bathroom, and Carl and Ninepence took care of the cobra. How often we have felt God's protection over the children from snakes and other pests! God is so GOOD!*

Snakes often came precariously close to where children slept. Emil Rilling once shot a snake that was weaving in and out of the gables of the house, and the snake dropped right on top of William's bed while he was in it. Thankfully, the screen lid of the bed, which Emil had specially constructed to protect the children, was closed.

Dorothy Strom told of a time when a snake plopped down in the exact place where two-year-old Gloria had just been taking her afternoon nap:

*A few weeks after arriving in the Zambezi Valley, I got our daughter, Gloria, up from an afternoon nap and then went back into the room to find a snake coiled up in the indented place where she had just been sleeping. With a shovel and broom that were just outside the door, we brought it to a messy death.*

# Perils of Health

While the missionaries were not immune to illness and injury on the field, God's protecting hand was often recognized in sparing them from diseases common to the area. When sickness and accidents did occur, numerous ones testified of how God intervened to spare lives that could otherwise have been lost or seriously debilitated.

## Parasites

Living in areas where malaria, bilharzia (schistosomiaisis), sleeping sickness, and other parasitic diseases were rampant, the incidence of these among the missionaries was amazingly low. Many believed they were divinely protected.

Martin Uppendahl wrote:

*We were very aware that to go into the tsetse fly area was to take a known risk. The Lord was good and faithful to protect His own, however, not only from sleeping sickness but also from a dozen or more other serious diseases and parasites in the Zambezi Valley.*

*At one point, while we were in the process of moving from Rukomechi to Urungwe, friends we had made at the newly developing Chirundu Sugar Estates were sent over to check what health precautions we were taking, as some of their staff were coming down with various health problems, including sleeping sickness, malaria etc. In our discussion with them we discovered that they were doing just about the same things that we were. The only difference had to be that our good Lord was taking care of us!!!*

Mildred Rogers Carnall told of how she would regularly wade through the Msengedzi and Hunyani Rivers in her early years on the field, carrying her Bible and flannelgraph materials in order to teach the Gospel in villages on the other side. She knew the danger of getting bilharzia but did not let that stop her. She reported:

*I chose places where the water was running, not standing, and I prayed that the Lord would protect me from the parasites—and He did. I never got bilharzia. Praise Him!*

## Serious Illnesses

God's protective hand was seen in regard to other serious illnesses as well. Dr. Dan Stephens credits God for the fact that no staff member at Karanda Hospital has contracted AIDS. With over 60% of the patients having HIV/AIDS and the hospital's lack of adequate means to protect its staff from the deadly virus, they have to rely on God as their Protector.

Others saw God protect their health, and sometimes their very lives, by specific, timely interventions which He orchestrated. Lynn and Judy Everswick gave a poignant example of this:

*Zimbabwe's independence had been declared in April 1980. Our five-year term was up, and we were due to go home in June. We really wanted to stay in the country for a sixth year, however, so we could be "bridge-builders" during this important time of transition in the country's history. Being deeply involved in ministry in both the Shona and European farming communities, we felt it was not a good time for us to leave and asked for permission to stay longer.*

*Dick Winchell, TEAM's general director at that time, insightfully responded by asking us to consult with our daughter Kim's school concerning the effect that delaying our furlough would have on her education, as she was due to enter high school. When we did, the headmaster told us that going home on schedule would be better for her in order not to affect her O level preparation.*

*We complied, and upon arrival in the States went for our regular medical check-ups. After his routine exam of Lynn, the doctor pronounced him to be in great health but asked if he had any questions or concerns he wanted addressed. Lynn only pointed out a black mole on his neck that Dr.*

*David Drake had suggested be checked.*

*The doctor decided to remove the mole. When the pathology report came back, we learned that it was indeed cancerous—a stage 2 melanoma. Because of its location on the crease of his neck in close proximity to the lymph nodes, the doctor said that Lynn had only a 25% chance to survive. This was obviously very shocking and grim news to us, and we immediately garnered as much prayer support as we could.*

*The doctor then did further surgery and unexpectedly announced that he had been able to excise the entire cancerous growth and it had NOT spread to the lymph glands. We couldn't have been more pleased and thanked God for His wonderful protection of Lynn's life. With five kids, and the twins being only 18 months, we weren't quite ready for him to go to be with Jesus.*

*When I asked the doctor how much longer it would have taken until it had gotten into the lymph nodes, he said he couldn't say for sure but waiting another six months would have been too late. We thought that the timing of our furlough was to benefit our daughter when God knew we needed to come home then to save Lynn's life. What a loving Father He is!*

Chris Goppert also told of a time when God orchestrated a timely medical intervention for his wife Joyce:

*In 1983, while on home assignment [furlough], Joyce fell on a flight of stairs, landing on her coccyx [tail bone], but she exhibited no immediate signs of injury. Three years later, however, during the Christmas holidays in Harare, she happened to sneeze and immediately felt sharp pain in her lower back, resulting in significant immobility.*

*At this time the Lord had so ordered our steps that I was under the care of Professor Levy, an outstanding, local neurosurgeon, for my own back problems. On the night of Joyce's sudden onset of severe lower back pain, the Lord impressed upon my heart the need to ring Prof. Levy to ask for advice, as Joyce was now bed-ridden.*

*He offered to stop in and have a look at Joyce at his first possible free moment. As promised, he paid the house call on Boxing Day (Dec. 26) and ordered some tests. Within days of the scans and x-rays, Prof. Levy operated and removed five bone chips which were intertwined with nerves. Immediately after surgery Prof. Levy met with me and informed me that had he not operated, Joyce would have been an invalid for the rest of her life.*

*God certainly provided the right doctor for that occasion. To top it off, Prof. Levy did not charge us a cent. We were so moved by his generosity that to show our gratitude, Joyce baked him a beautiful fruit cake, and I made a special clock face for him.*

Bud and Mandy Jackson believe that God intervened in a special way to spare the life of their 15-month-old daughter, Erin, when she was seriously ill too. Bud wrote:

*Erin developed a high fever the day we traveled to Wheaton headquarters just before our departure for Zimbabwe as TEAM missionaries in 1981. After taking her to a clinic, we struggled all day to keep her temperature from escalating too high. Ice baths, wet towels, and a fan all seemed to have little effect.*

*As Erin's condition declined, her symptoms began to make us suspicious of meningitis. We took her to the emergency room, and she was admitted to Dupage County Hospital where she came under the care of Dr. Ruth Feldmann, a wonderful lady doctor who had ministered a few years with TEAM in Pakistan. We believe she was a special gift from God in saving our precious daughter's life.*

*She was well-acquainted with the early symptoms of meningitis and knew how aggressive the disease could be unless combated in an equally aggressive manner. Therefore, she didn't wait for the results of a spinal tap culture to determine whether the infection was bacterial or viral before putting Erin on three different antibiotics.*

*As we waited and prayed for our dear little girl, Dr.*

*Dick Winchell, TEAM's General Director, ministered to us in a special way as we sat by Erin's bed. He shared many hugs with us, offered a few special verses of Scripture from his ever-present pocket Testament, and prayed with us as only he could. Lois Dunkeld Bishop, my fellow MK who was now a nurse, was a constant presence by our side too. Her medical understanding of the situation and calm demeanor was also a great encouragement.*

*Erin went through a very difficult time, including seizures and a coma, before the antibiotics took effect and she began to recover. God spared Erin's life and taught us some very valuable lessons that have remained with us over the years. The experience has also allowed us to minister much more knowledgeably to others in similar situations.*

## Life-Threatening Accidents

Sometimes the tasks the missionaries had to do under less than ideal circumstances exposed them to significant danger. God's protection was seen over and over again as He preserved their safety or prevented accidents that did occur from being more severe than they were.

Les Austin told about the extremely risky way in which Orla Blair dug a well outside his house at Hunyani.

*He would dig down in the soil until he hit shale. He would then make three holes in the shale with a chisel and put sticks of dynamite in them. He would then light the fuses and climb quickly out of the well on his homemade bamboo ladder.*

God marvelously protected him in this extremely risky procedure and also granted him success in digging his well.

Les Austin had a very close call himself when lightning struck the trowel he was holding as he was up on scaffolding building the hostel. Fortunately, the trowel had a wooden handle, which protected him. Russ Jackson saw it happen and thought Les had certainly been hit, but he was totally unaffected by it.

Emil Rilling had a more serious encounter with electrical power when he was trying to fix a lighting problem that occurred the night of the Homecraft School dedication. He received a powerful jolt of electricity and fell over backwards. He would have hit his head on the cement, but Norman Everswick was right there and able to break his fall. Though severely shocked, he bore no serious repercussions from it.

Lorraine Waite also felt the Lord spared her life when she was seriously injured in an accident on her new motor scooter. Her protective parents had never allowed her to have a bicycle or anything with wheels on it as a child. Nevertheless, while she was at Msengedzi during her first term, she decided to take a brave new step and get a Vespa motor scooter. Orv Dunkeld had picked it up for her and carefully went over all the instructions on how to use it. She tried it out by driving it up to the clinic, which went fine.

Then Dr. Sam and Emily Wall, who were there for language study, invited her to supper that night, so she decided to ride the motor scooter up to their house. This time things did not go so well. She reported:

> *Their house was on top of the hill, and the road had a bend in it with a lot of sharp rocks sticking up on one side. Suddenly when I got to this point, I couldn't remember which way to rotate the handle in order to slow down. I must have turned it the wrong way. I'm told that I landed on my head on those rocks with the motor scooter upside down and still running. The local villagers who saw it happen quickly ran and told the Dunkelds that I was dead.*
>
> *They came and discovered that I was alive but unconscious. They carried me up to the Walls' house on a camp cot. I regained consciousness a couple of hours later with Dr. Wall peering into my eyes. I apparently had suffered quite a concussion as well as a cracked temple bone. I realized that I would be laid up for awhile.*
>
> *After about a week we decided I could be moved and should see a neurologist in Harare. Bud Fritz drove me into town, and I stayed with Shirley Bradford.*
>
> *I didn't do too badly until I went to see Prof. Levy. He took x-rays and did a spinal tap. When I was finished, I*

*called Orla and Marguerite Blair to tell them I was ready to
come home. As I sat and waited for a long, long time, I got
dizzier and dizzier. After that experience I couldn't stand
any light. I had to have all the shades in my room pulled
down, and I could hardly stand to lift my head up for about
a week.*

*When I returned to the States for my first furlough, I
learned that one of the ladies from my home church had had
a real burden to pray for me in the middle of the night right
at about the same time as my accident. She had gotten up
and prayed fervently for me for several hours. It was a serious accident, but God enabled me to recover fully, and I
continued to ride my motor scooter.*

Lynn and Judy Everswick praised God for saving their daughter
from a life-threatening situation that occurred as they waited for a
rapidly flowing river to recede at a spruit. Judy wrote:

*We set up camp on the side of the road and made a little
fire so we could cook some lunch as we waited. In order to
pass the time, Lynn took a stick and started playing "fetch"
with our dog, Lance, throwing the stick into the water and
having him retrieve it. After awhile, when Lynn got tired of
playing, he came up for some tea.*

*Our daughter Kim was three or four years old at the
time, and when Lynn stopped playing with Lance, she
decided that she would throw the stick in the water for him
to chase. When Lance did not go after it, she reached out
from the edge of the river to retrieve it herself before it was
swept away. She reached too far, however, and her little
body tumbled into the raging water, which was doing a
dangerous swirl over the culverts before rushing over the
bridge and downriver.*

*Lynn saw her fall and was down to the river's edge in a
split second, but he could see no sign of her in the mud and
muck of the turbulent water. He knew that in just seconds
she would be swished around the circular flow of water and
be gone over the bridge.*

*His heart cried out to God for his little girl lost in that muddy water when all of a sudden he saw what looked like a small, light-colored mop floating under the water. It was Kim! He reached down and grabbed her by the hair just before she would have been swept away.*

*Never had a hug from a wet, little girl felt so good! Equally gratifying was the "Heavenly Hug" we felt from our Father, who is ever present to protect His little ones..*

Tom Jackson told about an equally harrowing experience when he accidentally ran over Tim, his seven-year-old son, in the hostel driveway:

*I was driving a pick-up truck, and I had "hung" the canopy in the garage so it would be easy to put it back on the truck when needed. This is what I was attempting to do on the day of this tragic accident. I was backing the truck from the front of the house, around the corner, and back into the garage. I rarely reversed into the garage like this, so that may have been one reason Tim did not cry out or yell for me to stop.*

*Anyway, unbeknown to me, Tim had come out the kitchen door at the back of the house looking for me. He had built a Lego object he wanted to show me. He reached the garage about the time I had started reversing. The Lego toy fell out of his hands, and he got down in the grass in front of the garage trying to pick up the pieces as the truck rounded the corner in reverse and headed his way. Again, I don't know why he didn't call out or get out of the way except that he was worried about his Lego pieces getting run over, and he must have thought I would stop before I reached the garage.*

*The first I knew he was there was when I heard a stran-gled cry like I had run over one of our pets. I slammed on the brakes, put the truck in first gear, and moved forward. I got out of the truck expecting to see one of our pets, and there was Tim lying all curled up. He couldn't breathe, and as I reached him, his eyes rolled up and he passed out.*

*I ran into the house and yelled to Lois, "I've run over*

*Tim. Call Emergency and tell them I am on my way."*

*I went out and found that Tim was breathing again. I gathered him up in my arms and laid him on the seat next to me and tore out of the driveway. He was trying to cry and breathe with difficulty, and I said, "Don't worry, Timmy, I will get you to the hospital as quickly as I can." Needless to say, we broke numerous speed limits.*

*The emergency staff was ready for us and immediately put Tim on a drip. I remember they didn't have a child-sized IV needle and had to use an adult one (one of the problems of health care in a third world country—supplies are often pretty limited). Anyway, the care they gave Tim was excellent. An x-ray showed some slightly cracked ribs and some small pockets of air that had been squeezed into his chest area from his lungs but nothing serious. He spent a night or two in hospital with me sleeping on the bench beside him. He had a wonderful time there receiving visits and presents and lots of TLC—and he had one very happy Dad!!*

*When I was driving to the hospital, I knew we might have lost Timmy, and so many things about him flashed through my mind. Looking back, I can't help but think that Tim's guardian angels were pushing on the vehicle, holding it back. If I had rolled right over Tim, he certainly could not have survived. The wheel must have just pressed up against him and squeezed him, coming to a stop before actually rolling onto him. The difference between Tim surviving and not must have been fractions of an inch.*

The Endicotts are grateful for God's protection of their daughter Linda when the family was visiting the Karanda station and Diane Powell and Anne Watson let her and her sister, Nancy, ride their horses. This went fine until Rick Froese's motorbike spooked the horse Linda was on. The horse took a sudden detour through a backyard with a metal clothesline. The horse fit under the clothesline fine, but Linda's face would have been seriously cut and scarred had she not had the presence of mind to put her hand in front of her face and duck as far as she could before falling off and landing on the ground in the only soft dirt amidst an area of rocks.

Her mother reported that every exposed area of her skin was embedded with dirt and cinders, and several of the nurses spent a long time cleaning her up and treating her bleeding hand. She still bears the scars on her hand, but the whole family praises the Lord that her hands bore the brunt of the clothesline and not her face or neck, which would have been much more serious.

Chris Goppert wrote about a time when he narrowly escaped serious injury or possible death:

*In 1973, I was involved in showing a film at Mavuradonha, which was also attended by some police who were in the area. As they climbed into their open-backed truck to return to base camp, one of their guns accidentally discharged. The rifle had been pointed directly at me at very close range, and the discharge missed me by inches.*

## Perils in Travel

Whether in the air, on the sea, or overland, travel always poses potentially life-threatening dangers. The TEAM Zimbabwe missionaries were constantly exposed to these in their extensive travels during deputation, en route to Zimbabwe, and on the field. When one considers the hundreds of thousands of miles they traveled with no loss of life or serious debilitation, God's protective hand is clearly seen. Accidents and "close calls" certainly happened, but these only served to make those affected more aware of His divine presence with them.

Martin and Wyn Uppendahl recalled their trip back to Africa after furlough on a large, new freighter and praised God for sparing their lives as it plowed through an extremely tumultuous sea, struggling to get out of the way of an oncoming hurricane. Then, just as relief seemed in sight, they found themselves in front of a second, larger and more powerful, hurricane. At this point Martin and Wyn, along with everyone else on board, including the captain and crew, feared for their lives—with good reason. Several times the ship leaned far over onto its side for over a minute before beginning to recover from a deep roll and steep pitch at the same time. The adults on board all knew that only by a miracle of God were they eventually able to sail into calmer seas.

On a much more frequent basis the missionaries faced the dangers of travel by road. Here again they recognized the hand of God granting them divine protection. Phyllis Rilling testified:

*One thing which has been continually apparent all through the years has been God's care for us on the roads. Many times we drove under potentially dangerous conditions, but God kept us from serious accident both on the field and on furlough.*

Melita Larson told of a journey she made under particularly dangerous conditions on some of Zimbabwe's most remote, dirt roads. She had graciously offered to drive one of the Karanda staff nurses to her home village after her mother had passed away. Melita described the rugged trip and precarious situations in which God protected them:

*Friday and Rachel Chimukangara, affectionately known as the "Chims," are both graduates of the Karanda Nursing School who have been on the hospital staff since the early 1980's. Mrs. Chim had an emergency Cesarean section on March 25, 1999, giving birth to a healthy, pre-term daughter weighing 2400 grams [5 lbs, 4 oz.].*

*By Saturday, April 10th, mother and baby were ready to travel, so we began our 704-kilometer [475-mile] journey, leaving Karanda at about 7:30 p.m. Altogether, we had six adults and a two-week-old baby in the truck. This included a pastor, a friend, and an older daughter of the Chimukangaras.*

*We stayed the first night at TEAM's guesthouse in Harare. On Sunday, the 11th, we drove on to Rusitu, a small village in the Chimanimani mountains, and stayed with Mrs. Chim's sister there.*

*At about 2:00 p.m. Sunday afternoon we left the last decent road and began the final, most difficult part of the journey, up a much-less-traveled, mountainous, dirt road. I found out, after we started, that only banana truck drivers use this stretch of road. Cars and busses will not attempt to navigate it. Many times we were acutely aware of the Lord looking after us. The truck made it through places it should never have been able to go without four-wheel drive.*

*The road was also filled with bad mud holes in which we got stuck a couple of times. The second time this occurred, we ended up with both the front and back wheels of one side of the truck hanging over the edge of an embankment with a river below. The men, with some help from passersby, literally had to lift the rear of the truck and move it bit by bit back onto the road. Then they had to do the same with the front end.*

*At 4:00 p.m. we finally reached the end of this extremely poor, 12-kilometer [7.5-mile] stretch of road. Then we had to walk the remaining distance up the mountain to the village. I parked the truck by the side of the road, praying that it would be safe, and began the climb upwards with the others. I was quite exhausted by this time.*

*The family was really surprised to see the Chimukangaras but glad they could come. We spent the night on the mountain and had very heavy rains, which continued into part of the morning as well. (It had been raining a lot in this area for six months.) All I could think of was how we would possibly get back over that awful road!*

*We began our return journey at about 1:00 p.m. Monday and got stuck twice in the first half-kilometer. I could see we were in for a long afternoon!*

*Soon we met a banana truck driver who was returning up the mountain because another truck, loaded with bananas, was stuck in the middle of the road further down. In spite of this news we all decided to continue. The banana truck driver was even willing to leave his truck behind and drive mine down to where the other truck was stuck. I readily accepted this as a gracious provision of the Lord.*

*The going was still very difficult, and we got stuck several more times. When we reached the other banana truck, it had just gotten freed from the mud, so we were able to proceed. Our return trip down this bad, 12-kilometer stretch of road took three hours!*

*I was never so glad to see a village as I was when we finally drove into Rusitu. We spent the night there, and the next morning Mrs. Chim was able to talk with the doctor and find out more about why her mother had died.*

*On Tuesday we traveled to Harare and spent the night there again. We finally arrived at Karanda late Wednesday afternoon. Mrs. Chim was tired, but she was feeling much better about her mother's passing, having been able to go home and see her family, her friends, and her mother's grave and to talk with the doctor.*

*I was thankful for the very real protection of the Lord on that difficult journey. All along the way I felt the reality of His promises in Psalm 121.*

Missionaries encountered many other dangerous situations on the Zimbabwe roads, but God was always with them. Several described instances when they felt His protective hand dramatically intervene to avert what could have been serious accidents.

Phil Christiansen frequently burned the candle at both ends during his time at Karanda, working at often strenuous, construction or maintenance-type jobs during the day and then doing his hospital lab work late into the night. Unfortunately, his sleep deprivation at times jeopardized his safety on the road, making him extremely thankful for God's protection.

He reflected on a couple of incidents when he was particularly mindful of this:

*One night I went sound asleep driving in the middle of Harare. I almost sideswiped a car but woke up just in time. On another occasion Barb and I were on the Mt. Darwin road coming home from Harare when I fell asleep. Barb poked me just in time for me to pull away from running into a stone wall.*

Don Hoyt had an even closer call in averting what could have been a very serious accident as he drove with his father-in-law, Dad Grigg, back to Mavuradonha one day in his Toyota station wagon. He described what happened:

> *The grass was high along the sides of the road, limiting visibility. As we came around a banked curve, veering into the other lane, we suddenly confronted a bus speeding toward us. With no time to get to the left of the bus [people drive on the left side of the road in Zimbabwe], I went up as far as I could on the right embankment.*
>
> *As the bus whizzed by, it skimmed off all the outermost attachments on the left side of our vehicle: the side mirrors, the door handles, the open wing window, etc. Dad Grigg was covered with broken glass, but we were not injured at all and could still continue driving the car on to Mavuradonha, praising the Lord for His protection.*

Lorraine Waite had a similar experience of encountering an unexpected vehicle in her path one night as she was returning to Karanda. She had taken about 18 local Shona people to Harare for an engagement party, and they were all returning in her pick-up truck. She described the supernatural intervention that helped her avert what could have been a serious accident:

> *I was going downhill into a little valley with a car coming toward me from the opposite side. Suddenly when I reached the bottom of the hill, I saw an ox cart right in front of me. It was painted black or dark blue, had no reflectors, was pulled by black oxen, and the Shona people riding in it were wearing dark clothing, making both them and the cart virtually invisible. By the time I saw them, I couldn't possibly stop fast enough to avoid hitting them.*
>
> *At that moment I felt hands come over my hands and steer me into the path of the oncoming car. Since the driver had a shoulder on his side of the road, he was able to steer off the road onto it while I got around the ox cart. If I had turned off the road on my side, we would have rolled down a steep embankment. Either the Lord Himself or one of His angels had intervened to keep us safe.*

Lynn Hoyt described another incident that seemingly involved the protective role of angels:

*Angels drive cars! I'm convinced of it! More than once over our 16 years in Zimbabwe we saw the Lord's faithful hand of protection over us as we drove the treacherous dirt roads in the bush.*

*An incident that particularly stands out in my mind occurred at Mavuradonha during our first term. Because we lived in the first house that visitors encountered as they came onto the station, they often stopped to get information from us.*

*One afternoon a huge truck loaded with school supplies came grinding up the hill, arriving at our home just as Don also drove up in our blue Opal. He quickly parked the car and hopped out to give the truck driver directions.*

*As I watched from a distance, I couldn't see the two men talking. I just saw the Opal move past the truck, jump over a deep drainage ditch, and proceed across a grassy hill toward the student dorms below. I could not understand why Don would be driving the car over the field like that.*

*Then I caught sight of him—running behind the car! By this time it had picked up considerable speed and was heading straight toward the drop-off above the roof of the boys' dorm.*

*Amazingly, the car suddenly veered left toward a large storage shed and a small fenced-in area where supplies were kept. Another slight turn took it to the side of the shed and into the fence where it stopped in a whirl of dust. Not a thing was damaged nor a person hurt! The angel driver left, sight unseen, and we all praised God for His protection! He had averted what could have been a tragic disaster.*

Sometimes God's hand of protection was seen in keeping missionaries from more serious injury when accidents did occur. Some walked away hardly scathed from accidents that could easily have been fatal.

When Carl and Donna Hendrickson moved their household from Rusambo to Kapfundi in 1959, their heavily-laden truck completely overturned; yet they all escaped serious injury. Donna wrote:

*All of our household items, including the kerosene fridge and petrol-driven washing machine, were packed into the truck bed. Carl and I, along with our four children, aged 7½ to 3, were in the cab. We stopped in Harare for supplies and gained another passenger, our co-worker Ray Finsaas, who needed a ride home to Kapfundi. This made three adults and four kids in the cab with our cook, Ninepence, riding on top of the load in the back.*

*Leaving the tarmac [asphalt] road out of Harare, we proceeded onto the rocky, dirt, washboard road for the last 55 miles into the mission station. Being April and the end of the rainy season, the grass was extremely tall and thick on each side of the road.*

*We were traveling at about 30-40 m.p.h. when suddenly out of the tall grass and onto the road right in front of us came a man riding a bicycle. To avoid hitting him, Carl turned into the tall grass on the right side of the road, not knowing what lay hidden in it.*

*After hitting a tree or two, the truck rolled completely upside down, throwing Ninepence onto the ground. The windshield of the cab was totally smashed, but what saved all of us inside from being crushed was the FRIDGE, which had been packed in the truck bed right up against the cab!*

*One by one we crawled out through the side window and took stock of our injuries. We had some noticeable bruises and tattered emotions but no broken bones and very few cuts. Ninepence, who had quite a fall, was the most bruised and had also injured his arm.*

*Very shortly a local vehicle came along, and the driver enquired as to what had happened. He was able to send word to Kapfundi, and Wilf Strom came out to rescue us. He drove me and the children back to the station while Carl and Ray, with help from local village men, worked to turn the truck right side up. The two men were then able to drive the slightly damaged truck on to Kapfundi as well.*

*God's protection and grace were very real to us in what could have been a much more serious accident. If the truck bed had not been so fully packed with the fridge up against* the cab, the story could have had a different ending. We were reminded of the promise that "The Lord is the one who goes ahead of you; He will be with you. He will not fail you or forsake you. Do not fear or be dismayed" (Deuteronomy 31:8; NASB). God still had lessons to teach us through this experience.

Roy and Mildred Carnall also praised God for minimal injuries when they rolled over in their Opal Caravan driving from Cape Town to Zimbabwe in 1962. They were returning from furlough in the States, and Mildred was driving. Roy was holding two-year-old Cora, who had been sick. Mildred described what happened:

*I was driving through the Karoo Desert with virtually no traffic and noticed that Cora had fallen asleep on Roy's shoulder. I suggested that he lay her down. As he did, she began to wake up, and my attention turned to her. I momentarily took my eyes off my driving and ran off the road. I then turned the wheels sharply back toward the road, which apparently broke the drive shaft, causing the car to go out of control. I kept braking, which probably saved our lives, but the vehicle rolled over one-and-a-half times. Thanks to God, we were all alive with only cuts and bruises!*

*An Afrikaans couple came by going south and stopped to give us what aid they could. Since our car was totaled, they drove Cora and me to the hospital in the nearest town of Colesberg. Then they reported the accident to the police, who went out to get Roy and had the car towed to a garage in town. In questioning him, the policeman asked Roy if he thought we had just been lucky or if God had had something to do with why our car was totaled and we were alive. Roy, of course, gave God the credit.*

*He and Cora ended up having a few stitches, and I, being six months pregnant with Jim, only had bruises. Our luggage was damaged but still usable. . . . Upon hearing of our accident, a church in Indiana sent a sizable donation, and we were able to buy a used Opal pick-up in Harare.*

Mary Danielson sustained slightly more serious injuries when she and Donna Kahlstorf had an accident while returning to Rusambo from Harare in 1965. They were not exactly sure how it happened but recalled seeing a snake crossing the road in front of them. Their next memories were of calling out to each other to see if they were both still alive after their vehicle had rolled over several times. It was completely wrecked, but they were both extremely grateful to the Lord that they were not more critically hurt.

In a prayer letter to her supporters Mary described her injuries and the effect the accident had on herself and others:

> *I was thrown through the door after the first turn-over while Donna stayed [in the car] till it stopped. That we escaped with our lives is a miracle of God's grace. I sustained a badly dislocated knee and several broken ribs while Donna had only bruises and scratches. . . .*
>
> *[After] having my leg in a cast for six weeks and being restricted in my activities for awhile, I have now almost fully recovered the use of my knee. I only missed three days of school as [the accident occurred] ten days before the new term began.*
>
> *It had a very sobering effect on the school, as God has [spoken] to each one of us through this experience. I have come to realize [how much] our lives are in God's hands, and it is only by His grace that [we] are spared for another day.*

Tom and Lois Jackson also praised God for sparing their lives when they totaled their car in a horrible accident as they were returning from holiday in South Africa. All four of their children were with them in the car, but the Lord protected them all. No one was hurt.

Bud and Mandy Jackson were also mindful of the Lord's protection in an accident they had while traveling on a gravel road behind a truck pulling a large trailer. Bud described what happened:

> *We had been following the truck for a number of miles when I decided to move forward into the dust cloud surrounding it with the intent to make our way past it. I*

*didn't realize that the truck had come to a stop and had moved far to the right in order to negotiate a sharp left turn.*

*When the rear of the trailer suddenly loomed out of the dust cloud before us, I tried to brake, but we skidded on the gravel and crashed into it. We were protected, however, by the "bull bar" on the front of our vehicle, which took the brunt of the collision. Had the elevated steel box of the trailer penetrated our windshield, we would undoubtedly have been seriously injured. We definitely felt the hand of the Lord with us that day.*

Dr. Dan and Julie Stephens had a terrifying accident in which they were sure they were going to be killed as they were driving to South Africa for holiday with their family. Julie described what happened and how God marvelously protected them:

*We were driving to South Africa on a busy road after dark when suddenly in front of us we saw a shower of sparks and heard a huge collision. Then, hurtling directly toward us on its side with sparks flying everywhere, was the detached tanker of a truck filled with spilling diesel. We were absolutely certain it would broadside us.*

*Dan quickly swerved off the road, so the tanker only hit our trailer, ripping it wide open. Miraculously, we sustained no injuries, the fuel tank did not explode, and no fire occurred.*

*When everything finally came to a rest, out of the otherwise deathly silence we heard a baby crying. As we got out of our car to investigate, we saw the mangled remains of the car in front of us and found a baby lying in the middle of the road. The parents of the child had been crushed to death. The drivers of the two semi-trucks that had sideswiped each other, causing the horrible accident, had run away. In the midst of such carnage we praised the Lord for His obvious protection of our lives.*

# Perils of War

The conditions of unrest in Zimbabwe that eventually led to the War of Independence developed gradually over the years. Even as it reached its height, it was a war fought in obscurity, almost always under the cloak of darkness. Missionaries rarely knew where the national combatants were located at any given time or where they would show up next. They learned to live in an atmosphere of tension and uncertainty.

As early as 1966, Ray and Myrtle Finsaas were warned that Hunyani station was going to be attacked by men coming on the bus that evening. The message arrived too late to be communicated via wireless to TEAM headquarters in Hatfield. Ray and Myrtle could do nothing but claim Psalm 91 and God's protection over them. Unable to sleep, they prayed all night long. The next day they learned that the men had been diverted to another location. God had faithfully answered their prayers and protected them.

Rusty Sherwood also received a warning just before he was ready to travel to Kapfundi with some Shona brethren to conduct a youth seminar there. He was told by the local people that this would not be a good time for them to go, as the people in the Kapfundi area had to "plow their fields." Since it was not plowing season, Rusty understood and heeded the warning.

A number of missionaries were confronted in various bush settings by strangers that questioned them in an unsettling way. While living at Chironga, Donna Kahlstorf had stopped on her way to the Kudyanyemba Church to pick someone up. As she waited for this individual, a strange man came out of the bush and over to the car to question her.

"How long have you been here?"

"A few years."

"Would you like to die here?"

"Well, I guess I have to die someplace. It may as well be here."

Then, after a few moments he told her she could stay and disappeared into the bush again. Donna was struck with how very peaceful she was in what she recognized was a potentially frightening incident.

As the war began to escalate, safety in traveling became an

increasing concern. Judy Everswick was driving 25 miles in her little VW bug every Tuesday from Bindura to Mtepetepa for a ladies' Bible study that started at 2:00. The curfew on travel in their area was supposed to begin at 4:00. The ladies always wanted to study for as long as they could, so getting back by curfew was always a push for Judy. She wrote:

*That 40-minute drive home was always a time of trusting God for protection as the long shadows of the mountains extended over the road—one that generally had weekly ambushes on it. I had such a peace as I drove, however, knowing that God was surrounding both me and the car.*

The roads out near the bush stations also became more dangerous. Driving in and out of Mavuradonha, Stew Georgia recalled times in which he drove past craters in the road where land mines had exploded. Eventually missionaries refrained from venturing out on the roads. In the meantime, however, no TEAM missionary was ever hurt by a land mine in Zimbabwe.

Because schools were becoming a frequent target for recruiting potential soldiers, tension increased for the missionaries at Mavuradonha. Reg Austin, serving as headmaster of the mission high school there, was well aware that the station was under observation.

This was confirmed when the combatants showed up at George and Pat Dee's home. They made no threats of harm, and George and his son, Jon, treated them in a friendly manner, serving them Cokes and giving them the medicines they requested from the clinic.

When they returned a second time, they were not as friendly. Instead, Stew Georgia was confronted at his house by heavily armed men, who compelled him to lead them to the homes of the chaplain and the boarding master of the high school. These two men were then brutally murdered before his eyes.

Marlene Georgia told of how the Lord ministered to her that night:

*I believe that God did much to protect me that night. I do remember that I was trembling and praying while Stew was gone—but in my mind I thought they were going to kidnap the student body as they had done just the week before at another nearby mission school. I think that was part of God's protection—that I was not even thinking that anyone would be murdered or that Stew's life was in danger.*

*The kids were home from the hostel but sleeping— another blessing. I found strength in Bible verses that came to mind, like Psalm 23 and Psalm 46:1 [KJV]: "God is our refuge and strength, a very present help in trouble."*

*Even when I heard the shot, I still thought that it was a warning shot to make the students cooperate. I was not surprised when Stew came back because I never thought otherwise. Of course, I was as devastated as he was when he told me what had happened.*

Dr. Roland Stephens commented on God's protection of the missionaries on the Karanda station:

*The incidents of God's protection over us during the war were numerous. Mortars lobbed at the hospital fell far short of their target. Our plane and vehicles were never attacked or damaged. We treated the injured on both sides of the conflict with no adverse repercussions. We received many threatening letters but none of the threats ever materialized.*

*Probably even more numerous were the times that we were divinely protected without knowing we were in danger. We heard after the hospital closed that a "hit list" contained the names of some of the staff here, so possibly closing the hospital saved some of our lives, as hard as that was to do.*

Ann-Britt Byrmo Smazik recalled an evening at Karanda when small arms fire broke out on the station just minutes after the midwives had left a party at Wilma Gardziella's house. Wilma called to make sure the students had arrived back at their dorm safely. Then she, Ann-Britt, and Judy Gudeman all sat in the hallway, praying and trusting God with very little fear. Ann-Britt stated, "I felt I was being held in the hollow of God's hand."

Joe and Olga Reimer were living at Karanda when the hospital was closed in 1978. They remained in Harare for six more months, helping to set up facilities for the makeshift nursing school that would enable the second and third year students from Karanda to finish their training.

As the Reimers' objectives were nearing completion, they began trying to arrange their trip home to Canada. Zimbabwe's main airline had already lost two of their planes, so seats were at a premium. They finally got tickets to fly out to Johannesburg on February 12, 1979.

The next day the very plane they flew on, bearing the same flight number and making the same trip to Johannesburg, was shot down, killing all passengers. Joe and Olga rejoiced in God's protecting hand on their lives. If they had flown one day later, they would have been killed.

## Perils in the City

Riots became a frequent hazard of urban life as various groups within the political mix of the now independent country expressed their dissatisfaction with assorted issues. Unfortunately, innocent pedestrians and drivers of vehicles could unintentionally get caught in the midst of one of these, putting them in danger of becoming casualties of the mob mentality that seemed to rule at these times. While missionaries were occasionally caught in such situations, they were always protected from physical harm by the Lord.

Bud and Mandy Jackson described a couple times when they experienced this:

*Mandy and I found ourselves stopped in traffic on one of the main streets in the city as an angry mob suddenly descended upon us with a frightening noise. Soon bricks and rocks were raining all around our vehicle. A government pick-up truck next to our car came under direct attack. The occupants escaped, wounded but alive, with their vehicle badly damaged. As the riot swept on, we were finally able to make our way to relative safety, but we passed overturned, burning vehicles and a great deal of collateral damage along the way.*

*Another time Mandy was traveling into the city to attend a Bible Study Fellowship session when she saw a large crowd gathered along the road ahead. At first, thinking that the people were waiting for a bus at the nearby bus stop, she proceeded on her way. By the time she realized that the crowd was actually an angry mob, she was caught in the midst of it.*

*Her car began to be pelted by various items from both sides, and a man lay down on the road in front of her vehicle to impede her forward progress. Another one smashed her windshield. She remarkably maintained her composure and kept moving slowly forward, steering around the man lying in the road, and eventually made her escape. Our car sustained some dents and a smashed windshield, but we were extremely grateful to God that the situation had not been more tragic.*

Kelley Ulrich told how the Lord protected her from being caught in a similar situation as she took her children to school one morning. Taking the back roads out of Hatfield, she was flagged down and warned by three ladies running in the opposite direction that she should not go on Chiremba Road, as "lots of trouble" was going on there. Kelley quickly changed her route and thanked the Lord for this warning.

Daylight robberies were also becoming commonplace in the city, particularly outside banks. Mandy Jackson had a firsthand experience with this as well. After coming out of Barclay's Bank one day, she used her remote door opener to unlock her car. Ordinarily she would press the central lock button as soon as she got in to lock both front doors again. On this occasion, however, before she even got the driver's door closed, she was startled by a young man who attempted to pull it open again. This resulted in a face-to-face tug-of-war between Mandy and the man. Mandy also "lay on the horn" in an attempt to attract the attention of someone who might be able to assist her. Seeing the strength of Mandy's resistance, the young man suddenly departed.

As Mandy quickly backed out of the parking space, the still unlocked, front passenger door swung open. She shuddered as she realized that the man at the driver's door must have had an accomplice, who had opened the front passenger door, most likely with the intent to grab her handbag while she was struggling with the man on her side of the car.

She was greatly relieved to confirm that her handbag was still tucked next to her on the seat! "Why it wasn't taken," she testified, "can only be explained as an act of the Lord's intervention—for which I was so grateful!"

Rita Ibbotson also had a scary encounter in the city. Because of the fuel crisis in Harare, she had to take public transportation to get to the Parirenyatwa Hospital for several days while she was observing their three-year nursing program with the intent of starting one at Karanda. At the end of her day the busses were usually full by the time they reached the hospital, having already filled up in the city center.

Rita described what occurred on this frightful day:

*A bus came along with no one in it and, without thinking, I climbed in. No sooner was I seated than I regretted my action. The conductor was drinking from a bottle and reeked of alcohol. Although other passengers were seeking rides along the road, the driver did not stop. I was uncomfortable to say the least and prayed a silent prayer for help.*

*Just ahead I could see a police checkpoint. The driver attempted to turn the bus around in order to avoid it, but he was unable to do so. I believe God provided that checkpoint to protect me from potential robbery or other danger. When we stopped, I said I wanted to get out. The conductor tried to stop me, but I insisted.*

The staff of the Word of Life Bookstore in Harare also had reason to praise the Lord for His protection during the precarious days after the war. They endured a very close call when a bomb exploded in the building directly behind them. While the bookstore sustained some damage, they were very grateful that no one in the store was injured.

The missionaries could not possibly avoid all situations of potential danger in the city. They carried on their necessary business knowing that God was with them. Julie Stephens testified, "I am sure the Lord protected us many times from what we were not even aware of as we walked the streets in town." The assurance of His presence gave them both peace and confidence.

# CHAPTER 11

# God Answered Prayers

*"The eyes of the Lord are on the righteous*
*and his ears are attentive to their cry."*
(Psalm 34:15)

One of the awesome ways in which God demonstrated His constant presence with His servants was in answering their prayers. His attentive ear and loving responses are seen throughout their missionary careers from the time they began preparing until the time their service was over and beyond. Sometimes the answers were so subtle they were not even noticed. At other times the answers came in virtually miraculous ways. What is reported here is but a minute sampling of the way God responded to the countless prayers of each of His servants on the Zimbabwe field and their faithful prayer warriors around the world.

## Logistical Needs

While answering prayers for logistical needs may pale in comparison to other more dramatic health and safety needs, God's work could never have been successfully accomplished through the missionaries' lives had He not intervened at many critical junctures to smooth the path before them. His partnership with them every step of the way was demonstrated in how He worked on their behalf, opening doors, moving obstacles, and granting special blessings in an extraordinary manner.

## Preparation Logistics

Many "missionaries-to-be" experienced God's obvious intervention as they pursued the education and training they needed to prepare for their service in Zimbabwe. When they unexpectedly received special favor or preferential treatment, they recognized the hand of God. This not only warmed their hearts but also gave encouraging confirmation that they were walking in His will.

Betty Mason Wolfe described such an incident:

> *My mother advised me, after graduating from BIOLA, to get either teacher's or nurse's training before I went to the field. I knew that I would never make a teacher, so I decided to go for nursing. My mother and I prayed together and then went to the Lutheran Hospital, which was the closest one to our home in Fort Wayne.*
>
> *It was January and they were taking in a new class in February. They had room for just 10 students and 10 had already been accepted. However, just that morning one had withdrawn. I was told to get a transcript of my high school grades, and before I had time to think about it, I was enrolled.*

Others saw God answer specific prayers in connection with their raising of support. To many, this was a challenging and often prolonged process, and they rejoiced whenever they saw God intervene on their behalf.

Dr. Sam and Emily Wall testified of how God responded to their special request to get to Zimbabwe by January 1958:

> *In our planning and preparation for going to Africa, we saw God work in some incredible ways. In July 1957, Emily and I were deeply moved to get to Zimbabwe in time for our oldest daughter to enter school at the commencement of the next school year, which in Zimbabwe was January 1958. She had been bumped around so much throughout my training*

*that we felt she finally needed to have a proper start for her education in Zimbabwe.*

*Accordingly, we made our bookings on a ship leaving in December 1957, taking by faith that we could raise our support by this time. TEAM undoubtedly thought we were being quite presumptuous, as we probably were.*

*To our surprise, funds did not come in from the sources on which we had counted. As our spirits sank, we found ourselves at one point praying, "Lord, we believe; help our unbelief!"*

*Our first encouragement came as we learned that an anonymous donor (still unknown to us) had given $5000 towards our support. Then we met with a doctor at 11:30 at night and visited for two hours. In the midst of a flu epidemic that was the only time he could see us. This man subsequently gave us $3500 and an operating room table.*

*On the night before our scheduled departure we learned that our full support had been pledged! God was faithful!*

When Doug and Nancy Everswick began raising their support, they also made a special request of the Lord. They had witnessed the hardships experienced by many missionaries whose supporters were spread from coast to coast in the U.S., making extensive travel necessary whenever they returned for home assignment. Doug and Nancy decided to ask God to supply their support from a relatively small geographical base. In the end, with the exception of a few individuals, all of their support came from within a four-hour drive of their home base in New Jersey.

God also intervened to help the missionaries in the final, "pulling up roots" stage of their preparation for the field. Frequently this was a time when significant transfers of property and responsibilities needed to occur.

Noël and Ann Liddle testified of how God helped to streamline this process for them:

*The arrangements in selling our Chicago house were almost unbelievable. The only explanation is that the Lord supervised the entire deal. We sold privately to save the Real*

*Estate Agent's large fee, and the buyer was my replacement in the schools. He . . . needed a house to accommodate his family, liked the house we were selling, and purchased it![1]*

## Travel Logistics

God's oversight was also greatly appreciated as the missionaries navigated through the complexities of the international travel system. No matter how good their planning was, many of the details needing to come together at the right time were completely out of their control—but not God's.

Ken and June Munger trusted in this as they left home in early December 1952, driving to Chicago in their one-ton truck loaded with all their personal effects. There they would board a cargo ship that would take both them and their truck to Africa. Their only problem was that they had not yet received their visas. Believing that God would resolve this problem before the ship sailed, they kept moving forward.

Upon arriving in Chicago, they learned that their ship was being delayed. Day after day they waited, eagerly anticipating notice of the new sailing date and the arrival of their visas. Finally, on December 27 they learned that the ship was ready to sail *and* that their visas were granted. June wrote:

*Ken went to get the visas stamped into our passports as I took a cab with our suitcases to the ship and boarded. Just minutes before the ship departed, Ken arrived with our visas.*

*When we asked why the ship had been delayed, no one seemed to have an answer. We felt sure that God had orchestrated this in answer to our prayer that we would receive our visas in time for sailing.*

Dick and Mary Ann McCloy experienced God's last minute intervention in a similar way as they were leaving for their first furlough in 1974. Mary Ann wrote:

*My passport needed to be updated and baby Esther's picture added before we could leave the country. We had*

*committed the matter to the Lord, but the day of our sched-
uled departure arrived with no passport in hand.*

*We proceeded with our last minute packing, still trusting
God. Just hours before our flight took off, our faith was
rewarded as the passport arrived via an airline stewardess
from South Africa on a flight up from Johannesburg!!!*

## Furlough Logistics

Returning for furlough, or "home assignment," often meant
confronting another set of logistical needs. This included arranging
for housing, a vehicle, and often schooling for the children, in addition to planning extensive travel itineraries to visit supporters. Once
again missionaries reported how God answered some of their
specific prayers in regard to these needs.

The McCloys were delighted with God's response to one of
their prayers as they approached furlough:

*With four teen-agers, ages 13, 15, 17, and 19, we asked
people to pray for a camper we could use so our kids would
have a consistent space of their own as we traveled rather
than having to sleep every night in a stranger's home. The
Lord answered superabundantly by giving us more than we
expected—an RV with bunks for each of them!!! What a
blessing!!!*

The Liddles also recognized the hand of God in providing their
transportation needs for their first furlough. They were able to
repurchase the Pontiac station wagon they had sold to their son
before going to Zimbabwe. They had bought this car new in 1973
and had asked God to keep it going until both of their children had
completed college. The Lord did that and more, now making it
available to them, nearly two decades later, to make a 10,000 mile
deputation tour.

# Medical Needs

Being cut off from ready access to advanced medical care, the
missionaries on the rural stations relied heavily on prayer when

they confronted major medical needs, either for themselves or the Shona people they were serving. Many testified of how God faithfully answered their prayers at these critical times.

Thelma Everswick told of a very trying night when God gave her special strength to assist a woman in labor:

> *It was the end of October, the hottest month of the year, when one of the school teachers came to our house at 2 a.m. pleading, "Please come and help. My wife is in labor." I got up and made my way to their house. The entire time I was in constant prayer asking for God's help, as I myself was almost due to deliver our fourth child. By 4 a.m. twin baby boys were delivered and all went well.*
>
> *I returned home hot and exhausted, but instead of going to bed, I told Norman, "We better go to town now." It was a long, uncomfortable drive, but by the next morning my own baby boy was safely delivered. How I praise the Lord for strengthening me and helping me at a time when I felt like saying, "I need help myself!"*

Marg Jackson, who ran the dispensary at Rusambo, told of a time when she needed special help for a woman who had just delivered a baby:

> *One time a lady had given birth to a little girl, but the placenta wouldn't budge and she was bleeding badly. I didn't know what to do. In our house on the station was a very old telephone that you could crank up and sometimes get through to Mt. Darwin. I didn't know if it would work, but I had to try.*
>
> *By God's grace it did work, and I was able to speak to the doctor at the clinic there. He told me to give the lady an injection of quinine to contract her uterus and help her get rid of the placenta. I did this, the bleeding stopped, and she lived. This was another time I was aware that many were praying for us.*

Verna Knapp described a time when God's answer to prayer

came in a rather unusual way but brought immediate resolution to the problem:

> *Our two-year-old daughter, Clariss Lee, had a habit of sucking her fingers, which were getting white and wrinkly. To prevent her from more sucking, we would wrap her hand lightly.*
>
> *One evening she came down with a fever, which remained high in spite of being treated by Ruth Ebbern, the nurse on our station. As the evening progressed and the fever did not subside, we prayed and considered taking her to the hospital.*
>
> *After praying, however, we saw that the wrapped hand was bothering her. Upon unwrapping it, we saw a pussy swelling on the back of her hand—the source of the infection and cause of the fever. This enabled Ruth to know how to treat it. By midnight the fever broke, and we thanked the Lord for answering our prayers.*

Donna Hendrickson Robinson shared how God answered prayer in a special way when serious illness struck her family:

> *In December 1959, we were packed and ready to leave on our first furlough. The day we were to leave the station (Tuesday), our three-year-old son, Wes, became very ill with a 105° fever and went into convulsions.*
>
> *We were so grateful to have our station nurse, Myrtle Finsaas, as a next door neighbor and called for her help. (Six weeks prior to this her daughter Ruth had been similarly sick and went into convulsions.) Dear Myrtle came and showed us how to hold Wes's tongue down when he was convulsing so he wouldn't swallow it. [An intervention that is no longer recommended during a seizure.]*
>
> *With these instructions for caring for Wes, we continued with our plans to drive into Harare to take care of last minute arrangements before leaving by plane the following Monday. As we traveled, Wes's fever subsided a little, and we were encouraged.*

*Upon arriving in Harare, however, it climbed up to 105°
again and was accompanied with more convulsions. We
consulted with Dr. Norman, and he prescribed antibiotics
and instructed us to put Wes in a tepid bath and keep a 24-
hour watch on him. We were so grateful to have three
nurses in the guesthouse at the time, who so lovingly helped
us do this and joined us in prayer for Wes.*

*The doctor also came over every day to check on him,
but no change occurred over the next couple days. When
Friday came and Wes was still not well, Dr. Norman told us
that if his temperature was not normal by Saturday noon, we
would have to cancel our flight to the States on Monday.*

*By God's providence nearly all of the missionaries on
the field were in town that weekend for Roy and Mildred
Carnall's wedding on Saturday afternoon. Everyone was
praying for Wes—and by Saturday noon his temperature
was normal!*

*When Dr. Norman came, he was amazed and let us know
that the medication was not what brought his healing.
Instead, it was Wes's own body fighting the infection. We all
knew it was God's loving answer to all our prayers. We
praised Him for restoring him to us, as we learned later that
we nearly lost him.*

*When we boarded our flight out of Harare on Monday,
we discovered that God had even provided a missionary
doctor and a nurse as passengers with us. We felt so loved
and safe and were grateful to be on our way home to have
Christmas with family we hadn't seen for over five years.*

Donna also saw God answer prayer when her husband, Carl,
became very sick at Rusambo. She described what happened in this
case:

*Rusambo is in the Mt. Darwin area and can be locked in
by rivers in the rainy season. Carl became very ill and
weak with a high fever. Our clinic nurse, Ruth Ebbern,
compassionately did all she could for him, but he was not
getting better.*

*As we prayed, we decided we needed to contact a doctor. Ruth drove our truck two miles to a local store, hoping to use their phone, while I stayed with Carl and our four young children. Ruth was able to contact the field office in Harare and learned that Dr. Wall just "happened" to be in town.*

*Doc and his wife, Emily, drove out immediately. After thoroughly examining Carl, Doc diagnosed him with severe pneumonia. He set up an IV with antibiotic and told me to watch it all night so it wouldn't run out. After much prayer and several days of care by Doc and Ruth, the fever subsided, and Carl slowly began to regain his strength.*

*Doc Wall said driving 150 miles to our home was the longest house call he had ever made. We praise God for a doctor ready and willing to treat a co-worker in desperate need and give us the confidence that he would have a good recovery.*

Dr. Wall was also instrumental in identifying the cause of the high fevers that Chuck and Scottie Pruitt's daughter, Cherie, was spiking about every two weeks from the time she was eight months old. Initially, she had been diagnosed with malaria and treated for that, but the fevers continued.

Dr. Wall asked Scotty to chart Cherie's fevers, taking her temperature every hour around the clock. This revealed a cyclical pattern and made Dr. Wall suspect undulant fever, which she could have contracted through drinking unpasteurized milk.

When Chuck and Scotty came to the States on furlough, they took Cherie to the Illinois Research Hospital where the diagnosis of undulant fever was confirmed. With no cure available, she continued to have fevers up to 105° every two weeks. Wherever they went on deputation, they would have to take her to a doctor or the hospital for treatment.

TEAM would not clear them for returning to the field until Cherie was fever-free for nine months, leaving their ongoing missionary career in question. Scotty told how God intervened and brought special healing to Cherie:

*Finally, we were home in Lisle, Illinois, and on Sunday evening Pastor Loving asked if Cherie was having a fever right then. I told him that she was just starting the fever cycle again. He responded, "Well, let's go over to the house and pray about this." He prayed, based on the authority of our call to the mission field, that the Lord would heal her.*

*The next morning he came over to see how she was, and she was out playing with her tricycle. The fever had never developed. She was 2½ then and never had a fever after that. In fact, she was our healthiest child. She never even had a cold until she was 16.*

Donna Hendrickson Robinson told about another time God answered prayer to bring healing to one of the teachers' sons on the Rusambo station:

*While we were stationed at Rusambo, Carl periodically needed to be away to teach refresher courses to pastors or to attend board meetings. This left me alone with our four children and no means of transportation or, frequently, communication if our radio transmitter was down.*

*On one such occasion in early 1959, Teacher White, a dear Christian friend, came and informed me that his baby son, Timothy, had been sick with a fever for several days. We had no nurse on the station at the time, and since Carl had taken our truck and would be away for a week, we had no means to take him to Karanda to see our mission doctor there either.*

*Having only a limited knowledge of medicine myself, I treated Timothy the best I knew, but we both felt that something more needed to be done. As we discussed the problem, God spoke to me, and I said, "Teacher, let us pray that God will heal Timothy. There are many promises in God's Word that tell us He will answer our prayers if we have faith and confidence in Him." We quoted several of these promises and then decided to spend the day in prayer. Teacher White spoke to the other teachers and the pastor, asking them to join in prayer for little Timothy during this trying time too.*

*That evening Teacher White came to report that Timothy was a little better. We kept on praying. The next morning he came and said Timothy was completely well! He had had a good night and was now feeling fine!*

*God had answered our prayers! How we praised him! This experience thrilled our hearts and strengthened our faith in believing God through intercessory prayer. "And all things, whatsoever ye shall ask in prayer, believing, ye shall receive" (Matthew 21:22; KJV).*

Don and Lynn Hoyt were grateful for God's response to a medical emergency that they had before they even got to the field. Their son Richie was born May 6, 1959, while they were doing their initial deputation. When he was three weeks old, he began projectile-vomiting accompanied by a dramatic loss in weight.

He was diagnosed with pyloric stenosis, a major blockage in the valve between his stomach and intestinal track. Don wrote:

*. . . His initial treatment was medicinal and seemed to be working, although he was eventually hospitalized in New Jersey.*

*At the same time this was happening, we were scheduled to attend TEAM's Candidate School in Chicago. With assurance from the medical staff at the hospital that Rich was stable and would improve, we reluctantly left him to the caring oversight of Lynn's parents and continued with our plans to go to Chicago.*

*On our way, however, as we stopped to spend the night with friends in Ohio, we received a call from Lynn's parents that Richie's condition had become critical, and he had been transferred to the Children's Hospital in New York City for surgery. We immediately turned around and drove all night, committing our precious little one into the Lord's hands.*

*When we arrived at the hospital, his condition was startling! He was as thin as a war orphan and had tubes coming from his head and feet. . . . An impressive young surgeon [chosen as "Surgeon of the Year" by LIFE magazine] spoke with us and carefully described the corrective*

*procedure that Richie needed. He also explained the seri-
ousness of Richie's condition, stating that he had the lowest
metabolism of any living child he had ever seen, which
made him a very poor candidate for surgery. Therefore, they
wanted to delay surgery as long as possible, hoping to build
up his strength so he had a better chance to survive the
operation.*

*After two days of waiting, the surgeon announced that
Richie's condition left him with no option but to operate
immediately. He grimly told us that he could only give him a
50/50 chance to survive. With total dependence on the Lord,
we gave permission for the surgery.*

The Hoyts also informed the doctor of how many people were
praying for this little guy, including their families, their church, and
everyone at TEAM Candidate School. They were all praying,
"Lord, save this little boy for a special ministry." And God did! The
surgery was successful and little Richie began gaining weight
immediately.

More answers to prayer followed. Just after Rich was born and
all seemed well with mother and baby, Don had left his employment with a manufacturing company in Newark, NJ, and had taken
a job with a landscaping company, feeling the summer sun and
physical activity would better prepare him for missionary life in
Africa. His new employer did not offer health insurance, so Don
and Lynn anticipated a prolonged delay in getting to Zimbabwe as
they worked to pay off the large medical debt accumulated with
Richie's illness.

As they laid this problem before the Lord, a friend suggested
that Don contact the insurance provider from his previous job. With
little confidence that this would be productive, Don followed
through with this. To his amazement he learned that his insurance
premium had been paid for three months just shortly before he left
the company. Therefore, his coverage was still in effect!

This meant that all of Richie's expenses were covered and Don
and Lynn were free to continue their preparations for the mission
field. Don wrote, "This was certainly a provision of the Lord and
great confirmation that we were moving under His direction." What

a joy it was for them to celebrate Richie's first birthday in Zimbabwe!

God also answered the "special ministry" part of the prayer made for little Richie. Growing up to be a spiritually sensitive and directed child, Rich knew even in high school that he was going into ministry. With his wife, Anne, and their four children he has served with TEAM in Chad since 1987.

Clarence and Gladys Cedarholm faced a similar crisis when their third child, John, was born in March 1956 in Zimbabwe. Gladys wrote:

> *He seemed well and healthy, but for the next two days he couldn't keep any milk down. We were informed that he had pyloric stenosis and surgery would be necessary to correct the condition. Nevertheless, the doctors decided to wait another day or two to see if the problem might resolve on its own.*
>
> *When no improvement came, John was transferred to another hospital for surgery, which was scheduled for the next morning. As prayer went up on his behalf, a remarkable change took place overnight. The only explanation the doctor could give was that John did not have pyloric stenosis after all, but most likely the valve muscle had just been in spasm. WE felt God had answered our prayers, and we were delighted to share this with those who were attending to him.*

Diane Powell Hawkins told of another time when God wonderfully intervened for the baby daughter of her lab assistant:

> *Enock Chakubva's wife, Esther, had given birth to a healthy baby girl named Emily. However, within a few weeks they brought her back to the hospital with breathing problems. Soon her breathing stopped altogether, and she was rushed back to the operating room where we had our ventilator, and resuscitation efforts were begun.*
>
> *As the hours passed and many prayers ascended on behalf of this child, I would periodically check on her condition. At one point I was told that her eyes showed no pupil-*

*lary response to light, which seemingly meant that she had suffered significant brain damage from the lack of oxygen and therefore had little hope of ever being a normal little girl, even if she did survive.*

*For some reason the hospital staff did not give up on little Emily and continued doing their best to save her life, all the time praying for God's intervention. Enock's family gathered on the verandah outside the OR door awaiting the fate of their dear little one. My heart went out to them. How could I reach out to them at this time of crisis? As I returned home at the end of the day, I decided to take them some tea and sandwiches to show how much I cared. I felt that it was only a matter of time until they would be given the dreaded message of her passing.*

*Early the next morning I heard a knock at my door. I quickly grabbed my robe and went to see who it was. There stood Enock returning the tray and dishes I had brought the night before. I had to ask the inevitable question, feeling that certainly little Emily had died sometime during the night. I could not believe my ears when he told me that she was still alive and doing better! Not only did little Emily survive, but she grew up to be a perfectly normal child! How I praised God for this answer to prayer!*

# Protection

Missionaries on the rural mission stations relied on God for their protection as much as for their health—and He was no less apt to answer. Even the MKs realized the potential dangers of the African bush. Nancy Hendrickson Snyder wrote:

*I remember doing lots of praying for Dad and the other missionaries when they went on their hunts and when they were asked to catch leopards or lions that were causing problems in a village. I was always afraid that they would climb a tree at night to watch and find the leopard in that same tree or fall asleep and have the leopard or lion get them or a poisonous snake would find them. I had a vivid imagination, and it kept me praying for protection for our men a lot.*

Emil Rilling wrote a story entitled "The Lion Hunt" in which he described such an incident:

*We had not been at Mavuradonha very long when some men came walking up to the station from Chiswiti Village, about 20 miles away, down in the Zambezi Valley. They were asking for help.*

*A pride of lions, about half a dozen in number, had been troubling the village. The villagers' cattle were all kept in one pen at night. This pen is called a kraal and is usually round. At night the lions would circle around the outside and frighten the cattle, putting them into a high state of excitement and fear. Finally, the lions would give off a smell by urinating. This would cause the cattle to stampede, and no matter how strong the kraal, they would break out. Then the kill would be made.*

*The men of the village devised a scheme. They built a wall, perpendicular to the wall of the kraal, extending out about 50 feet. Then they strewed the area with thorns, so the lions would have to walk a long way around to continue circumventing the kraal. In making the wall, however, they left a gap where it joined the kraal, just big enough for a lion to walk through. In this gap they hung a wire cable in the form of a snare, in hopes of snaring the lead lion.*

*The plan worked, and a big male lion, leading the pride, walked through the gap and found himself tied up in the snare with the cable around his neck and behind his left front foot. It couldn't choke him, but the harder he thrashed, the tighter it became. He just thrashed and thrashed until everyone in the whole village was awake. Finally, he twisted the cable off, but by that time he was exhausted. He ran to the nearest bush and hid—right in the village! (The rest of the pride ran off and were never seen again.)*

*When we heard the story, Norman Everswick said, "We've got to help them." Norman, Chuck Pruitt, and I climbed into the truck with our guns. Two national teachers also went with us, Teacher Tiago and Teacher Alufai.*

*When we arrived at Chiswiti Village, the men showed us where the lion was. He hadn't moved. Women, children, and older people were afraid to come out of their huts. As we approached, however, the lion bolted out of the bush, up a ravine, through more bushes, and across cornfields.*

*It had rained the afternoon before, so the ground was soft and the spoor was easy to follow. We followed his trail, along with about 80 of the villagers. For several hours we walked in the heat of the midsummer sun in the Zambezi Valley. Our clothes were wringing wet. The lion kept just far enough ahead of us that we could not get an accurate shot at him. Finally, exhausted, he sat down in a dense grove of bushes. We were so close we could hear his breathing, but the foliage was too dense to see him.*

*Norman said, "I'm going into the bush here to look for a chance to shoot." Chuck went somewhere else. I said, "Not me, I'm going around there where I see a trail going through the bush. I think I will be able to get a clearer shot from further away." (Most of these bushes are hollow underneath.)*

*All of a sudden the lion saw me, let out a roar, and charged! He was probably about 60 feet away. He bounded about 20 feet with each leap. By the third leap I was able to aim a God-directed shot. The bullet hit him in the shoulder, shattering his whole front shoulder complex. The lion dropped only about 10 feet away from me and was unable to get up.*

*After this first shot I was getting a little bit nervous. In putting a second cartridge into the gun, I failed to draw the bolt back far enough to eject the old cartridge. This returned the spent cartridge to the chamber. I realized what I had done, so I quickly ejected the old one properly, put a new one into the gun, and fired the fatal shot. The bullet hit the lion between the eyes, and he slumped down.*

*Norman saw the lion charging. He tried to shoot, but his gun jammed! When the lion charged, all the village men fled. They melted away like butter. Only Teacher Tiago stood with me! After the lion was dead, we all gathered around and had a prayer of thanksgiving to God! . . .*

*About four years later, when we were on furlough in Alberta, Canada, we were invited to a meal at the home of my high school physics teacher. After the meal he said, "I have been waiting four years to ask you a question. What happened January 15, 1954, at 3:00 in the morning? That night I awoke with a tremendous burden for prayer, especially for Emil Rilling. I got up and prayed earnestly for about an hour. The burden did not lift. Then I got my wife up and both of us prayed for you for another hour. Finally, the burden lifted, and we went back to sleep. Think back," he said, "and tell me what happened."*

*So we reached back in our memories and realized this was the exact time when I was on this hunt, and I was charged by the lion! How thankful we are for those who obeyed the Lord's burden to pray!*

Russ Jackson also described a frightening encounter with a wild animal in which he had to rely solely on God for his protection:

*Leopards were abundant in the Zambezi Valley and would often try to break into my hen house and chicken run. Many times at night when we would hear a commotion out at the chicken house, I would quickly put on my head torch, take the shotgun, and go out to protect my precious chickens, our only source of eggs.*

*On one such occasion I remember putting the 12-volt battery pack supplying my head torch in my pajama pocket as I hurried out to the back yard. Sure enough, in the beam of my head torch I could see the shining green eyes of a large leopard.*

*I had learned from experience that the surest and safest way to shoot a leopard was to move slowly forward, getting close enough to distinguish its unmistakable spots. On this night the leopard moved off into the bush behind our house, so I quietly and carefully followed.*

*When I was close enough to see him clearly, I raised my*

*shot gun to shoot. Then, just at that very tense moment, the leopard moved under a low clump of trees. When I bent down to get a clear shot, the battery fell out of my pajama pocket, pulling the wire from my head torch and causing me to be suddenly be left in total darkness.*

*I remember the feeling of utter panic, standing there knowing the leopard was only a few yards from me. The leopard, of course, had perfect night vision, and all I could do was hope and pray for safety as I walked slowly back to the house. Once inside, I breathed a huge sigh of relief, thanking God for His special care of me that night.*

Dr. Dave and Karen Drake had a perilous experience occur at a spruit crossing near Karanda Hospital. Dave wrote:

*The visiting college students had been working hard in the hospital for several weeks and were excitedly anticipating this evening's outing. We would be taking them for an authentic Shona meal in a local village.*

*It was October, the month the rains usually start, but we didn't anticipate a problem that day. The Kadzingasais' village was only five miles away, near Chironga, so it would be just a short jaunt over there and back.*

*When the time arrived, Karen and I, along with three-year-old Brad, two-month-old Heather, and the three students, all crammed into our old Peugeot station wagon for the short drive to the village. By the time we arrived, a gentle rain had begun falling, so we were ushered one-by-one into the Kadzingasais' hut with an umbrella.*

*As the sadza, chicken, and muriwo were set before us, the students were given instructions on how to eat them Shona-style with their fingers. They thoroughly enjoyed this new experience, and we became so absorbed with eating the delicious food and interacting with them and our hosts that we temporarily forgot about the weather.*

*As we continued to eat, however, the rain came down harder and harder. It eventually became so loud that we could hardly hear each other speak at the table. Warned by this, I felt we needed to head back to Karanda, as we had several spruits to cross. With such a heavy downpour these could fill quickly with flash floods.*

We all piled back into the old Peugeot and started down the road. Soon we came to our first spruit. It was indeed flooded, but as we came downhill in our approach, I could still make out the markers on either side of the submerged causeway. Using these for guidance, I drove slowly forward, confident that with care I could get safely across.

Then, quite unexpectedly, just as I was fully onto the causeway, a sudden surge of water came down the rushing stream, hitting the car from the side and killing the engine. We were not particularly alarmed, as we knew that water levels in these spruits often recede as quickly as they rise. So we just sat and waited, certain that we would be able to push the car to the other side and get help once the water went down.

Instead of receding, however, the water continued to rise. The strength of the current was also increasing. Floating logs and other debris were striking the car as they careened down the now raging stream. Our nonchalance quickly changed to grave concern, as we realized that the force of the water could easily sweep us off the side of the causeway.

With adrenalin rising, we hastily considered what we could do to resolve our predicament. The only option we could think of was to see if Karen and the students could get out of the car on the downstream side, hang on with all their might, and push the car to the other end of the causeway while I steered.

Eager to try any possible solution, they bravely eased themselves out of the car. Almost immediately, however, they realized the current was far too strong and were forced to abandon that plan.

As they climbed back into the car, the seriousness of our situation became even more real. By now the water had seeped into the car up to the level of the seats, and we were crouching on top of them. There was a 10-foot drop off the *leeward side of the causeway. If the car was swept off it, some of us might make it downstream to safety but certainly not all of us, especially with Heather being only two months old and Brad three years.*

*We realized we were entirely dependent on God to intervene on our behalf and began earnestly calling upon Him to stop the rain and diminish the strength of the current coming against our car. We prayed, sang, and claimed God's promises for what seemed like an eternity. Gradually, the rain subsided, and the water receded to the point that we were able to get out and push the car to the other end of the spruit, where we opened the doors and let the water out.*

*Our plan was then for me to walk the four miles back to the hospital and get George Smazik to rescue us with the tractor. As I prepared to set out, I grabbed my trusty flashlight, turned it on, and was utterly dismayed when it gave one flicker of light and burned out. Now what was I supposed to do?*

*I had no choice except to attempt following the winding bush road on my own in the dark. With no moonlight able to seep through the thick, overhead clouds, the darkness was so great that I could not even see the road by my feet, let alone anything ahead or alongside the road. The only source of illumination I had to guide me that night was the lightning. Every time it flashed, I would check the road ahead as far as I could see and run that distance. Then I would slow to a walk until the lightning flashed again.*

*I did this all the way back to Karanda and managed not to go off the side of the road even once. This was divine intervention. At one point I had literally bumped into some people coming along the road from the hospital. It was so dark that even though we could hear each other, we could not make out figures. Once again I was totally dependent on God for both safety and guidance.*

*When I finally reached the station, I quickly summoned George, and we drove back in his pickup to get the others. On the way I filled him in on the details of our ordeal and how God had faithfully kept us safe.*

*We had only gotten about a mile from the hospital when in the headlights of the truck we saw a large python, four to six inches in diameter, stretched across the entire road. I gasped to think that I had just walked that road in the dark! I couldn't help but wonder what other dangers God had protected me from on that lonely, dark journey. I was more aware than ever that His angels had truly watched over me!*

*After picking up the others and bringing them back to our home, we had a wonderful time sitting around our big, round table praising God and thanking Him for showing us His unbelievable mercy in helping us out of our precarious situation. He had once again proven His faithfulness in never leaving us nor forsaking us!!*

God's faithful protection of His children continued through the years and was dramatically evidenced as He intervened to save the lives of two missionaries who were on holiday at Mana Pools in July 2004. Lynne Hawkins and short-term worker Kim Combs had joined Dick and Mary Ann McCloy and their daughter Becky for five days of R & R at this popular wildlife preserve.

As they set up camp, they noticed two old buffalo that had been thrown out of the herd. Having lost this protection, they tended to stay near the camp, where they feel safer.

Lynne described how she and Kim became much more acquainted with one of these massive animals:

*The first night out, at about 8 o'clock, Kim and I went to the outhouse before settling in for the night. We knew we needed to stay alert because of the wild animals around. As we walked back to the camp, we walked slowly, talking softly and looking around for buffalo or elephants. We stopped at the water tap, which is about three feet high and eight inches square, to wash our hands.*

*Then, halfway back to camp, one of the old male buffalos walked out from the trees and stood about 10 feet in front of us in the clearing. We stopped and stood still. Then, without any provocation, it turned and started for us!*

*Kim was in front of me, as she had the flashlight. Her*

*instinctive response was to run, but she tripped and fell just as the buffalo was about to reach her. She thought she was surely on the way to heaven at that point, but she had the presence of mind to roll out of the buffalo's path so she wouldn't be trampled.*

*With Kim down, I became the target! I started backing up slowly with the angry buffalo keeping step with me just two feet away.*

*By God's grace I made it back to the water tap—for what little protection it would offer. My only plan was to do my best to keep it between me and the huge, horned head of the buffalo as he started chasing me around it, first one way then the other.*

*Then suddenly he stopped and threw his head around the tap, attempting to gore me. I let out a mighty scream as I was sure this was it for me, but by God's grace the tip of his horn had been broken off and fell just short of my leg.*

*After that he stopped, and we just stood, one on each side of the water tap, staring into each other's eyes. He was so close I could feel his breath.*

*The McCloys heard me scream and came out of their tents to see what was happening. They and Kim stood watching in horror and praying earnestly for my safety.*

*As for myself, I began pleading, "God help me!" over and over. I wasn't praying for deliverance because I knew my death was inevitable. I was just asking God to help me through the terrifying and painful experience it would be.*

*After a couple of minutes, however, the buffalo turned and walked away. At first I just stood there—stunned. Then I slowly began to stumble towards our camp. The others lovingly rushed to help me.*

*When I reached the camp, I was physically shaking and breathing heavily as my body, mind, and emotions began reacting to the traumatic reality of what had just happened. To think that both of us were still alive was unbelievable to me!*

*As I look back at the whole incident, I see a string of miracles that God worked to spare our lives. The only injury in the attack was that Kim broke her wrist when she fell. To me, God did the impossible in an impossible situation. Very few people ever live to tell a story like this.*

Fire was another hazard of living in the bush country of Africa, especially in the dry season. Bill Warner recalled a windy day at Chironga when a grass fire jumped the Ruia River and spread so fast that it was burning chickens before they could run away. It burned the teachers' houses and reached a missionary storage house, setting off dynamite stored in it, which blew the roof off. In the midst of great anxiety over the further loss this fire could cause, Bill went out and prayed fervently that the wind would shift—and it did.

Clarence and Gladys Cedarholm had a close encounter with fire as well. They had just returned from furlough in 1966. After getting David and Lois settled into the hostel in Hatfield, they drove to Msengedzi to fill a short-term need there for a few weeks before moving to Chironga. Gladys wrote:

> *One evening after dark a Shona man appeared at the door requesting some petrol. The mission policy was not to give or sell petrol to a stranger, so he left unhappy at my response.*
>
> *Shortly after this we noticed the large storeroom adjacent to the missionary dwelling was on fire. Remembering that petrol drums were in that storeroom, Clarence quickly ran to roll them out of the building while I went to awaken John and Ruth and get them safely outside should the fire spread further.*
>
> *Upon seeing the building on fire, four-year-old John exclaimed, "Oh, we're really going to have to ask Jesus to 'hep' us." Even he knew this was a time for prayer.*
>
> *Jesus did help us. We were spared from being caught up in that fire. He also enabled Clarence to roll out the petrol drums before the fire reached them, although he about collapsed with exhaustion afterwards. This was another example of God's care and protection upon us in those early years of our missionary service.*

# Guidance

God was also faithful in answering prayers when the missionaries reached critical junctures in their lives and needed guidance as to the direction He wanted them to go. Being strongly committed to following His will, they generally bathed such situations in much prayer. Usually, God graciously showed them the path to take and confirmed it in their hearts with a real sense of peace.

Perhaps one of the most life-altering decisions encountered by some of the single missionaries involved opportunities for marriage. Sometimes these arose while preparing for the field. Others occurred as romances developed on the field or when missionaries returned home for furlough.

Pat Meador faced an especially difficult decision in this regard as she proceeded through her educational journey towards mission service. When she arrived at Moody Bible Institute for her freshman orientation week, an urgent prayer request was circulating for a student from Michigan who had had to drop out of school because of cancer. She soon learned that this was Dick Dunkeld (son of Orv and Helen Dunkeld), who had been diagnosed with Hodgkin's Disease.

While his prognosis had originally seemed quite grim, he surprisingly improved and was able to return to Moody the following year, joining Pat's sophomore class. The two were soon introduced, as Dick was a friend of Pat's roommate, who was also from Michigan. Pat described their initial relationship:

> *As I got to know Dick, my only interest was to glean all I could about life as an MK growing up on the mission field. He quickly shattered the mostly negative stereotypes I had of such kids being resentful and maladjusted. He not only seemed very well-adjusted, but he also loved Zimbabwe, which he considered his real home, and wanted to return as a missionary.*

Despite Pat's initial intentions their relationship grew. With Dick doing well through another year, the doctors dared to hope that they had caught and treated the cancer in time to effect a cure.

By the end of their senior year Dick and Pat were engaged.

Their plans for marriage reached a real crisis the following fall, however, as Dick's Hodgkin's Disease returned. By this time Dick was in business school in Michigan, and Pat was studying at the University of Kansas. She described this difficult time and how God ministered to her:

> *Somehow I was able to continue studying enough to keep my grades up. What I remember most about that year, however, was the agony—longing to be more closely involved with what was happening with Dick, questioning whether we should continue our plans, and wondering what the future held.*
>
> *Then, one unforgettable spring day I was sitting in the Student Union building on campus deep in prayer. Suddenly I changed my plea from "Lord, please show me if you don't want me to marry Dick," to "Lord, I give him up and will only continue if You clearly say to go ahead."*
>
> *When I truly gave up my plans and dreams, that "peace . . . that passeth all understanding" (Philippians 4:7; KJV) absolutely flooded my heart. I walked out with a lighter step than I could possibly have imagined an hour before. I knew without a doubt that God had given me the green light and that He would take care of me whatever came.*

Soon Dick began to improve again. He finished his business school course, and on August 27, 1966, he and Pat were married.

The following year they attended TEAM Candidate School with the desire to go to Zimbabwe as missionaries. Contrary to all logical expectations, Dr. Kaarsgard gave his medical approval for their acceptance. This was largely because of the fact that Dick already knew the language and culture of the Shona people and, in fact, considered Zimbabwe "home." In addition, the field desperately needed his accounting abilities in their plan to centralize their book-keeping system.

Pat graduated from her studies in January 1968. That spring they began deputation, and on December 7th they flew to Africa. In the Lord's perfect timing Dick was able to complete the basic set-up of the new bookkeeping system before his condition worsened once more. After just two years on the field, they sadly returned to the United States. This time, in spite of their access to more advanced treatment possibilities, nothing seemed to help.

Fifteen months later Dick's doctor asked if they would like to return to Zimbabwe. Having totally given up all hope of that possibility, they were stunned! Then they learned that back on the field Dick's parents had been urging the TEAM leadership to allow Dick to die "at home," which for him was Zimbabwe.

TEAM was willing to do this on the condition that Pat would remain in Zimbabwe as a missionary after Dick's death. That was the only way they could justify the expense of sending them back to the field. Pat, who had been wondering what the Lord wanted her to do after Dick's passing, testified:

*There was no doubt at all in my mind what the Lord was saying in answer to my question. The door couldn't be open any wider; I just had to walk through it.*

Dick, Pat, and Dick's sister, Lois, all flew to Zimbabwe in early February 1972, moving in with Orv and Helen at Chironga. While Dick was too weak to do much of anything, he enjoyed visiting with the many Shona people and missionaries who came to see him. Then, late in March, on Palm Sunday, God chose to take Dick from his earthly "home" to his heavenly home.

A widow at 27, Pat was nurtured and supported by her fellow-missionaries as she moved to the Karanda station to continue her missionary service there. She began teaching English and Bible at the nursing school and serving as the hospital secretary. Soon she also became dorm "mom" to the female nursing students.

God's plans for her were not complete yet, however. During her first furlough He brought another man and another decision into her life. Soon God once again gave her peace in becoming Mrs. Dennis Christensen. While she never returned to Zimbabwe, she remained a TEAMmate, joining Dennis on the Netherland Antilles field.

Other missionaries had the opportunity for marriage arise while they were on the field. When proposals came from fellow-missionaries or individuals planning to join TEAM's work in Zimbabwe, the decision process was less complicated, as it did not involve changing one's envisioned course of missionary service. Nevertheless, being sure of God's will before entering these unions was just as important.

John Wolfe was a South African working in Zimbabwe who had become acquainted with the work of the TEAM missionaries in the Zambezi Valley and was very interested in becoming a part of it. At the same time he also became fond of a certain single missionary named Betty Mason, who was serving at Msengedzi. As they prayed about getting married, Betty reported, "The Lord gave me a greater peace and assurance that this was His will than even my call to be a missionary." They were married on December 11, 1954, and served the Lord together in Zimbabwe for 25 years.

When getting married meant leaving missionary service in Zimbabwe, the decision was generally more difficult, and those involved wanted to be very sure of God's leading. Bev Nelson was one of those individuals. From the time she was nine years old, she wanted to work in a mission hospital in Africa. As she set her course in that direction, God led her to Karanda Hospital in Zimbabwe. Here she felt her dream was finally being fulfilled.

Just a few years later, however, she received a proposal from Stan Line, a TEAM missionary serving in Columbia. The two had met at Candidate School, and during those three weeks they became what Bev thought was "just friends." Bev admired him, but he wasn't headed for Africa, which had always been her dream.

Now she had a huge decision to make, and she wasn't sure at all what God's will for her was. She wrote of her struggle and how God graciously guided her:

> *My supporters were people who had known me all my life. They knew I wanted to be missionary in Africa and had followed my preparations for this through the years. If I were to leave to get married, how would that affect them? Was their support because of an interest in Africa? Would I be letting them down? How could I know that this whole thing wasn't a temptation of the flesh?*
>
> *TEAM didn't have a medical ministry in Colombia, nor were plans for such feasible. Was I now to put those years of*

*training on the shelf? Though we had corresponded for these three years, how could I really be confident that I knew Stan? Our letters hadn't been with that purpose in view.*

*Had I been on the outside advising someone in this situation, I would have reacted just as some did to me: "How can you even think of it?" Others, who knew us both, gave me strong counsel to accept the proposal and transfer mission fields.*

*But it was MY life and future in question, and the decision couldn't be made by others. I needed to get away where I could spend much time in prayer and the Word, and God provided the perfect place for me. Rusty and Jo Sherwood were going on vacation and needed someone to take over the clinic at Rusambo.*

*What a haven that proved to be for me! It was one of the most wonderful times with the Lord that I've had. His presence and direction were so real. I left Rusambo without a doubt in my mind—nor has there ever been in these 35 years since I became Mrs. Stan Line.*

*I've used all of my nurse's training here right from the beginning, not in a mission hospital but as it fit around responsibilities of the home. After our children left for college in the States, I began doing volunteer nursing at a cardiology hospital and am now in my 14th year there. It's not a mission hospital, but it's my mission field.*

Diane Powell had a similar decision to make, but hers came when she returned home after her first full term. Her experience living on the Karanda Mission Station and being a part of the TEAM Zimbabwe family was nothing but wonderful. Nevertheless, as a medical technologist, she found herself professionally bored with the limited lab work possible in such an isolated mission hospital. Branching off into youth work was much more satisfying, but her weakness in the Shona language kept her from being able to have anything but superficial conversations with the kids. She had to rely on national helpers to do most of the discipling, which was also frustrating.

In addition, she struggled with her singleness. As her furlough approached, she began praying that if God had a husband for her, He would prepare the way before her, but if He didn't, that He would give her contentment in being single.

A month before leaving Zimbabwe, Diane was astonished to receive a very thick letter from a pastor in Iron Mountain, MI, who had recently lost his wife to cancer. Unbeknown to her, Diane's best friend from high school had given him her name and a recent prayer letter of hers.

As she returned to the States and her relationship with this man developed over the next months, she faced a real struggle. Had God truly answered her prayer and "gone before her," or was Satan using her "weakness" to keep her from fulfilling God's will for her in Zimbabwe?

In the end she put her trust in the loving nature of her heavenly Father and accepted that He had truly orchestrated their meeting— just as she had asked Him. With that confidence, on July 9, 1977, she became Mrs. Tom Hawkins—a pastor's wife and instant mother to two young girls.

God knew what lay ahead for Diane and the loving support she would need at her side as the unresolved issues of an abusive childhood could no longer remain submerged. Today she and her husband have an international ministry to adults who were severely abused as children. This became God's new "mission field" for Diane. While she never returned to service in Zimbabwe, she left a big part of her heart there and thanks God for the limited years she was able to serve Him there—and the opportunity to write this book.

While in each of these cases God led the missionaries forward into marriage, this was not always the case. For some individuals He clearly indicated that this was not the direction in which He wanted them to proceed. Usually these committed missionaries obediently complied with His will.

God's guidance was needed for other situations that arose along the course of missionary service too. Mary Danielson faced this when she returned to the States with Muriel after Rudy had died. Many thought that she should not return to the field as a single mother with a four-year-old daughter. Mary was troubled by that advice, however, as God had called her to be a missionary, and in her mind that was not dependent on being married.

A group of women at Wheaton Bible Church agreed to pray with her for guidance in this matter. As they prayed together, they were all convinced that God wanted her back on the field. With this renewed assurance Mary wrote to the mission, asking if they would consider sending out a single missionary with a small child. Dr. T.J. Bach quickly responded, informing her that everyone at mission headquarters was praying that she would go back, as the need for teachers in Zimbabwe was so great.

Once she was back on the field, she needed the Lord's guidance again. To be back among her dear Shona friends at Msengedzi and living in the house that Rudy had built was a real joy. She quickly recognized, however, that the needs there could be readily filled by the additional missionaries God had brought to the field, whereas teachers were definitely needed for the advanced students attending school on the mountain station of Mavuradonha.

While reading her daily devotions one morning, Mary came to Haggai 1:7-8 [KJV], which spoke to her heart: *"'Consider your ways, Go up to the mountain, and bring wood, and build the house; . . . and I will be glorified,' saith the Lord."*

A house at Mavuradonha had been partly built but still needed doors and windows. To Mary, God's guidance was clear, and she and Muriel joyfully moved to Mavuradonha. For the next 10 years Mary taught Bible and English to hundreds of students from the surrounding area who attended school there.

Bud and Lolly Fritz faced a critical situation that needed God's guidance as they neared the end of their third furlough. The war of independence had begun in Zimbabwe, and the field chairman sent a telegram to inform them that if they brought their youngest son back to the field, he would have to go into the army for three years before being eligible to return to the States for college.

Suddenly they needed the Lord's guidance in a major way! Did He want them to return to the field anyway, or should they remain in the States for another year in order to get both of their sons into college before returning? Bud wrote:

*God answered by reminding me that Samuel had two sons who disobeyed the Lord and did not follow in the ways of their father. Eli also had two sons who rejected the Lord because of Eli's unfaithfulness in teaching them. I believe that God was leading us to remain in the States and complete the training of our sons before we ventured out to the foreign field again.*

The Fritzes ended up transferring to TEAM's Trinidad field and serving several years there. Then they returned to the United States, and Bud became the director of Leadership in Training (LIT) on special assignment from TEAM.

After a difficult first term on the field, Dr. Dan and Julie Stephens needed clear direction from the Lord and peace in their hearts about returning to Zimbabwe after their first furlough. Dan wrote:

*God met all of our support needs, provided for all the projects I had dreamed of doing at Karanda, and supplied all the equipment I had wanted. The furlough time had been wonderful, but the Lord assured us that He wanted us back on the field. We went.*

Marian Wilterdink needed guidance from the Lord regarding the time to make her final departure from Zimbabwe, the country in which she served for 51 years. She was so devoted to teaching the Bible to the schoolchildren there, as God had clearly called her to do, that she had returned to carry on in this role even after her official retirement from TEAM.

She described how God answered her prayer:

*At the end of 2002, conditions in the country and in the retirement home where I lived continued to deteriorate, causing such stress. So I prayed, seeking the Lord's will as to whether I should stay there or return to the States. My main concern was whether my leaving would mean that my students would no longer have a Christian Bible teacher.*

*Then I was reminded of the Dorothea Mission, which had five Christian nationals who taught thousands of students each day in the heavily populated townships. Without being given a reason, they had been told they must stop teaching the Bible in the townships in which they had* been working. So I asked them if they would be interested in taking over my Bible classes in the five schools in which I taught.

They excitedly responded that this was an answer to their prayers too. So I took them to the schools and introduced them to the headmasters, who were thrilled to know that their students would still be taught the Bible after I left—and so was I.

## Miraculous Answers

Sometimes the answers to prayer that God gave were simply miraculous. The odds that a certain event would happen at precisely the needed time were far too great to attribute it to happenstance or natural occurrence. Dave Voetmann reported such an incident when he and a group of men were hunting near Hunyani. They wanted an elephant to provide meat for an Evangelical Church Bible Conference. He wrote:

> . . . I flew [some of the Karanda men] to Hunyani where we joined George Dee, Ray Finsaas, and some Shona trackers for the hunt. It was September and still in the heat of the dry season.
>
> When we got there, we all piled into Ray's old Jeep and drove into Mozambique. Soon the Shona men found fresh elephant tracks. . . . We were all so excited that we took off running with only one water canteen and a few oranges in our pockets. . . . We trailed the elephants all afternoon until late in the evening when we finally began hearing them up ahead crunching brush as they ate and moved along.
>
> By this time only George and I were keeping up with the fast-moving trackers. They were crumbling leaves and letting them drift to indicate the wind direction. George and I followed closely as we circled around the herd to get downwind from them, creeping closer and closer. We could now clearly hear their stomachs rumbling, their snorting, and the cracking of brush as they moved and broke off branches to eat.

*Then we began seeing black patches of hide through the trees. Our thoughts were racing. What way would they run when we shot? What protection was there for us if they charged?*

*As we approached to a final position, we used a 6-foot high anthill as cover. We took aim, and at the count of three we both shot at the same elephant. With adrenalin pumping and our heart in our throats, we heard the most horrendous noise as the entire herd trumpeted and stampeded, leaving a path of broken trees 30 feet wide through the brush.*

*When all quieted down, we approached to claim our prize. By this time it was late in the evening, and slowly the others in the party caught up and joined us. It was too late to return to the jeep, so we built a fire, roasted some elephant meat, and bedded down to spend the night there beside the elephant. With the glowing eyes of wild animals visible around us and the almost constant succession of hyenas and other creatures making noises in the brush, some of us got very little sleep.*

*By the next morning we were all hungry and even thirstier. Having left the Landrover in such a hurry the day before, we hadn't taken any of the water from Ray's 30-gallon barrel that he had so wisely brought with us. The evening before we had come across a dead tree with a hole at ground level with water in it, so the trackers went back there to fill our only canteen before we headed back to Ray's Landrover.*

*We all loaded up with as much meat as we could possibly carry. George, in typical fashion, had the largest load, and as we trudged along in the heat of the Zambezi Valley's dry season with no water, he began to get delusionary. Believing that we were close to the Jeep, he told the rest of us to go on and leave him to find his own way out, which we refused to do.*

*With very few options available, someone said in an almost facetious, wishful manner, "Let's pray for rain." Within minutes a small cloud the size of Elijah's began forming just over us. Soon it was raining in the parched*

*Zambezi Valley in September!*

*After being revived and refreshed by the rain, we headed out through the bush again. With the incredible ability of the Shona trackers we eventually found our way back to the very spot where Ray had parked his Jeep. God had so clearly shown us His miraculous, protective, caring hand on that trip that we had a lot more than meat to share at the conference!*

Mary Danielson told of another time when God brought rain in a most unexpected manner. Many were praying about the dire water situation at Rusambo at the end of the dry season in 1973. One day the men came up from the dam and reported that they had pumped the last water remaining in it. Mary wrote:

*All that was coming through the pipe was mud and an occasional frog. We took stock of the water supply on hand in the tanks and decided that with careful rationing it might last a couple of weeks. That was for drinking and cooking but there was still the washing and bathing. An early flash storm had filled some holes in the nearby river so that was a help.*

*Then that very noon the dark clouds began to gather, and for nearly two hours the rain poured down on the Rusambo area. It came so quickly that it did not have time to soak in, so it filled the dam. We just couldn't believe our eyes. The work on raising the spillway had just been finished thirty hours before. Would it hold as the water rose . . . ? We prayed and it held. . . So praise the Lord with us for answered prayer.*

Others saw God intervene in supernatural ways when they broke down on isolated bush roads. Dick and Mary Ann McCloy described such an incident when they were driving out to Chironga for language school the very first time, pulling a trailer behind their car:

*As we drove along over the corrugated Chesa road, there was suddenly a bigger bump than usual. Dick felt a drag on the car as well, so we stopped, got out, and looked at the trailer. It had one wheel up in the air due to a broken pipe underneath that had dug into the ground.*

*As we stood there and looked at it, Dick said, "Let's pray." As we finished, a group of men came out of the bushes and helped us get the trailer back on the ground properly, and the pipe going into the round ball underneath, but there was no way to fasten it back together.*

*Just then, we saw a cloud of dust coming towards us on the road, and a big welding truck pulled to a stop. The driver welded the pipe to the ball, and went on his way into Harare. Even before we had asked, God had sent the answer on its way.*

Carl and Donna Hendrickson had a somewhat similar experience. Donna wrote:

*While living at Msengedzi with the Sherwoods, we took a weekend trip by truck to Mazarabani for meetings. The roads were dry and sandy. As we drove down a deep spruit and started up the other side, we became stuck with both front and back wheels in deep sand. Jo Sherwood and I decided to lay out our picnic lunch on the dry sandy river bed, and we all enjoyed some refreshments under the hot sun. Julie and Wes played in the sand as we pondered what to do.*

*No way could Carl and Rusty push the truck either way. We laughed and prayed and wondered what the Lord had in store for us. After a while in that lonely dry desert we heard a car coming towards us. A government employee came along with a land rover, attached his chain to our truck, and pulled us out. God always has an answer and a plan so we can rest in Him.*

## Ministry Needs

From the beginning the missionaries recognized their dependence upon God for the effectiveness of their efforts to win souls and build the Church in Zimbabwe. Ministry needs were thus a frequent focus of their prayers. At times God answered in quiet, behind-the-scenes ways: preparing hearts, directing paths, and empowering the Word that was taught. At other times His answers came in a more overt manner, resulting in an outpouring of praise for His faithfulness.

When Orla and Marguerite Blair moved from Hunyani to open a new work at Chinhoyi, they prayed for a Shona helper who could work with them and serve as a go-between in making contacts with the local people. Marguerite told how God marvelously answered this prayer along with several others:

*On our first Sunday in Chinhoyi, we went to the hospital to inquire if we could hold a service there. We were delighted when those in charge welcomed us with open arms.*

*Then, as I began giving out tracts in the hospital yard, I was so surprised when a woman looked up at me and asked, "Are you Mrs. Blair?" It was Mrs. Kakunguwo! Her husband, Frank, had been involved with the boarding school on the Mavuradonha station before coming to work in Chinhoyi, so they were familiar with the TEAM missionaries and their work.*

*Meanwhile Orla was circulating in the men's ward, and there he met Mr. Kakunguwo. What a delight it was to connect with this fine couple! God was answering our prayers! Not only did we have services for both the men and the women in the hospital that Sunday, but we also found a lovely Shona couple to help us with the work in Chinhoyi.*

*As we visited with the Kakunguwos, we learned that they had been unable to find a place in Chinhoyi where they could live together. As a result, Mrs. Kakunguwo was living in the single women's quarters and her husband in the single men's quarters.*

*We joined them in praying about this and saw God answer another prayer, giving them a nice little house in a suburb. Orla helped move their meager belongings into this little house. Then they knelt at a chair and thanked the Lord for this provision.*

*At the side of their house I started leading women's meetings. The two men ministering together in the evenings in their suburb, out at the citrus estates, in the farm compounds surrounding Chinhoyi, and in outlying villages.*

*We were so thankful to the Lord for giving us such an honest and dependable co-worker. He always had a radiant smile and a vibrant testimony and was so energetic in the work of the Lord.*

*Eventually Frank Kakunguwo came to Orla expressing his desire to enter full-time service for the Lord. We helped sponsor him and his wife at our Evangelical Bible School at Kapfundi. Then, upon graduation, he became the pastor of the Evangelical Church in Chinhoyi. Some years later he was called to be the chairman of all TEAM's churches in Zimbabwe. What a servant of God he was! He served in that capacity for some years and then became the chaplain at the Mavuradonha boarding school where he eventually died a martyr's death.*

Mary Danielson's letters reveal some of the answers to prayer she experienced in the ministries in which she was involved as well as her deep appreciation for her prayer supporters back in the homeland. In a letter written in February 1956, she reported on recently answered prayers at the Mavuradonha boarding school where she was teaching:

*As we labor out here and the burden seems so great at times, we have that confidence that there are many of you in the homeland who are sharing the burden in prayer with us. It seems like the beginning of this school year brought us no end of troubles in getting the necessary arrangements made for teachers and pupils alike. One by one the problems were solved, and now less than a month after the start of the school year, everything seems to be running smoothly, and the Lord is blessing the work with souls being saved.*

Later, when she was leading the Evangelical Homecraft School at Rusambo, Mary shared another specific answer to prayer regarding an urgent staffing need:

*It was the opening day of school, and no teacher [was] available for the first-year class. There were thirty-five pupils and only a student from last year to help carry on the work. It looked discouraging, but that first night when I was sitting contemplating how we could possibly manage, there was a knock at the door, and there stood one of my former teachers. She had finally received my letter, asking if she would consider coming back. She answered but I did not receive [her letter]. So with no word from me she got on the bus and train and bus again and after three days reached here. She felt compelled to come and see if I still needed help. So God answered your prayers and mine. . .*

Throughout the years, staff needs have often been a matter of prayer on the field. With many short-term doctors and other medical staff helping to meet the needs at Karanda Hospital, the staff situation there fluctuated frequently. In a prayer letter Kiersten Hutchinson shared how God answered prayer for additional staff there at a time when she was feeling quite stretched:

*Many of you may have sensed how overwhelming the situation out here can be. Part of me was worried that I might not be able to carry the load. Yet God is always faithful. He has provided not one, but two, Christian national doctors. That brings us to five practitioners [a rare occurrence]!! This is remarkable considering that three local hospitals have no doctors at all!*

*The blessing has been a lighter call schedule and a more reasonable workload. The challenge is that the patient load seems to be increasing as well! We did 44 C-sections last month compared to 100 for all of last year.*

Nancy Everswick once found herself in need of a mature teacher to help in her growing Sunday school. She felt that all of the ladies currently in the church were baby Christians and needed to hear the pastor's sermons. God answered her prayers by sending a new couple to the fellowship who were mature believers. The wife was even an experienced Sunday school teacher.

Donna Kahlstorf wrote a story entitled "Reading by Heart,"

telling how in answer to prayer God supplied a helper to meet the need of a local village woman in the Chinhoyi area:

*I supervise [some Bible school students teaching] a little Sunday school that meets under a tree with sacking for pews. Most of the members of the class are boys and girls, but one day an older woman came. She had a baby on her back, [her face was scarred, her clothes were plain,] but Mai James came every week. She often said, "If I could only read. Can you teach me to read?" I told her of a reading class at the church, but she could not attend because of her work.*

*Several weeks later a quiet little man, Baba Wilson, began coming regularly. He sat apart from the women— Shona style. He seemed to blend in with the dry grass surrounding the stump on which he sat. He was a [quaint] fellow with a large growth on his forehead. But his face was a sunburst of smile wrinkles.*

*One day after class he was upset. He came to me and said, "What was the word today? Where was it found in the Bible? What did it say?" [The student teacher] had reviewed several lessons but had omitted the memory verses. When I finally realized what he wanted, I gave him a memory verse and he was happy. He pulled out a little note-book and slowly printed each word. Curious, I asked him, "Why were you so eager to get a verse today, and why are you writing it in your book?"*

*He explained, "Mai James wanted with all her heart to learn to read, and I wanted to help her, but I had no text-book. I have been making my own book for her by copying the verse each week. I help her learn it very well by heart. Then I teach her the words. She can read some of it well."*

*I thought to myself, "She only thinks she can read. She is only reciting what she has memorized. I will test her. I pointed at different words in her book—she read them! She had learned to read the words and memorize all the verses in a few weeks.*

*This little man with the baggy pants and unusual bump on his head had the heart to teach her. He couldn't fail using the greatest textbook in the world and the Master Teacher as his guide.*

*Teachers should be trained, pupils should be clever, and textbooks should be colorful; but God can use the crude, the colorless and the simple for His glory.*

Dr. Bill Warner described an answer to prayer that deeply impacted him as Word of Life Publications (WLP), TEAM's literature ministry, was trying to get Scripture lessons into the public schools:

*I'll never forget how God answered prayer in our early days of WLP. While traveling alone on a train to the Evangelical Fellowship of Zimbabwe board meeting in Bulawayo, I had had the idea of producing Scripture readers for the mandatory Religious Education classes in the public schools.*

*When I returned, we worked hard to produce our first Shona Scripture reader in a very short time. I then traveled across the country promoting it to headmasters, only to return to Harare and learn that all book orders for government schools would be handled by Textbook Sales (TS).*

*That evening was our weekly TEAM Hatfield staff prayer meeting. I told Joyce to go ahead of me as I contemplated whether I should call TS right away. As I looked to the Lord for guidance, I felt I was to wait on Him, so I went on to the meeting myself. When I arrived, I explained the situation to the group, and we went to prayer.*

*After a short time the phone rang. A gentleman asked to talk to someone with WLP. I took the phone and found myself talking to TS, who had heard from headmasters around the country wanting the Scripture readers! God had answered our prayers! When we received our first government check, I rejoiced in their support of Christian publishing.*

In recent years Dick and Mary Ann McCloy saw God answer a special prayer of theirs as they worked in the public schools in the Harare area. They had been showing Bible drama videos in the

Religious Education classes, but with the AIDS crisis sweeping the country, they bravely requested permission to show a video entitled "Sex Has a Price Tag." They wanted to show it to the entire Marlborough School and prayed earnestly that God would work this out.

Mary Ann described what happened:

*By the time we finished showing the weekly Scripture Union Bible drama, the headmaster had left for the day. We were informed that he would let us know the following morning if we could show the video on the consequences of premarital sex. In faith we left the black plastic curtains in place because they take a long time to put up when both sides of the hall are all glass!*

*When we arrived the next morning, the office staff told us, "This is World Teachers' Day, but the Ministry of Education has announced that the teachers must teach—not have a holiday. So we have decided that you can show your video—and that will give them their holiday!*

*We showed the video to all the girls before break and to all the boys after! Many, many of them made commitments to keep sex for marriage and to maintain faithfulness in marriage. Thank you, Lord!*

Mary Ann also shared how God answered her prayers in another ministry opportunity she had:

*While Lynne Hawkins was on home assignment, I was privileged to take over her two ladies' Bible studies. These two groups were about as different from each other as night and day. The morning group consisted of young mothers from Southerton, most of whom were related to each other. The afternoon group was primarily made up of older ladies from the Marlborough side of town. Most of them had grown children and several were widows.*

*I prayed, "Lord, these groups are in such different stages of life with totally different needs. You know their needs. Please give me the illustrations and examples that will help make the Scripture practical to each of them."*

*By the end of the day I would always be amazed at how the discussion of the same Bible passage had gone in two utterly different ways in the two groups. God answered prayer and met their needs and mine too!!*

Don Hoyt shared a dramatic answer to prayer that the Mavuradonha High School staff experienced during some very troubled days. When he and Lynn returned to assume teaching positions there in 1968, the atmosphere was very different than it had been when they taught there a few years earlier. Don wrote:

*Days were filled with tension as the war for independence was escalating in the area. The students found themselves caught between their loyalties to their people and their need and appreciation of the missionaries.*

*At that time the insurgents were kidnapping entire student bodies and taking them to Mozambique for training. The students anticipated this possibility occurring during the night from their dormitories, but no kidnapping occurred at Mavuradonha. The students responded, however, with food strikes and discourtesy in the classroom, refusing to show the usual respect when their teachers came into the classroom, etc.*

When Reg Austin went on furlough, Don became principal of the school. This was a very stretching year for him. In the midst of all the tensions he regretfully had to expel some students for cheating.

He continued describing the situation:

*The student body was so out of sorts, and the underpinnings of unrest were so prevalent. Humanly speaking, I felt totally inadequate to address the situation. All of the staff were concerned and praying for a breakthrough.*

*Then out of the blue one day we received a radio message from TEAM headquarters in Harare informing us that a Gospel team of five students from Taylor University was available for ministry in Zimbabwe. They were supposed to go to South Africa but had been refused entrance because one of the team was Congolese and another Kenyan. Headquarters wondered if Mavuradonha could use them for a week-end. We agreed to let them come, and Dave Voetmann flew them out.*

*They arrived on Friday afternoon and immediately went down to the dining hall and ate with the students, establishing instant rapport with them. It was so beautiful to see. Saturday morning they played soccer with the boys, and the rapport continued to grow.*

*Saturday night they had a meeting, and the team sang and gave their testimonies. Sunday morning Philip Muinde from Kenya shared his testimony of growing up in Kenya and going to a mission school. He was extremely open and frank about how he was one person when he was on the mission compound and another person when he was off of it. As he described this hypocrisy in his life and how the Lord had to deal with it, he hit the students right where they were.*

*When he finished speaking, he gave an invitation for those who wanted to get real with God. I sat there saying to myself, "Philip, this isn't going to work. These kids are too hard."*

*Then, to my amazement, someone got up and joined Philip at the front, then another and another, and eventually almost the whole student body went forward. I was emotionally overwhelmed and deeply convicted about my own lack of faith.*

*As a result of that service virtually all the students formed themselves into Bible study groups. As Lynn and I walked down to the school early in the mornings, we would see groups of students studying under the trees or by the rocks. The dramatic change that occurred lasted for the rest of the year, and many strong Christian leaders came out of those classes.*

Doug and Nancy Everswick told of how God answered their prayers in supplying a house for them as they were preparing to begin ministry in the Mvurwi area. When they had initially checked on what was available, they were told that nothing suitable was currently on the market.

They continued to pray about this, and one day while in Harare they "happened" to speak with someone about this need. She told them of a woman who was only going to be in the country for a week and had come for the purpose of selling a piece of property in Mvurwi with a house on it. They met with her the next day in Mvurwi and discovered that the house was perfect. God provided just what they needed, and the property later turned out to be ideal for building a church on as well.

Training national church leaders to reach their own people was one of the major goals of the missionaries virtually from the beginning of their work in Zimbabwe. Many answers to prayer occurred as God brought a formal Bible school into being and nurtured it into a fully accredited theological college with a predominantly Shona staff.

While several missionaries held short-term Bible schools at Msengedzi and Rusambo, the theological college that exists today had its roots in a group of six students Norman Everswick began teaching on the Mavuradonha Mission Station in 1953. Thelma Everswick wrote:

*These men found it difficult even to read at first, but they improved as they read the Scriptures daily. In the end they became great witnesses for the Lord.*

One of the missionaries on the station (possibly Mary Danielson) shared the excitement they felt when these students finished their yearlong course of studies:

*The first students of our Bible school have completed their [initial] course of study. They have been here a year. Now they leave for their appointed places of [pastoral internship]. Those of you who have been praying for them will rejoice with us for their earnestness and zeal. These men have caught something of the preciousness of the Word of God, and their hearts have been kindled aflame with a passion for the lost. They are [few] in number, but they are a beginning in the filling of our great need of evangelists. May*

*God be pleased to use them in a great way in the days ahead.*

The writer also revealed the vision that existed to carry this ministry forward and the recognition of the prime importance of prayer to enable this:

*In the future a Bible training school will be necessary, but between now and then there is need for much prayer. . . . We must look to God for the future to provide our every need.*

God honored those prayers as the next year Moody Bible Institute gave $4,000.00 to build a classroom building and ten thatched huts and kitchens for families on the new station of Kapfundi. This enabled the men's wives and families to join them, and the wives could also be taught by some of the missionary ladies. Construction was completed, and the fledgling Evangelical Bible School moved to its new facilities in 1955.

Marie Schober revealed how the school's programs had expanded by 1958:

*During the past year three men completed the evangelist's course (two years of classroom instruction and one year of internship). Several women have completed one year's Bible training. Trained evangelists are few in number, but their value to the Lord has been strengthened by their Bible school background.*

*Three-month Bible courses are being added on the local level to train villagers as lay evangelists, so sorely needed in these early days of the indigenous church.*

*The Light of Life correspondence course on the Gospel of John, offered in the Shona language and English, has a large enrollment of over 4,000 students. The course on the Book of Acts is being translated for those who finish the course on John.*

The Light of Life correspondence course ministry actually predated the Bible school. Norman Everswick had initiated it at Mavuradonha in 1951, translating lessons that Dick Hillis had been using in India. In 1958, this ministry was also moved to Kapfundi with Marian Wilterdink taking over its leadership. It provided the means for men and women who were unable to come for formal classes to study the Bible as well. New courses were continually added.

These Bible lessons, available in English and Shona, were able to penetrate into many areas where missionaries and local evangelists were scarce. They even made their way into Mozambique and Malawi. Russ Jackson and Chuck Pruitt introduced them to prisoners they visited in the Harare area and enrolled many students among the inmates there. Over the years tens of thousands of individuals were enrolled with a large percentage accepting Christ as Savior. This extremely fruitful ministry became an official extension of the Bible school in the early sixties when Donna Hendrickson took over leadership from Lydia Eichner.

God continued to bless the Bible school, sending more and more students eager to be taught the Word. In 1960, a three-year English Bible course was established for students with a Standard 6 or higher education. In 1965, a three-year Christian Education course for female students was started with the objective of training them to minister to Shona women and children.

Each of these courses placed a strong emphasis on practical experience. Students were given at least two ministry assignments every week. They would be observed by a staff member and given feedback on ways to improve their effectiveness.

By 1965, the staff realized that the rural setting in which the Bible school was currently located was not adequately preparing men for the growing number of churches being established in urban settings. Therefore, the decision was made to build an entirely new campus in Chinhoyi, an urban community serving a large farming district.

Roy Eichner, who was serving as principal at that time, shared some of the many prayers that God answered in the process of this immense undertaking:

*When the decision was approved by the field to move the Bible school from Kapfundi to Chinhoyi, many missionaries gave a generous portion of their tithe to launch the project. After that the few missionaries on the Bible school staff were responsible to raise the rest of the funds needed, a challenge that loomed like a mountain before us.*

*By faith we moved forward and were able to obtain a choice piece of land in Chinhoyi. The initial funds received from the missionaries were sufficient for us to start the building process as well, so we immediately began working on the plans. Reg Austin, who had had some architectural drawing experience, drew a site plan with every building we envisioned needing. Then he drew plans for each building.*

*Our next task was to find the right man to supervise the construction process. The committee overseeing the project requested the Field Council to release a particular mission-ary couple to do this. We had every confidence they could carry this responsibility very well. However, because of a shortage of staff on the field, our request to use this couple or, in fact, any other missionaries could not be granted.*

*This was a major disappointment, as our small Bible school staff could not possibly continue the daily schedule of teaching at Kapfundi if any of us had to oversee the build-ing in Chinhoyi. Our only option was to increase our prayers that God would somehow supply this need.*

*We were somewhat encouraged when we received a message from our field chairman, Orla Blair, telling us that he had someone to consider for this position and that this individual was willing to come to Kapfundi to meet with us the following Saturday. Since this was not a missionary, our staff met to decide what we could offer this man for a salary. This was a cost on which we had not planned. We wanted to offer a fair salary, but in the end we realized what we could pay him was much less than he could get anywhere else. We looked forward to meeting him with mixed emotions—joy that he would consider the job but fear that he would reject it because of the low salary.*

*Saturday arrived, and we were thrilled when Orla intro-duced us to George Till (brother of Cecyl), and informed us of his many years of experience in construction. As we shared our vision with him and showed him our plan, we sensed that he was as excited about the project as we were.*

*This made me dread all the more telling him what we would be able to pay him. When the moment came, I took a deep breath and revealed that figure. To our great surprise George replied, "Roy, if you are going to force me to take a salary, I won't do the work. I'm doing this for God!"*

*Then he went on to explain that he had been born to missionary parents and had accepted the Lord as his Savior at an early age. In his teens, however, he turned from the Lord, and only as he neared retirement did he come back to Him—at quite a personal price. Now he was looking to the Lord to use him. "I can't preach or teach," he said, "but I have a lifetime of experience in construction. I would be honored if God could use me to build this Bible school campus."*

*We were overwhelmed by this offer. Certainly God had answered our prayers and supplied the man He desired to use for our project in His own time and way.*

*As George brought together a construction crew and they started building, we made a commitment to Field Council that we would never go into debt with this project. Whenever the funds ran out, we would stop building. After the initial gifts from the missionaries were exhausted, we kept praying for God to supply the finances for one building after another.*

*God faithfully answered our prayers again and again, always supplying what we needed. He usually did it one building at a time, however, so our faith would continue to be exercised and grow through the whole experience.*

*Once George informed us that he was almost finished with a building and would soon be ready to start on the next one—but we had no more money. With only a few days of work remaining for the builders, we figured that if the funds did not arrive by Wednesday at 5 p.m., we would have to give them notice. As we had done all along, we shared the need for prayer with the students. We were all learning valuable lessons in faith together.*

*Monday came, and we eagerly checked the mail for some news of funds arriving. There was nothing. On*

*Tuesday it was the same. We all held our breath as we picked up the mail bag on Wednesday morning, but still it held no news of funds.*

*Later that day someone suggested that we make a second check on incoming mail at 4 p.m., which we had never done before. At the very last minute God honored our faith! There was a letter from headquarters informing us that a substantial gift had come in, and it would, in fact, cover the cost of the most expensive building on campus, the auditorium. What praises ascended to heaven from our staff, students, and work crew!!!*

In just over two years, 21 buildings were erected on the campus entirely debt-free. Each of them was viewed as a miracle of God coming into reality in response to the prayers of His children.

As the new site neared completion, the Bible school staff had another decision to make. What was the best timing for making the physical move from Kapfundi to Chinhoyi? Roy continued:

*Many things had to be taken into consideration. Should we move during the November to January school holiday and try to get settled in before the new school year began? Should we move earlier to avoid the potential problems of the rainy season, which usually started in October? Should we wait longer so that all the finishing details in the staff dwellings would also be completed? After considerable debate and prayer, we decided to move during the school holiday.*

With much planning and teamwork the massive move of staff and school took place. As the missionaries settled into their new homes, the carpenters often served as their alarm clocks as they arrived to complete various finishing details.

During this time another specific prayer request was brought to the Lord. Roy explained:

*Though all of the buildings had been internally wired for electricity, we lacked the outdoor cable, which had to be shipped from South Africa and was hard to find. We had received no promised or anticipated date of delivery, but its arrival became a specific matter of prayer, especially in our Wednesday evening prayer meetings. The older MKs were home from the hostel for the holiday and joined the younger ones in praying not only that the cable would arrive soon but that, if it was God's will, they could have electricity by Christmas.*

*In the meantime George Till and Bud Fritz made sure that everything was ready so the cable could be installed in the shortest amount of time when it arrived. The expectations were high for all of us but especially for the MKs. In faith that God would answer their prayers, the various families put up their Christmas trees with lights and all.*

*Finally the cable arrived, and it was "all hands on deck" to get it on the poles and connected to the houses. The countdown to Christmas was getting closer by the day. On Christmas Eve morning the men were finally ready to call the inspector to check it out and pull the switch. By God's grace it passed inspection, and by supper time on Christmas Eve we had electricity!*

*The lights on the Christmas trees shone with special significance that year, reminding us all of God's delight in not only supplying needs but also giving special gifts to His children when they pray. What a blessing this was for all, but especially the MKs!*

In April 13, 1968, the new facility was dedicated at an official ceremony with TEAM General Director Vernon Mortenson and his wife present. Before Dr. Mortenson brought the main message, Roy Eichner acknowledged the tremendous answers to prayer the new Bible school represented and the field's vision for how God would use it:

*. . . This new campus has been the result of the prayers of Christians in [Zimbabwe] and around the world. Today we wish to publicly thank the Lord for what He has accomplished. . . .*

*While we realize that a new campus is not an end in*

*itself, we look to God to send men and women who know Jesus Christ as their personal Savior and who have a thirst for His Word to study with us that they, in turn, will leave the Evangelical Bible School as spirit-filled laymen and full-time workers zealous to do the will of God, to reach others for Christ, and to establish strong local churches. . . .*

Then, after Dr. Mortenson spoke, Norman Everswick led in prayer, again giving glory to God for His role in bringing this new Bible school campus into being:

*We thank Thee, O God, for Thy faithfulness. . . . as we bow on this occasion and witness all that has been done. We see these beautiful buildings and this campus that has been built and prepared, and how glad we are, Lord Jesus, that we can recognize Thee in all of it. Truly, Lord, Thou hast made these things. Thou art the giver of every good and perfect gift. Thou hast done what humanly could not be done but which has been done because of dependence upon Thee with our hearts in prayer and thanksgiving even on this grand occasion. . . .*

In 1976, another milestone occurred for what was now being called the Evangelical Bible College (to distinguish it as being on a higher level than a secondary school). As Carl Hendrickson, who was serving as principal, was facing an upcoming furlough, the staff and board of the school felt the time had come to train nationals to take over its leadership. Edgar Bumhira, a teacher who was also serving as vice principal at that time, was the person they felt God was leading them to prepare for this role. Carl continued mentoring and training him with this in mind, and when Carl left on furlough, Mr. Bumhira became the first Shona principal of the Bible college. At the same time Donna Hendrickson had trained Engeline Nduna, a graduate serving as matron of the female students, to take over as office secretary.

In the late eighties the need for a national to serve as the college librarian was also recognized, and the staff began to pray for a suitable person. Ann Liddle was currently serving in this position and, with this goal in mind, began observing the students and their skills within the library. Her attention was drawn to a young man by the name of David Matsveru. When she approached him to ask about his plans after graduating, he gave her the most expected answer of a Bible college student: "Be a minister."

Ann decided to plant a seed for thought in his mind, however, and asked if he had ever considered being a librarian. When he replied that he had not, Ann challenged him to pray about this.

Several weeks later he came back and told her, "I feel that the Lord is leading me to be a librarian." Ann greatly encouraged him in this decision, impressing upon him how he could do this job as a service to the Lord and would probably have opportunities to preach too.

As the school continued to grow and draw students from as far away as Malawi and Mozambique, thoughts also emerged in the late eighties of upgrading its academic standards to be recognized and accredited by the Accrediting Council for Theological Education in Africa (A.C.T.E.A.). Dorothy Strom initiated the preliminary steps toward this goal. When her husband, Wilf, was elected as Field Chairman and they moved to Hatfield to take over this responsibility, she essentially handed the baton to Noël Liddle. Working under Mr. Isaiah Chiswiti, the principal, Noël led the process of writing an extensive Self-Evaluation Report. He described the amount of work involved:

> *The entire staff worked long, hard hours in the committee work of analyzing, evaluating, and upgrading the school administration, the curriculum, the teaching staff, student services, and physical facilities. All this was done concurrently with regular classroom and extra-curricular duties. Nobody could foresee that it would take four years to complete this work.*[2]

After more than 20 years on the lovely Chinhoyi campus, a vision developed for moving the college to Harare. Being located in the capital city would make it accessible to commuter students as well as qualified adjunct staff. Since TEAM had already moved its headquarters and hostel from the Plot to a new site in Marlborough, those vacated 15 acres with extensive buildings in place seemed like an ideal new location for the college.

When both of these proposals, the upgrading and the relocation, were presented at the annual field conference, they were unanimously approved. Once relocated and accredited, the school would take on the new name of Harare Theological College (HTC).

By this time Dr. Onesimus Ngundu, who had been both a student and a staff member of the college, had returned from receiving advanced theological studies abroad. He had graduated from Edinburgh University with an M.A. degree and from Dallas Theological Seminary with a Th.D. degree. His arrival back on campus to take over the principalship of the college with these outstanding credentials had been highly anticipated.

The physical move of staff, students, school, and library was an enormous logistical task, designated to occur under the direction of Dick McCloy over the Easter holidays of 1991. As he took on this responsibility, Dick prayed earnestly that God would superintend a smooth move. He shared some of the specific ways in which God faithfully answered his prayers:

> *To move us, most removal companies wanted Z$25,000 plus a steep percentage for insurance. The Lord led us to a company that quoted us a price of Z$15,000, and we would not need to pay insurance!*
>
> *Then, about four weeks before the scheduled move, the Liddles wanted to know if they could move the library two weeks ahead of time. I was sure the removal company would not go along with this at such late notice—but, they agreed!*
>
> *This ended up helping us in several ways. We were able to use this smaller move as a trial run to help us organize better for the main move. It also meant we would not have to worry about the library at that time. In addition, with no competing activity Ann Liddle, as college librarian, was able to assure that the entire library was transferred in proper catalogued order.*
>
> *God's hand was also evident on the day of the big move. The quotation we had received from the removal company was based on the use of three huge removal vans with their*

*trailers. In the end it took 6-8 van loads to get everything transferred, and this was done AT NO EXTRA CHARGE!!!*

*Unknown to us, the Lord had led us to one of His servants in the company who could make such a decision. This man had often visited Word of Life Bookstore to buy books by Warren Wiersbe, so he was acquainted with TEAM's ministry.*

1991 was also the year that David Matsveru graduated. He began working part-time in the HTC library while taking library science courses at the Harare Poly-Technical Institute. When he received his diploma, he took over Ann Liddle's position as librarian for the college. He also became the pastor of the Epworth Evangelical Church around this time.

God's timing was perfect, as this transfer of responsibilities took place just as Noël and Ann Liddle were seconded to the Baptist seminary in Gweru. They felt they were leaving the HTC library in very good hands and spoke highly of Mr. Matsveru's capabilities:

*David is highly professional in his work and has a great deal of ability and ambition. This has led him to study for a degree in Library Science at Botswana University.*

In January 1992, the school's Self-Evaluation Report was finally completed, and the A.C.T.E.A.'s Visitation Examination Team was invited to the campus. They spent a week examining the total functioning of the school. The Exit Report they presented to the staff indicated that accreditation at the Diploma Level had been achieved.

1n 1998, A Tutorial Research Degree Program was added to the curriculum. Dr. Onesimus Ngundu described how it works:

*The degree programme . . . seems to be one of the working models for theological education in developing countries like Zimbabwe. Students do most of the work on their own during the week and come for tutorial sessions on Thursdays.*

While the Hatfield campus served the needs of the college for many years, a decision was made in 2004 to move the college to a downtown location near the University of Zimbabwe. This was necessary because of the changing economy and mushrooming costs of maintaining an entire campus with both living and educational facilities in Hatfield. The move to the city also provided a more convenient classroom and library location for the rapidly growing tutorial research program.

In a recent letter Dr. Ngundu wrote:

*HTC has become the largest, multi-racial, degree-offering college in the country. Most of the largest, white and multi-racial churches plus three colleges in Zimbabwe are now under the leadership of HTC graduates. We see HTC as [a strategic] part of God's work in Zimbabwe. . . . HTC continues to prepare people for ministry at the Degree and Diploma levels.*

God had so faithfully answered the prayers of the entire field, probably far beyond their original intentions, in bringing into being this quality institution, which He is using to train Christian leaders for all of Zimbabwe and beyond. Only eternity will reveal the full scope of the fruit reaped for the Kingdom of God through its graduates.

This college serves as a symbolic capstone of the work God did in the largely unreached portion of Zimbabwe to which He had called scores of ordinary people to spread the Gospel and build the Church. Through their obedient service He had faithfully accomplished this goal. In a vast area once characterized almost solely by animism, a mature Church has been firmly established and placed into indigenous hands.

When Bud and Mandy Jackson made a return visit to Zimbabwe, Mandy's homeland, in December 2000, they reported on their firsthand look at the state of that Church in the midst of extreme trials. Bud, currently serving as an area representative for TEAM Canada, shared his observations, beginning with his thoughts as they descended into the Harare airport:

*From the window looking out, Zimbabwe appeared the same as always. . . . As the bush, rocky outcrops, and foot-*

*paths became ever more distinct, I was struck by the realization that I carried in my heart a mixture of great sorrow and sincere gratitude—sorrow for what I knew of the social and economic situation we would encounter once we landed and gratitude for what we knew God had been doing in the hearts and minds of our co-workers and fellow believers.*

*The next morning I sat over a typical Zimbabwe breakfast at a street-side cafe and reflected on our first few hours in Zimbabwe. Christmas was approaching, but the festive atmosphere this year was tainted and torn. The physical structures around me had deteriorated. . . . The unseen realities I knew to exist spoke more loudly, however, in the faces of the people of all races who passed to and fro, trying to make the best of a bad situation. So much around me was the same as I had remembered it; so much was different.*

*Mandy and I had approached this trip with a prayer that we might be used of God to bring encouragement to His people. We returned to Canada trusting that we had been, but we were more impressed that the predominant flow of ministry had been the other way around—all credit to the crucible and God's presence.*

*Paul wrote, "Momentary light affliction is working for us an eternal weight of glory" (2 Corinthians. 4:17 NASB). It's one thing to look back in the history of the Church and remember that the Church has been its strongest during difficult times. It is another thing to find oneself confronted by that reality in the meeting of hearts and minds, face to face, in the midst of turmoil. We observed the grace of God at work in the hearts of people at the point of extreme and came away refreshed by the blessing that they were to us.*

*As I write this, it strikes me that much of the reason why Christians in Zimbabwe have been able to rise spiritually to the challenges they have faced can be attributed to the ministry of intercession that has been entered into by people around the world who have cared and acted. Time and again, we were thanked for having passed on words of encouragement that had come from praying people from other countries. Time and again, we were confronted by the evidence of answers to those prayers; in some instances in the outworking of circumstances but more significantly in the inworking of the Spirit of God.*

*Mandy and I returned to Canada excited about what lies ahead this year. While we maintain our prayerful concern for Zimbabwe and her people, we have come away confident that God really is carrying out an eternal agenda. God's control is being applied, not simply in making the best of a bad situation, but more in the direct outworking of His purposes.*

*We have also returned with a deep appreciation for our co-workers in Zimbabwe. They are rising magnificently to the exciting challenge of ministry in such a place as that, at such a time as this. We are evermore aware of the great army of intercessors of which we are a part, but, most of all, we have a deeper appreciation for the One who accomplishes all things.*

To Him we present our tribute of praise!

---

[1] Noël Liddle, *A Million Miles of Miracles* (Bulawayo, Zimbabwe: Baptist Publication House, 1995), p. 60.

[2] Ibid., p. 72.

# APPENDIX

# TEAM Zimbabwe Missionaries 1938—2005*

| NAME | CATEGORY** | DATES OF SERVICE |
|------|------------|------------------|
| Abuhl, Bert & Donna (Hendrickson) | ST | 1993—1994 |
| Agriss, Steve | CM | 1981—1989 |
| Anderson, Ruth Married Dick Regier 1957 | CM | 1955—1957 |
| Archer, Grace | ST | 1983—1984 |
| Asa, Beverly | CM | 1966—1978 |
| Austin, Leslie & Lillian | CM | 1951—1954 |
| Austin, Reg & Carol | CM | 1957—1981 |
| Beach, Wilbur Married Jean Schmidt 1955 | CM | 1953—1955 |
| Beach, Wilbur & Jean | CM | 1955—1990 |
| Befus, Mildred | CM | 1957—1961 |
| Berge, Scott & Maryanne | ST | 2002—2003 |
| Betts, ElLois | CM | 1987—1990 |
| Blair, Orla & Marguerite | CM | 1946—1976 |
| Bloom, Merle & Kay | CM | 1953—1958 |
| Borowski, Barbara | ST/CM | 1983; 1986—1995 |
| Bradford, Shirley | CM | 1960—1971 |
| Brown, Helen St. Claire | CM/AS | 1964—1972 |

| | | |
|---|---|---|
| Bruton, Warren & Lois | CM | 1951—1987 |
| Burslem, Dr. Fiona | ST | 1970—1972 |
| Byrmo, Ann Britt | CM | 1973—1986 |
|     Married George Smazik 1986 | | |
| Byrmo, Martin & Margaretha | CM | 1961—1978 |
|     Affiliated with Swedish Alliance Mission | | |
| Byrd, Effie Mae | CM | 1951—1960 |
| | | |
| Canode, Fred & Charmaine | AS | 1981—1983; 1985—1987 |
| Carnall, Roy & Mildred | CM | 1962—1987 |
| Caseboldt, Mildred | AS | 1969—1974 |
| Cedarholm, Clarence & Gladys | CM | 1953—1978 |
| Chatow, Sheryl | AS | 1974—1976 |
| Chick, Dorothy | CM | 1970—1971 |
|     On loan from TEAM South Africa | | |
| Christiansen, Phil & Barb | CM | 1959—1970 |
| Christiansen, Jon & Kathy | CM | 2004—Present |
| Classen, Eldon | ST | 1981—1982 |
| Clemenger, Dr. Alan & Donna | CM | 1960—1961 |
| Congdon, Dr. Rob & Nancy | AS | 1989—1990 |
| Cook, Sam & Dorothy | AS | 1967—1970 |
| | | |
| Danielson, Mary | CM | 1942—1980 |
| Danielson, Rudy & Mary | CM | 1938—1942 |
| Dee, George & Pat | CM | 1953—1979; 1982—1994 |
| Doyle, Sean & Kim | ST | 2002—2003 |
| Drake, Dr. Dave | CM | 1966—1975 |
|     Married Karen Holritz 1975 | | |
| Drake, Dr. Dave & Karen | CM | 1975—1991 |
| Driedger, Merv & Myrl | CM | 1963—1968; 1971—1976 |
| DuBert, Phil & Karen | CM | 1990—Present |
| Dunkeld, Dick & Pat | CM | 1968—1970 |
| Dunkeld, Lois | ST | 1972—1973 |
| Dunkeld, Orval & Helen | CM | 1941—1960; 1970—1982 |
| Dunkeld, Pat | CM | 1972—1973 |
| | | |
| Eagles, Carol | CM | 1991—1996 |
| Ebbern, Ruth | CM | 1952—1977 |
| Edds, Helen | CM | 1965—1968 |
| Eichner, Roy & Lydia | CM | 1957—1975 |
| Elzinga, Dr. | ST | 1995 |

| | | |
|---|---|---|
| Endicott, Bob & Betty | CM | 1969—1974 |
| Everswick, Dale | CM | 1973—1985 |
| Everswick, Doug & Nancy | CM | 1984—Present |
| Everswick, Lynn & Judy | CM | 1969—1983 |
| Everswick, Norman &Thelma | CM | 1946—1986 |
| | | |
| Fierke, Frank & Hazel | AS | 1980—1981 |
| Finsaas, Ray & Myrtle | CM | 1957—1972 |
| Fritz, Bud & Lolly | CM | 1957—1977 |
| Froese, Dr. Rick & Joanne | CM | 1961—1989 |
| Fuller, Dr. Earl | AS | 1970—1974 |
| | | |
| Gardziella, Walter & Wilma | AS | 1974—1976 |
| Gardziella, Wilma | CM | 1961—1981 |
| Georgia, Stew & Marlene | CM | 1965—1982 |
| Goldsmith, Susan | ST | 1986—1987 |
| Good, Randy & Marilyn | CM | 1970—1976 |
| Goppert, Chris & Joyce | CM | 1973—2004 |
| Goppert, Sonja | ST | 2000—2001 |
| Gregory, Joe & Rita | CM | 1978—1982 |
| Grigg, Richard & Inez | AS | 1967—1976 |
| Grigg, Richard | AS | 1983—1985 |
| Gudeman, Judy | CM | 1961—1978 |
| Gustafson, Goldye | CM | 1971—1972 |
| Gustafson, Marcie | ST/AS | 1985—1986; 1989—1992 |
| | | |
| Hamstra, Bev | AS | 1987—1989 |
| Hawkins, Lynne | CM | 1967—Present |
| Hendrickson, Carl & Donna | CM | 1954—1977 |
| Hendrickson, Janet | AS | 1973—1975 |
| Holritz, Karen | CM | 1973—1975 |
|     Married Dr. Dave Drake 1975 | | |
| Hotchkiss, Glenn & Dorothy | CM | 1957—1961 |
| Hoyt, Don & Lynn | CM | 1960—1976 |
| | | |
| Ibbotson, Rita | CM | 1988—Present |
| | | |
| Jackson, Paul & Mandy | CM | 1981—1998 |
| Jackson, Russell & Margaret | CM | 1948—1982 |
| Jackson, Tom & Lois | CM | 1976—Present |
| Johnson, Bud & Audrey | ST | 1991—1992 |

| | | |
|---|---|---|
| Kahlstorf, Donna | CM | 1955—1995 |
| Kappesser, Amy | ST | 1984—1986 |
| Kinesberger, Dr. Gerda | ST | 1991—1994 |
| On loan from an Austrian mission | | |
| Kinney, LaVonne | CM | 1967—1974 |
| Knapp, Chuck & Verna | CM | 1953—1964 |
| Kraft, Kyla | CM | 1984—1986 |
| Married Don Lester 1987 | | |
| | | |
| Lanegan, Bonnie | CM | 1973—1985 |
| Larsen, Dorothy | CM | 1960—1965 |
| Larson, Melita | ST/CM | 1984—Present |
| Lester, Don & Kyla | CM | 1987—2001 |
| Liddle, Noël & Ann | AS/CM | 1987—1992 |
| Longnecker, Karen | CM | 1972—2005 |
| Ludlow, Bev & Ted | CM/MAF | 1968—1970 |
| Ludwig, Marcia | ST | 1986—1987 |
| | | |
| Mann, Judy | ST | 1979—1980 |
| Marsh, Iona | ST | 1984—1985 |
| Marshall, Gordon & Jean | CM/MAF | 1974—1978 |
| Mason, Betty | CM | 1951—1954 |
| Married John Wolfe 1954 | | |
| McClenahan, Richard & Dorothy | AS | 1996—2000 |
| McCloy, Dick & Mary Ann | CM | 1994—2005 |
| McCloy, George & Edith | ST | 1973—1974 |
| McGlothin, Barry & Karen | CM | 1986—1989 |
| Medaris, Bob & Fran | AS | 1967—1980 |
| Milligan, Bob & Stephanie | ST | 1990—1991 |
| Mooi, Dr. Len & Karen | ST | 1987—1988 |
| Mortenson, Pat | CM | 1966—1975 |
| Mossberger, Sharon | ST | 1986—1987 |
| Munger, Ken & June | CM | 1953—1961 |
| Munger, June | ST | 1965 |
| | | |
| Nelson, Bev | CM | 1962—1965 |
| Nelson, Lillian | CM | 1948—1951 |
| Married Les Austin 1951 | | |
| | | |
| Olsen, Carol | CM | 1954—1957 |
| Married Reg Austin 1957 | | |

| | | |
|---|---|---|
| Ott, Eunice | CM | 1944—1956 |
| | | |
| Parker, Judy | CM | 1986—Present |
| Powell, Diane | AS/CM | 1971—1976 |
| Prescott, Marshall & Alice | CM | 1955—1959 |
| Pruitt, Chuck & Scottie | CM | 1953—1986 |
| | | |
| Ratzlaff, Cliff & Jeanette | CM | 1955—1969 |
| Reddington, Naomi | AS | 2004—Present |
| Regier, Dick & Ruth | CM | 1957—1979; 1986—1995 |
| Reimer, Joe & Olga | CM | 1976—1979 |
| Repke, Bob & Rhoda | CM | 1964—1968 |
| Rilling, Emil & Phyllis | CM | 1953—1990 |
| Roeper, Wyn | CM | 1955 |
|     Married Martin Uppendahl 1955 | | |
| Rogers, Mildred | CM | 1955—1959 |
|     Married Roy Carnall 1959 | | |
| Roth, Dr. Gisela | CM/DMG | 1987—1992; 1994—1998 |
| Rousseau, Dave & Susan | CM | 1989—Present |
| | | |
| Sander, Cynthia | AS | 1976—1978 |
| Schober, Marie | CM | 1953—1963 |
| Sherwood, Rusty & Jo | CM | 1958—1977 |
| Smazik, George | CM | 1980—1986 |
|     Married Ann-Britt Byrmo 1986 | | |
| Smazik, George & Ann-Britt | CM | 1986—1993 |
| Smith, Paul & Helen | CM | 1957—1983 |
| Stahle, Otto & Peggy | CM | 1960—1970 |
| Stephens, Dr. Dan & Julie | CM | 1991—Present |
| Stephens, Dr. Roland & Kathy | CM | 1962—78; 1995—Present |
| Stermer, Dorothy | CM | 1988—1990 |
|     Retired from Japan | | |
| Storm, Guy & Karen | CM | 1987 |
| Strom, Brenda | AS | 1981—1984 |
| Strom, Faith | AS | 1964—1966 |
| Strom, Gloria | AS | 1974—1976 |
| Strom, Lorne & RuthAnn | AS | 1988—1990 |
| Strom, Wilfred & Dorothy | CM | 1953—1982; 1985—1990 |
| | | |
| Thomas, Hermede & Phyllis | CM | 1985 |
| Till, Cherith | CM | 1968—1978 |

| | | |
|---|---|---|
| Traynor, Marilyn | CM | 1971—1975 |
| Ulrich, John & Kelley | CM | 1999—Present |
| Uppendahl, Martin & Wyn | CM | 1950—1961 |
| Valente, Frank & Linda | AS | 1995—1996 |
| Voetmann, Dave & Marilee | CM/MAF | 1964—1968; 1970—1974 |
| Waite, Lorraine | CM | 1957—1991 |
| Wall, Dr. Sam & Emily | CM | 1958—1962 |
| Warner, Bill Jr. | CM | 1955—1957 |
|     Married Joyce Kukard 1957 | | |
| Warner, Bill & Joyce | CM | 1957—1969 |
| Warner, William Sr. | AS | 1966—1968 |
| Watson, Anne | AS | 1971 |
| White, Welton & Betty | AS | 1975—1981 |
| Williams, Ray & Marti | CM | 1984—1992 |
| Wilterdink, Marian | CM | 1951—2002 |
| Winchell, Karen | AS | 1977 |
|     Married Phil DuBert 1988 | | |
| Wolfe, John & Betty | CM | 1954—1979 |
| Zuelesdorf, Dr. Elizabeth | CM/DMG | 1987—1991 |

**Abbreviations: CM: Career Missionary; AS: Associate Missionary; ST: Short-Term Missionary

MAF: Missionary Aviation Fellowship; DMG: German Missionary Fellowship

*Although a diligent effort was made to obtain accurate information on each missionary who served for at least a year in Zimbabwe, we were unable to verify every listing and apologize for any inaccuracies or omissions.*

Printed in the United States
40032LVS00007B/70-189